The Collected Works of
James M. Buchanan

VOLUME 17
Moral Science and Moral Order

James M. Buchanan,
Fairfax, Virginia, August 1993

The Collected Works of

James M. Buchanan

VOLUME 17

Moral Science and Moral Order

LIBERTY FUND

This book is published by Liberty Fund, Inc., a foundation
established to encourage study of the ideal of a society of free
and responsible individuals.

𒂼𒄀

The cuneiform inscription that serves as our logo and as a design
element for Liberty Fund books is the earliest-known written appearance
of the word "freedom" (*amagi*), or "liberty." It is taken from a clay
document written about 2300 B.C. in the Sumerian city-state of Lagash.

2nd printing (2023), printed on demand by Lightning Source, Inc.

Library of Congress Cataloging-in-Publication Data
Buchanan, James M.
Moral science and moral order / James M. Buchanan.
p.   cm. — (The collected works of James M. Buchanan ; v. 17)
Includes bibliographical references and index.
ISBN 0-86597-245-1 (hc.). — ISBN 0-86597-246-x (pbk.)
1. Political science—Economic aspects.   2. Political ethics.
3. Ethics.   I. Title.   II. Series: Buchanan, James M.
Works.   1999 ; v. 17.
JA77.B84   2000
172—dc21   99-42627

ISBN: 978-0-86597-246-9

LIBERTY FUND, INC.
11301 North Meridian Street
Carmel, Indiana 46032
libertyfund.org

Contents

2. *Belief and Consequence*

3. *Moral Community and Moral Order*

4. *Moral Science, Equality, and Justice*

5. *Contractarian Encounters*

Foreword

The British and Scottish Moralists of the Enlightenment period would have felt very comfortable with James Buchanan.[1] Like them Buchanan may be seen as a "man of letters" who concerns himself with fundamental problems of moral science and moral order. But, also like them, Buchanan is not a secondhand dealer in old ideas. On the contrary, taking as inspiration classical philosopher-economists (in particular Adam Smith), Buchanan not only proposes new applications of the neoclassical economic paradigm, he also addresses, in innovative ways, fundamental issues of his discipline and beyond.[2]

Since, in developing his own arguments, Buchanan almost always goes back to fundamental principles first, much of his work has a certain philosophical ring to it and, quite often, a very strong one. Thinking only of such papers as "The Relatively Absolute Absolutes" or "Ethical Rules, Expected Values, and Large Numbers" and books like *The Limits of Liberty* or Buchanan's and Roger Congleton's joint work *Politics by Principle, Not Interest: Toward Nondiscriminatory Democracy,* it is obvious that the present volume

1. For more on British and Scottish Moralists, see the excellent anthologies by David D. Raphael (ed.), *British Moralists* (Oxford: Oxford University Press, 1969); and Louis Schneider (ed.), *The Scottish Moralists on Human Nature and Society* (Chicago and London: Chicago University Press, 1967).

2. James M. Buchanan, "Adam Smith as Inspiration," in *The Academic World of James M. Buchanan,* ed. Byeong-Ho Gong (Seoul: Korea Economic Research Institute, 1996), Korean translation only, is reprinted in *Ideas, Persons, and Events,* volume 19 in the series. A good example of what was a new application of the economic paradigm is Buchanan's seminal paper "An Economic Theory of Clubs," *Economica* 32 (February 1965): 1–14, reprinted in *Externalities and Public Expenditure Theory,* volume 15 in the series. *Cost and Choice: An Inquiry in Economic Theory,* reprinted as volume 6 of the Collected Works, addresses fundamental issues of economics, as do many of the papers in part 1 of volume 12, *Economic Inquiry and Its Logic.*

must leave out a considerable portion of Buchanan's philosophically relevant writing.[3] In addition, there are parts of books, like Buchanan's comment "Marginal Notes on Reading Political Philosophy," which appeared as an appendix to *The Calculus of Consent,* that may also seem conspicuously missing in a volume with a title such as this one.[4] Despite these gaps, the editors feel that the essays assigned to this seventeenth volume of the Collected Works are representative of Buchanan's philosophical views.

Because Buchanan's concerns and perspectives connect to other literature more familiar to philosophers than to what we take to be Buchanan's standard readership, we have tried here to highlight several of the more conceptual issues in Buchanan's approach, to sketch the inherent philosophical logic of the approach, and to connect it to a broader philosophical literature. In so doing, we have interpreted our role as editors somewhat more expansively than in the introductions to the other volumes. We trust that no apology for this decision is required because the reader will find philosophical reflection on Buchanan's basic philosophical views as fascinating as we do.

In the papers reprinted in part 1 of this volume, "Methods and Models," Buchanan characterizes his own methodological position. Special attention may be drawn to the paper "The Related but Distinct 'Sciences' of Economics and Political Economy."[5] It is philosophically highly significant that he separates these two "sciences" in terms of their distinct views of the world. And the significance of Buchanan's distinction between the two worldviews

3. James M. Buchanan, "The Relatively Absolute Absolutes," in *Essays on the Political Economy* (Honolulu: University of Hawai'i Press, 1989), 32–46; and "Ethical Rules, Expected Values, and Large Numbers," *Ethics* 76 (October 1965): 1–13, are reprinted in volume 1 in the Collected Works, *The Logical Foundations of Constitutional Liberty,* as representative of central aspects of Buchanan's philosophical views. *The Limits of Liberty: Between Anarchy and Leviathan* (Chicago: University of Chicago Press, 1975) and James M. Buchanan and Roger D. Congleton, *Politics by Principle, Not Interest: Toward Nondiscriminatory Democracy* (Cambridge: Cambridge University Press, 1998) are reprinted in this series as volume 7 and volume 11, respectively.

4. James M. Buchanan and Gordon Tullock, "Marginal Notes on Reading Political Philosophy," in *The Calculus of Consent: Logical Foundations of Constitutional Democracy* (Ann Arbor: University of Michigan Press, 1962), 306–22, volume 3 in the Collected Works.

5. James M. Buchanan, "The Related but Distinct 'Sciences' of Economics and of Political Economy," *British Journal of Social Psychology,* Special Issue, *Social Psychology and Economics,* ed. Wolfgang Stroebe and Willi Meyer, 21 (part 2, June 1982): 175–83.

can presumably best be understood in philosophical terms. We refer here to the work of the philosopher Peter Strawson, who conceptually distinguishes an "objective" from a "participant's attitude" to social interaction.[6] If we adopt the objective attitude toward other human beings, we treat them as parts of the natural environment and their deeds as natural events. Influencing other human beings amounts to manipulation, pure and simple. As opposed to that, an individual who is adopting the participant's attitude treats other as fellows and as independent sources of value. He sees and respects them as members of his moral community.

In Buchanan's basic philosophical view of the world, a distinction corresponding to that between the participant's attitude and the objective attitude can be made. It applies to those who are just players in one of the games of life as well as to those who analyze such games. A player can approach other players as participants in the game but also as objects of manipulation. Likewise, an analyst may conceive of himself as being situated outside the social interaction that forms the object of his analyses, or he may serve as a participating analyst who, in the last resort, views himself as a member of the moral community he analyzes. Likewise, we can adopt a participant's attitude toward our fellows even in making operative or within-rule choices. But, more typically, we will perceive them as fellow participants at the constitutional level of choosing and justification of the rules of the game rather than at the operative level of choice. Again, we can, on both the constitutional and operative levels, adopt an objective attitude. Buchanan denies none of these, or any other, combinations. He insists only that we are not restricted to adopting the objective attitude. We *can* and, in general, *do* conceive of ourselves as members of moral communities.

Buchanan's notion of moral community may be less "moralistic" than Strawson's, but Buchanan's distinction between others as objects of manipulation and others as fellow participants in ongoing social interaction has the same general spirit as Strawson's. Not to use other individuals merely as means but always to respect them as persons is clearly part of Buchanan's basic normative convictions. It is appropriate, therefore, that Buchanan, in his essay "A Hobbesian Interpretation of the Rawlsian Difference Principle,"

6. See Peter F. Strawson, *Freedom and Resentment and Other Essays* (London: Methuen, 1974).

characterizes his own position as "quasi-Kantian."[7] He thinks that in forming our (normative) judgments, not only as theorists but also as citizens, we command the faculty to perceive social interaction as subject to constitutional choices that we can make in mutual agreement. The Buchanan-type contractarian political economist should therefore focus on suggesting such choices of rules. Once the rules are in place, individuals make their own autonomous decisions within this "legal cum moral" order and produce, from the interaction of these decisions, a social outcome.

The instructive parallels between Kant's and Buchanan's views of the world go even further. In a characteristically Kantian move, Buchanan seems to assume that, by conceiving of ourselves as participants in a process of agreement seeking, we, to a certain extent, "create" the world in which we act. Looking at the world with a participant's attitude, we organize our perception in a specific way and, at least in a way, become members of a world that differs from the one perceived by those who adopt an objective attitude toward others. This world is not merely characterized by social interaction. It is rather a moral community in which, to some extent, norms of mutual respect reign because the members of the community perceive and acknowledge each other as moral subjects.

"Contractarian political economy," conceived as the moral science of that world, leaves no room for the derivation of social engineering prescriptions that seek to determine and to bring about an optimal result of social interaction independent of the choices made by its participants. But Buchanan himself insists that we can and must look at the world through an objectivist window as well.

Alongside (contractarian) political economy, there is the science of economics, in which the objective attitude prevails. In economics, typically, the focus is on operative, or within-rule, choices. It is assumed that, in the context of such choices, individuals seek to get their own preferred ways rather than restricting themselves to the realm of mutual advantage.[8]

---

7. James M. Buchanan, "A Hobbesian Interpretation of the Rawlsian Difference Principle," *Kyklos* 29, fasc. 1 (1976): 5–25. Also see part 5 of this volume, "Contractarian Encounters."

8. Henry Hazlitt's *The Foundations of Morality* (Princeton: University Press of America, 1964) refers to the closely related concept of "mutualism" as a fundamental principle

The distinction between adopting an objective attitude and adopting a participant's attitude extends to the level on which the analyst of social interaction is operating, too. That is not to say, though, that those who, in their analyses, assume that individuals approach each other with an objective attitude need themselves share this attitude. The Buchanan-type political economist must rather always approach the world with both attitudes. It may seem impossible to adopt simultaneously the participant's attitude of political economy and the objective attitude of economics. One can reduce the tension between these two views of the world by arguing that the participant's attitude should be adopted on the level of constitutional decision making, while the objective attitude is of primary importance for analyzing operative choices. But for those who have to switch between attitudes, the tension between the objective attitude and the participant's attitude remains.

Buchanan is not a "natural economist" who cannot do otherwise than to perceive of human behavior as driven by selfish motives and to approach humans with an objective, almost solipsistic attitude.[9] On the contrary, Buchanan insists on the feasibility of the contractarian moral science of political economy. He rejects an economic science based exclusively on a model of human behavior in which each individual tries to manipulate others to his personal advantage only. And he deems it methodologically inappropriate for the scientist not to perceive of himself as a participant of social interaction. This rejection should not, however, be confused with a rejection of methodological individualism. Quite to the contrary, Buchanan insists on a strictly individualistic approach. It may seem appropriate, therefore, to add some further comments on the issue of (methodological) individualism versus collectivism in moral science here.

On one level, the methodological individualism versus collectivism dispute boils down to a question about the structure of scientific laws. To put it simply and crudely, the question is whether or not sound explanations and predictions of social phenomena contain independent variables that repre-

---

of moral science and moral order. Hazlitt's is, in that regard, quite close to Buchanan's contractarian approach but certainly somewhat less Kantian.

9. James M. Buchanan, "The Qualities of a Natural Economist," in *Democracy and Public Choice: Essays in Honor of Gordon Tullock,* ed. Charles K. Rowley (Oxford: Basil Blackwell, 1987), 9–19, reprinted in volume 19 of the series, *Ideas, Persons, and Events.*

sent genuinely collective phenomena. The discussion of this question is a virtual minefield and too complex to be addressed here.[10] As for our present concerns, we may, fortunately, remain open as to whether or not there are well-corroborated laws based on genuinely collective independent variables in the best social science explanations. For even if such laws existed, Buchanan would insist that, for purposes of intervening in the course of the world, the values of collective variables cannot be chosen collectively. In Buchanan's view, choices, in the true and proper sense of the term, are of necessity always made by individuals. Even if the collective entity faces alternative options that concern it as a whole, and even if in a process of collective interaction one of these options emerges, it is not "chosen" collectively. To look at the process in which collective results are determined as if the collective entity would choose them is not innocuous; rather, it promotes a serious distortion of our view of the social world.

In his critique of social choice theory, Buchanan does not deny that we can describe the relationship between profiles of individual choices and social outcomes by a so-called collective choice function. But for him it is not meaningful to refer to this mapping as representing collective choices. As he puts it in "Rational Choice Models in the Social Sciences":

> Even if the collective entity, as such, confronts the alternatives, the only genuine choices made are those of the individuals who participate in the decision process. Given a decision rule, individuals "choose," and such choices may be evaluated in accordance with rationality precepts. From this participation by separate persons, the decision rule or institution generates an outcome which may be a different one from those that the collective confronts. No one "chooses" this outcome, however, and it is an error of major proportion to attribute to the choosing process, as such, any rationality precepts.[11]

---

10. One of the best overviews of this dispute was written by Buchanan's longtime collaborator and coauthor Viktor Vanberg and is titled *Die zwei Soziologien. Individualismus und Kollektivismus in der Sozialtheorie* (Tübingen: J. C. B. Mohr [Paul Siebeck], 1975).

11. James M. Buchanan, "Rational Choice Models in the Social Sciences," in *Explorations into Constitutional Economics,* comp. Robert D. Tollison and Viktor J. Vanberg (College Station: Texas A&M University Press, 1989), 37–50, reprinted in this volume.

This quotation expresses one of Buchanan's most fundamental philosophical convictions very well. Like an iceberg of which you can see only the tip, it
may seem harmless at first sight. Yet, thinking through its implications and
relating it to traditional welfare economics and Kenneth Arrow's social choice
theory, it has extremely far-reaching implications.[12]

Why this is so is most easily seen if we apply to it the distinction between
the objective attitude and the participant's attitude introduced earlier. We
can then say that once we adopt a participant's attitude, we accept, by implication, that other individuals are independent centers of decision making
whose decisions are beyond our direct control. So, in other words, it is always
the case that "each of the others chooses" and that "I choose," but never that
"we choose." And neither can "I" or the "collective as a whole" virtually
make "their choices for them."

The paper "An Ambiguity in Sen's Alleged Proof of the Impossibility of a
Pareto Libertarian" insists on this simple point.[13] It has not been well received by the social choice theorists who think that it is based on a simple
misunderstanding. But the misunderstanding may be entirely on their side.
Within Buchanan's perspective, the adherent of the concept of genuinely collective choice is, in the last resort, forced to look at social interaction as a
kind of screenplay in which all the roles for all the individuals are fixed in
every detail in advance while the collective result is determined by executing
the instructions of the play's script.[14] Ascending to the higher level of fixing
a "choreography" for later actions that would then not require anymore
separate choices would be the only way to "choose" a collective result by the
coordinated action of several individuals.

But in Buchanan's view, justifying the notion of "collective choice" in that
way does not help the social choice perspective. For even if we neglect the

12. Kenneth J. Arrow, *Social Choice and Individual Values* (New Haven: Yale University
Press, 1963). Some of the implications are also acknowledged by leading social choice the-
orists such as Amartya K. Sen, for example, in "Rationality and Social Choice," *American
Economic Review* 85, no. 1 (1995): 1–24.

13. James M. Buchanan, "An Ambiguity in Sen's Alleged Proof of the Impossibility
of a Pareto Libertarian," *Analyse & Kritik* 18 (September 1996): 118–25, reprinted in this
volume.

14. See *Analyse & Kritik* 18 (September 1996). The entire issue is devoted to the discussion of collective choice.

fact that the whole construction is somewhat absurd (since, first, we never agree on a screenplay, and then we behave as if we were puppets on a string who do not have any further choices), the very act of accepting and rejecting the screenplay would have to be accomplished by separate persons. These individuals would have to signal their agreement or dissent to the screenplay by their separate (individual) acts—which are all they can control—and thus they choose in the strict sense of that term. At some ultimate level, "participation by separate persons" under some rule rather than the "collective choice" of a collective result would be taking place. What is chosen, at this level, are the acts of signaling assent or dissent, not the collective outcome. In the last resort, then, individuals make the relevant choices, and it is not the collective result that they choose.

Yet, many of those who would admit that the collective result, properly speaking, is not "chosen" would at the same time insist that people, as a matter of fact, do have "we-intentions."[15] They do form value judgments for the collectivity at large. They do think in terms of such collective choices. Even if collective results or their selection can emerge only as a side effect of choices that are always individual, we do form our opinions of right and wrong in terms of value judgments for the collectivity, and we can describe the process by a collective choice function. This, in turn, can induce us to make specific individual choices when participating in those processes in which collective outcomes are determined. Though the influence of "we-intentions" on individual market choice may be of minor or no importance, in politics how individuals choose to act (for example, vote) may strongly depend on their intentions for the collectivity at large.[16]

However, even if we think of social welfare functions as representing "individual intentions for the collective" rather than as representing actual

15. On related issues, see also Raimo Tuomela, *A Theory of Social Action* (Dordrecht: Reidel, 1984).

16. On related issues, see Geoffrey Brennan and James M. Buchanan, "Voter Choice: Evaluating Political Alternatives," *American Behavioral Scientist* 28 (November–December 1984): 185–201, reprinted in volume 13 of this series, *Politics as Public Choice;* and James M. Buchanan, "Individual Choice in Voting and the Market," *Journal of Political Economy* 62 (August 1954): 334–43, reprinted in volume 1 of this series, *The Logical Foundations of Constitutional Liberty.*

choices, Buchanan would argue that the formation of these several individual value judgments—there would be as many social welfare functions as there are individuals—would not make sense for individuals who are seeking interindividual agreement. Individuals who, adopting a participant's attitude, subscribe to the quasi-Kantian principle of interindividual respect and at the same time believe that the choices of their fellows are beyond their direct control cannot represent their intentions by a social choice function. By their own construction of social interaction there can be only individual choices. So why formulate an individual welfare function for the collective at all?

In Buchanan's individualist political economy, this question is rhetorical. There is no legitimate use for the concept of "choice for the collective as a whole." Not even in forming individual judgments of right and wrong may we give up the participant's attitude of seeking the genuinely individual agreement of others. And since this applies to our commonsensical judgments, it should apply with added force when we form judgments in moral science.

The preceding remarks highlight some central features of Buchanan's distinctive approach to moral science in general. In particular, they should be kept in mind when "encountering" part 5 of this volume, "Contractarian Encounters." Forming our opinion on what "good" and "just" social institutions might be and consulting our "constitutional interests," it may so happen that we all concur, or at least conceivably could concur, on the same views. Conceiving of ourselves as participating in a process of seeking agreement on mutually advantageous solutions to social problems rather than as merely trying to get our way is the basic contractarian perspective. As was argued before, however, the fact that individuals can adopt an objective attitude must not be forgotten. For instance, adopting the corresponding economic perspective, Buchanan arrives at the conclusion that individuals, on the constitutional level, might have good reason to accept the Rawlsian difference principle as a guideline for creating social institutions precisely because they foresee that their operative, or within-rule, choices may be made in a Hobbesian manner. Based on his own intuitive insight into what is discussed in the more technical game-theoretic literature as the problem of subgame perfectness, Buchanan shows that individuals who cannot bindingly commit to specific courses of action on the constitutional level might have good reasons to support the Rawlsian difference principle as a way of securing the self-enforcing character of their agreement.[17]

Taking into account what Buchanan himself has to say in part 3 of this volume, "Moral Community and Moral Order," one may have second thoughts on the limits of communities for which the participant's attitude is supposed to be operative at the constitutional level. In the end, a more particularistic vision of moral order may emerge than is fully compatible with the implied universalism of quasi-Kantian contractarianism. Here, clearly, Buchanan's philosophical contractarianism confronts some of the problems that are nowadays raised by the so-called communitarian philosophers. We cannot address these problems here. Let it suffice to note that certain basic tensions are characteristic of the works of all eminent moral scientists. It comes as no surprise, therefore, that they emerge in the work of Buchanan as well.

In fact, Buchanan himself is very good at spotting tensions and problems in the work of his fellow contractarians. A case in point is his criticism of Nozick's theory of the minimal state, as developed in "The Libertarian Legitimacy of the State" and "Utopia, the Minimal State, and Entitlement."[18] In particular, Buchanan's question as to whether the famous basketball player Wilt Chamberlain should be perceived as being entitled to his full income in a society to which he immigrated or only to the income that he could command in his preimmigration environment should be borne in mind by all defenders of entitlement theories of justice. The question also draws attention to the more general and fundamental philosophical issue of whether or

---

17. On these insights, see also James M. Buchanan, "The Samaritan's Dilemma," in *Altruism, Morality and Economic Theory*, ed. Edmund S. Phelps (New York: Russell Sage Foundation, 1975), 71–95, reprinted in volume 1 in the series, *The Logical Foundations of Constitutional Democracy*; and, in a similar vein, Thomas C. Schelling, *The Strategy of Conflict* (Oxford: Oxford University Press, 1977, 1960). The two seminal papers of the technical game theoretic literature are Reinhard Selten, "Spieltheoretische Behandlung eines Oligopolmodells mit Nachfrageträgheit," *Zeitschrift für die gesamte Staatswissenschaft* 121 (1965): 301–24 and 667–89; and "Reexamination of the Perfectness Concept for Equilibrium in Extensive Games," *International Journal of Game Theory* 4 (1975): 25–55.

18. James M. Buchanan, "The Libertarian Legitimacy of the State," in *Freedom in Constitutional Contract: Perspectives of a Political Economist* (College Station: Texas A&M University Press, 1977), 50–63; and "Utopia, the Minimal State, and Entitlement," *Public Choice* 23 (Fall 1975): 121–26, in part 5 of this volume.

not any claims to justice exist independent of predefined communities or prior to conventional rules and institutions. Except for the quasi-Kantian respect for the autonomy of the individual as a decision maker and a source of value, Buchanan certainly would take sides here with the "conventionalists," who think in terms of "morals by agreement" and do not believe in the existence of any objective standards of justice that are ultimately "found" rather than "invented."[19]

Throughout his academic career, Buchanan has commented on the fundamental issues addressed in this volume. As always, he can best speak for himself. But it may be helpful to bear in mind some of the connections and links to other philosophical topics when addressing the papers in this collection. This holds particularly true for part 4, "Moral Science, Equality, and Justice," in which Buchanan applies his characteristically individualistic perspective to some central normative issues of social and moral philosophy, and also for part 2, "Belief and Consequence," in which he discusses certain epistemological questions that are related in one way or another to the constitution of his basic view of the world.

Hartmut Kliemt
University of Duisburg
1998

---

19. This, of course, alludes to David Gauthier, *Morals by Agreement* (Oxford: Oxford University Press, 1986), and to the subtitle of John L. Mackie, *Ethics: Inventing Right and Wrong* (Harmondsworth: Penguin, 1977), in which a skeptical ethical view close to or at least compatible with Buchanan's is worked out in some philosophical detail.

PART ONE

Methods and Models

Economics and Its
Scientific Neighbors

There exists something that is called "economics."[1] Courses in this something are offered in most universities; departmental faculties exist as separate administrative units. Specialized professional positions, in both private and public industry, are held by "economists." Professional journals and many books are written, printed, and presumably read, which libraries and bookshops catalogue under "economics." All of this creates the presumption that there is some widely shared common language, some special communication network among those who qualify as professionals, which makes for efficiency in discourse. Such a language is a necessary condition for science, but it is not a sufficient one. The efficiency in discourse must be measured also against the standards of science, which are those of understanding, not utility, of predictive ability, not platitudes, of objectively detached interpretation, not reasoned justification.

From *The Structure of Economic Science: Essays on Methodology,* ed. Sherman Roy Krupp (Englewood Cliffs: Prentice-Hall, 1966), 166–83. Reprinted by permission of Prentice-Hall, Inc.

1. In a recent paper, labeled explicitly as an "essay in persuasion," I called for some shift of emphasis in the attention of economists, and by implication for a somewhat modified conception of "economics" as a scientific discipline. My criticism was directed primarily at the post-Robbins concentration on the allocation problem independent of the institutional-organizational setting. In essence, my plea was for a re-emphasis on the central role of human behavior in the exchange relationship, or the theory of markets, broadly conceived. I shall not repeat here the arguments therein presented, and I shall limit to the maximum extent that is possible normative judgments about the appropriate boundary lines for the discipline that we variously define as "economics." See my "What Should Economists Do?" *Southern Economic Journal,* 30 (January, 1964), 213–22.

To an extent at least, "economics" qualifies as a science under these criteria. I propose to begin with this "economics" as empirical fact and to examine in some detail the relations of this science with its neighbors. Preliminary to the central questions it is useful to make some general observations about the development of "economics" itself. Insofar as one who is himself inside the discipline is able to discern movements in the whole, to me economics seems to be currently undergoing two apparently contradictory trend changes. The independence of "economics" in any broad disciplinary sense is rapidly breaking down, while, at the same time, specialization among the subdisciplines, within economics, is increasing apace.

Was "economics" ever so independent of its scientific neighbors as the bureaucracy of professional specialization makes it seem? Its subject matter emerged, scarcely a century ago, from "political economy," which, in its turn, sprang classical and full-blown from an earlier "moral philosophy." The scientific origins of economics lay hidden from their early expositors, and classical political economy was explicitly prejudiced toward reform. Its emphasis was on *improving* the institutions commanding its attention; *understanding* such institutions was always a secondary, even if necessary, purpose. Improvement did, as we know, materialize; the social transformation dictated by the classical precepts was, to an extent, realized.

The practical success of classical economics was responsible, in part, for its scientific undoing. The distinctions between scientific propositions and proposals for social reform were blurred from the outset. This led critics, who quite properly disputed classical prejudices toward social structure, to attack, and to appear to attack, the central propositions of the scientific analysis. This confusion has plagued economics and continues to plague it even now. The physical sciences have, by and large, escaped this confusion, and herein lies their prestige. Only in the recent discussions of the hydrogen bomb and radiation has there appeared anything akin to the elementary confusion between positive prediction and normative engineering that has pervaded economic discussion. Economists have, from the beginning of the discipline, been in the position faced by J. Robert Oppenheimer. And they have, unfortunately for the science, chosen much as he seems to have done. As a result, the interests of economists have been rarely, if ever, wholly scientific, and, on occasion, have been explicitly ascientific. The personal inclination toward social involvement has proved too strong for most, even for those who shun the limelight and who remain, physically, within the ivoried towers. In this perspective, Pareto stands dominant over a narrowly confined group of lesser figures.

What Is Economics?

The science advanced, nonetheless, despite the noise generated by inconsequential argument, and there has been, and remains, content in the words "economics" and "economist." Before the relationships among this science and its neighbors can be discussed, brief note of what this content is seems in order. What is the common language? What are the simple principles? How does one identify an economist?

By way of illustration, I propose to design here a simple conceptual experiment. One of the ancient Greek philosophers is credited with the statement: *Anything worth doing is worth doing well.* As our conceptual experiment, let us suppose that we select a randomly drawn sample from the general population. We give each person in the sample the adage cited above, and we ask him to comment upon it. We then observe their comments and attempt some sort of classification.

No single test could, of course, possibly be wholly conclusive, but it seems quite possible that the simple experiment proposed here would, in fact, provide us with a rough and ready manner of classifying economists and distinguishing them from the general public of which they form a part. There would be, in other words, a characteristic economist's response to the adage which would not be shared by large numbers of other persons. Additional, and more discriminating, tests could, of course, be devised which would further delineate the economists from the remaining community of scientists. But these need not be elaborated here since the single experiment is sufficient to illustrate the elemental principles of the science.

The economist's stock-in-trade—his tools—lies in his ability and proclivity to think about all questions in terms of *alternatives*. The truth judgment of the moralist, which says that something is either wholly right or wholly wrong, is foreign to him. The win-lose, yes-no discussion of politics is not within his purview. He does not recognize the either-or, the all-or-nothing, situation as his own. His is not the world of the mutually exclusives. Instead, his is a world of adjustment, of coordinated conflict, of *mutual gains.* To the economist, there are, of course, many things worth doing that are not worth doing well since he is trained, professionally, to think in terms of a continuous scale of variation both in doing things and in criteria for judging them done well.

The theorems that are of relevance to the economist are all constructed from this simple base. These may be germane to the choices, the decisions, of individual persons, of organizations of persons, or of social groups. Care must be taken at this stage, however, to insure that too much is not claimed for the economist. His domain is limited to the behavior of individual persons in choosing among the alternatives open to them. This behavior provides the raw material for the economist, and his theory of economic aggregates is built on foundations of sand if the elemental units, behaving individuals, are overlooked. Individual persons choose among alternatives that they confront; their choices are not mutually exclusive; they do not choose on an either-or basis. Instead, they select the "goods" and reject the "bads" through choices of "more or less." There are few, if any, demonstrably universal "goods" which are desired independent of quantity variation; and, similarly, there are few, if any, demonstrably universal "bads." It is for this reason that the economist does not speak, indeed cannot speak, of "goods" and "bads" separately from the choices made by individual persons.

By examining such choices, the economist can, however, place some restrictions on human behavior patterns. He can develop testable hypotheses about behavior, which observations can refute. Once he has succeeded in identifying what individuals, on the average, consider to be "goods," the economist can predict that more of any "good" will be chosen the lower its "price" relative to other "goods." This is the central predictive proposition of economics, which can be all-encompassing provided only that the terms "goods" and "price" are defined in sufficiently broad and inclusive ways. This central principle amounts to saying that individuals, when confronted with effective choice, will choose more rather than less.

As such, this remains a very elementary, and, to the economist, self-evident, proposition. But the economist's task is that of extending the range of its application and usefulness. Individuals choose among the various opportunities that they confront, but, in so doing, they cannot treat other individuals as they can the physical environment. One means of choosing more rather than less is choosing to engage in trade; in fact, this is the pervasive means through which man has expanded his command of "goods." The institutions of exchange, of markets, are derived, therefore, from the mutual interactions of individuals who are continuously engaged in making ordinary choices for more rather than less. As a "social" scientist, the primary function of the economist is to explain the workings of these institutions and to predict the effects of changes in their structure. As the interaction process that he examines becomes more complex, it is but natural that the task of the economic scientist becomes more intricate. But his central principle remains the same; and he can, through its use, unravel the most tangled sets of structural relationships among human beings.

The economist is able to do this because he possesses this central principle—an underlying theory of human behavior. And because he does so, he qualifies as a scientist and his discipline as a science. What a science does, or should do, is simply to allow the average man, through professional specialization, to command the heights of genius. The basic tools are the simple principles, and these are chained forever to the properly disciplined professional. Without them, he is as a jibbering idiot, who makes only noise under an illusion of speech. The progress of a science is measured by the continuing generalization of its principles, by their extension into new applications. Economics is not different in this respect from any other science. Its progress is best measured by the extent to which its central propositions are pushed outward, are stretched, so to speak, to explain human behavior as yet unexplained, to provide new predictive understanding of institutions emerging from human behavior. Viewed in this light, John von Neumann's contribution lay in extending the principles to apply in a wholly new set of situations confronting the individual. Game theory takes its place within the expanded kit of tools that the economist carries with him.

Contrast this with the Keynesian and post-Keynesian attention on macro-economics and macro-economic models. Does this "theory" provide the economist with an additional set of tools? Does this extend the application of the central principles of the discipline? Unfortunately, the answer must be negative here. Precisely because it has divorced itself from the central proposition relating to human behavior, modern macro-economic theory is really no theory at all. It has evolved, and remains, a set of models for the workings of economic aggregates, models that have little predictive value. Lord Keynes, of course, recognized this, and it was for this reason that he tried to tie his theoretical structure to basic psychological propensities. These propensities, which were designed to replace the more simple neoclassical behavioral propositions, have never fulfilled the role that Keynes must have hoped for them, and the modern model builders seem largely to leave even these out of account.

Macro-economic theory may, of course, attain the status of science, when and if its propositions carry predictive implications. However, when it does so, it will be a wholly new science, not that of economics. And its practitioners will not be classified by the characteristic responses of economists to the simple conceptual experiment carried out above. It is the divergence of macro-economics from the central propositions that is tending, today, to create serious problems of communication within the confines of the same discipline that is professionally classified as "economics." Increasingly, it becomes difficult for those who have specialized in macro-economics to communicate with those who start from the traditional base.

Spillouts to and Spillins from the Neighborhood Sciences—a Schematic Presentation

The discussion to this point has been concerned with what "economics" is. This preliminary has been necessary before raising the main questions of this essay, those which concern the relations of this science to its disciplinary neighbors. Full-length, and useful, methodological essays could, of course, be written covering the relations between economics and each and every one of the neighborhood sciences. Obviously, selectivity and condensation are essential here. It will perhaps be helpful, nonetheless, to present, briefly and schematically, the totality or quasi-totality of relationships. It seems reasonable to think of these as falling broadly within two sets. First, the contributions that economics can make to the other sciences or disciplines can be presented. These external effects can be called "spillouts," following another usage of this term by Burton Weisbrod. Second, the essential contributions that neighborhood disciplines can make to economics may be arrayed. These are, similarly, called "spillins."

In this section I shall present an array of spillouts and spillins, with only limited explanatory discussion under each heading. For simplicity in presentation, I have organized the material such that a single term represents the spillout contribution of economics to each discipline and a single term represents the spillin contribution of each other discipline to economics. Those relationships which will be discussed in more detail in the following sections are marked with an asterisk.

What Can Economics Contribute to Its Neighbors?
 To Engineering——an Attitude*
 To History——Constraints
 To Humanities——dashes of Reality*
 To Law——Limitations*
 To Mathematics——Applications
 To Physical Science——an Appreciation
 To Political Science——a Theory*
 To Psychology——a Challenge
 To Statistics——Problems

The above is, of course, shorthand. And, as with much shorthand, the schema may raise more issues than it resolves. Some brief clarification may be attempted here for those items which cannot be elaborated on in more detail below.

Economics can impose on the study of history essentially a constraining influence. The reconstruction of past events is circumscribed by the predictions that can be made concerning man's responses to his economic environment, and the viability of institutional arrangements may, in a sense, be tested. In fact, one of the interesting developments in economics, which amounts to an extension of its simple principles, involves the work of economic historians in applying data from past years to test the central hypotheses.

Economics offers little to the pure mathematician, at least at first hand. However, to the applied mathematician, the problems posed by the economist can offer fascinating and fruitful challenges to his ingenuity. And, to the extent that the "twisting" of pure theory by the applied mathematician generates a secondary reaction from the purist, there may be ultimate influence on the development of pure mathematics itself.

The physical scientist can, I think, learn much from the economist. Essentially, he can learn humility as he appreciates the limitations of science and scientific method in application to the inordinately complex problems of human relationships. To the extent that he can learn that, by comparison, his own problems are indeed elementary; despite his great achievements, he becomes both a better scientist and a better citizen.

To the psychologist, economists offer a standing challenge. Provide us with a better explanatory behavioral hypothesis! Economists know, of course, that ordinary utility maximization does not "explain" all behavior, or even a predominant part of it. Their success is, however, measured by the relevance of this hypothesis. Psychologists object to the economists' behavioral assumptions, but they have not provided sufficiently explanatory alternative hypotheses for the development of a general theory of human behavior in social structure. Perhaps they will do so; the challenge remains with them until they do.

The statistician is in much the same position as the applied mathematician, if, indeed, these two need be distinguished at all. The tests that economists seek, the aid that they request from him in devising such tests, may open up areas of research that otherwise remain closed.

What Can Economics Learn from Its Neighbors?
    From Engineering——a Warning*
    From History——Hope
    From Humanities——Inspiration
    From Law——a Framework*
    From Mathematics——a Language
    From Physical Science——a Morality*
    From Political Science——Data
    From Psychology——a Damper
    From Statistics——Design*

We may now examine, quite briefly, those spillins to economics, and to economists, from disciplinary neighbors not marked with asterisks on the above listing and thus not reserved for further elaboration.

The idea of progress that pervaded liberal scholarship in the two preceding centuries has, to an extent, disappeared. Nevertheless, history teaches economists, and all others whose subject matter is human civil order, that there is ultimate hope. Man may, and does, behave badly, by almost any standards, on many occasions. Yet learning more about how he does behave can mean only that, ultimately, he may choose to reform his institutions so as to bridle his impulses properly. History should teach the economist that the grievous mistakes of past epochs need not be repeated in future. History should provide him with hope.

The arts and the humanities have been too long neglected by economists, through simple error and confusion. The "goods" that men pursue should in no manner of speaking be conceived as vulgarly materialistic, in the common-sense terminology. The economist takes man essentially as he is, and he observes man selecting his own "goods," while shunning his own "bads." But as affluence allows man to rise above the subsistence minima, his "goods" expand to include those things that only the arts and the humanities discuss. Man wants to want better things; he wants to change his own tastes, and he deliberately chooses to modify his own listing of the "goods" that matter to him. It is appropriate that competent research scholars are now devoting attention to the economics of the fine arts.

The language that mathematics provides to economists, supplementary to their own, is widely recognized and understood. Its contribution to the productivity of economists, at the margin, may be questioned, but the integral of the product function must be large indeed.

What can political science, in its traditional disciplinary organization, contribute to the economist? Basically, it provides him with a record, data, of socio-political structures that he may, if he chooses, utilize in conducting his conceptual and actual experiments. Governments tend to do many things, and many of them foolishly. Political scientists keep the institutional record.

Psychology always threatens to undermine altogether the economist's simple principles, to make his model as a house of cards. Human behavior is erratic, nonrational, and often wholly unpredictable. Nonlogical explanation often supersedes logical explanation. The psychologist, by emphasizing the nonlogical, the "deeper" motivations and urges that guide the human psyche, chips continuously at the economist's predictive models. To an extent, these models remain in a state analogous to Newtonian physics, while the psychologist hopes to achieve the relativity breakthrough. To date, he has not succeeded, but the economist who is wise always keeps out a weather eye.

The two listings, those for spillouts and spillins, are not complete, and the brevity with which the relative directional contributions have been discussed has surely served to confuse as much as to enlighten. And especially for noneconomists, the necessary sketchiness may have served to raise more red flags than intended.

The Important Spillouts from Economics to Neighbor Disciplines

I now propose to discuss the four important spillout relationships marked with asterisks in the above listing more thoroughly.

ENGINEERING

In the simple schema on page 9, I suggested that economics contributes an attitude to the engineer and to the engineering sciences. With the latter term, I refer to all those studies that are instrumentally oriented toward the accomplishment of specific objectives. That is to say, the aim of the science is not understanding, but rather improving, making things work. Under this heading, therefore, I place not only physical engineering, as usually conceived, but also business engineering, most often labeled as business administration, and, likewise, social engineering.

As I have suggested, economists have often conceived themselves primarily as social engineers, and their interests have been more oriented to improvements in social structure than to predictions of a scientific character. This has led, and continues to lead, to much confusion. There is, of course, no reason why social engineering need not be a legitimate activity, in certain limits. But the activity of the social engineer is not that of the economic scientist.

Similarly, with the business engineer. It is one of the many American tragedies in education that has caused economics to be blanketed with business administration in professional association. Again, the business engineer serves a proper task, but a wholly different one from the economist. However, and this should be noted with some emphasis, the business engineer stands in precisely the same relation to the economist as the social engineer. The presumptive arrogance of those who call themselves economists and act as social engineers while scorning the role of the business engineer should be called promptly to account.

Having defined what I mean by "engineering" and "engineer," I can now elaborate what I mean by saying that the economist can contribute an "attitude" that is extremely helpful, as ample evidence reveals. The economist is trained to think in terms of alternatives; his attitude is one of searching among available alternatives for some optimal solution, and the study of the behavior of persons as they carry out such search. Engineers, far too frequently, fail to embody, as a "natural" thought pattern, sufficient concern for *alternatives.* They tend, by contrast, to think in terms of defined objectives and of specific means.

The best example of the economist's contribution to engineering in this respect is provided by the whole field of operations research. Here the central idea is essentially that of searching out from among the available alternatives and examining the possibility of accomplishing the same objectives with other alternatives, arrayed finally in accordance with some acceptable criteria. A predominant share of the developments in this area of study belongs to those who are trained, professionally, as economists.

The *attitude* that is relevant here is the one which emerges quite naturally from a concentration on the allocation of scarce means among alternative ends—the traditional definition of an economic problem. To many of my professional colleagues, this attitude is the peculiar talent of the economist, and he works always essentially as an engineer. I do not, of course, deny his value to the engineer, be this technical, organizational, or social, but I prefer to divorce this spillout effect from the central principles of economic science. This is not, of course, to deny that the contribution made by economists here is highly productive. It is essential that some professionals specialize, explicitly, in measuring and analyzing the relative costs of alternatives. And, given the state of the scientific world as it is, economists are better equipped to do this than almost anyone else. In the process, however, I should emphasize only that they work as engineers, not as economists.

HUMANITIES

Scholars in the humane studies should maintain at least a nodding acquaintance with economics and with economists. The spillout contribution here is that of imposing reality upon man's natural proclivity to dream. The economist, almost alone, takes man as he exists, and he does not spend his effort in dreaming of man's perfectibility. To the humanist, therefore, the economist's prospect is indeed a dismal one, and his concern with baser motives of man is held to scorn. This is as it should be; the humanist should not be expected to "love" the economist as fellow scholar. Indeed, his very purpose is to stretch the economist's model of ordinary man beyond its natural limits, and his success is measured by his ability to do so. The economist serves to provide the base from which the humanist begins. Essentially, the economist represents an ever-present Hobbesian realism standing counter to the innocent romanticism of all Rousseaus.

Utopianism is not the disease it once was, and to the extent that it has disappeared, the economist's constraints now have less value for the humanist than before. Even the last vestiges of utopianism, represented by the romantic conception of the ever-benevolent bureaucracy, the all-embracing despotism of the state, seems to have been dealt a crushing blow by the turn of events through history. Perhaps there is need now for a new utopianism rather than for its opposite, which seems reflected in the modern waves of disillusionment and despair. What is the future for humane studies in an absurd world? Perhaps the role of the economist has come full circle: Is it too much to claim that sober realism can, in fact, focus renewed attention on attainable human order? When it is finally recognized that man is neither the noble savage nor beset with original sin, the elemental rationality that is central to the economist's model may too become the stuff of dreams.

Law

The medium through which human beings impose constraints on their own interaction, one with another, is provided by the law. The simple principles of economics impose limitations on the operation of these constraints, much as the simple principles of physics impose limitations upon the engineer's working models of machines. Law can modify the conditions under which human beings choose among alternatives; it cannot directly affect the behavior in choosing. Economics seems to generate nonsensical statements by its critics, but none takes precedence over the discussion about the "repeal of the law of supply and demand." Intelligent and sophisticated men, who remain economic illiterates, talk as if human behavior in choice situations can be modified by legal restraints, as opposed to modifications in the conditions for choice. And on the basis of such discussion laws are enacted and enforced which have the effect of preventing the attainment of the very objectives that they are designed to promote.

Minimum-wage laws provide perhaps the best single example. Reasonable men support such legislation on the grounds that the poorer classes will be aided. The effect is, of course, the opposite, as the simplest of economic principles must state. By requiring the payment of a legal minimum wage, employers must choose fewer of the lowest paid workers rather than more. Low-productivity workers must be unemployed, or must shift into employments not covered by the legal restrictions. The laws harm the poorer and less-productive workers.

Such examples could be multiplied. The laws enacted in the ignorance of simple economic principles can do great damage, yet we observe little progress in the recognition of the limitations that economics should impose on legislation. This is the continuing despair of economists who want to see their science applied in practice.

POLITICAL SCIENCE

To orthodox political scientists, it may seem the height of presumptive arrogance to say that economics can provide "a theory" for explanation and prediction of political decisions. Nonetheless, it is becoming increasingly evident that the important theoretical advances in the explanation of political phenomena have been made primarily by those who approach the subject matter as economists. The reason for this is not far to seek. The political scientist has not, traditionally, incorporated a theory of human behavior into his structure of political process. To him, "theory" has never implied prediction. Instead, political theory has suggested normative philosophical discourse on the objectives and aims of political order. Little, if any, positive science is to be found in this tradition.

The economist, shifting his attention to man's behavior in reaching collective decisions in concert with his fellows in some political arrangement, brings with him, ready-made so to speak, a basic behavioral postulate. He is able, through its use, to make predictions, to advance hypotheses that are conceptually refutable. He does so in the full knowledge that the predictive value of his propositions is much less than that for the corresponding propositions relating to man's behavior in the strictly defined market relationship. He is prepared to accept the fact that his "explanation" of politics falls far short of completeness. But he can claim that he has a "theory of politics," of the way men do behave in collective decision making.

It is essentially this "economic" approach to politics that has come into attention as an important interdisciplinary area of scholarship since the 1940's. Work here remains in its infancy, but scholarship will surely accelerate over the decades ahead.

Important Spillins to Economics from Other Disciplines

Having discussed the four most important spillouts, the contributions that economics and economists can make to its scientific neighbors, I shall now discuss spillins. The "exchange" among disciplines is clearly multilateral, and the economist can learn much from the larger world of scholarship. Writing this paper as an economist, I find it more difficult to discuss spillins, which are more or less unconsciously allowed to affect our thinking, than I find it to discuss spillouts.

ENGINEERING

In the schema above, I have suggested that the contribution of engineering to economics consists of a "warning." Stated in an obverse way, we can say that the engineering sciences offer a constant "temptation" to the economist, and he must ever be on his guard lest he forget his own special position in the scientific world. The argument here is much the same, in reverse, of that offered above concerning the economist's contribution to the engineer. The economist's task is not properly that of *improving*, or making things work, whether these things be technical equipment, a business organization, or the social system. These are engineering tasks, and the economist must warn himself not to assume the role of the engineer too readily. There are specific contributions that the economist can make to engineering, as discussed above. But engineering is engineering, not economics. And the engineer, be he business, social, or technical, can best contribute to the development of economic science if he acts jealously concerning the intrusion of economists in his field. Professionally, the engineer should refuse association with the economist, and he should shun all attempts of the latter to enter into the confines of his discipline. "Management science" should be isolated and should isolate itself from economic science. But so should "social engineering," or "the science of social management," which far too many economists claim as their own bailiwick.

LAW

What can the study of law contribute to economics? The answer is clear, but its implications are too often overlooked. Economics seeks to explain human interactions within an emerging-evolving institutional setting, and this setting is best described in terms of the set of laws that condition human choices. The essential subject matter for the economist consists of human behavior in social institutions, not of human behavior in the abstract. The tendency of economic theorists to overlook this simple fact provoked the reaction of the American institutionalists, a reaction which surely was misguided in its emphasis, but which, nonetheless, pointed up a serious deficiency in the evolution of economic science. Imaginative and critical work in economics remains to be done in extending the applications of principles to the legal setting that is actually observable in a specific society.

To what extent are the rules, the laws, the institutions of social order assumed to be variable in the implied setting of theoretical welfare economics? The economist who has examined this literature will know that there is no answer suggested. Yet it is surely evident that the whole exercise has little significance until and unless such questions are answered. If, in fact, no laws are to be changed, Pareto optimality is automatically attained by each individual acting within the constraints imposed upon him. The whole discussion of Pareto optimality must, therefore, imply some change in the laws governing human conduct. But just which laws are to be subjected to change? Are overriding constitutional provisions to govern the changes that are allowed? These questions shall not be answered here, but merely raising them will suggest the need for some greater tie-in between the structure of economic theory on the one hand and the legal-institutional framework on the other.

How should such work begin? The logical starting place seems to be with the institutional structure that actually is observed. To this factual base can be applied the theoretical analysis. Fruitful results should emerge from such institutional theorizing. It is in such a context that productive work on the economics of property relationships has been done, and is being done, by such economists as Armen Alchian and Ronald Coase.

PHYSICAL SCIENCE

Frank Knight has said that economists should learn *morals* not method from the physical sciences. There is a point in what Knight says, and it is worth discussing. The physical scientists are scientists in a fuller sense of this emotive term than are most economists. They have been able, with rare exceptions, to conduct reasoned argument critically and dispassionately without the ideological overtones that have plagued effective communication among economists. They have a higher respect for "truth"; at least this appears to be the case to one who stands outside their pavilions. Perhaps this is because their standards are more precise; this, in itself, breeds a scientific morality that social scientists seem to lack. Hobbes is widely credited to have made the statement that general agreement would never have been reached on the proposition that two and two add up to four if it had proved to anyone's interest to argue otherwise. To an extent, this is surely true. The physical sciences have advanced so rapidly because their own advances have been divorced from direct social implications. Economics, and economists, have been placed at a great disadvantage because they cannot, even if they try, divorce their theory from social implication.

Should economists try to be pure scientists? Should they seek truth independent of values? This continues to be a debated question, and the fact that it is debatable, or thought to be so, suggests the state of the science. Gunnar Myrdal, and others, argue that there are no independent propositions; that the "truths" in economics emerge from basic value postulates that had best be stated at the outset of discussion. Taken seriously, this position removes all scientific content from the discipline and reduces discussion to a babel of voices making noise. The economist, to maintain his self-respect, must hold fast to the faith that there does exist an independent body of truth in his discipline, truth that can be discerned independent of value judgments.

THEORETICAL STATISTICS

Rutledge Vining has impressed upon me the contribution that theoretical statistics can make to the economist and to the study of economics. Practitioners in our discipline have been too prone to look directly at the instan-

taneously observable results of economic process and to infer from these implications that carry both theoretical and policy content. Statistical theory
forces a recognition of the temporal sequences of results that are observable
and the variations in distributions over time. The very presence of randomness in the economic universe seems to have been largely neglected in the
formal development of the theory that we use. Once we begin to recognize
that each and every event in time-space is not predetermined but contains
some randomness in its generation, direct inferences from instantaneously
observed results become much more difficult.

To what extent can the distribution of income among persons be explained by random variation? To what extent can the distribution of persons
over space be explained by random selection? It is clear, once such questions
as these are asked, that until and unless we can have some approximate idea
as to the answers we cannot really evaluate the implications of any observable
distribution. In designing his conceptual experiments, the economist cannot
now fail to allow for the relevance of randomness, or chance, in determining
outcomes. This makes the refutation of his hypotheses much more difficult, of
course, but it is best that he proceed without false hopes of rigor that does not
exist. Truth is not so easy to come by in a world of uncertainty, but, once having recognized this, we are better off as scientists.

Theoretical statistics can contribute to the design of experiments, and to
the economist's thinking about design, in yet another way. The statistician
recognizes that he does not choose directly among outcomes, allocations, or
distributions. His choice is among *rules* that will restrict or confine the range
of possible outcomes and among the criteria through which the operation of
these rules shall be judged. This attitude is of major importance to the economist, and it can teach him a major lesson. The overemphasis on allocation
problems has taught far too many economists to think in terms of directly
choosing allocations of resources, distributions of income, etc. Reflection on
this indicates at once that such variables are not within the range of social
choice, even if social choice be accepted as appropriate for the economist's
advice. The society chooses among the several possible rules which restrict
or condition human behavior. These rules will generate outcomes, which
may be examined in terms of allocations or distributions. Once the emphasis
is shifted to the choices among rules, however, the whole structure of discussion of welfare criteria is shifted, and with obvious advantage.

Specialized Interdependence—a Specific Example

In the introduction I suggested that two trends could be observed in the development of modern economics. First, the independence of the science from its neighbors seems rapidly to be disappearing, while, at the same time, professional specialization within the discipline is proceeding apace. These are, at first glance, contradictory trends, but upon closer examination the contradiction disappears. What seems to be happening in most instances is the emergence of a new orientation of professional specialization, and one that has not, as yet, found its place in the structure of professional organization and educational curricula. It becomes increasingly clear that the channels of effective communication do not extend throughout the discipline that we variously call "economics," and that some "economists" are able to communicate far more effectively with some scholars in the noneconomic disciplines than with those presumably within their own professional category.

I shall illustrate this development, which I think can be generalized for several areas, with reference to a single cross-disciplinary field, one with which I have personally been associated. I refer to the work that has been done by economists in extending the simple principles of their discipline to political decision making, to the making of decisions in a nonmarket context. As I have suggested earlier, much of the early work was done by economists, but more recently a few political scientists have been directly engaged in this field of scholarship. At the same time separate but closely related work has been done in other areas. Economists who have worked on the "theory of teams," on the "economics of information," on the "theory of organization" have all been concerned with similar constructions. Psychologists who have been concerned with small-group theory, all scholars who have worked in game theory, and especially with nonzero sum cooperative games, also fall into the cross-disciplinary field that is emerging. There are even a few philosophers who, in their concern with what is called "rule-utilitarianism," fall among the interdisciplinary communication network.

Through this development, it becomes far easier, and more interesting as well as more productive, for the economist who works with nonmarket decisions to communicate with the positive political scientist, the game theorist, or the organizational theory psychologist than it is for him to communicate with the growth-model macro-economist, with whom he scarcely finds any common ground. This specialized interdependence, if it is, in fact, general over several emerging specializations, can be expected to result, ultimately, in some movements toward professional institutionalization. To an extent, this has already happened in such areas as regional science. These movements should not be discouraged by the inherent conservatism of established disciplinary orthodoxy. Insofar as interdisciplinary specialization emerges genuinely from the changing channels of effective scholarly communication, steps taken to further such communication, while breaking down traditionally established disciplinary lines, represent added efficiency.

Conclusions

The starting point for this essay has been the empirical embodiment of "economics" as a scientific discipline. I have deliberately interpreted economics narrowly, as a science and as a positive set of conceptually refutable propositions about human behavior in a social organization. The normative content that is often alleged to be present in the discipline has been simply defined as outside the pale of discussion here. This is, I think, as it should be, although I recognize that many highly competent methodologists will sharply disagree with my position on this. There is, I submit, positive content to the science that is economics, and it is this positive content that is currently deserving of stress and emphasis, both on the part of its own practitioners and on that of its neighboring scholars. The role of the economist, at base, must be that of attempting to understand a certain type of human behavior and the prediction of the social structures that are emergent from that behavior. Ultimately, the economist must hope that his simple truths, as extended, can lead to "improvement" in the structure of these institutions, through the ability of institutions to modify the conditions of human choice. But improvement must remain his secondary and subsidiary purpose; he verges dangerously on irresponsible action when he allows his zeal for social progress, as he conceives this, to take precedence over his search for and respect of scientific truth, as determined by the consensus of his peers.

This does not imply that the economic scientist must remain in the realm of pure theory and shun all discussions of economic policy. There can be, and should be, a theory of economic policy. And the economist, by analyzing the results of alternative lines of action, can be of great assistance to the social decision maker. But, as such, the economist has no business at playing the social engineer. He can hope that his light will ultimately be used to generate some heat, but he should live with his hope and refuse to become an activist. He can point out to men the opportunities for reorganizing their social institutions in such a way as to achieve the goals that men desire. But the final choices in a free society rest with individuals who participate in that society. Men may choose to live primitively and to refuse to recognize the simple principles that economists continually repeat. If they so choose, they will so choose, and it is not the task of the economist, or anyone else, to say that they "should" necessarily choose differently. The task of the economist, and of economic science, is done when the simple propositions are presented.

If the economist can learn from his colleagues in the physical sciences, and learn in sufficient time, that the respect for truth takes precedence above all else and that it is the final value judgment that must pervade all science, he may, yet, rescue the discipline from its currently threatened rush into absurdity, oblivion, and disrepute. In the large, he does not seem to be learning, and, if anything, the physical scientist seems more in danger of accepting the perverted confusion that has plagued the economist through generations. But there are a few encouraging signs, and these are to be found in the genuinely exciting areas of specialized interdisciplinary interdependence that are blossoming in full flower. A second ray of hope lies in the attitude of the young scholars, in economics as well as its neighbors. Their attitude is properly critical of all ideologues. To the emotionally committed socialist or libertarian, who parades also as economist, these young scholars may appear as disinterested, lacking passion, as "cold fish." But to the extent that they are, economics is gaining stature as a science and is shedding off its burdensome overgrowth of social involvement. The economics that may gain full stature as a science will not excite the reformers who have occupied too many of its chairs in past decades, but to those who seek for truth the discipline will be worthy of their efforts.

The challenge remains with those who are and will become economists. The pessimist observes the prostitution and worries about scientific morality. The optimist seizes the rays of hope and projects the millennium. The final response will depend perhaps as much upon the unpredictable evolution of social institutions, guided only in part by rational choices, as on the deliberate decisions made by the professionals.

BIBLIOGRAPHY

Alchian, Armen, and W. R. Allen, *University Economics*. San Francisco: Wadsworth, 1964.

Coats, A. W., *The Role of Value Judgments in Economics*. Monograph 7. Charlottesville, Va.: Thomas Jefferson Center for Studies in Political Economy, 1964.

Friedman, Milton, *Essays in Positive Economics*. Chicago: University of Chicago Press, 1953.

Hutchison, T. W., *Positive Economics and Policy Objectives*. London: G. Allen, 1964.

Kirzner, Israel M., *The Economic Point of View*. New York: Van Nostrand, 1960.

Knight, Frank H., *Intelligence and Democratic Action*. Cambridge, Mass.: Harvard, 1960.

————, *On the History and Method of Economics*. Chicago: University of Chicago Press, 1956.

Myrdal, Gunnar, *The Political Element in the Development of Economic Theory*, trans. P. Streeten. London: Routledge, 1953.

Vining, Rutledge, *Economics in the United States of America*. Paris: U.N. Educational, Scientific, and Cultural Organization, 1956.

The Domain
of Subjective Economics
Between Predictive Science
and Moral Philosophy

We . . . are in part living in a world the constituents of which we can discover, classify and act upon by rational, scientific . . . methods; but in part . . . we are immersed in a medium that . . . we do not and cannot observe as if from the outside; cannot identify, measure, and seek to manipulate; cannot even be wholly aware of, inasmuch as it . . . is itself too closely interwoven with all that we are and do to be lifted out . . . and observed with scientific detachment, as an object.

—Isaiah Berlin

Introduction

Any discussion of the methodology of subjective economics must at once confront an elementary fact along with a necessary hypothesis. That fact is that, in any science of human behavior, the observer is himself among the observed. The hypothesis is that human beings *choose*. Without this hypoth-

From *Method, Process, and Austrian Economics: Essays in Honor of Ludwig von Mises*, ed. Israel M. Kirzner (Lexington, Mass.: D. C. Heath, 1982), 7–20. Reprinted by permission.

I am indebted to Pamela Brown and Karen Vaughn for helpful comments. Precursory ideas to those developed in this chapter are present in my essays "General Implications of Subjectivism in Economics" and "Natural and Artifactual Man" in my book *What Should Economists Do?* (Indianapolis: Liberty Fund, 1979).

esis the activity of the observer becomes meaningless exercise. The fact and the accompanying hypothesis impose constraints or limits on any "positive economics," if the model is taken from those sciences within which these attributes are missing. The natural scientist remains separate from the objects of his observation, and, despite the acknowledgment of the possibility of mutual influence between observer and observed, there remains the basic category differentiation. Furthermore, the simple ability to put these words together in a meaningful sentence distinguishes me, as a man, from those objects of science that most resemble me, the higher animals. By the process of writing a sentence, I am choosing what I create; I am not merely reacting to external stimuli, at least in a sense readily amenable to prediction.

In summary terms, the *subjective* elements of our discipline are defined precisely within the boundaries between the positive, predictive science of the orthodox model on the one hand and the speculative thinking of moral philosophy on the other—hence, the chapter's title. For our purposes, I define *moral philosophy* as discourse that embodies an explicit denial of the relevance of scientific explanation. Note that this approach does not require a categorical rejection of the relevance of empirically testable, positive hypotheses concerning certain aspects of human behavior commonly labeled "economic." Nor does the approach rule out the relevance of normative moral philosophy. The approach emphasizes, instead, the existence and the importance of the area between empirical science and moral philosophy. It denies that these categories of thought span the universe of relevance. On this point, I think that my own professor, Frank Knight, and Ludwig von Mises would have been in substantial agreement. Both would have been extremely critical of the modern economists who seek to rule out any nonempirical economics as nonscientific and, by inference, normative. Both these seminal thinkers would have been comfortable with a science of subjective economics, although they might have differed somewhat on the relevance of any other part of our discipline.

Adam Smith and Classical Economics

Classical economics has been almost universally interpreted as an attempted, and ultimately failed, effort to derive an objective and predictive theory of the relative values of commodities. The central features are perhaps best exemplified in Adam Smith's famous deer-beaver illustration, which I shall use here. Smith's hypothesis was that one beaver would "naturally" exchange for two deer in that setting where two days of labor are required to kill a beaver and one day of labor to kill a deer. I want to ask the following question: Even if we grant all the required presuppositions of the Smith model, do we then derive a genuinely predictive theory of the relative values of beaver and deer? Or do there remain necessarily subjective elements in the inclusive explanatory model, even within such an extremely restricted setting?

The required presuppositions are familiar. Deer and beaver must be "goods" to all potential consumers and producers: labor must be a "bad." Labor is the only productive resource, and units of labor are completely homogeneous. Further, each commodity must be producible at constant returns. But we must recall that Adam Smith was seeking to explain *exchange* values. The restrictions of the model, even if fully realized, do not explain the emergence of exchange, and, in the strict sense, no exchange would take place in the setting postulated. If the input ratio is two for one, precepts for rationality suggest that each behaving unit will attain an equilibrium adjustment when the two-for-one ratio is equated to a two-for-one valuation ratio for the two goods. There is no subjective element in the analysis, as I have deliberately limited the scope for the term *subjective* here.

Adam Smith and classical economics were not, however, interested in explaining individual behavioral adjustment. Smith was interested in explaining *exchange* values. And, to explain these, he had to explain the emergence of exchange itself. To do so, he must have incorporated an additional presupposition not listed. The productivity of labor when specialized must be higher than when unspecialized. Smith's emphasis on the importance of the division of labor suggests, of course, that this presupposition was indeed central to his explanatory model. But why would exchange emerge in the first place? Here Smith resorted to man's "propensity to truck, barter, and exchange one thing for another."[1] The critical role of this propensity in

---

1. Adam Smith, *Wealth of Nations*, Modern Library Edition (New York: 1937), 13.

Smith's analysis has been too much neglected in interpretations of his work. But with this propensity, Smith places a subjective element at the heart of the whole explanatory model. He quite explicitly contrasts the actions of man with the animals in this respect when he says that "nobody ever saw a dog make a fair and deliberate exchange of one bone for another with another dog."[2]

In some preexchange setting, the exercise of the "propensity to truck"— behavior that must necessarily have been different in kind from that which had been reflected in established patterns (and, hence, predictable scientifically, at least within stochastic limits)—allowed man to discover the advantages of specialization and to create the institutions of exchange within which relative values of commodities come to be settled. The person who initially imagines some postspecialization, postexchange state and who acts to bring such a state into existence must engage in what I shall here call "active" choice. He must do more than respond predictably to shifts in the constraints that are exogenously imposed on him.

An economy (if indeed it could be called such) in which all persons respond to constraints passively and in which no one engages in active choice could never organize itself through exchange institutions. Such an economy would require that the constraints be imposed either by nature or by beings external to the community of those participants who are the passive responders. In either case, such an economy would be comparable in kind to those whose participants are the "animal consumers" examined by John Kagel and Raymond Battalio, and their coworkers.[3]

Even at the level of Adam Smith's most elementary discourse, there are two interpretations that may be placed on his analysis. If Smith is read as relatively unconcerned about the emergence of exchange institutions, and if he is assumed simply to have postulated the existence of specialization, it may be argued that his aim was to present a positive, predictive theory of the relative values of commodities. On the other hand, if Smith is read as primarily or centrally concerned with explaining how exchange institutions

2. Ibid.

3. See John H. Kagel et al., "Demand Curves for Animal Consumers," *Quarterly Journal of Economics* 96 (February 1981): 1–16.

emerge, he becomes a thoroughgoing subjectivist in that he resorts to that particular propensity that distinguishes man from other animals. There could be no predictive science concerning the exercise of this propensity, since to predict here would imply that the direction of all future exchanges would be conceptually knowable at any point in time.

The two interpretations of Smith's basic analysis differ in their *explananda*. The first involves an explanation, or attempted explanation, of relative exchange values of commodities. The second involves an explanation of exchange institutions themselves. That which can be predicted (conceptually) can be explained with an objective or scientific theory. That which cannot be predicted can be explained (understood) only by a subjective theory. If this basic methodological duality had been accepted at the outset, much confusion in the history of economic doctrine, then and now, might have been avoided. Subjective economics, properly, even if strictly, defined, occupies an explanatory realm that is mutually exclusive with that properly occupied by positive economics. If this much is granted, however, the relative significance of the two realms of discourse for the inclusive understanding of human interaction becomes clear. Positive or predictive economics becomes largely an exercise in triturating the obvious; subjective economics can offer insights into the dynamics through which a society of persons who remain free to choose in a genuine sense develops and prospers.

In subsequent parts of this chapter I shall illustrate this basic argument by reference to somewhat misguided and at least partially confused efforts to emphasize the subjective elements in economic theory, broadly defined. I shall discuss the so-called subjective-value revolution and its transformation into the modern neoclassical synthesis. I shall discuss also the dimensionality of economic theory to show that the dimensionality problem should be considered separately from that of operationality of theory. A discussion of the particular Austrian variant of neoclassical economics, as exemplified notably in the works of Mises, follows with particular emphasis on his insistence of the praxeological foundations of the discipline. The following section discusses the potential applicability of subjective and objective economic theory, and I shall offer a provisional explanation for the relative dominance of the latter in the postclassical century. Finally, I shall summarize the argument and draw some inferences for the direction of research.

The Subjective-Value Revolution of the 1870s and the Subsequent Neoclassical Synthesis

As noted previously, classical economic theory was widely interpreted as an attempt to derive a predictive theory of the relative values of commodities.[4] Classical economics was acknowledged to have failed in such an attempt. Emphasis came to be placed on the specific difficulties that could not be satisfactorily met with the classical models. The diamond-water paradox remained; the classical effort to explain relative exchange value by objectively measurable costs of production could not survive.

The so-called subjective-value revolution, presented in various ways in the early 1870s by Jevons, Menger, and Walras, was explicitly aimed at resolution of the prevailing difficulties in the classical explanation of exchange values. The early contributions here demonstrated that relative values depend on schedules of evaluation on both sides of the markets for goods, on demand and supply. But we must ask a question here that has not, to my knowledge, been frequently posed. To what extent does the economic theory of Jevons, Menger, and Walras, or their neoclassical successors, embody genuine subjective economics as I have defined this term? Despite its label as the subjective-value revolution in economic theory, are there any necessarily subjective elements in the inclusive explanatory models that were offered in place of the discarded classical edifice?

I suggest that the label *subjective* may be misleading in application to this theory of exchange values, notably so as the initial contributions were redeveloped and refined into the neoclassical synthesis of the twentieth century. The marginal-utility theory of the 1870s embodied the central notion that values are determined at the appropriate margins of evaluation and that the locations of the margins are relevant. The diamond-water paradox was thereby resolved satisfactorily. But there is nothing in the whole analytical framework here to suggest that the evaluation schedules (those of demand and supply), which simultaneously interact to determine the location of the

---

4. This statement should be qualified to limit its relevance to the core problem of economic theory, that of explaining how an economy allocates resources and distributes product. Classical economics has been differently interpreted as offering a theory of economic development or growth.

margins and hence exchange values, are not, themselves, *objectively determinate,* at least in a conceptual sense. There is nothing in neoclassical economic theory that precludes the universalized existence of simple reaction patterns of behavior on the part of all persons in the economy, reaction patterns that, even if more complex, are still analogous to those that might empirically describe the behavior of rats. Once individual-utility functions are formally specified, individuals whose behavior is thereby depicted cannot choose differently. Choice, as such, cannot remain in any such formulation.

I am not suggesting here that the objectification of the solution to the problem of determining relative exchange values of goods (and bads) was necessarily central to neoclassical theory. It was not. The earlier classical effort was aimed to provide a single, and simplistic, objective measure of relative exchange values that might be both readily understood and empirically estimated. The neoclassical effort, in contrast, was primarily aimed at resolving difficulties at the level of logical coherence and rigor. There was a shift of emphasis from attempts to provide empirical bases for measurement toward attempts to offer understanding of the whole logical structure of economic interaction. For the latter purpose, the issues involved in making empirical estimates or predictions about relative exchange values do not take on critical significance. These issues tend to be overshadowed by those concerning the derivations of proofs of the existence of solutions to the complex interdependencies that the economy embodies. That the empirical measurability or predictability of exchange values does not occupy center stage in orthodox neoclassical theory should not, however, be taken as evidence that, conceptually, such measurability is categorically impossible. The focus of neoclassical economic theory, in comparison with classical, is shifted from empirical estimates to analyses of structures, but there is nothing directly in neoclassical theory that implies the absence of conceptual predictability. If utility and production relationships are ascertainable, solutions exist and are determinate. It is meaningful in this context to make an attempt to compute equilibrium prices.

The Dimensionality and Data of Economic Theory

My purpose in this section is to clarify possible confusion and ambiguity that may arise from my somewhat restricted definition of subjective economics and from my claim that the term *subjective-value revolution* as applied to the contribution of the 1870s may be, in this context, misleading.

It is necessary to distinguish carefully between the definition of the dimensions of the space within which the operations of economic theory are performed and the operationality of the theory itself. My narrowly restricted definition of subjective economic theory is relevant only to the second of these subjects. As I have limited the term here, subjective economic theory embodies those elements of explanation of the economic process that cannot be operationalized in the orthodox sense of predictive science. For those elements of economic theory that can be operationalized, however, I have advanced no presumption whatever about the dimensionality of the space.

Confusion necessarily arises at this point between the claim that any economic theorizing must take place within a subjective-value dimension and the totally different claim that, because of the subjective dimensionality, an operational theory is not possible. The first of these claims must be accepted. Economic theory is surely concerned with evaluations, with values. It is totally misleading to think of physical dimensionality here. Goodness and badness are qualities that are assigned to physical things, to commodities or services, by personal evaluations.

The naive and simplistic efforts by the classical economists to derive a predictive theory of relative exchange values tended to obscure the value dimension and generated the absurdity that commodities may be produced by commodities somehow independent of the evaluation put on these by persons. In the sense that it emphasized and brought to full realization the essential value dimension, it is appropriate to label the 1870s effort as a subjective-value revolution. But, as I have noted, this corrective shift in implied dimensionality of the space for the application of economic theory carries with it no direct implication for the potential operationality of the theory itself. Indirectly, of course, there is the obvious implication that only if economic theory applies within a value dimension could there arise any issue of nonoperationality. Subjective economics could hardly be discussed in any analysis of variables in pure-commodity space. On the other hand, however, there is nothing in the value dimension itself that logically prohibits the derivation of a fully operational science. Whether or not such analysis is possible depends not on dimensionality but instead on the possible uniformity of valuations over persons.

A related source of confusion involves the informational requirements that a thoroughgoing recognition of the value dimensionality of economics places on any putative scientist who seeks to derive empirically testable hypotheses. F. A. Hayek, in particular, has emphasized the value dimensionality of economic theory and the informational implications of this attribute for the organization of society.[5] Markets utilize information efficiently; they do not require extensive centralization of information about individual evaluations. And, indeed, the informational requirements for a centrally planned economy may be practically insurmountable. There is nothing in the basic Hayekian insight, however, that precludes the possible derivation of a set of conceptually refutable hypotheses about the evaluations of all persons over all goods and services.

In earlier works I have stressed the subjectivity of costs, and I have tried to show how errors arise in applications of economic theory when this basic dimensionality is overlooked.[6] In the restricted classification scheme that I have suggested in this chapter, however, there is nothing in my analysis of cost, as such, that precludes the derivation of a set of conceptually refutable hypotheses, which is, of course, the criterion of a predictive theory. Costs are, of course, related to choices, but if there are sufficient data on the environment of a past choice and if the chooser's behavior is, in some sense, predictable on the basis of observed uniformities, choices may be judged ex post. Practically, the subjective-value dimension of economic behavior may make enforcement of any cost-price rule impossible, but such application of the predictive science cannot be deemed conceptually impossible.

Mises and Praxeology

Mises explicitly denied that economic theory can be operational in the orthodox meaning of this term. Economic theory was, for Mises, necessarily a priori; it offered a pure logic of choice. In taking this extreme position methodologically, Mises seemed to be aware that attempts to force economic theory into the straitjacket imposed by the requirements for predictive science

---

5. F. A. Hayek, "Economics and Knowledge," *Economica* 4 (1937): 33–54.
6. *Cost and Choice* (Chicago: Markham, 1969).

must, at the same time, deny to persons who act the possibility of making genuine choices.

I shall confess here that I have never been able to appreciate fully the Misesian emphasis on praxeology or "the science of human action."[7] Central to this conception is the purposefulness of all human action. Man acts always with a purpose; he seeks to replace a state of relative dissatisfaction with one of relative satisfaction. However, an observer can never get inside anyone else; he can never know what a person's purpose is. Hence, there is no way, even conceptually, to predict what action will be taken in any particular circumstance. A person chooses that which he chooses, and when he so chooses, he must anticipate that the chosen course of action will yield a net increment to his satisfaction. Although he may err, we can never infer, ex post, that he acted irrationally.

At its most general, this Misesian theory of choice is totally nonoperational. It can "explain" any conceivable course of action that a person might be observed to take; the obverse is, of course, that the theory can really "explain" nothing at all. Mises himself did not worry about nonoperationality as such, presumably because his reliance on introspection provided him with a basis for sorting out meaningful from meaningless explanations. To return to the Adam Smith illustration, Mises could claim to have explained why exchange institutions emerged from the vision of some person who imagined the mutual advantages of specialization and exchange. Mises could also explain the relative values of deer and beaver quite simply as those exchange ratios that emerge from the purposeful choice behavior of participants in the exchange process, whose acts of participation or nonparticipation are themselves purposeful.

Misesian economic theory becomes strictly subjective economics in my earlier definition of the term. But my basic criticism of Mises is that he claimed far too much for the subjective economics domain. He seemed to

---

7. Thomas Nagel's fascinating review of Brian O'Shaughnessy's recently published two-volume book suggests that at least some of the attention of modern analytic philosophers is turning to what seems to be a Mises-like a priori conception of human action. See Thomas Nagel, "The Self from Within," review of Brian O'Shaughnessy, *The Will: A Dual Aspect Theory*, vols. 1 and 2 (Cambridge: Cambridge University Press, 1980), in *London Times Literary Supplement*, 27 March 1981, 327–28.

want to preempt the whole territory when he totally rejected the existence of any relevant domain for what I have called positive or predictive objective economic theory. This somewhat overzealous extension of methodological frontiers may be at least partially responsible for the relatively limited reception that the ideas of Mises have had among economists, catholically classified.

The basic Mises conception of praxeology seems flawed in that it appears to incorporate two quite distinct sorts of human action, one of which may be analyzed scientifically and empirically in the orthodox sense. Consider two examples: (1) A man is walking along a road; he sees a car approaching; he jumps to the side of the road to avoid being run down. His action here is purposeful. It is surely aimed at removing a potential state of dissatisfaction and replacing it by one that is preferred. (2) A man is walking along a road barefooted. His feet are sore. He sees some cowhide and he imagines the possibility of shoes. He acts to make the shoes from cowhide. (My thanks to Israel Kirzner for this example.) This action is purposeful, and it, like the first, is surely aimed at replacing a state of dissatisfaction (sore feet) with one that is preferred.

But Misesian praxeology, as I understand it, would seem to include both examples within the realm of human action that theory seeks to analyze and to explain. I submit, however, that they are categorically distinct. The first action need not reflect conscious, active, or creative choice; it can be interpreted as an animal-like response to a change in the external environment. It is reflective of behavior that might have been scientifically predicted. It is the sort of action that could describe the behavior of rats as well as men. By evident and sharp contrast, an animal could never take the second sort of creative action, which becomes uniquely human.[8] The Misesian praxeological umbrella that seems to encompass both sorts of action does not allow the sophisticated discrimination that must be made between the two. Indeed the Misesian emphasis on treating all human action as if it were like the second example tends to foster a critical response that involves the danger of neglect of the very type of action that subjective economics properly emphasizes.[9]

8. I ignore the tool-using action of some primates. My purpose is conceptual classification rather than ethology.

9. My criticism of the Mises-Austrian position in this section (although it was developed independently before I knew about Nozick's paper) closely parallels that taken by

The Mutually Exclusive Domains
for Economic Theory

There are patterns of human behavior in economic interaction that are subject to conceptual prediction about which empirically testable hypotheses may be derived. There is a legitimate domain for predictive economic theory. Or, to put my point differently but somewhat more dramatically, in some aspects of their economic behavior, with appropriate qualifications, men are indeed like rats.[10] They are essentially passive responders to economic stimuli; they react; they do not choose. They are programmed, whether genetically or culturally, to behave in potentially predictable ways to specific modifications in the constraints that they face. The scope for this predictive theory of economic behavior is enormously extended when it is acknowledged that it is the behavior of some average or representative member of a group that is to be predicted here, not the particularized behavior of an individual.

The recognition of the domain of an operationally meaningful economic theory does not carry with it any implication concerning the practical usefulness of this theory in making predictions in the real world and/or in using such predictions to control man's behavior in that reality. There remains the awesome gap between the science that embodies conceptually refutable hypotheses and that science that embodies definitive refutation or corroboration. The familiar distinctions between the human and the nonhuman sciences involving controls on experiments arise here, along with the informational problems noted briefly earlier. Nonetheless, ultimate empirical content remains in the theory, regardless of actual testability, and the elaboration of the structure of relationships can add to our understanding of economic reality.

Robert Nozick in part 2 of his paper "On Austrian Methodology," *Synthese* 36 (1977): 353–92, especially pp. 361–69. For an informative critique that is somewhat differently directed, see Willi Meyer, "Erkenntnistheoretische Orientierungen und der Charakter des ökonomischen Denken," in *Zur Theorie marktwirtschaftliches Ordnungen*, E. Streissler and C. Watrin, eds. (Tübingen: Mohr, 1980), especially pp. 82–91.

10. The qualifications refer to the obvious differences in the complexity of response patterns as between man and rat. I am not saying that men are like rats in any descriptive sense. My purpose, to repeat, is conceptual classification, not accuracy in description.

There are also aspects of human action that cannot be subjected to explanation in an operationally meaningful theory of economics. Any attempt to derive even conceptually refutable hypotheses about such action would amount to epistemological confusion. I have labeled this domain that of subjective economics or subjective economic theory. The objects for analysis are the *choices* of persons, which cannot be genuine choices and at the same time subject to prediction. Theory or analysis can be of explanatory value in this domain without the attribute of operationality in the standard sense. Theory can add to our understanding (*verstehen*) of the process through which the economic world of values is created and transformed. Subjective economics offers a way of thinking about economic process, a means of imposing an intellectual order on apparent chaos without inferentially reducing the status of man, as a scientific object, to something that is not, in kind, different from that of animals.[11]

The limits of this vision of economic process must be recognized, however, along with its advantageous insights. Subjective economic theory can be of little assistance in an explanation or understanding of the allocation of values or in predicting general responses to changes in constraints imposed on actors. Since this theory advances no claim to prediction, it can, at best, suggest that any predictions made will likely prove to be wrong, indeed must be wrong to the extent that its own domain of choice is allowed operative range.

The purpose of the explanatory exercise determines the appropriate domain of economic theory to be employed. If this purpose is that of control of the economy through some manipulation of the constraints within which persons respond, the first domain of positive, predictive economic theory is the only one that holds out any scope for assistance. To the extent that this theory can isolate predicted response patterns to shifts in imposed constraints (to an increase or decrease in taxes, for example), those persons who participate in making political decisions (who may, of course, also be mem-

11. The work of Israel Kirzner exemplifies subjective economic theory in the sense defined here. Few critics could argue that Kirzner's discussion of entrepreneurship and the role of the entrepreneur in the competitive economic process is not explanatory in the ordinary meaning of the term. See Israel Kirzner, *Competition and Entrepreneurship* (Chicago: University of Chicago Press, 1973).

bers of the group whose reaction behavior is being predicted by the economists) make their choices among alternative constraints on the basis of better
information. The predictions of the economists have value, and this value
commands a price. It is, therefore, not at all surprising that the efforts of economists shifted toward the predictive-science domain during the century-long
period of increasing controls over national economies. Faith in the efficacy
of such predictive science for assistance in controlling the economy perhaps
reached its apogee in the 1960s, after which skepticism emerged from its dor-
mancy. The very failures of the predictive science of economics suggest the
necessity of allowing for the existence of that domain of human action not
amenable to scientistic explanation.

As the purpose of inquiry shifts toward understanding the sources of
value creation with some ultimate objective of encouraging the establishment and maintenance of an environment within which human choices are
allowed to take place relatively free of imposed constraints, we should expect economists to direct more of their attention to the domain of subjective economic theory.

Of Rats and Men

I have found a discussion of the methodology of subjective economics impossible without first defining what I have called the "domain," and my discussion in the chapter has been almost exclusively limited to definitional issues. After considerable intellectual floundering, my proposed classification
of the two domains of economic theory emerged from a consideration of the
very interesting laboratory experiments of rats and pigeons that have been
conducted by Kagel, Battalio, and their colleagues. It seemed evident to me
that this experimental work was scientific in a sense fully analogous with that
carried out by our noneconomist peers in the natural sciences. And yet, as
this work has revealed, rats have been shown to choose rationally, to respond
predictably to stimuli, to react to "prices," and in many respects to behave as
true (even if simple) "economic men." It is possible to derive demand and
supply schedules for rats. That part of economic theory, therefore, that analyzes human behavior of the sort that is also evidently descriptive of rat behavior must be categorized as a genuinely predictive science.

The residual aspects of human action that are not reducible to rat-like responses to stimuli, even in the much more complex human variants, define the domain for a wholly different, and uniquely human, science—one that cannot, by its nature, be made analogous to the positive-predictive sciences of the orthodox paradigm.

There is surely room for both sciences to exist in the more inclusive rubric that we call economic theory. We must acknowledge that in many aspects of their behavior, men conform to laws of behavior such that such behavior becomes subject to scientifically testable prediction and control through the external manipulation of constraints. But we must also acknowledge that men can choose courses of action that emerge only in the choice process itself. Men create value by the imagination of alternatives that do not exist followed by the action that implements the possibilities imagined.[12]

Perhaps the methodology of subjective economics, once the definition of its domain is accepted, can best be advanced by a deliberate attempt to sweep out thought patterns that are carried over from its positivist counterpart. I cannot, in this concluding section, discuss such steps in particular, but one example indicates my meaning. It has been suggested that subjective economic theory necessarily draws attention to the elementary fact that choices are made under conditions of uncertainty. Any attempt, however, to carry over the modern analysis of individual choice under uncertainty to the genuine choice making that is the subject of subjective economic theory reflects intellectual confusion. How can anything remotely resembling a probabilistic calculus be applied to choices that are among alternatives that come into being only through the act of choice itself? The human beings whose choices occupy the thoughts of G. L. S. Shackle could never be reduced to the status

12. Methodologically, it is important to insist that the two domains be treated as mutually exclusive. Unless this precept is strictly adhered to, the operational status of the predictive theory may become meaningless. Suppose that an hypothesis derived from this theory is empirically refuted. The theorist cannot be allowed to fall back on an essentially subjective economics explanation to the effect that utility functions have shifted, that persons have exercised genuine choice. He should, instead, be forced to acknowledge the falsification of his hypothesis about behavioral reality. To resort to presumed shifts in the reality itself while holding to the central hypothesis is methodologically illegitimate.

For a fascinating discussion of a related problem that arises in the relationship between moral and predictive theory, see David Levy, "Rational Choice and Morality: Economics and Classical Philosophy," December 1979, mimeo.

of rats, even superintelligent ones.[13] In my view, no economist other than Shackle works exclusively within the domain of subjective economic theory, as I have defined it here.

Any methodological advance must build on the work of Shackle. But as many scholars have already found, the next steps are not easy. The advances themselves will, of course, be genuine choices in the full Shackleian sense. They cannot be predicted. But there is surely some relationship between the objects of attention and the imaginative results that emerge. So long as modern economists devote their considerable intellectual energies, and imaginative skills, to the search for empirically testable regularities in human conduct, they will succeed in extending the scope of applicability for the man-as-rat metaphor to describe economic theory. To the extent that modern economists use their own imagination in efforts to understand more fully those aspects of human action that reflect man's own distinctive imaginative ability to choose his own reality, we can expect new insights about the process of economic interaction to emerge.

13. Among Shackle's many books, see, in particular, *Epistemics and Economics* (Cambridge: Cambridge University Press, 1972) and *Imagination and the Nature of Choice* (Edinburgh: Edinburgh University Press, 1979).

The Related but Distinct "Sciences" of Economics and of Political Economy

The *raison d'être* of natural science is to provide knowledge and to control natural processes. Most economists believe that they should practise economics in the same manner, i.e., accumulate knowledge of the behaviour of men and of the economy that enables the powerful to control other people's behaviour with increasing efficiency. This paper argues that in doing so, economists forget the moral basis of their science and thereby miss the *raison d'être* of economics. The true purpose of the distinctive "science of political economy" is to design alternative legal structures and to evaluate their potentialities in enhancing efficiency in the exploitation of the mutuality of advantage. This means that the "science of political economy" is *categorically* distinct from the "science of economics." The former uses the knowledge of behavioural regularities, which the latter may discover, in order to allow the community of free individuals to make informed institutional choices. This approach has, as a necessary prerequisite, a different conception of human nature from that used by the "science of economics," which characterizes human beings as mere net-wealth maximizing beasts. Such an assumption makes the stability of civil order totally incomprehensible. The "science of political economy" also leads to quite different consequences as

From *British Journal of Social Psychology*, Special Issue, *Social Psychology and Economics*, ed. Wolfgang Stroebe and Willi Meyer, 21, part 2 (June 1982): 175–83. Reprinted with permission from the copyright holder, The British Psychological Society.

to a proper understanding of government and of society. The paper discusses the differences between a morally indifferent "science of economics," or behavioural theory, and a morally relevant "science of political economy" and urges social scientists to remember the basic truths of their forefathers, the moral philosophers of the 18th century.

"Science," in a narrowly defined sense that is descriptive of the "hard-science" disciplines, is explicitly positive. Scientists are presumably concerned with the discovery of the apparent reality that exists, that is "out there," or (if they are somewhat more sophisticated) with the construction of models that enable refutable predictions to be made about the consequences of particular experiments. Science is about the "is," or the conjectural "is," not the "ought." It rarely occurs to the "scientist" to ask himself or herself about his or her *raison d'être*. Why does science have ultimate "social" value? Once this question is so much as raised, however, the limits of the strictly positive posture are very soon exhausted. By more or less natural presumption, "science" is valued because it is precursory to its usefulness in control. Physics, as positive science, is antecedent to the miracle of modern technology, the space flights and the hydrogen bomb alike.

"Know the truth and the truth shall make you productive." This implicit motto has served science well, and especially so until the emergence of the awful moral questions raised in the middle and late years of our own century. Knowledge of how the physical universe operates has allowed man to assume increasing control over the "natural processes" that he observes about him. And, again excepting the new moral issues of our times, this control, made possible by the application of science, has been largely unidirectional in effect. It has dramatically improved man's lot. But how is "improvement" measured? By man's own evaluation—this offers the only satisfactory response. But the normative step taken in such a response should be acknowledged. "Improvement" follows upon the control made possible by science; therefore, science "ought" to be pursued; there is apparent normative support for the exercise of the scientist's talents.

Man is of the world and his activities are "natural processes." Does it not then follow that increasing knowledge about man and his activities has its appropriate place in science? And should we not expect that such advance will yield results comparable to those demonstrated to have emerged from other aspects of general scientific development? Why should there exist a categorical difference between the "science of man" and the science of anything else?

These questions point to unidirectional answers if the normative purpose of science is forgotten. The necessary linkage between increasing scientific knowledge and "improvement" is provided by the control that the knowledge potentially offers, control that may be exercised to further objectives that individuals themselves evaluate positively. Can the "sciences of man" be made to correspond to the non-human sciences in this respect?

Robinson Crusoe as Positive Scientist

Consider Robinson Crusoe alone on his island. In one sense, much of his behaviour can be interpreted as that of a positive scientist who is making and testing hypotheses. "This red berry makes me ill; this blue berry makes me well. Fish abound in the eastern lagoon; sharks are in the western lagoon." Crusoe is testing hypotheses about his own body and temperament as well as about the external elements of his new environment. He is engaged in pursuing a "science of man," as well as all of the other sciences. His standard of living improves, by his own reckoning, as he applies the newly acquired knowledge, as he controls the environment, and himself, in the light of this knowledge.

Let us now shift to Crusoe's situation after Friday is on the island. Friday is now a part of Crusoe's natural environment, and Crusoe will have an incentive to acquire knowledge about this part as much as any other. He will, therefore, continue to behave as a positive scientist. He will advance and test hypotheses. As he does so, knowledge is acquired, and, as applied, this knowledge will allow Crusoe to control Friday's behaviour. As he does this, Crusoe will be able to improve his own well-being, in his own terms. For purposes of illustration, even if a departure from Defoe's narrative, suppose that Crusoe discovers that Friday is extremely superstitious about serpents, even to the extent of fearing images of serpents. Having made this discovery, which is genuinely scientific in the full sense, Crusoe can, by drawing images in the sand, modify Friday's behaviour in ways that seem desirable to him.

The story to this point neglects Friday's ability to behave also as a positive scientist. Robinsoe Crusoe is a part of the new natural environment for Friday, and the latter, too, will engage in advancing and testing hypotheses about Crusoe's behaviour. The two positive scientists, Crusoe and Friday, are discovering aspects of their environment, and they are controlling this environment through application of their scientific discoveries, each to the improvement of his own standard of living, as he himself evaluates it. Crusoe is "exploiting" Friday's superstitious fear of serpents; Friday is "exploiting" that which he learns about Crusoe. Each person, individually, is better off than he would be without the bit of scientific knowledge that he has discovered.

Adding Up

The moral of our illustrative Crusoe-Friday story should be clear. Each person, acting as a positive scientist and applying his discoveries for his own purposes, finds the activity rewarding. But, because there are now *two* sentient beings interacting *each upon the other,* there is no *a priori* basis for claiming that "science," as practised in the illustrative story, improves well-being for the group of two persons. The normative support for "science" as an activity that seems so self-evident in both our introduction and in Crusoe's one-man setting, now seems questionable when applied to interactive behaviour. Science, as applied, implies control, and control for individualized private purposes need *not* lead to mutual gains.[1]

The problem that Crusoe and Friday confront in living together is *not scientific* in the standard sense, and no matter how rapid the advances in scientific knowledge by one or both persons, the problem will remain one of mutual adjustment one to the other. There is no reality "out there" to be discovered that will be of assistance in accomplishing this mutual adjustment. Each person may come to know the properties of all of the elements in the natural environment, and each person may model the behaviour of the other

1. We should stress that in the interactive setting any scientific knowledge can be used to damage some persons for the benefit of others. Crusoe's possible discovery of a plant that would induce sycophantic behaviour by Friday would be equivalent to the discovery of Friday's serpent mania.

with reasonable accuracy in a variety of interaction situations. To the extent that Crusoe (Friday) discovers that Friday (Crusoe) will act in certain ways in response to increments or decrements in his stock of goods, each person may use something we might call "economic science" in making his predictions about the behaviour of the other. But so long as each person acts independently, the setting will remain one of a non-cooperative game. In such a game, "science" can, at best, indicate to the players something about optimal strategy selection. We suggest that a society of many persons is simply the Crusoe-Friday setting with complications.

The Imagination-Evaluation of Alternative Institutions: The "Science" of Political Economy

Let us suppose, however, that Crusoe (or Friday) *imagines* (dreams) a different world, one in which he and Friday (or Crusoe) remain alone on the island, but one in which the interaction between the two persons becomes cooperative. But what imaginary scenarios are feasibly worth consideration? Crusoe could, of course, imagine himself and Friday to be wholly different creatures, but he may reckon that such thoughts would reflect idle dreams. Within the realm of feasible scenarios in which both persons remain recognizable specimens of what they are observed to be, Crusoe (or Friday) can still imagine alternative "possibles," to introduce a useful term from G. L. S. Shackle here. A world in which each person refrains from the exploitation of the other person's known vulnerability might be a better world for both persons. In his imagination of this alternative interaction, Crusoe is required to engage in "science" of a categorically different sort from that which describes his search for "truths" about the edible qualities of berries or the superstitions of Friday.

What is required here is some imagination of the behaviour of the other persons that is categorically different from the straightforward *reaction* pattern that would consist simply of a set of predicted responses to changes in the environment. Crusoe, acting as a positive scientist in the simplistic sense, and subsequently acting on the knowledge gained, can develop a set of predictions about Friday's reactions to external stimuli (Friday can, of course, do the same with Crusoe). This set of predictions will *not*, however, be of direct assistance in the imagination of the interaction that follows from a "leap out of anarchy," a "shift from the independent adjustment equilibrium," a "move out of the dilemma." Crusoe (or Friday) must imagine a *person* who is, in a sense, *morally equivalent* to himself in order to examine the prospects for mutual gains. Furthermore, he must model the predicted working properties of the interactive setting within which each party behaves within the limits of agreed-on rules of conduct. The "science of political economy" describes this process of institutional evaluation.

An interaction with an animal could never provide the basis for such an imaginative construction. The difference between human and animal interaction was acutely sensed by Adam Smith in a passage that economists have too much neglected. Smith lodged the sources of human progress squarely in man's propensity to "truck, barter, and exchange one thing for another," and he specifically stated that no one had seen "a dog make a fair and deliberate exchange of one bone for another with another dog."[2]

Self-seeking within Constraints

It is essential to understand the precise meaning of the term "morally equivalent" in the discussion above. Crusoe need not imagine Friday to be "moral" in the ordinary sense of this term; he need not project or model Friday as a benevolent person, one for whom Crusoe's interests matter as well as his own, even to the slightest degree. That is to say, Friday need not be required to "love" Crusoe, and vice versa, in the potentially productive interaction that will guarantee mutuality of advantage. Friday may be modelled as a self-seeking autonomous person, but one whose predictable behaviour is constrained voluntarily within the limits of mutual gain.

The central contribution of 18th-century moral philosophy was the recognition that such limits could be drawn, both conceptually and in institutional reality. Without such recognition, there is no escape from the attitude that man must be "ruled" so long as he remains immune from the full acceptance of the moral precepts of the church. Free man, as a legitimate philosophical idea, emerged only when it was recognized that the indicated behavioural limits were *minimal*, in the sense that they fall far short of

2. A. Smith, *The Wealth of Nations* (New York: Modern Library, 1937; originally published in 1776), book 1, chapter 2, 13.

some standard of "ethical perfection" or "universal love." To the mediaeval philosophers, man could not be free *because* he could not attain sainthood.

To modern economists, the wheel has come full circle. Many of them model man as a net-wealth maximizer in *all* aspects of his behaviour. They fail to see that man cannot be "free," in any normatively meaningful sense, unless he is constrained within the limits of mutual advantage. Unchained man *is* a beast; this is a simple and elementary fact that must be acknowledged by us all. And, as we have argued above, whereas intelligent "beasts" may be very skilled in the usage of what may be called "economic science," until and unless they acknowledge the normative relevance of imposing limits on behaviour, they cannot evaluate alternative schemes of cooperative social order. They cannot act as "political economists." "Economic science," defined and used analogously to the hard sciences, requires that some persons be putty subject to the manipulation and control of others.

More specifically stated, the 18th-century contribution was to construct the bridge between *Homo economicus* on the one hand and "social welfare" or "group interest" on the other. Mandeville, Hume, and Smith did not invent the notion of self-seeking, autonomous man. Such a person had been around for centuries, and he had been emphatically brought to philosophical consciousness by Thomas Hobbes in the 17th century. By building on the Hobbesian contractual insights, and by postulating the possible existence of the limited sovereign in the sense articulated by John Locke, the 18th-century philosophers demonstrated that, within such constrained behavioural limits, the self-interested motivation on the part of individuals might promote the welfare of the whole community of persons.

To return again to the Crusoe-Friday illustration, and to concentrate only on the calculus of one party, Crusoe, we can see that he must imagine how the two parties might interact in a *limited* or *constrained* setting, where each party is motivated by self-interest, but where the exercise of this interest is itself constrained by some adherence to mutually accepted "law," which may itself be morally derived, externally imposed, evolved as custom, or contractually established. The "imagination" of such "an economy" of self-seeking persons who make their own choices within a system of law becomes a "scientific" construction, but it is one that is categorically distinct from that which straightforwardly models persons as beasts and which embodies no limits on maximizing behaviour.

The Sciences of Economics and
of Political Economy

There are two quite different uses or applications for the exercise of the scientific imagination in relation to the interaction behaviour of persons within an economy under law. By postulating self-seeking behaviour of *other* persons, within the legal limits, the individual, acting as "scientist," can make and test predictions about their behaviour, and these predictions may prove useful either for their own sake, or for improving the well-being of the scientist or those for whom he acts as agent. The predictive "science of economics" is positively valuable to governmental agents, business firms, and private individuals. Persons can "play better games" if they can predict their opponents' strategy more accurately.

But there remains a categorically different exercise which we may call the "science of political economy." Its purpose is to evaluate the structure of the constraints, "the law," with some ultimate objective of redesign or reform aimed at securing enhanced efficiency in the exploitation of the potential mutuality of advantage. This science of political economy requires more than the making and testing of predictions about behaviour under an existing set of constraints, some given system of laws, although the latter "science" will, of course, continue to be a necessary input in the exercise. The second "science," however, also requires some comparison of the results observed within an existing system of constraints and those that might be predicted to emerge under alternative systems. For the simple reason that it does not now exist, the results of an alternative set of constraints can never be observed. Alternative structures exist only as potentialities, as constraints that persons might *create* by their own choices, from the void as it were, and not from some reality "out there" waiting to be explored and discovered. At this level, the discovery metaphor which has proven useful in describing the search activity of ordinary science becomes positively misleading in application to the comparative analysis of alternative constraints structures.

It is in its failure to distinguish between the two distinct sciences that it inclusively embodies that modern economics often defaults on its very *raison d'être*. By modelling their own activities in the exploration-discovery metaphor of the ordinary sciences, and by misunderstanding the positive-normative relationship between science and control, modern economists often inadvertently lend support to the efforts of the subset of persons who seek always to treat other persons as potential responders to control stimuli, support to those putative authoritarians who act on behalf of and as agents for the modern state apparatus. Often in wholesale ignorance of what they are about, modern economists may invent the shackles by which they, along with their fellows, are bound by the modern state.

Predictive Science, Behaviour, and Choice

Man cannot be, at one and the same time, a behaving animal subject to scientific prediction *and* a choosing agent that remains immune from control by the manipulation of rewards and punishments. This fact is applicable both for the single person and for the collectivity of persons in the "representative" or "average" sense. To put the point differently, there is no way to "explain" the existence of civil order among persons by resort to the predictive science of behaviour alone. The 18th-century philosophers knew this; their modern counterparts have forgotten it.

Crusoe must initially imagine Friday to be a person, like himself, who acknowledges the desirability of imposing limits on the behaviour of *both* parties, but who would, necessarily, reject the imposition of constraints unilaterally. The leap from anarchy into order is at the same time a leap "beyond predictive science." In a very real sense, civil order requires mutual agreement on and acceptance of the trading ethic, or, more simply, mutual respect for contractual agreement, for promise keeping. Civil order is based on *exchange*, in the most inclusive meaning of this term. Civil society requires and implies reciprocity in dealings among its members.

But what is "truth" in reciprocal dealings? Predictive science is, by its nature, unidirectional in its search for and discovery of "truth," an attribute of the reality presumed to be "out there," quite independent of the means through which it is ascertained or discovered. "The red berries are poisonous"—this scientific statement exists for Crusoe quite separately from the means through which he has found out about its validity—*both* he and Friday can improve their lot, and on their own terms, by simple trade based on comparative productive advantage. This latter becomes, for Crusoe, a speculative hypothesis that he may test only by suggesting it to Friday and by securing the latter's agreement, agreement that must be expressed be-haviourally in terms of adherence to the limits of mutual gain.[3]

Within the agreed-on limits, Crusoe may, indeed, model Friday as *Homo economicus,* as one who seeks to gain private advantage and who is uncon-cerned about the well-being of his partner across the exchange relationship. Reciprocally, Friday models Crusoe's behaviour in a similar way. It is impor-tant to recognize, however, that, in adhering to the limits, both parties may violate the strict *Homo economicus* postulate of net-wealth maximization. Each trader may stop short of maximal exploitation of his privately defined advantage, not from any benevolent concern for the well-being of his trading cohort, but instead from some recognition that the mutuality of gain to all parties is the *sine qua non* of stable civil order. Indeed it may be argued that behaviour based on a recognition of such limits as here discussed is appro-priately defined as "rational" under an inclusive definition of rationality.[4]

From Simple to Complex Society

As we shift attention from the simple two-person interaction to a many-person community, however, any model of behaviour that requires voluntary adherence to the limits of mutual advantage for *all* persons must be ques-tioned. Crusoe might well imagine a two-person society that incorporates mutual agreement on behavioural constraints that will be honoured; he might reckon plausibly on enlightened or long-range self-interest motiva-tion to lead each of the two parties to extend precepts of rationality to in-clude predicted behavioural feedbacks. But to imagine such voluntaristic limits on behaviour in the many-person setting may become scientifically naïve, in the sense that any attempts to organize one's own behaviour on such a prediction of voluntaristic limitation may lead to disastrous per-sonal consequences.

In a many-person, complex society, it becomes necessary to model the

3. J. M. Buchanan, "Positive Economics, Welfare Economics, and Political Economy," *Journal of Law and Economics* 2 (1959): 124–38.

4. For a modern discussion, see J. R. Lucas, *On Justice* (Oxford: Oxford University Press, 1980).

actors as if they do not voluntarily restrict their behaviour to the limits defined by the mutuality of gains. Such models of behaviour do indeed embody the *Homo economicus,* or net-wealth maximization, assumption in the strict sense. But these models are *not* used as inputs for prediction and control in the sense of ordinary science. They are, instead, to be used for the purpose of allowing the individual (each individual) to make informed and sophisticated choices among alternative institutional constraints, constraints that are to be mutually acknowledged and accepted by all parties, and which are to be *externally enforced* by the sovereign.[5]

In the complex society, the enforcement role of the sovereign, of government, cannot be romantically neglected; this role must be squarely acknowledged. The sovereign must "enforce the law," "keep the peace," or, in the terminology of this paper, must "keep the self-seeking behaviour of persons within the limits of mutual advantage." The scope and range of the authority granted to the sovereign will critically depend on the analytical results that emerge from the construction of models of interaction. And it is in precisely the construction of such models that the *Homo economicus* postulate about human behaviour assumes maximal value. Only by examining the workings of models in which all persons are postulated to behave exclusively as self-seeking maximizers of privatized or individualized net wealth can appropriate "limits of law" be defined and entered into the lists for effective constitutional dialogue. It would be folly to model persons as saints for the purposes of generalizing the results to form a basis for "the law" to be enforced by the sovereign agent. But, on the other hand, to model persons in *Homo economicus* terms for this purpose of deriving constitutional structure is *not* the same thing at all as advancing predictions that persons will necessarily behave as *Homo economicus,* even in some average or representative sense. The legitimate "science of political economy"—of interaction among persons who behave in accordance with precepts of net-wealth maximization—is not, and should not be conceived to be, analogous to that "science of economics" which is conceived to be exclusively concerned with the gener-

---

5. For an extended treatment of the bases for employing the *Homo economicus* model in institutional comparisons, see G. Brennan and J. Buchanan, "Predictive Power and Choice among Regimes: The Monopoly Example" (Center for Study of Public Choice, Blacksburg, Va., 1981, mimeographed).

ation of refutable hypotheses. The "positive science of political economy," which does embody persons behaving as net-wealth maximizers, does not have as its ultimate normative purpose the accumulation of predictive knowledge about behavioural relationships in the observable real world, knowledge that may be of ultimate assistance in enabling some sovereign master to control those whose behaviour is so analysed. Political economy has, instead, the ultimate purpose of enabling persons to analyse their own behaviour, along with that of others, in some imagined state and, from such analysis, to define the appropriate or desired set of constraints that will be then embodied in the law assigned to the sovereign for enforcement.

Models of the Sovereign

Modern economists, who do not spend much thought on methodological questions, might not object strenuously to the distinctions sketched out above. If pressed, they would presumably agree that the knowledge about economic reality that they seek is primarily useful in genuine political economy as an input in the dialogue about constitutional-legal reform. Having done so, they would return to their chores, leaving open the whole set of issues raised concerning models of the enforcing agent, of the sovereign, of government, of persons who act on behalf of the modern state.

A major deficiency in the political-legal-social philosophy of the 19th and 20th centuries has been the failure to model the behaviour of the sovereign, or, more precisely, to model the behaviour of those persons who are empowered or authorized to act on behalf of the state or government. This failure has been far more pervasive than any like failure to model what we may call "private man." The latter has often been modelled as *Homo economicus* for the legitimate purposes of assisting in the dialogues on law reform. By contrast, "public man" has rarely been modelled at all, save implicitly as "saint." This perversity in analysis has come to be recognized, and partially corrected, only through the influence of public choice theory in the years since 1960.[6]

---

6. As in all shifts in ideas, there are antecedents or precursors. The Italian public finance theorists and sociologists, who worked in the last part of the 19th century, did introduce models of the "ruling classes" that have much in common with modern public choice theory constructions. And, of course, Machiavelli himself is the father of all such

The reason for the perversity lies partially in the confusion about "economic science" and the "science of political economy" previously noted. "Public man," the agent who acts in the name of the sovereign, the elected legislator, the judge, the bureaucrat, the person who chooses among the options that restrict and confine the liberties of the citizen, cannot be conceptually modelled as behaving to further his own self-interest, *and at the same time,* justified or legitimated in his functional role on some grounds of "general good." By contrast and comparison, the profit-seeking businessman (Adam Smith's butcher) can be modelled as wealth-maximizing while at the same time justified as furthering the "general interest." As noted above, however, the self-seeking in the marketplace must be assumed to be limited or constrained by the bounds of mutual advantage, even if the necessity of assuming such limits is not often explicitly recognized.

How can models of "private man" and "public man" be made consistent one with another? "Public man" must be modelled in self-seeking terms if his behaviour is to be compared with those persons who interact in the accepted models of markets. But how, then, can any "public man" role be justified at all?

The recognition of limits can be helpful in resolving what seems to be a dilemma here. It becomes necessary to differentiate between the predictive science of behaviour, the "science of economics," and the modelling of interaction patterns for the purposes of designing appropriate legal and constitutional constraints, the "science of political economy." In the latter, only by modelling "private man" as exclusively seeking to maximize net wealth can the legal framework, the "laws and institutions," of the marketplace be designed so as to further the "general interest" and to prevent the undue exploitation of man by man. Comparable principles should tell us that "public man" must be similarly modelled and for the same reasons. The person who is placed in a position to act on behalf of the state must be modelled as a net-wealth maximizer in his own right if the legal-constitutional constraints that define his authorized powers and his behaviour within those powers are to be appropriately designed. "Public man," like his counterpart in the market,

---

models. For a summary of the Italian public finance contributions, see J. M. Buchanan, *Fiscal Theory and Political Economy* (Chapel Hill: University of North Carolina Press, 1960).

can be constrained to behave within the limits of mutual gains. "Public man" need not be allowed powers of exploiting his fellows provided that his behaviour is appropriately restricted.

The purpose of the scientific construction that embodies *Homo economicus* is the same as between the two patterns of interaction, as between the relations of persons within markets and the relations of persons within politics or government. "Economic theory," as it has emerged and developed, has been almost entirely devoted to analysis of persons within markets, and even here with a neglect or oversight of the ultimate purpose of the whole exercise. Prior to the "public choice revolution," there was essentially no comparable theory of the interaction of persons within politics. In the absence of such a theory, persons who act on behalf of the sovereign were implicitly modelled as saints, with the predicted consequences. There was near-total loss of the 18th-century wisdom that recognized the necessity of constraints on the agents of governance. There was a developing failure to understand and to appreciate the *raison d'être* of constitutional limits on government and governors. There emerged the awesome normative gap in elementary social philosophy, a gap that seems clearly to be attributable to the absence of a scientific theory used in its appropriately constructive sense. It is perhaps not exaggeration to suggest that millions of citizens in many modern states might have been spared the agonies and terrors of collectivism in almost all of its embodiments had the "science of political economy" been properly rather than improperly used.

Conclusion

Economists will, of course, continue to engage in both the "science of economics" and the "science of political economy." In the former role, they will try to construct more satisfactory models of human behaviour within historically observed institutional structures, with empirical tests being used as an important criterion of scientific progress. These efforts must go forward, and there is nothing in my argument of this paper that suggests otherwise. Economists must, however, understand that the underlying normative purpose of the whole exercise is that of facilitating comparison of institutional alternatives. "Economic science" is not to be conceived as offering assistance to selected agents who seek to use scientific knowledge to control others.

Even if these warnings are heeded, however, the role of the economist, as scientist, is not limited to "economic science," as defined here. In the comparison of institutional alternatives, the "science of political economy" emerges to occupy a role that is perhaps more important than its predictive counterpart. In the ultimate sense, this science, too, finds its normative purpose in *control*, that which is exercised upon our behaviour by the selection of the institutional-constitutional constraints within which we interact one with another. But the vital distinction between the use of science to assist in the control of subjects-objects (animate or inanimate) and the use of science to assist in the self-imposed control of the behaviour of those who are simultaneously the controllers and the controlled must be kept in mind.

Rational Choice Models
in the Social Sciences

I. Introduction

By profession and discipline I am an economist, and some of my work has involved the extension of the economist's model of rational choice behavior to areas of human interaction other than the market, broadly defined. I shall first discuss several elements of this basic model: (1) methodological individualism, (2) utility maximization, (3) the structure of constraints, and (4) the levels of choice. These elements are, of course, interrelated, but they can provide a useful scheme for organizing the essay. Following the treatment of these elements, I shall, in Section VI, examine the purpose of the whole analytical enterprise. Finally, in Section VII, I shall isolate one glaring omission in my discussion of rational choice and suggest some of the implications of this omission.

II. Methodological Individualism

The central presupposition of any and all rational choice models, including those of the economist, must be the definition of the choosing-acting agent as the individual human being, the unit equipped with some presumed ca-

From *Explorations into Constitutional Economics,* comp. Robert D. Tollison and Viktor J. Vanberg (College Station: Texas A&M University Press, 1989), 37–50. Reprinted by permission of the publisher.

I am indebted to Peter Bernholz, Frank Forman, David Levy, Robert Tollison, and Viktor Vanberg for helpful comments.

pacity to evaluate options or alternatives and to choose among them. Many of the sophisticated analyses of rationality in choice simply take this presupposition as given, but its central importance should be emphasized. Only individuals choose; only individuals act. An understanding of any social interaction process must be based on an analysis of the choice behavior of persons who participate in that process. Results that are predicted or that may be observed in social interaction must be factored down into the separate choices made by individuals. In ordinary discourse, confusion abounds from failure to take this step. For example, a corporation does not "choose" among alternatives; the choices of individuals, acting as agents for the corporation, are the relevant subjects for meaningful inquiry.

Several qualifications must be placed on this elementary presupposition. First of all, methodological individualism does not imply or require that individual choice behavior is invariant over changes in the institutional setting, that persons choose always "as if" they exist in social isolation, one from another. Acceptance of the classic Aristotelian proposition that man is a social animal reflects, in no way, a criticism of the individualistic presupposition. Persons behave differently in differing social interactions, and these differences are important (see Section V below). The individualistic postulate suggests only that, regardless of the social setting, all choice behavior is finally individualistic.

A second caveat is that methodological individualism, as a framework for conducting social science, does not imply anything at all about the objectives sought by those who choose. To say that only individuals choose among alternatives suggests nothing whatsoever about what these alternatives are or how the individual arrays or orders these. There is no implicit inference that these choices are or are not "narrowly self-interested." The rational altruist and the rational egoist can fit equally in the model's structure. The individualistic postulate identifies the unit to which rationality precepts are applied; it remains silent on the objects of choices.

A third inference that must be clarified concerns the differentiation between the set of alternatives for choice faced by the individual participants and the results of the choice process in which many persons participate. This relationship is perhaps the most difficult "principle" for noneconomists to understand, and, indeed, we may suggest that a thorough understanding of this "principle" is the most distinguishing feature of the economist, as such.

The discovery and elaboration of this principle were the crowning achievements of the eighteenth-century moral philosophers, from whose work economics, as a discipline, emerged. The idea is often summarized in the phrase "unintended consequences." The network of economic exchanges, in which many persons participate in various capacities, generates results that may be described in terms of "allocations" and/or "distributions." These results may be evaluated by observers, while at the same time it is recognized that these results are "chosen" by no one. There is no "allocative choice," as such, in a functioning market economy; individuals choose, not among resource allocations or distributions, but among the alternatives that each person, separately, confronts. Personally, I chose to present this lecture, a choice that affects the allocation of economic resources today only in a very small way.

An important methodological principle surfaces at this point. Because allocative-distributive "choices" are not made, the aggregative results do not lend themselves to evaluation in terms of the criteria developed in rational choice models which are, as noted, applicable only to the individual's selection among options. While it may be legitimate to use the terms "efficient" and "optimal" in evaluating the results of an individual's choosing process (see Section III below), the more familiar usage of these terms in regard to aggregative results that emerge from the simultaneous choices of many persons must be recognized to be categorically different. In this second usage, "efficiency" and "optimality" are potential properties that are related to individual choices only through an indirect nexus that cannot be adequately treated here.

A fourth inference to the individualistic presupposition is closely related to that just discussed. Because choice behavior is limited to individual choosing agents, the precepts for rationality that may be used to evaluate individual choice cannot be extended to nonindividual entities in any direct sense. The familiar extension is to the collective, as such. There may arise settings in which only the collective seems to confront a selection among alternatives. The decision process must generate a single result from among several options available. The political unit, the state, must (1) go to war, or (2) maintain the peace. It is natural linguistic usage to refer to the state as "choosing" among the options, and from this to infer directly that the decision process of the state should exhibit the rationality properties of the individual.

Careful attention to the basic individualistic presupposition would prevent such an extension. Even if the collective entity, as such, confronts the alterna-

tives, the only genuine choices made are those of the individuals who participate in the decision process. Given a decision rule, individuals "choose," and
such choices may be evaluated in accordance with rationality precepts. From
this participation by separate persons, the decision rule or institution generates an outcome which may be one from those that the collective confronts.
No one "chooses" this outcome, however, and it is an error of major proportion to attribute to the choosing process, as such, any rationality precepts.

Failure to appreciate the illegitimacy of such an attribution made economists' mid-century search for social welfare functions seem initially to be
an appropriate exercise. And, even in 1985, economists remain who act as
if such functions are meaningful constructions. In this context, Kenneth
Arrow's impossibility theorem appeared surprising only to those who failed
to understand the restrictive limits imposed by the individualistic presupposition.[1]

III. Utility Maximization

The second element in the economist's model of rational choice behavior is
summarized under the rubric "utility maximization." In its most general
sense, this rubric refers only to the "as if" maximand for individual choice
behavior, with the content of this maximand left totally open ended. Terms
such as "happiness," "satisfaction," or, simply, "X," might be substituted for
utility. At this level of generality, there is no suggestion that the maximand
contains the same specific arguments for different persons, or that the same
person's maximand contains the same arguments over extended time. In the
limit, there is not even the notion that there exists a single common denominator, such as utility, in which all arguments may be expressed. In a purely
formal construction, operationality of the utility-maximization hypothesis is
limited to criteria for consistency in observed choice behavior. With no specification of the arguments, there is no means of predicting directions of behavioral response to changes in constraints. Utility maximization implies
only that persons "choose what they choose" in a noncontradictory fashion.

A less empty but still quite general formulation involves the specification
of arguments in the utility function, along with the signing of these argu-

1. K. Arrow, *Social Choice and Individual Values* (New York: Wiley, 1951).

ments as positively or negatively valued. There need be no presumption that the chooser maximizes some common denominator of evaluation such as "utility." All that is required is that, so long as an argument is classified as a "good," the chooser will seek more rather than less of it.[2] For example, so long as measurable net wealth is defined to be positively valued by the individual, regardless of how insignificant this argument might be relative to other "goods" (prestige, status, friendship, peace, privacy, tranquility, etc.), hypotheses about changes in the individual's choices under changes in constraints may be advanced, hypotheses that can be tested empirically.

The standard economist's textbook model is more specified. The individual is presumed able to evaluate "goods" and "bads" in terms of a unidimensional denominator, "utility," and is presumed also to seek to attain a maximum achievement level, given the constraints faced. Further, the chooser is presumed able to internally trade off "goods" and "bads," one against another. This model allows for the derivation of testable hypotheses, over and beyond those derivable from the less specified model.

More ambitious effort involves some specification of the trade-offs among the arguments in the utility function, a specification sufficient to allow the derivation of refutable hypotheses that amount to predictions about patterns of behavior defined in some absolute rather than in a relative sense. The most familiar example here is the hypothesis that individuals seek to maximize net wealth, or that this argument dominates choice behavior. This construction really substitutes the wealth-maximization hypothesis for the more general utility-maximization one.

Critics of the economist's general model of utility maximization have tended to interpret the whole framework for analyzing individual behavior in terms of the most restrictive hypotheses rather than the more flexible, and more general, formulations. And critics often consider themselves to have destroyed the efficacy of utility maximization, as an hypothesis of rational choice, when they point to empirical refutations of the wealth-maximization hypothesis. Economists themselves have been partly responsible for this bi-

---

2. See G. Becker, "Irrational Behavior and Economic Theory," *Journal of Political Economy* 70 (February, 1962): 1–13; I. Kirzner, "Rational Action and Economic Theory," *Journal of Political Economy* 70 (August, 1962): 380–85; and J. Buchanan, *What Should Economists Do?* (Indianapolis: Liberty Fund, 1979).

ased interpretation of their models of choice behavior. In their sometimes overly zealous attempt to introduce empirical content into their research inquiries, modern economists may have been led to incorporate too readily the wealth-maximization hypothesis. Wealth is objectively measurable; other possible arguments are less amenable to the observer's calculus.

IV. The Structure of Constraints

The third element in the economist's model of choice behavior involves the relationships between precepts for rationality and the structure of the constraints that are faced by persons in varying choosing roles or positions. "Individuals maximize utility subject to constraints"—the central, and simple, principle here is that the choice which qualifies as rational under one set of constraints is not that which qualifies under another set. That is to say, the utility-maximizing choice behavior of an individual depends on the constraints that define and describe the set of alternatives that are available. (Failure to recognize this simple principle has led sophisticated intellectuals to mouth absurdities about public policies in the modern welfare state setting.)

The dependence of choice on constraints is straightforward in the elementary economics textbook exercise in which the individual, as consumer-buyer, is constrained by his income-wealth, along with the set of prices for the market alternatives. In the more general setting, the constraints may not be reducible to a single numeraire value. The individual making the choice may be subject to a whole set of conditions, only some of which may be binding.

Another familiar emphasis of the elementary economics textbooks must be carefully qualified before acceptance. We find frequent reference to the resource and technology constraints that limit the feasibility space for "the economy," considered as a functioning organization. This reference is misleading in that neither "the economy," nor its political agent, "the state," chooses. Only persons choose, and the single person is affected in his behavior by economy-wide resource scarcities only insofar as these are translated into effects on his own endowments or choice options. Within an individual's private calculus, there is a resource constraint, which becomes almost equivalent to the income-wealth constraint, and, of course, the whole set of individual constraints must be consistent with the total resource availability in the economy. Similarly, the individual can choose only among alternatives that he actually confronts, which implies technical possibility.

The emphasis on economy-wide rather than on individual constraints has been partly responsible for a serious omission in analysis. If we adopt the methodological imperative that all choice analysis be reduced to inquiry into individual behavior, the importance of *institutional* constraints becomes evident. The feasible choice options open to the individual are, in part, determined by the institutional setting. I shall defer, until Section V, the analysis of rational choice *among* constraints, as contrasted with the economist's model, which concentrates attention on choice *within* exogenously given constraints. In the standard framework, recognition of the importance of introducing institutional constraints has led to developments within economic analysis that have extended the explanatory power of the rational choice model, horizontally as it were, by examination of the incentive structures of alternative institutions.

Several areas of research inquiry embody developments worthy of notice here. "Property rights economics," much of it based on the seminal work of Armen Alchian, had been influential both in the emergence of "law and economics" as a subdiscipline in its own right, and in the construction of what is sometimes called the "new institutional economics."[3] A second major extension of the explanatory power of the economist's basic model of rational choice, again in the horizontal sense noted, originates at the University of Chicago with the work of Gary Becker and his colleagues. Becker uses the basic model to develop a general theory of social interaction, but his central contribution has been to our understanding of individual behavior within households and families.[4] Also deserving of notice in this respect is much of the analysis in public choice, inclusively defined. The choice behavior of persons located in bureaucratic positions, analyzed by Tullock, Niskanen, and others, is now acknowledged to yield refutable predictions that are helpful in understanding how bureaucratic institutions operate.[5]

3. A. Alchian, *Economic Forces at Work* (Indianapolis: Liberty Fund, 1977).

4. G. Becker, *The Economic Approach to Human Behavior* (Chicago: University of Chicago Press, 1976).

5. G. Tullock, *The Politics of Bureaucracy* (Washington, D.C.: Public Affairs Press, 1965); W. Niskanen, *Bureaucracy and Representative Government* (Chicago: Aldine, 1971).

The choice behavior of the individual in a large-number electorate has also been subjected to exhaustive analysis. This behavior is worth discussing in some detail since it can illustrate well the effects of the choice setting on rational behavior. The first choice faced by the person in a large-number electorate is that involving the act of voting itself. Even if the individual places a relatively high value on the differential effects of the alternatives that the collective faces, rationality precepts may dictate abstention.[6] If, for any reason, this choice threshold is passed and the individual plans to vote, the individual may not find it rational to acquire more than cursory information about the alternatives. Beyond this, even if the individual decides to vote and does acquire some information about the alternatives, he may rationally use participation to express whim and prejudice rather than valued interests.[7]

The large-number electoral setting, in particular, illustrates the point made earlier that the results generated from the collective-decision rule, say, majority voting, are "chosen" by no one. In an election between Candidate A and Candidate B, these alternative collective results are *not* the alternatives for choice as faced by any individual, as voter. The voter faces starkly different alternatives—the "lever marked A" and the "lever marked B." There is only a probabilistically very small correspondence between the individual's act in the voting booth and the collective results generated from the choice behavior of the many persons along with the decision rule in being.

For purposes of discussion here, the relevant point of emphasis is that rational choice precepts dictate totally different behavior in divergent institutional settings. Consider and compare an individual's choice among alternatives in the market and his choice among alternatives in a large-number election. The same person, with the same rational norms, will act differently in the two cases, even when the differentials in value placed on the alternative results are identical. In the market, confronted with a choice between a restaurant dinner and a book purchase, there is a direct one-to-one correspondence between choice and consequence. If the market prices of the two options are the same, and the individual places a differential value of ten

6. A. Downs, *An Economic Theory of Democracy* (New York: Harper, 1957); G. Tullock, *Towards a Mathematics of Politics* (Ann Arbor: University of Michigan Press, 1967).

7. G. Brennan and J. Buchanan, "Voter Choice," *American Behavioral Scientist* 28, no. 2 (November–December, 1984): 185–201.

dollars, in utility, on the dinner, the person knows that, having made his choice, he will enjoy the consequences. Before making the choice, he has an incentive to invest effort in information about the alternatives. If he chooses wrongly, if he makes an error, he alone will suffer the consequences. In the voting booth, by sharp contrast, the linkage between an individual choice and the consequence is almost totally absent.[8] The individual will remain "rationally ignorant," since there is little or no return from additional information. Even if the individual values one alternative more than the other, and by the same ten dollars as before, he is unlikely to participate at all, and, if he does so, there is no assured prospect that he will even vote for the alternative that he most highly values.

Note that the difference in choice behavior here stems exclusively from the differences in the institutional-incentive structure within which the individuals confront choices and not from any differences in the specification of arguments in the utility function or from any differences in the precepts for rational choice behavior. The person who sincerely acts exclusively from what he thinks to be the "public interest" has precisely the same incentive for remaining rationally ignorant in the voting booth relative to the marketplace as does the person who acts exclusively in his own interest, narrowly defined. Recognition of the effects of the institutional setting on rational choice behavior, and on observed results of choices made in different settings, would do much to eliminate the proclivity of many social scientists to introduce one model of behavior for market interaction and another for politics.

V. The Choice within Constraints and the Choice among Constraints

An important extension of the economist's basic model of rational choice has been a shift of attention, *vertically,* to the choice among constraints themselves, as opposed to the standard presumption that constraints faced by choosers are exogenously determined. Clearly, such presumption seems legitimate when reference is to the overall resource or technological limits of "the economy." But, as previously noted, "the economy" does not choose.

8. J. Buchanan, "Individual Choice in Voting and the Market," *Journal of Political Economy* 62 (1954): 334–43.

Once we recognize that institutional structures, as well as the individualized endowment constraints, define the potential boundaries of choice, the prospect of deliberative selection among these structures emerges. If persons can choose among the constraints that are imposed on their own within-constraint choice behavior, surely we should be able to analyze the first set of choices in some fashion analogous to that employed for analyzing the second- or lower-level choices. This shift in the level of choice extends the model of rational choice vertically as contrasted with the horizontal extensions embodied in the nonmarket applications mentioned earlier.

A generalization of the evolutionist paradigm may suggest that, although institutions of social interaction do change through time, these changes can emerge only through the long process of cultural evolution. According to this perception, it is not legitimate to infer that basic institutions of social order, basic rules for the socio-economic-legal-political "game," can be deliberately "chosen" in any manner analogous to the choices among options that are available to persons, in a collective decision process, within an existing set of institutional rules.

Such a stance would seem, however, to close off the most constructive avenue for social reform or improvement. If the institutional constraints are assumed to be beyond the range of choice and control, and, further, if, within the constraints that exist, individuals choose in predictable patterns, there remains little or no scope for "reform," as such, apart from moral preaching. The whole exercise of political economy is eliminated. This exercise is the demonstration that, within certain sets of constraints, individual utility-maximizing behavior, even if narrowly self-interested, can generate overall results that may be "better," under agreed-on criteria of evaluation, than those results predicted to emerge under alternative sets of constraints. Normative evaluation of institutional arrangements implies that a potential modification of such arrangements is possible, that the rules of social interaction are subject to directed change.

Economists do not find such vertical extension of rational choice models amenable to analysis with their familiar tools, and it is not, therefore, surprising that relatively few of them have made efforts in this direction. Choice, as such, requires the limitations of alternatives, and the very notion of utility maximization implies that, if subject to control, the set of alternatives should be as inclusive as possible. Why should anyone choose deliberately to restrict the available choice set, to reduce the range of options?

Economists' prejudgments on such a question stem from their analytical models rather than from any empirical observation of behavior. Persons do impose constraints on their own behavior, both as individuals and as members of socially interacting groups. They deliberately adopt rules that restrict situational responses. It is useful, however, to distinguish between the choice of individualized constraints and the selection of general constraining rules or laws.

The "economics of self-control" is now emerging as an important area of inquiry. Work by Schelling, Elster, and Shefrin and Thaler may be noted here.[9] The relatively more important area is, however, the one that involves constraints that are imposed *generally* on the choice behavior of all persons in a community. These constraints emerge, or may emerge, from a radically different calculus on the part of the individual, and from a calculus that is much more readily brought within the rational choice calculus emphasized by economists. Once it is acknowledged that institutions enter as constraints on individual choice behavior, and once we allow institutions to be treated as variables subject to reform or change, the potential for selection from among alternative sets of institutions seems to follow. In expressing a preference for a *general rule,* one that will equally constrain the behavior of *all* persons in a community, the individual is, effectively, trading off the possible negative value of losing his own freedom of action (of having his choice set constrained) in exchange for the positive value that he expects to secure from the constraints imposed on the behavior of others, behavior that he anticipates may impact on his own well-being in a negative fashion. Ideally, the individual may prefer that his own behavior be exempted from the application of a constraining rule. There may be no explicit desire for self-control with respect to the activity that is constrained. Practically, no such individu-

---

9. T. Schelling, "Self-Command in Practice, in Policy, and in a Theory of Rational Choice," *American Economic Review* 74, no. 2 (May, 1984): 1–11; J. Elster, *Ulysses and the Sirens* (Cambridge: Cambridge University Press, 1979); A. M. Shefrin and R. Thaler, "An Economic Theory of Self Control," Working Paper No. 208, Center for Economic Analysis of Human Behavior and Social Institutions (Stanford, Calif.: National Bureau of Economic Research, 1977).

alized exemption from a general rule is feasible. The individual supports the introduction and enforcement of a general rule because the benefits from "control of others" are valued more highly than the costs, measured by loss of self-liberty.

The area of inquiry into the choices among alternative sets of general rules, which has been called the "theory of constitutions," "constitutional political economy," or, even, the "theory of law," involves both positive and normative elements. The individual, in determining what is, for himself, the most preferred set of general rules, applicable to his own as well as to others' behavior, must call on his analytical skills in modeling the expected working properties of alternative sets of rules, or changes in such rules. Only after this essentially positive analysis is complete can the individual make an informed judgment as to the preferred set.

This extension of rational choice modeling to the "constitutional choices" of an individual seems straightforward enough until the necessarily collective action of the whole rule-making exercise is recalled. As in the within-rule settings for collective decision discussed earlier, where the mutually exclusive alternatives are, somehow, emergent from a process involving the participation of many persons, no individual effectively faces the final choice options in any sense analogous to that treated in orthodox rational choice models. This severe limitation on any simple application of such models in either within-constraints or among-constraints large-number settings must be acknowledged. The predictive-explanatory power of rational choice models is reduced, not because the participants depart from rationality norms for behavior, but because these norms themselves are not related so closely to identified arguments in individual utility functions as is the case in strictly private choice settings.

VI. The Purpose of the "Scientific" Enterprise

The economist's model of rational choice behavior was initially developed for application in market interaction, the whole set of voluntary exchange relationships in which persons participate as buyers and/or sellers of final products and/or resource inputs. What I have called horizontal extensions of this model involve attempts to analyze behavior in other than ordinary market settings, behavior of persons in family interactions, of persons as potential criminals, as managers of nonproprietary organizations, as legal contractors, as adjudicators, as charitable contributors, as rent seekers, as public choosers, as team members. By contrast, what I have called vertical extensions of the economist's model involve attempts to analyze behavior where the objects of choice are shifted upward to the constraints or rules that will limit or restrict subsequent within-constraint choices. These attempts may apply to the individual's effort at self-control or to the participation of many individuals in constitutional evaluation, with a view toward possible changes in the generalized institutional setting within which the choices of all persons in the community are made.

It is these extensions, both horizontal and vertical, of the economist's model of rational choice that raise most of the hackles of noneconomist critics, who accuse economists of disciplinary imperialism and who admonish us to "stick to our lasts." The most familiar of these criticisms may be discussed in terms of the separate elements of the model examined. There would seem to be relatively little basis for serious concern about the individualistic postulate. Those who prefer to conduct inquiry into the relationships among classes, states, and other organizations as such, and without attempts to reduce analysis to the individuals who participate, do not, in my view, pass muster as social scientists in any useful sense of the term. Or, to put it more charitably, let me say that there seems little prospect of constructive dialogue between the methodological individualists and those whose work commences with nonindividualistic organic units as building blocks.

We can engage in more constructive discussion with those research scholars who accept the individualistic postulate, but who criticize utility-maximizing models. As I have noted earlier, there is little objection to be raised as long as the arguments in the utility functions remain nonspecified. Objections are raised primarily to the predominant place economists tend to assign to private net wealth as a motive force in choice behavior, and particularly in nonmarket interactions. These objections warrant discussion here, and they allow me to call attention to the purposes of the whole scientific enterprise.

To what end do we construct and use the rational choice models of individual behavior? Do we seek only to be able to predict patterns of behavioral response to changes in constraints? Is our objective wholly descriptive? Or do we seek to use our models to assist in the same ultimate reform in the constraint structure? The central point to be made here is that the methodological legitimacy of the wealth-maximizing model may depend on the purpose to be served. If the purpose is restricted to that of empirical prediction, we seek corroboration (or nonrefutation) of the hypotheses that the model implies. On this count, the wealth-maximizing model may fall short of economists' expectations, in nonmarket settings in particular, and its critics may appropriately point to the descriptive limits of *Homo economicus,* and especially as extended beyond markets.

On the other hand, if the purpose of the wealth-maximizing model is that of offering a basis for institutional-constitutional evaluation and reform, the descriptive limits of the model may not be critically destructive to its introduction and use. "Best fit" models in the strictly predictive sense may not offer the appropriate base for making institutional judgments. A deliberately chosen bias toward the "worst case" behavioral model may insure against disproportionate losses emergent under potentially realizable worst cases.[10]

The point here was clearly understood by both David Hume and John Stuart Mill. Citations seem warranted.

> Political writers have established it as a maxim, that, in contriving any system of government, and fixing several checks and controuls of the constitution, every man ought to be supposed a *knave,* and to have no other end, in all his actions, than private interest.[11]

> The very principle of constitutional government requires it to be assumed that political power will be abused to promote the particular purpose of the holder; not because it is always so, but because such is the natural tendency of things, to guard against which is the especial use of free institutions.[12]

Let me not be misunderstood here. The argument does not defend the use of the narrowly restricted economic model of behavior independent of its

---

10. For extended treatment of this point, see G. Brennan and J. Buchanan, "The Normative Purpose of Economic Science," *International Review of Law and Economics* 1 (1981): 155–66.

11. David Hume, "On the Independency of Parliament," in *Essays, Moral, Political, and Literary* (Indianapolis: Liberty Fund, 1985), 42.

12. J. S. Mill, *Considerations on Representative Government,* volume 19 of *Essays on Politics and Society, Collected Works* (Toronto: University of Toronto Press, 1977), 505.

descriptive qualities. The predictive model is relevant for the selection of the presumptive model of behavior that can serve as the basis for making institutional comparisons. The positivist attributes of the model of choice interact with the normative usage. My emphasis on this point here is largely to warn against the somewhat naive criticism to the effect that because politicians and bureaucrats are not really observed to behave like the economist's models, then these models provide no basis for evaluating alternative constitutional structures.

If the raison d'être of social science is to advance discussion of potential institutional-constitutional reform, we must acknowledge both the dependence of individual choice alternatives on the institutional-constitutional constraints and the possible variability of such constraints. Rational choice models, as such, remain sterile exercises until and unless the ultimate end objective for analysis is specified.

Personally, I remain unconcerned about the inclusion or exclusion of the vertical extensions of analysis, discussed above, in the domain of rational choice modeling in some taxonomic sense. I fail to see how "social science," as such, can establish a claim to legitimacy unless it can claim some contribution toward understanding human behavior and, further, that this enhanced understanding can offer assistance in institutional-constitutional change.

VII. Choice, Ignorance, and Uncertainty

One glaring omission will have seemed obvious from my treatment of rational choice models to this point. Nowhere have I introduced the critically important distinction between rational choice behavior under conditions of full knowledge and choice behavior under ignorance and/or uncertainty, a distinction that has commanded the attention of many modern choice theorists, and which affects the potential linkage between the analytical models of interaction and the predictive usefulness of these models, along with the implications for normative policy change. In a very real sense, choice, as such, assumes meaning only under conditions of ignorance/uncertainty, as Shackle has repeatedly emphasized, and the individual necessarily chooses among "alternative futures," none of which can be known before choice and only one of which can be experienced after choice. This central fact insures that the whole utility-maximizing apparatus assumes meaning only in some reconstructive and explanatory sense. In its most general formulation, "to choose" reduces to "doing the best one can," under the particular circumstances faced, circumstances that are described by time, place, and setting.

Because of my own sympathies for the Shacklean position, which carries quasi-nihilistic methodological implications for much of social science, including economics, I may conclude by calling into question the initial wisdom of those who invited me to write this paper. I am a long way from being the most ardent advocate for rational choice models in the social sciences. On the other hand, and in partial justification for my acceptance of the challenge, I fail to see how inquiry can proceed at all unless we reduce analysis to the choice behavior of individuals. From such a base, the social sciences, broadly defined, have added and can add to our understanding and explanation of the social-interaction processes that we observe and in which we participate.

Care must be taken lest we claim too much for our "science," however, and especially lest we slip into the arrogant presumption that any "science" of behavior offers direction to some persons who seek control over the choices of others. Let us not think of the "science of economics" or of anything else as providing the basis for proffering advice to some benevolent despot. Ultimately, our "science" becomes constructively useful only if it can serve as an input into the never-ending discussion among all persons, ourselves included, on ways and means to modify the existing set of general rules so as to achieve higher levels of commonly shared values.

An Ambiguity in Sen's Alleged Proof of the Impossibility of a Pareto Libertarian*

Abstract: "Minimal liberalism," in Sen's strict definition, is impossible, because any "social state," once chosen, freezes all of its components, thereby removing any prospect of further assignment of choice making authority.

My purpose here is to identify a basic ambiguity in A. K. Sen's initial note in the *Journal of Political Economy,* an ambiguity that remains in the later

From *Analyse & Kritik* 18 (September 1996): 118–25. Reprinted by permission of the publisher.

Prefatory Note (April 1995): I appreciate the decision of the Editors, through the intercession of Professor Hartmut Kliemt, in offering me the opportunity to publish belatedly this note, which was written in September–October 1976 for seminar presentation at the Center for Study of Public Choice, then at Virginia Polytechnic Institute and State University in Blacksburg, Virginia. At that time I made no attempt to publish the note because, in the seminar presentation itself, the argument was so severely criticized by my colleagues that I lost confidence and concluded that, somehow, I must have been confused. Then or now, I have been unable to understand and appreciate the source of the criticisms. Only one Xerox copy of the note was circulated beyond my office, mailed to a welfare economist in England, shortly after the seminar. Hence, my surprise three years later when I received an inquiry from Professor Amartya Sen asking me where the note was published. Sen indicated that he wanted to use my note as a reference for students, and seemed surprised at its fate. He has, since that time, made several references to the note. I should also indicate here that I have made no concerted effort to examine the post-1976 literature on the Pareto-liberal paradox in order to bring the argument "up to date" as of 1995.

elaboration of his thesis, and one that has somewhat surprisingly not been specifically discussed in any of the several critical reactions that have been variously published.[1] In his note, Sen claimed to prove that the Pareto principle conflicts with the rule or principle of Minimal Liberalism, which he has rechristened as Minimal Libertarianism in his 1976 paper. I shall show that Sen's rule of minimal libertarianism is self-contradictory. When the rule or principle is reformulated so as to make it consistent with what seems to have been Sen's intent, the alleged conflict with the Pareto principle can be shown to be nothing more than the familiar inefficiency of independent adjustment or Nash equilibria under conditions of Pareto-relevant externalities.

The alternatives for comparison in Sen's analysis are "social states," with "each social state being a complete description of society including every individual's position in it."[2] His Condition L (Liberalism) is defined as follows: "For each individual i, there is at least one pair of alternatives, say (x,y) such that if this individual prefers x to y, then society should prefer x to y; and if this individual prefers y to x, then the society should prefer y to x."[3] This more restrictive condition is then replaced by the lesser requirement that at least two persons in the society, rather than every person, must each be decisive over one pair of alternatives. This difference in defining the rule of liberalism or libertarianism is not relevant to my argument, and it may be neglected in what follows.

Having defined the rule of liberalism, Sen then proceeds to prove that it is inconsistent with Condition P (the Pareto principle) which he defines in the standard manner. His alleged inconsistency here is wholly irrelevant, however, because the principle or rule of liberalism, as defined, is self-

1. A. K. Sen, "The Impossibility of a Paretian Liberal," *Journal of Political Economy* 78 (1970): 152–57; for a complete listing of both the criticisms and Sen's responses, see A. K. Sen, "Liberty, Unanimity and Rights," *Economica* 43 (1976): 217–46. The two critics who have come closest to raising the central point of this note are Peter Bernholz ("Is a Paretian Liberal Really Impossible?" *Public Choice* 20 [1974]: 99–107) and Christian Seidl ("On Liberal Values," *Journal of Economics/Zeitschrift für Nationalökonomie* 35 [1975]: 257–92). As I shall note later, however, neither Bernholz nor Seidl directly attacks Sen's argument at its most vulnerable point, with the result that neither criticism has been effective in dislodging Sen's adherence to his main theorem.

2. Sen, "Impossibility of a Paretian Liberal," 152.

3. Ibid., 153.

contradictory. This stems from the elementary fact that not more than one person could ever be assigned so much as a single choice over alternatives, provided that these alternatives are defined as "complete descriptions of society including every individual's position in it." This fact follows from the mutual exclusiveness of the alternatives themselves. Hence, the assignment of decisiveness to a single person necessarily precludes a similar assignment to any other person in the society.

To illustrate this point, let us introduce a simple two-person example, where complete social states can be easily described. Person 1 and Person 2 may be clean-shaven or bearded. All other aspects of their environment, including behavior, are arbitrarily fixed. There are only four possible social states, as follows:

(x) Person 1 clean-shaven; Person 2 clean-shaven;
(y) Person 1 bearded; Person 2 clean-shaven;
(z) Person 1 clean-shaven; Person 2 bearded;
(w) Person 1 bearded; Person 2 bearded.

Let us now define these four mutually exclusive and distinct alternatives as x, y, z and w, the notation introduced in Sen's formal proof of his theorem. Sen proceeds as follows: "Let 1 prefer x to y, and 2 prefer z to w. And let everyone in the community including 1 and 2 prefer w to x and y to z. There is no contradiction for 1 and 2, for 1 simply prefers w to x, x to y and y to z, while 2 prefers y to z, z to w and w to x. . . . But by Condition L^* society should prefer x to y and z to w, while, by the Pareto principle, society must prefer w to x and y to z."[4]

The contradiction lies in the inference that Person 1 can somehow be assigned the choice between x and y while, *at the same time*, Person 2 is assigned the choice between z and w. But it should be evident from the example that the choice of either x or y by Person 1 will, in fact, preclude any exercise of choice between z and w by Person 2, and vice versa. Since the four social states are mutually exclusive, by definition, it follows that not more than one person can be allowed to be decisive, either between any two of the alternatives or among those in the whole set. The assignment of decisiveness to Person 1 as between the pair x and y rules out z and w as alternatives be-

4. Ibid., 154.

tween which Person 2 could possibly be allowed to choose. Such an assignment of decisiveness is equivalent to an initial specification of "property rights."

In accordance with the preference rankings used in Sen's proof, neither x nor z is Pareto-optimal. Either one of these two possible initially chosen points (depending on whether Person 1 or Person 2 is assigned the right of choice) is Pareto-dominated, the first by w, the second by y. If Person 1 is, for some arbitrary reason, assigned the right to choose only between x and y, but any move from either one of these positions is allowed upon unanimous consent, then society will shift to position w, which is Pareto-optimal. Similarly, the assignment of the initial right to select between z and w to Person 2 will produce first z and then, by unanimous agreement, y. In this interpretation, however, it is difficult to understand why a single person should be assigned only the choice between two selected alternatives from among the whole set, rather than the more inclusive choice among all of the alternatives. In the latter case, Person 1, given the right to choose, would select w directly; Person 2, given the right to choose, would select y directly. Hence, the assignment of decisiveness to either person would necessarily produce a position on the Pareto-optimality surface.

In his criticism of Sen's analysis, Peter Bernholz argued that under the "rule of liberalism," individuals do not have the right to choose among social states.[5] As I shall indicate below, Bernholz's claim is correct under a reformulated and internally consistent rule of liberalism. However, Sen's statement of the rule, his Condition L or L^*, does quite explicitly grant to the individual a right to choose between a pair of social states, defined on his own terms. In response to Bernholz, Sen could suggest that as a normative principle liberalism is indeed concerned with such a right.[6] Furthermore, he could respond that: "Given the rest of the world, Jack's choice over the 'measure' of sleeping on his belly *is* a choice over two 'social states.' "[7] Indeed it is. But no such choice could simultaneously be allowed to Jill, whose sleeping position must be fixed in Jack's "rest of the world."

---

5. Bernholz, "Is a Paretian Liberal?" 100.

6. A. K. Sen, "Is a Paretian Liberal Really Impossible? A Reply," *Public Choice* 30 (1975): 112.

7. Sen, "Liberty, Unanimity and Rights," 228; italics in original.

Person 2

		Clean-Shaven z'	Bearded w'
	Clean-Shaven x'	$(x'z')$ a, c	$(x'w')$ b, c'
Person 1			
	Bearded y'	$(y'z')$ a', d	$(y'w')$ b', d'

Figure 1

Seidl's distinction between technologically separable and nonseparable social states also involves an implicit and indirect recognition of the contradiction.[8] But, as with Bernholz, Sen could, and did, respond by pointing out that "the result of defining liberalism in the existential form is that if it is denied then *j* loses his right to decide singlehanded on the 'regime' . . . *as well as his right to sleep as he likes . . .*"[9] By existential form, Sen here refers to his own Condition *L* (or *L**), as defined. My point may be restated in this context as follows: If *j* is indeed given the right to decide singlehanded on the regime *as well as on everything else, i* cannot possibly be granted a similar right.

But Sen surely does not mean what he appears to say in parts of his formal proof and in some of his responses to critics. To determine just what he has in mind we may refer to his examples. In these it seems clear that he is not implicitly defining the choice alternatives for an individual as complete descriptions of society. In terms of our own example above, Sen would want to define the possible alternatives for Person 1 as the two states of his own face, independent of the state of Person 2's face. Similarly for Person 2. Complete descriptions of the possible social states embody two separate components, and it is mutually consistent to assign each of the two persons control over one of these two. What we have here is a two-person interaction, which may be readily illustrated in simple matrix form, as in Figure 1. We may now de-

8. Seidl, "On Liberal Values," 262ff.
9. Sen, "Liberty, Unanimity and Rights," 228; italics in original.

fine the social states by their two components, as shown in the separate cells of the matrix. We may use x' and y' to describe the pair of alternatives over which Person 1 may be allowed control, and z' and w' to describe the pair of alternatives over which Person 2 may be allowed control. (The primes are added here to suggest that these alternatives are *not* the same as those denoted by x, y, z and w above.) We can now define the four possible social states as $x'z'$, $x'w'$, $y'z'$ and $y'w'$. In this setting, which seems to be in conformity with the discussion in Sen's examples, the individual rankings provided in parts of his alleged proof may be quite differently interpreted. We can interpret Person 1's preference of x' over y' to mean that given any state of the environment (in this case Person 2's behavior) Person 1 will prefer being clean-shaven to wearing a beard. Similarly for Person 2. There is row dominance for Person 1, column dominance for Person 2. In terms of the ordinal utility payoffs represented in the matrix illustration, we know only that for Person 1, a exceeds a' and b exceeds b', while for Person 2, c exceeds c' and d exceeds d'.

In this setting, it is possible to introduce a meaningful statement of the libertarian rule or principle. This would suggest that each person should be allowed control over a particular element—in our illustration, over the state of his own face. Hence, Person 1 should be allowed to choose between x' and y', while Person 2 should be allowed to choose between z' and w'.[10] The solution that would emerge from the operation of this rule is $x'z'$. From a knowledge of the rankings of the ordinal payoffs, as interpreted above, we know *nothing* about whether this solution or outcome is or is not Pareto-dominated by some other social state. In the relationships between payoffs noted, b' may be less than, equal to or greater than a, while d' may be less than, equal to or greater than c. If b' is greater than a, and d' is greater than c, we then have the familiar prisoners' dilemma setting, in which both parties can reach agreement on a shift away from the wholly independent adjustment outcome toward the jointly efficient solution to the interaction. There is surely nothing at all new or "deeply illiberal" in this.[11]

Both to him and to most of his critics, Sen's results seem more significant

---

10. This meaning of the principle is clear in Sen's later reformulation. See item b on p. 217 of his "Liberty, Unanimity and Rights."

11. Sen, "Impossibility of a Paretian Liberal," 157.

than they are because of the fundamental confusion between the evaluation of complete social states and the evaluation of elements within these states, and because in switching between his examples and his formal proof, Sen mixes these two quite different conceptions. As a consequence, Sen's overall argument seems to imply a more pervasive inconsistency between Pareto-optimality and the rule of liberalism, properly reformulated, than occurs in the familiar externality analysis.

This may be demonstrated readily by looking directly at Sen's initial example in the interaction setting introduced above. Let us replace the four states of society depicted in Figure 1 by the following:

I.   Person A reads *Lady Chatterley's Lover* (*LCL*); Person B reads *LCL*.
II.   Person A does not read *LCL*; Person B reads *LCL*.
III. Person A reads *LCL*; Person B does not read *LCL*.
IV.   Person A does not read *LCL*; Person B does not read *LCL*.

In Figure 2 we may put this in matrix form analogous to that of Figure 1. Sen's discussion leaves out the social state depicted in Cell I, but its inclusion does not violate the spirit of his example. He then tells us that A, the prude, ranks outcome IV above III, which in turn is valued more highly than II. We may add I as A's lowest ranked outcome. Hence, from Sen we get the payoffs for A arrayed as follows: $b' > b > a' > a$. For Person B, the lascivious, adding I, we get: $c > c' > d > d'$. Note that these are ordinally arrayed payoffs over the full set of *complete* social states. In this they differ from the orderings in the discussion of Figure 1, which were only over pairs of the four complete

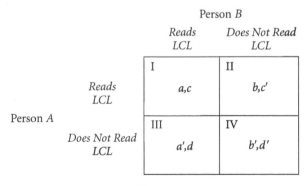

Figure 2

states. In the orderings discussed in Figure 1, there was no way of comparing the as and bs for Person 1, or the cs and ds for Person 2. Application of the libertarian rule, therefore, might or might not produce a Pareto-optimal outcome or solution. In Sen's example, however, his explicit ranking of social states rather than the mutually compatible, individually controllable elements of these states, guarantees that the independent adjustment outcome will be nonoptimal. Note that in Figure 2, if Person A is allowed to select his own reading matter, and if Person B is allowed to do the same, the outcome in Cell II is produced. This libertarian outcome is Pareto-dominated by that in Cell III by Sen's rankings. By comparison, there is no way for us to know, without additional information, that the $x'z'$ outcome in Figure 1 was similarly Pareto-dominated.

Nowhere in his analysis, either in his original note, in his several replies to critics or in his 1976 elaboration, does Sen refer to the assignment or starting-point problem. If the purpose is limited to that of deriving an ordering over complete social states, there is no issue of assigning or partitioning rights among separate persons. But if individuals are to be allowed to interact, one with another, to produce social outcomes, their separate assignments in the interaction process must first be specified. It is at this point that the rule or principle of liberalism or libertarianism, as reformulated in this note and earlier as interpreted by Bernholz, may be sharply distinguished from its alternatives. Sen is concerned about the presence and potential influence of "meddlesome preferences" in social outcomes. The rule of liberalism assigns to each person a protected domain or sphere of private action that he can, if he desires, enforce as a part of any social outcome. At this level, the rule of liberalism may be contrasted with that of extreme collectivism, where no such protected domains for individual action exist.

As it is normally invoked, the Pareto principle does not enter into the analysis of initial assignments, where pure conflict is presumed to prevail.[12] This principle or norm emerges only at a post-assignment or post-constitutional level of analysis. Once individual rights have been assigned or partitioned, the Pareto criterion does offer a means of evaluating potential transfers of rights

12. In my book *The Limits of Liberty* (Chicago, 1975), I extend the Pareto norm backward so to speak to explain conceptually the leap from Hobbesian anarchy. But this is by no means the orthodox or standard usage of the Pareto construction.

among individuals. At this point, "meddlesome preferences" may reenter. If a person is assigned the right to determine his own reading matter, he can guarantee the enforcement of this right as a part of the observed social outcome. If, however, someone else places a higher value on this person's reading habits than he does himself, the Pareto norm would suggest the mutuality of gains from a transfer. In the end, the"meddlesome preferences" may prevail, but only if those who hold them are willing to pay for their exercise.

The ambiguity that I have identified in this note seems to lie at the base of Sen's antipathy to the Pareto principle or norm. If "rights" are somehow interpreted to allow persons to choose among complete social states, it follows from the earlier analysis here that mutually advantageous exchanges of rights are not possible. Since only one person can choose among complete social states, no one else possesses any "choices" that he might subsequently "trade" or "exchange." In such a setting, the Pareto-superiority of alternative social states must seem "ill-defined."[13] This peculiarity disappears immediately, however, once we recognize that the rule of liberalism does not, and, indeed, cannot assign rights to choose among complete social states to anyone. Persons are assigned rights to control defined elements which, when combined with the exercise of mutually compatible rights of others, will generate a social state as an outcome of an interaction process, not of a "choice," as such, by either one or many persons. In this context, "rights" may be exchanged among persons, and it is precisely in the evaluation of potential exchanges, be these simple or complex, that the Pareto criterion comes into use.

13. Sen, "Paretian Liberal Reply," 112.

Choosing What to Choose

In exclusive interactions, persons impose internal constraints that restrict the choice set to those alternatives considered to be attainable within the "rules." Persons do not behave opportunistically whenever the occasion permits. The market process is facilitated by widespread adherence to norms of reciprocation. An example of opportunistic behavior that violates such norms is the deficit financing of modern governments.

> . . . a norm of conduct, and fitting sphere which stops its wandering everywhere.
>
> —C. Day Lewis, "On Not Saying Everything" (as cited by John Bayley, *New York Review of Books,* 14 January 1993, 28).

1. Introduction

When the organizer of this conference on "Bounded Rationality" invited me to participate, I responded with the suggestion that I might write something on "Rationally Bounded Rationality." As it has turned out, my efforts to fulfill the contract here have proved to be much more difficult than I anticipated. I had a vague idea of what I wanted to include in the paper, but articulation of a coherent argument proved to be a severe test for my analytical and rhetorical competence.

From *Journal of Institutional and Theoretical Economics* 150 (March 1994): 123–44. Reprinted by permission of the publisher.

I am indebted to my colleague Viktor Vanberg for helpful comments on a *totally* different draft paper initially prepared for the same conference.

My difficulties were, in part, grounded in my implicit acceptance of too much of the mind-set of the economist, as the discussion below will indicate. Earlier drafts were centered on temporal externalities as related to the meaningfulness of utility trade-offs among time periods in recognition of changing personal identity through time. This subject matter remains important and surely deserves much work, but any such detailed analysis of individual choice in a presumed isolated setting seems less important than a more basic inquiry into the basic logic of constrained *individual* choice in social interaction. This paper does not go beyond such preliminary effort. I shall use analytical tools that are familiar from economics, but the central points to be developed do not fit well within the domain of economic theorizing. I introduce the tools of economics primarily to demonstrate their explanatory limits rather than their explanatory potential.

The paper is organized in five parts followed by a summary conclusion. Section 2 introduces the elementary economics exercise of utility maximization subject to a budget constraint, with the purpose of demonstrating its relatively narrow usefulness. The critical dependence of economic behavior on moral rules clearly emerges. In section 3, I introduce an example of behavior that is not limited by moral norms, that which is reflected in the deficit financing of governmental outlay. Section 4 considers some of the ambiguities that the examples contain. Section 5 generalizes the discussion beyond the narrow confines of the examples, and section 6 concludes the paper.

2. The Rules of the Market

Consider the exercise in chapter 2 of the standard elementary textbook in economics. The individual, who is presumed to be exogenously endowed with some economic value, in monetary or commodity units, enters a market or exchange relationship that allows the purchase of goods at fixed prices. The individual's preference over goods is independent of the constraints defined by the endowments and the prices confronted. Utility is maximized when the rate of trade-off in utilities is matched by the rate of trade-off dictated by the exchange opportunity.

Why should the individual restrict behavior to that which allows only for choices that lie within the budget line? Why does the individual trade at all?

By stealing, cheating, or defrauding potential trading partners, the individual may secure a preferred bundle of goods by giving up a smaller share of the endowments initially possessed than that required in the trading process. The elementary exclusion of all such opportunistic behavior from analysis relies on the presumption that the effective "price" of any good obtained opportunistically is as high as or higher than that which confronts the person in the straightforward exchange relationship.

Such a presumption can be challenged empirically. Observation suggests that the objectively measurable "prices" of goods attainable by opportunistic behavior may be much lower than those prices available in markets. In this case, any "economic" explanation of the widespread adherence to the rules of market requires some attribution of high levels of risk averseness to all traders. Economists cannot readily respond to the question: Why do so many persons trade? Or to the converse question: Why is there no more criminal behavior?

The noneconomist has a much easier time of it here. Many persons abide by the standards of conduct that we observe because they act only within a set of self-imposed constraints. Many persons do not behave opportunistically, even when the possibilities of apparent advantage are present, because they adhere to certain moral precepts or norms. If this descriptive claim is accepted, however, the whole basis of the elementary exercise sketched out above is called into question. The effective constraints are no longer exogenous; the individual behaves only within an internal or endogenous set of constraints. Somehow and for some reason, the individual has chosen the set of prospects from which further choices are to be made.

The economist needs to be totally quiescent when confronted with evidence that potential traders do not seem to behave opportunistically on most occasions. There may be economic reasons why an individual chooses to act only with the implied rules for voluntary exchange. Adam Smith emphasized the importance of "the discipline of continuous dealings."[1] The existence of the exit option for all traders exerts behavioral control on those who expect trading relationships to continue through time. If a trader cheats, customers

---

1. A. Smith, *The Wealth of Nations* (1776; Indianapolis: Liberty Fund, 1981).

will shift to alternative sellers (buyers), and in a well-functioning market, exit involves relatively low cost.[2]

It should be noted that the influence of potential exit on behavior occurs only if the large-number anonymity of the stylized market is not descriptive of reality. And, as markets become more extensive geographically, the anonymity of dealers across sides of the market tends to increase, to be replaced only in part by the emergence of trade names and reputational capital. And even with an operative exit feature present, in each particular transaction the individual must act in accordance with a self-imposed constraint.

The set of endogenous constraints within which an individual is observed to choose may not be understood to be subject to conscious choice. As David Hume and, latterly, F. A. Hayek have emphasized, persons may abide by codes of conduct or personal rules of behavior that have emerged over a long period of cultural evolution, a process that is neither understood by those who are affected nor directed by anyone's intent.[3] The morality that described reciprocal dealing in the marketplace may reflect behavior that is not consciously "moral" to the participants themselves.

Nonetheless, we should recognize that the efficacy of any market order depends critically on the endogenous behavioral constraints that are in existence, and, further, that, to an extent, these constraints may, themselves, be "constructed." As the citizens of the former Soviet Union are discovering in the 1990's, the behavioral constraints that are necessary for a functioning market economy do not emerge spontaneously, at least within a limited time period, even if the formal institutional structures are largely in place. If the necessary personal constraints are not present, or if they have been and are eroding where once they were existent (the United States of the 1990's?), increased resource investment in both policing and preaching becomes more productive. More effective enforcement of legal sanctions against opportunistic behavior (theft, fraud, breach) can move the objective constraints faced by potential traders closer to the descriptive features of the economic model, al-

---

2. For a generalized game theoretic discussion, see R. Congleton and V. Vanberg, "Rationality, Morality and Exit," *American Political Science Review* 86 (1992): 418–31.

3. F. A. Hayek, *Law, Legislation and Liberty*, vol. 3, *The Political Order of a Free People* (Chicago: University of Chicago Press, 1979).

though value is necessarily lowered relative to that which might be generated in the presence of genuinely endogenous constraints. At the same time, resource commitment to "preaching" is also suggested. The powers of public persuasion may at least be marginally effective in transmitting a sense of values that include adherence to the generalized morality of the marketplace.[4]

The argument to this point may be accepted. The participants in a market order must, at least to some considerable degree, choose among a restricted set of alternatives that is defined internally by rules that have themselves either been chosen explicitly or been passed along in some evolutionary process. But what has really been "explained" by this statement? Why do many persons seem deliberately to act contrary to the dictates of their own preference orderings? How can those alternatives be rejected that seem, objectively, to promise higher utility yields than those alternatives eligible for choice? Something remains amiss in the standard economists' treatment, even as amended.

Consider figure 1, a basic diagram in the elementary textbook. The individual whose calculus is under examination holds an initial endowment measured by X and confronts the budget line B which indicates the rate at which units of X may be traded for units of Y through entry into voluntary exchange. In this exercise, utility is maximized at E, where the required tangency emerges. Suppose, however, that units of Y are available through nonexchange behavior (e.g., theft) at an effective "price" shown by the slope of T. Why will the individual move to or stay at E? What is to prevent movement directly to G, the position that promises to yield maximal utility under the T constraint, as indicated in the standard ordinal utility mapping represented by the indifference contours?

There is a contradiction involved in suggesting that the individual will internally constrain choice behavior as dictated by the market constraint, B, when the less restrictive constraint, shown by T, exists. The contradiction is removed once it is recognized that the construction in figure 1, as normally interpreted, is incomplete, and thereby misleading in a critically important respect. The error lies in the implied presumption that the preference order-

4. J. M. Buchanan, *Ethics and Economic Progress* (Norman: University of Oklahoma Press, 1994).

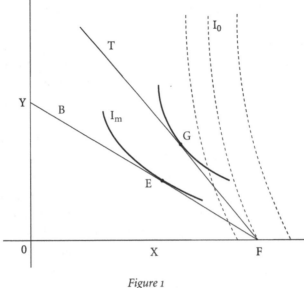

Figure 1

ing depicted is over only X and Y, defined to be objectively identifiable final goods, even if these are stylized along all of the standard quality dimensions. The good Y that is obtainable through voluntary market exchange is categorically different, in terms of its evaluation against X, from the good Y_0 that is obtainable through nonmarket opportunistic behavior. The ordering over goods cannot be separated from the means through which goods are expected to be secured.

The individual's ordering as between X, the good in the initial endowment, and Y_0, the good that might be available through nonmarket or beyond-market behavior, may be like that shown by the set of dotted indifference contours in figure 1. And, if this mapping is descriptive, as between X and Y_0, the preferred position is at F, the corner solution in which none of the good Y_0 is chosen. The three-good bundle finally selected when Y is available through exchange includes the quantities of X and Y, indicated at E, along with the zero quantity of Y_0.

The amended construction eliminates any contradiction between apparent utility-maximizing behavior and the imposition of endogenous constraints. The budget line, B, becomes, indeed, the *market* opportunity line, and all positions beyond the indicated limits are nonfeasible. The portions of the standard utility contours drawn outside the boundaries are both meaningless and misleading.

A critic of my argument might, at this point, concede that I have succeeded in patching up a bit of the elementary economic analysis of choice. But what are some of the implications? I suggest that the amended construction is helpful in providing an introduction to analyses of choice among constraints that is grounded on quite different foundations from those that are familiar, those that invoke perceptual error,[5] preference convexities,[6] or inconsistency in dynamic utility maximization.[7] Note, in particular, that once the domain of choice alternatives is itself chosen by adherence to the endogenous constraint, the individual will not have internal rational reasons for further restrictions on the choice set. If the budget line, B, includes within its limits all of the options that are available from voluntary exchange actions, there should be no basis for shutting off any of the included possibilities. The economists' familiar prejudices against the rationality of deliberative choices made in order to constrain choices become relevant here, but only as applied within the domain so defined.

Note also that the amended construction allows rule-constrained behavior to emerge from a rational calculus that is no way out of the ordinary. To choose not to choose the good Y, or any other good, that may be potentially available through means that are morally nonpreferred seems no different from choosing not to choose bananas because they may not "taste good." The constructions allow moral tastes or values to be introduced directly into the choice calculus, and to exercise an influence that is on all fours with other tastes and values.

Still another critic, this time from inside the economists' establishment, might lament my lapse from the sometimes tortuous separation of "economic science" from its foundations in moral philosophy. Does not my analysis here plunge economics back into necessary discourse about morals? My response is perhaps clear; the attempted separation between economics and

5. R. Heiner, "The Origins of Predictable Behavior," *American Economic Review* 73 (1983): 560–95.

6. D. Levy, "Utility Enhancing Consumption Constraints," *Economics and Philosophy* 4 (1988): 69–88.

7. J. Elster, *Ulysses and the Sirens* (Cambridge: Cambridge University Press, 1979).

morals was, at best, an illusion that simply cannot be sustained. Economics models persons as maximizers of utility, but arguments in utility functions include rules that restrict the range of choices that are made.

3. Rules of Fiscal Prudence

In section 2, I have used one of the basic constructions in elementary economics to suggest that choice behavior is widely restricted by adherence to endogenous constraints, whether or not these are consciously selected. Many persons are not observed to take advantage of each and every apparent opportunity for differential gains in trading relationships, even when they do not seem to be inhibited by the potential for exit by trading partners. I have not specifically discussed the possible origins of the standard rules of the marketplace. For economists, however, the welfare analysis is familiar. Resort to opportunistic behavior on the part of one party to an exchange harms the remaining party. And if each party attempts, simultaneously, to take advantage of the other, both parties suffer. The exchange prospect degenerates into a market version of the prisoners' dilemma (PD) of game theory. The implication is that both (all) parties in market exchange transactions can secure benefits by adherence to rules of behavior that dictate avoidance of differential advantage seeking. There are reciprocal gains from trade as reflected in an agreement on market rules.

The direct beneficiary of a choice on the part of one potential trader to play by market rules, that is, to choose to restrict the choice set to those alternatives that can be attained without seeking differential advantage through nonmarket means, is the cross-exchange trading partner. And, as noted earlier, there is an economic basis of sorts for adherence to market rules if the cross-exchange partner has an exit option available at relatively low cost and/or if such partner may, reciprocally, also resort to nonmarket sources for differential advantage. Voluntaristic adherence to the rules offers a plausible resolution of the PD setting that surrounds almost any trade or exchange relationship. Restrictions placed on the choice sets by both traders may reflect a mutual recognition of the reciprocal nature of market activity.

The generalized economic basis for choosing to play by market rules (value for money, money for value) disappears in those settings where one of two potential traders seems to possess unique access to utility enhancing opportunities. If someone knows that a potential trading partner has no prospect for exit from the relationship, and, further, possesses no means of retaliation against possible exploitation, only some "taste" for "playing fair" will generate voluntary restriction on the choice set. (In terms of the PD analogue, only the Row player has an effective strategy choice; Column must play the cooperative strategy. Only a "taste" for fair play by Row can produce the joint cooperative solution.)

I have suggested that, in many exchange transactions of the ordinary sort, persons will restrict the set of choice options to those that fall within the generalizable rules of reciprocal dealings, and that the market order works well only because of, and to the extent of, such endogenous constraints. It will be useful, however, to introduce a second institutional setting within which persons fail to restrict the set of choices in like manner, and where opportunistic behavior is widely observed, with potentially disastrous consequences. In this case, the argument becomes normative in its implications that persons *should*, indeed, choose to constrain their own choice options.

I refer to the proclivity of many modern democratic governments to finance current outlay through deficits. As representatives of citizens and acting as authorized through the collective agency of government, politicians choose opportunistically to finance public programs by debt rather than by taxation. In supporting this fiscal behavior, citizens are, in effect, approving the act of "stealing" from taxpayers in subsequent periods. By so doing, citizens living currently are able to secure governmental program benefits at "prices" lower than costs.

The simple construction of figure 1 can be applied. In effect, deficit financing allows current choosers to locate at G, the deficit financing equilibrium, rather than at E, the tax financing equilibrium, because they do not restrict the set of choices to those defined by the analogue to the limits of voluntary exchange. Future taxpayers, if they could be brought into an explicit exchange relationship with current citizens, would never agree voluntarily to the "terms of trade" that deficit financing involves.[8]

The practice of modern governments in democracies to finance programs

---

8. Unless, of course, the funds secured from borrowing are used exclusively to purchase income yielding assets that will allow for full servicing and amortization of the debt instruments.

with debt indicates that citizens do not consider "stealing" from future tax-payers to be morally reprehensible, at least not sufficiently so as to cause them to impose restrictions on the choice options that are acceptable. They do not evaluate "program benefits financed by debt" differently from "program benefits financed from taxation"; the three-dimensional bundle analogous to the construction in figure 1 above is not applicable.

Future taxpayers have no recourse. They do not have available an exit option, unless default on public debt should be considered. And they do not have means through which current citizens might be penalized reciprocally for their actions. Any resolution of the deficit dilemma requires a shift in moral attitudes, as might be indicated by a public willingness to place deficit financing "out of bounds." So long as governments are constitutionally authorized to finance public outlay by debt and so long as citizens do not treat such financing as unacceptable, there will be no basic change in fiscal practice. Failure to choose the boundaries on the fiscal choice set must sap the productivity of the market economy.[9]

4. Ambiguities Considered

I have grossly oversimplified the argument by introducing, in section 2, the example where observed adherence to market rules is acknowledged to be mutually beneficial to all participants in the economic nexus, and by introducing, in section 3, the example where failure of persons, acting through political agency, to adhere to the fiscal analogue of market rules is acknowledged to be differentially harmful to all persons who remain in the political community in later periods. In both of these discussions, I have presumed that there is little or no ambiguity involved in defining and in understanding the distinction between behaving within and without the rules that might be chosen to restrict the range of acceptable choices.

Any such presumption may be questioned. What does it mean to say that in a particular exchange a trader acts by the rules of the market? At a first

9. See J. M. Buchanan, "Moral Dimension of Deficit Financing," *Economic Inquiry* 23 (1985): 1–6, for treatment of the moral dimension of debt issue; J. M. Buchanan, *Public Principles of Public Debt* (Homewood, Ill.: Richard Irwin, 1958); and J. M. Buchanan and R. Wagner, *Democracy in Deficit* (New York: Academic Press, 1978), for a more general discussion.

cut, we might say that such behavior requires an initial acceptance of and respect for the rights claimed by the cross-exchange party. But what sort of choice behavior is dictated when and if the rights claimed by the cross-exchange party are considered to be illegitimate?[10] What if the person who brings good Y to the marketplace is known to have stolen the stocks from some third party? Clearly there is a difference between "the good Y that is stolen from someone who has stolen it from others" and "the good Y that is stolen from someone who has acquired it legitimately." The relevance and importance of the delineation and widespread acceptance of owner-ship claims to resources, both human and nonhuman, for any introduction of rules that might constrain acceptable choice sets should be clear. Again, as participants in the economies of former Soviet territories are finding out, until and unless conflicting claims to properties can be settled, at least to some working level, there can be little progress toward an extended market order.

The mutual acknowledgment of property claims is, however, no more than a preliminary stage toward the facilitation of mutually advantageous trading relationships. If we move beyond the simple exchange of physically homogeneous commodities, the quality of goods and services traded may be influenced by the behavior of the producer-supplier. And, in all such cases, ambiguity must arise in the definition of what quality of good or service is consistent with market norms. What is proper "value for money"? And, for the individual trader, the question, what quality of product do I expect to secure in exchange for my sacrifice of value? Should I fudge a bit on quality if I expect my cross-exchange partner to fudge? The elements of a PD setting emerge until and unless trading partners establish and maintain standards for market behavior that impose limits on acceptable internal choices. The potentiality of exit and entry from and into trading relationships will, of course, place some bounds on opportunistic behavior along quality dimen-sions. But markets would work very imperfectly if these were the only effec-tive influences.

Even if property claims are mutually respected, and even if quality consid-erations are absent, there remains the set of issues that might arise when traders think that offered terms of trade are unfair or exploitative. Will a

10. See J. M. Buchanan, *The Limits of Liberty* (Chicago: University of Chicago Press, 1975).

worker provide "a day's work for a day's wage" if he thinks that the wage rate, itself, is exploitative? Or will the worker take advantage of opportunities to shirk? The loss in overall economic value that may have been due to the classical-Marxist "scientific" claim that labor produces all value is scarcely imaginable. The Marxist-inspired adversarial relationship between employer and employee, a relationship that remains present in many modern industrial settings, tends to legitimize opportunistic behavior on the part of both parties to labor contracts. In the traditional labor negotiations between unions and firms, the PD setting is acknowledged, and neither party to negotiation is expected to consider internally imposed limits on the range of acceptable choice alternatives. The mutuality of gain from the basic exchange of labor service for value tends to be overwhelmed by the efforts to secure differential advantage. The observed contrast between this market for labor services in unionized sectors of industrial economies and other markets offers an indirect measure of the value of the endogenous constraints on choice sets in these other markets.

Ambiguities may also arise under more careful examination of the example introduced in section 3. What is the basis for my suggestion that balance in the budget is the fiscal analogue to "trading fairly" with later generations? It becomes relatively easy to enter the sometimes murky discourse about obligations to future generations. And at a much more mundane level, questions of defining budget balance may arise, and especially when efforts are made to separate public consumption outlay from public investment outlay.

The presence of ambiguities that emerge in the discussion of either example introduced does not, however, affect the thrust of my argument. There is no need to define with precision just what the rules of market behavior are in particular settings in order to understand the distinction between opportunistic behavior aimed at securing differential advantage and behavior that is within fair-play limits, even while remaining self-interested. And there is no need to enter controversy over detailed fiscal measurement in order to understand that future generations of taxpayers are exploited by the carryover of large public debt burdens.

5. Generalizations

The examples are helpful for my two-fold purpose: first, to advance the positive claim that many persons engaged in interactions with others do place restrictions on the set of choice alternatives they confront, and, second, to advance the normative argument that, by so doing, persons insure outcomes that are "better" in some meaningful sense. But the behavior of persons in direct market exchanges and in the political "exchanges" reflected through the fiscal process do not exhaust the whole range for interpersonal and intergroup relationships. And the argument that persons do, and should, adopt and adhere to rules that serve to constrain the set of acceptable choice alternatives can be immediately extended or generalized to apply to all interactive behavior.

I have suggested elsewhere that much of human activity takes place in a setting described as one of "ordered anarchy," by which I refer to the simultaneous presence of apparent order and an absence of formal laws governing behavior.[11] How is such ordered anarchy possible? If the private spheres of separate persons intersect, what is to prevent the emergence of conflict? What precludes the simultaneity of claims by separate persons to the same "resources," "places," or "positions"?

The answer suggested by my argument here is that interacting parties choose to constrain their separate choices in such a fashion as to create nonintersecting and therefore nonconflictual outcomes. Persons do not often collide one with another on crowded sidewalks; each walker eliminates spaces that others are expected to occupy from the set of choices among which a selection is made. Persons do not talk simultaneously in nonstructured discussion; each participant chooses to restrict speech until there is a pause in conversation.

The habits, customs, conventions, and manners that characterize behavior in many social settings that we commonly observe are the outward manifestations of the endogenous constraints that are imposed on their own behavior by the individuals who participate. For many, perhaps most, of those who claim membership in socially organized communities, a descriptive model of behavior would require recognition of the presence of endogenous constraints on choice options. That is to say, the argument may be widely generalized over many activities, including market transactions.

A comparable generalization cannot, however, be made over persons.

11. J. M. Buchanan, *Liberty, Market and State* (New York: New York University Press, 1986), chapter 11.

While many persons seem, indeed, to choose to abide by rules that restrict the range of allowable choices in situations of potential conflict, not all persons will do so. There will remain persons who will behave opportunistically when there exist apparent gains. It is because of the failure of these persons, perhaps a relatively small subset of a community's total membership, to impose constraints on their own behavior endogenously, that formal laws become necessary along with those institutional structures that facilitate exercise of the exit option. But the "laws and institutions" should always be considered to be supplementary to and complementary with the operative set of moral rules that prompt persons to constrain their own choice behavior. Differing societies at differing stages of development will embody differing mixes of these basic elements of order. A community that contains a larger number of members who exhibit a sense of fair play, mutual respect, and reciprocal understanding has less need of formal laws and can avoid many of the social costs of enforcement by comparison with a community with a larger share of "natural criminals."

6. Conclusion

I want now to relate the argument advanced in this paper to the inclusive subject matter of the conference, "Bounded Rationality." In my understanding of the term here, bounded rationality involves variations of analyses that stem from a central hypothesis to the effect that persons cannot consider all of the alternatives in the choice sets they confront because of an inherent limit to cognitive capacities. In conscious or unconscious recognition of this limit, individuals adopt simplifying rules that severely restrict the choice set, thereby allowing for an exercise of the rational faculty only within a highly confined subset.

My argument is fully consistent with and complementary to the familiar bounded rationality hypothesis. Whereas the latter finds its origins in the psychology of individual choice, the argument here finds comparable origins in the morality of individual choice. The two separately grounded subsets of choice alternatives over which an orthodox calculus may be exercised need not, of course, correspond. And if both sources of endogenous constraints are operative, only the intersection of the two subsets becomes relevant for utility-maximizing choice as analyzed in the standard economists' model.

Because of cognitive capacity limits, individuals must choose within rules; they act only within what we may call personal psychological "constitutions." But they also act within personal moral "constitutions," for the straightforward reason that they have moral tastes (values).

I am now surprised, belatedly, that most efforts of economists, including my own, to derive a logic of personal rule-following have "jumped over" the rather elementary logic of moral constraints traced out above. The object in most such analyses has been that of demonstrating the conditions under which it may become rational for an individual to be constrained from doing what he wants to do, the conditions under which direct utility loss is incurred in order to accomplish some more inclusive purpose. The neglect of the more central logic of constrained choice may stem in part from the economists' practice that defines preference orderings over "goods," independent of the processes through which "goods" are potentially made available. A more straightforward reason for economists' proclivity to proceed as if moral constraints do not exist may be located in the effort to extend the logic of individual choice in a Crusoe setting to individual choice in social interaction.

I should emphasize the limits of my efforts in this paper. It is possible to advance the positive claim that persons in social settings do constrain the set of choice alternatives they confront by imposing moral criteria on processes of interaction with others. It is also possible to justify the normative claim that a social order in which persons act within such moral constraints works better than an order where choice behavior is not so confined. However, there is no attempt here at explaining *why* persons may impose moral constraints on their own behavior. Modern philosophers[12] and game theorists[13] are making valiant efforts to get some handles on this important puzzle in behavioral science. In these modern treatments, as in the precursory arguments of both Hume and Kant, moral rules emerge from a tacit understanding that opportunistic individual behavior is not generalizable over all members of a community, and from tacit agreement on constraints limiting such behavior.

---

12. J. Rawls, *A Theory of Justice* (Cambridge: Harvard University Press, 1971); D. Gauthier, *Morals by Agreement* (Oxford: Oxford University Press, 1985).

13. K. Binmore, *Game Theory and the Social Contract,* vol. 1, *Playing Fair* (Cambridge: MIT Press, 1994).

Finally I return to my initial response to the invitation to prepare a paper for this conference. I suggested that I work on "rationally bounded rationality." Is it privately rational for an individual to impose morally based constraints on the set of choice alternatives that is confronted?

If consistency is all that is required for choice to be classified as rational, there is no difficulty in making an affirmative response to the question. If, on the other hand, criteria for rationality are extended to include objectively measurable "goods," no matter how defined, then any moral constraints on behavior must be "nonrational." Relatively few modern economists are willing to push the objectifiability of their "science" into such an extreme operational requirement. If "goods" are acknowledged to be defined ultimately by the subjective evaluations of participants in social interaction, qualities of these "goods" must surely include moral attributes of the processes of acquisition.

Law and the Invisible Hand

I have often argued that there is only one "principle" in economics that is worth stressing, and that the economist's didactic function is one of conveying some understanding of this principle to the public at large. Apart from this principle, there would be no basis for general public support for economics as a legitimate academic discipline, no place for "economics" as an appropriate part of a "liberal" educational curriculum. I refer, of course, to the principle of the spontaneous order of the market, which was the great intellectual discovery of the eighteenth century.

The principle is perhaps best summarized in Adam Smith's most famous statement:

> It is not from the benevolence of the butcher, the brewer, or the baker, that we expect our dinner, but from their regard to their own interest. We address ourselves, not to their humanity, but to their self-love, and never talk to them of our own necessities but of their advantages.[1]

Sir Dennis Robertson put the same point somewhat differently when he said that the economists' task was that of showing how to minimize the use of that scarcest of all resources, love. And he urged his fellow economists to emit warning barks whenever they observed proposals that required love for their effective implementation.[2]

The understanding of this principle is extremely important for the shaping of attitudes toward the economic process. To those who do not under-

From *The Interaction of Economics and the Law,* ed. Bernard H. Siegan (Lexington, Mass.: D. C. Heath, 1977), 127–38. Reprinted by permission of the publisher.

1. Adam Smith, *The Wealth of Nations* (Modern Library Edition), 14.
2. D. H. Robertson, *Economic Commentaries* (London: Staples, 1956), 148–49, 154.

stand this principle, either from a lack of formal instruction in economics (or because of perverse formal instruction which is by no means uncommon), or from some failure to sense its fundamental elements from ordinary perceptions of social reality, the economy has no "order." The man of habit may seldom think, but if he is forced, for any reason, to look about him, failure to understand this principle requires some resort to "miracles" to explain such a simple fact as the observed presence of tomato juice on his grocer's shelves each time he goes to the supermarket. In this situation, the man of habit is highly vulnerable to persuasion by those who, from either ignorance or design, propose to subvert the workings of economic process. If the continuing availability of tomato juice is brought to the level of political consciousness, either by the chance occurrence of some exogenous event or by the deliberate effort of a demagogue, the economic illiterate would quite naturally tend to embrace governmental controls purportedly aimed at insuring stability in supply (of tomato juice or of anything else). The whole *raison d'être* of economics, as a discipline with some didactic purpose, lies in its potential for reducing to a minimum the numbers of persons who remain illiterate in this sense.

By implication if not directly, I have advanced here what is essentially a *political* justification for the understanding of this principle of spontaneous coordination. But there are two other, and different, justifications for understanding this principle that must be discussed. First, it has been alleged by Robert Nozick, in his much-acclaimed book, *Anarchy, State, and Utopia*,[3] that "invisible-hand explanations" of reality are intellectually-aesthetically more satisfying than alternative explanations. Nozick offers complex philosophical reasons for this that I cannot fully appreciate, but the common sense basis of this justification seems clear enough. We place positive value on those sorts of understandings-explanations that allow us to predict, even when there is no prospect of control. Contrast the Newtonion (and post-Newtonion) explanations of the movements of the planets with those which required explicit intrusion of "God's will." The economic sophistication that allows us to know why the tomato juice is on the grocer's shelves and to predict what will happen if there is some increase in the demand is something of intrinsic value in its own right.

3. Robert Nozick, *Anarchy, State, and Utopia* (New York: Basic Books, 1974).

A second, and more familiar, justification for understanding the principle of spontaneous coordination lies in the direct efficiency applications. We know that there will be tomato juice on the grocer's shelves, but we know also that we shall get *more* tomato juice, *more* potatoes, *more* shoes—more economic value generally if we allow market forces to operate than if we make attempts to interfere. If we can then accept aggregate economic value as an appropriate objective, an instrumental argument for understanding the coordinative principle is provided.

Or, we may introduce Michael Polanyi's application of the same principle to the organization of science. If we are interested in discovering the unknown, we had best allow individual scientists free reign in their searches. The jigsaw puzzle that is confronted can best be "solved" by allowing different persons to look for differing subpatterns, especially since the "big picture" has no defined borders and since no one knows what this would look like even with borders imposed.

It is useful to distinguish the three justifications for understanding the principle of spontaneous coordination which we may label the *political,* the *aesthetic,* and the *economic.* The failure to separate these may have been a source of some confusion in application. As a different example consider, not the supply of an ordinary commodity on the grocer's shelves, but the dumping of litter on the beaches near San Diego. (We assume, for now, that there is no law against dumping such litter.) We should be able to observe the results; beautiful beaches uglied by litter. We can explain and understand this result in the selfsame way that we understand the tomato juice on the grocer's shelves. Persons do not dump litter on the beach because they are evil or malevolent. (Such persons may exist, but they are surely in a tiny minority, even in the world of the late 1970s.) Persons dump litter on the beach because to do so is in their own self-interest, which may be either narrowly or broadly defined. This does not imply that the persons who dump litter do not value a clean beach more highly than a littered beach; almost all will do so. But the private, personalized cost of cleaning up their own litter is probably greater for most persons than the differential value of the marginal change in the total appearance of the beach that their own activity can produce. In a large number setting, the change in the total amount of littering brought about by the change in the behavior of one person may be relatively insignificant. Hence, it may be to each person's interest to continue to litter, while deploring the overall appearance of the beach.

This is, of course, a familiar example to economists, an example of external diseconomies, of the generation of public bads, of a generalized prisoners' dilemma. Some economists would go on to suggest that the observed results arise because of the absence of property rights in the commonly used resource, the beach. If this scarce resource were assigned to some person or group, it would then be in their interest to maintain standards of cleanliness, to internalize the externalities, and in so doing to insure economic efficiency. My purpose here, however, is not to discuss the particulars of this example, or to raise the more general issues concerning the uses to which various "market failure" constructions have been put. My purpose is the quite different one of illustrating that "invisible hand explanations" may be as applicable to "orders" that are clearly recognized to be undesirable as to those that are recognized to be desirable. We have "explained" the observed pattern of litter on the beach by looking at the behavior of persons, each of whom is maximizing his own utility. Out of this behavioral interaction, a result emerges, an order of sorts, which was not designed by anyone. It was not intended by any of the actors in the process.

We may now apply our three separate justifications of the basic principle of spontaneous coordination to this example. The "order" which emerges, the littered beach, has been produced by anarchy; there is no politically or governmentally orchestrated control or regulation which produces the result. We fully understand that the results emerge from the working of the "invisible hand." We can, as in the other examples, secure some satisfaction in our ability to explain these observed results in such a way as to make them seem "natural," as having been generated by rational utility-maximizing behavior on the part of the separate individuals involved in the interaction. The aesthetics of understanding the principle of order do not seem different from those present in the more familiar meat-bread-potatoes examples from Adam Smith.

An appreciation of the workings of the invisible hand also allows us to recognize that the littering of the beach will be kept within bounds, within the limits that are indeed explainable by individual utility-maximization. Anarchy need not generate chaos; the public beach need not be weighted down with tons of garbage in the absence of specific regulation and control by government-political authorities. For any given population, and for any given set of ethical norms of behavior, anarchy in the use of the acknowledged common resource will produce some equilibrium, one that can be predicted and described in general terms by resort to the economist's set of tools.

It is in the economic, rather than the aesthetic or the political, characteristics that our beach-littering example dramatically differs from Adam Smith's butcher, baker, and candlestick maker, or from the other standard and familiar examples drawn from classical and neoclassical economics, including my earlier tomato juice one. In the latter examples, an understanding of the principle of spontaneous coordination enables us to predict that we shall get more meat, more bread, more candlesticks, more tomato juice by allowing the forces of individual utility-maximization to work independent of direct political regulation (assuming, of course, a well-defined set of legally protected property rights). And if we make the widely acknowledged value judgments that more is better than less and that individuals are better able to judge their own welfare than anyone else, we can label the results to be efficient. In somewhat more technical economist's jargon, we can say that the workings of the market generate Pareto-efficient results, which means that, under the standard conditions postulated, there will exist no possible rearrangements which could make one person better off without harming someone else.

But we cannot do this in our beach-littering example. In the equilibrium attained under anarchy here, under the uninhibited and unregulated utility-maximizing behavior of persons acting each independently or separately, no single person has an incentive to change his behavior, no incentive to reduce the amount of littering that he does. However, if *all* or even a relatively large number of persons should change their behavior in this way, by reducing the amount of littering, *everyone* might be made better off as a result. And "better offness" is here defined in precisely the same way as before, namely by the persons themselves. Each person who uses the beach may find himself with more utility after the general change in behavior than before. And no one would find himself with less utility than before the change. This is merely another way of saying that the results produced by the operation of the invisible hand, by the independent and separate utility-maximizing behavior of persons, are not necessarily efficient in the economic sense. The principle of spontaneous coordination, properly applied to our beach-littering example, allows us to understand and to explain the possible economic inefficiency that would characterize the anarchistic equilibrium just as it allowed us to understand and to explain the possible economic efficiency of the anarchistic equilibria (with well-defined property rights) in the market examples drawn from Adam Smith. The principle of spontaneous order, as such, is fully neutral in this respect. It need not be exclusively or even primarily limited to explanations of unplanned and unintended outcomes that are socially efficient.

So much for a very sketchy and capsule summary of the elementary principles of theoretical welfare economics. This is all by way of introduction to my basic purpose, which is that of examining the potential applicability of the principle of spontaneous coordination to human activities that are not normally classified as "economic," activities that are not normally discussed in terms of the production-exchange-trade of "goods" or "bads." More specifically, I want to look carefully at the emergence and evolution of "the law," which I define here broadly to include the whole set of legal institutions. I want to discuss the applicability of the principle of spontaneous coordination to legal institutions and to go beyond this to the implications for legal reform, notably for constitutional change. My discussion and analysis will be critical of the position that seems to be taken by Professor F. A. Hayek, a distinguished Nobel laureate in economics, and a social and legal philosopher whose ideas I respect and admire.[4] In his specific attribution of invisible-hand characteristics to the evolution of legal institutions, Hayek seems to have failed to separate properly the positive and the normative implications of the principle. Interpreted in a strictly positive sense, the principle of spontaneous coordination can do much to add to our understanding of legal institutions. But this understanding and explanation can be equally helpful in assessing the efficient and the inefficient elements of the order that we may

---

4. The Hayek position is expressed most fully in *Law, Legislation and Liberty,* Volume 1, *Rules and Order* (Chicago: University of Chicago Press, 1973). My criticism is based on what I interpret to be the basic thrust of Hayek's argument, gained from a careful reading of his book. In particular places, Hayek seems to concede many if not all of the points that may be advanced in opposition. My purpose here is not one of exegesis, but is instead that of offering hopefully constructive criticism.

observe, actually or conceptually. "The law" as it exists can probably be classified as some admixture of the bread-meat examples of Adam Smith and of the beach-littering example that I introduced earlier. In order to derive normative implications, we must carefully discriminate. The forces of social evolution alone contain within their workings no guarantee that socially efficient results will emerge over time. The historically determined institutions of legal order need not be those which are "best." Such institutions can be "reformed," can be made more "efficient." The discussions of such potential reforms should, of course, be fully informed by an understanding of the principle of spontaneous order. But warnings against unnecessary and ill-timed interferences with legal institutions should not extend to the point of inhibiting us against efforts at improvement, which seems to me to be the position Hayek's argument forces upon us.

I shall elaborate this argument in several stages. A basic point that I stress in almost all discussion is the necessity of recognizing that "we start from here." Any evaluation or analysis of social institutions must commence with the status quo for the evident reason that this describes that which exists. For present purposes, there exists some body of law; there is in being a set of legal rules, legal institutions, and these may be described. A major part of law school training is indeed little other than the transmission of this description.

And it is surely appropriate for qualified scholars to devote intellectual energies to what may be called the "positive history" of these institutions. In such a history, some understanding of the principle of spontaneous order can be helpful. The legal historian who searches for some explicit or planned design in the existing structure, in whole or in every part, is surely destined for frustration. In a very important sense, as Hayek stresses, law "grows"; it is not "made." The legal historian must explain the sources of this "growth" as best he can, and by resorting to "invisible hand" explanations he can add clarity and understanding. But certain parts of the law are also "made" and have been explicitly designed for the accomplishment of particular purposes. The historian must classify the elements of law into these two sets. Explanation and classification—perhaps the work of the positive historian is complete when he has done these tasks.

For those who seek to evaluate the existing structure of law, however, the records of the positive historian offer little more than preliminary inputs.

Return to the beach-littering example, and suppose that a careful history "explains" the absence of either a set of behavioral standards or more formally imposed constraints on private behavior. Population growth alone might explain why those behavioral standards that were deemed appropriate a half-century past may be inappropriate at the present time. But what is the conceptual basis upon which an evaluative judgment of "inadequacy" or "undesirability" may be established? How can the analyst attribute "inefficiency" to the results that he observes when the historian has explained how these results have emerged?

It is at this point that Hayek's argument seems misleading. He seems to suggest that those institutions that have evolved spontaneously through the responses of persons independent to the choices that they faced embody efficiency attributes. But, as the littering example is designed to demonstrate, an explanation of the results by the operation of "invisible hand" responses need not carry with it normative overtones.[5] But how can norms be introduced? It is here that my own position becomes what Hayek would call "constructivist," a term that he uses pejoratively. In order to distinguish my positive constructivism from constructivism of the idealist type, however, I should add the word "contractarian." My answer to the question posed is straightforward. We may evaluate any element of the existing legal structure in terms of its possible consistency with "that which might emerge" from a genuine "social contract" among all persons who are involved in the interaction.[6] This test applies equally to those elements of legal structure that may have evolved without conscious design or intent and to those elements which may have been quite explicitly "laid on" for the achievement of a particular purpose at some time in the past. The evaluative analyst must test all "law" on such "as if" contractarian criteria. But from such tests he can do nothing other than advance hypotheses of possible "failure." His understanding of the principle of order allows him to hypothesize that all of the beach-using persons would *agree* on some rule that would constrain their littering behavior, would agree on a change in the law that is in existence with respect to

5. My position seems to be close to that taken by Ernest Gellner in a lengthy critique of W. V. Quine. Ernest Gellner, "The Last Pragmatist: The Philosophy of W. V. Quine," *Times Literary Supplement*, July 25, 1975.

6. My position is developed in some detail in my book *The Limits of Liberty: Between Anarchy and Leviathan* (Chicago: University of Chicago Press, 1975).

littering behavior. The ultimate test of his hypothesis is observed agreement on the change suggested.[7]

I am not clear as to how Hayek would classify this basically contractarian position that I have sketched. It seems clearly to fall within the "constructivist" category in the sense that it does "provide a guideline for deciding whether or not existing institutions (are) were to be approved."[8] But the position is not at all "rationalist" in the sense that rationality norms are applied to the group, as such. If properly qualified and interpreted, the contractarian position offers a plausibly acceptable alternative to both Hayek's implicit attribution of efficiency to whatever institutions emerge from an evolutionary process and to the rationalist conception which posits the existence of a group mind. Hayek's criticisms of the latter position, which I fully share, seem to overlook the contractarian alternative, and his strictures may be taken, perhaps misleadingly, to apply equally to the contractarian construction.[9]

To imply, as Hayek seems to do, that there neither exists nor should exist a guideline for evaluating existing institutions seems to me to be a counsel of despair in the modern setting. There are, of course, many elements of the existing legal structure that would, without doubt, qualify as "efficient" in the technical Pareto sense. This would be true with respect to those elements that might have evolved in some evolutionary process, and in the absence of any design, and to those elements that might have been explicitly selected. There need be no relationship between the historical origins of a legal institution and its current efficiency properties. The latter relate exclusively to the institution's ability to command assent in comparisons with effective alternatives that might be suggested. In every case, the "as if" contractarian test

7. The basic methodological position outlined here is discussed more fully in my paper "Positive Economics, Welfare Economics, and Political Economy," *Journal of Law and Economics* 2 (October 1959): 124–38.

8. Hayek, *Rules and Order*, 10.

9. I say "perhaps misleadingly" here because in the Preface to *The Mirage of Social Justice*, Volume 2, *Law, Legislation and Liberty* (Chicago: University of Chicago Press, 1976), Hayek states that he considers his own objectives to be closely related to those of John Rawls, as expressed in the latter's *A Theory of Justice* (Cambridge: Harvard University Press, 1971). The fact that Rawls is an avowed contractarian suggests that Hayek may not apply his constructivist-rationalist criticisms to the contractarian approach, properly interpreted.

must be applied, and existing institutions should be provisionally classified as "possibly efficient" only after meeting such a test. Note that efficiency in this restricted sense is not at all comparable to any concept of efficiency that may be defined with respect to the utility function of a particular individual or even of a group of individuals. That which is Pareto-efficient is that upon which all persons assent, at least to the extent that they fail to agree on any particular change.

Hayek properly stresses that many institutions that have emerged without conscious design are, nonetheless, efficient in the sense defined. But he fails to note that they must be subjected to the *same* test as those which are to be classified as inefficient.[10] There are surely many elements of legal structure that may be provisionally classified as inefficient in the Pareto sense. For these, explicit and deliberately designed proposals for reform can be, and should be, advanced by those whose competence offers them an understanding of the principle of spontaneous coordination. Framework proposals for change can be, and should be, "constructed" and then presented for possible approval or disapproval by the members of the relevant public, the participants in the interaction. The economist can, and should, suggest the enactment of a rule, a law, that would impose fines on persons who litter the beach, a rule that is deliberately constructed for the attaining of an end result, the cleanliness of the beach.

This example may, however, be somewhat misleading for two reasons. First of all, the example is deliberately designed to suggest that *all* persons can be made better off by a simultaneous and fully symmetrical change in behavior, and without the necessity of introducing more complex compromises, compensations, multidimensional exchanges, political log rolling, or side payments. Even for most strictly economic examples, things are not likely to be nearly so simple as in the beach-littering case. Consider a situation in which the participants are not symmetrically engaged in the activity that creates potentially undesirable results. Consider mining activity in the desert, say, Death Valley. A few persons secure gains from undertaking this

10. In her summary paper on Hayek's work, Shirley Letwin suggests that Hayek does allow for "inefficient" outcomes under spontaneous adjustments. But she does not reconcile such recognition with the primary normative thrust of Hayek's argument. See Shirley Letwin, "The Achievements of Hayek," mimeographed paper circulated for Mont Pelerin Society Meeting, Hillsdale, Michigan, August 1975.

activity; to these persons the expected private benefits exceed the expected private costs. Many other persons, the set of nonminers, may be damaged slightly by the uglying of the desert that mining necessarily involves. Assume that there is in existence no law against mining and that the desert is not privately owned. Is the observed result inefficient or efficient? The economist who seeks to reach a provisional or hypothetical judgment here must reckon the costs that would be imposed on those who are now miners, whose behavior would necessarily be constrained by a new law, against the benefits or gains that would be promised to nonminers by the possible change in the level or type of mining activity. If the existing situation, with no law, is considered to be "inefficient," there must be some set of compensations possible which could "pay off" or "bribe" the persons who are engaged in mining, which would induce them voluntarily to modify their behavior. This example is considerably more complex than the simple beach-littering case, but neither example presents difficulties in defining the end results to be evaluated.

A second source of misconception may arise from these strictly economic examples, however, precisely because of the apparent ease with which the end result objectives are defined. For the more general elements of legal structure, the definition of an objective may itself be one of the most difficult steps in the process. Consider a familiar but highly useful example, the rules for ordinary games. Whether by some evolutionary and nonplanned process or by deliberate invention, an existing game is defined by its rules in being. Are these rules efficient in the orthodox Pareto sense? How can we apply the "as if" contractarian test? Would the players generally agree on any change?

This problem poses difficulties conceptually because it becomes almost impossible to specify the objective that might be sought through rules changes. There is nothing approximately akin to "cleanliness" or "natural beauty" here. Criteria of "fairness" may be adduced, but what can "fairness" mean independent of agreement.[11] The criteria for improvement in the rules that define the

---

11. Hayek (in *Rules and Order,* 76) notes that no one has probably succeeded in explicitly articulating the rules that define "fair play." This is in apparent contrast to the economist's articulation of the conditions that define efficiency, as normally understood. Even here, however, the contrast is not so great as it might seem, since the economist's criterion, like that of the observer of other social games, must ultimately reduce to agreement among participants.

general game are necessarily more internalized by the participants than they are in the beach-littering example. In the latter, there is apparently an agreed-on standard of valuation (a clean beach is "better" than a dirty one), which the observing analyst can call upon in his development of suggested hypotheses for change. The tests of the hypotheses are identical; the agreement among participants. But the task of the analyst in advancing reform proposals is conceptually more difficult in the one case than in the other; the constitutional analyst must be considerably more sophisticated in his prognoses than the economic analyst who advances suggestions for economic policy changes.

My argument may be broadly accepted, but there remains the question: Why is a scholar with the sophistication of Hayek led to attribute efficiency to the results of the social evolutionary process, an attribution that makes such results analogous with those that emerge from the operation of markets, *within* a defined legal framework? Failure to understand the principle in the latter case has led, and will lead, to many ill-conceived and damaging interferences through the intrusion of political-governmental controls. But are not these intrusions themselves a part of general social evolution? How can Hayek adduce norms that will allow him to adjudge such interferences to be "out of bounds," while elevating the overall legal structure to a position that should not be called into question by potential constructivists? Surely Hayek must acknowledge that the rules that *emerge* (which need not be "constructed") to constrain market adjustments may themselves be inefficient. But what is his own test? While he seems to allow for reform, for "legislation" to correct for evolutionary aberrations, he offers no criteria for judgment. Hayek is, I think, led into what we must classify finally as a logically inconsistent position because of his implicit fear that politically orchestrated changes must, in most cases, produce social damage. He has been, I think, overzealous in transferring his wholly justified criticism of those who have failed to understand the workings of the invisible hand in the operation of markets *constrained by law,* to the unjustified and partially contradictory criticism of those who seek to evaluate the emergence and operation of law itself in constructivist-rationalist terms.

In my discussion to this point, I have not distinguished between *nomos* and *thesis,* to introduce Hayek's terminology for the "law of liberty" and the "law of legislation" respectively. At base, my criticism of the invisible-hand or evolutionary criteria for evaluation applies equally to both. But it may be useful to outline Hayek's own distinction here. His emphasis is on *nomos*, that body of law that emerges from the separate decisions of judges in a process of spontaneous adjustment.[12] The evolution of the English common law is his historical model, and the implication is clear that the results that emerge from this process are somehow assumed to be "efficient" and that attempts to interfere with these results are likely to be harmful. As my argument has indicated, I see no reason to expect that the evolution of independent judge-made law insures efficiency or optimality.[13] Hayek elevates this set of legal institutions as prior to and conceptually different from legislation, which he defines as designed or constructed rules that direct the activities of governments. He has relatively little to say about criteria for evaluating legislation, which does not emerge from the invisible-hand process.[14] It is nonetheless clear that he assigns "legislation," which would include constitutional law, to a relatively insignificant role in the whole legal structure. *Nomos*, the law of liberty, "lawyer's law"—Hayek strongly suggests that this exists independent of and prior to "legislation."

Hayek's emphasis becomes almost the inverse of my own at this point. In a positive, empirical sense, many of our social-legal institutions have "grown" independent of design and intent. But man must look on *all* institutions as potentially improvable. Man must adopt the attitude that he can control his fate; he must accept the necessity of choosing. He must look on himself as man, not another animal, and upon "civilization" as if it is of his

12. Bruno Leoni has also analyzed judge-made law in a model of adjustment analogous to the working of a competitive market order. See Bruno Leoni, *Freedom and the Law* (Princeton: Van Nostrand, 1961).

13. Richard Posner is more specific in his claim to the effect that the decisions made under common law rules are guided by considerations of economic efficiency. See his *Economic Analysis of Law* (Boston: Little, Brown and Company, 1972). For my own criticism of Posner's argument, see "Good Economics—Bad Law," *Virginia Law Review* 60 (Spring 1974): 483–92.

Posner's claim is, however, less sweeping than Hayek's in one sense. Posner argues that the evolution of the common law has insured the satisfaction of criteria of economic efficiency, defined in the narrow sense. While he implies that this has also been socially desirable, he does not specifically make this the only criterion for the broader "social efficiency."

14. Presumably Hayek will deal with legislation more fully in the projected third volume of *Law, Legislation and Liberty*, which is not yet in final form.

own making.[15] In some final analysis, Hayek's position may be taken to reflect a basic European attitude which is sharply different from the American. The European classical liberal, who is well represented by Hayek, can and perhaps should stress the evolutionary sources of many of the institutions that stand as bulwarks of individual freedom. The American cannot, and should not, neglect the fact that his own heritage of freedom, although owing much to its European antecedents, was deliberately "constructed" in large part by James Madison and his compatriots. Theirs were no invisible hands. They set out to construct a constitutional framework for the "good society," which they defined implicitly as "free relations among free men." For two centuries, their construction has stood the test. But who would dare, in 1976, to suggest that constitutional improvements are not possible, that the observed erosion of our traditional liberties cannot be reversed by deliberately designed reforms, motivated by something akin to the initial Madisonian vision? Americans, because they are Americans, must place their faith in man's ability to impose rules of law upon himself rather than in the rules of law that the historical process imposes upon him.

15. I make this statement in order to contrast it explicitly with the following statement by Hayek: "Freedom means that in some measure we entrust our fate to forces which we do not control; and this seems intolerable to those constructivists who believe that man can master his fate—as if civilization and reason itself were of his making." (F. A. Hayek, *The Mirage of Social Justice*, 30.) Of course, Hayek would acknowledge that some aspects of civilization are of man's making, just as I would necessarily acknowledge that some aspects emerge from the "growth-like" processes of social evolution. What is important, however, is the difference in emphasis or thrust here, a difference that has important implications for the development of attitudes toward the potentialities for social reform.

On Some Fundamental Issues
in Political Economy
An Exchange of Correspondence

James M. Buchanan and Warren J. Samuels

The letters printed below are published by the correspondents with the hope that they will stimulate discussion and creative rethinking about some fundamental and interesting issues that are often ignored in the conduct of economic analysis and research and the application of traditional tools and concepts. The issues, we are aware, are not novel. Our conflicts and apprehensions replicate, in varying degree, past methodological controversies. But we are convinced that the fundamental nature of the topics argued warrants continuing reexamination. Just as each generation of economists has the burden of interpreting for itself the history of the discipline, each generation also confronts, directly or indirectly, the problem of the methodological foundations of economic analysis. Moreover, as the discussions in the letters illustrate, methodological issues are closely related to normative or policy positions, although the relations are often ambiguous and equivocal.

Each reader will have to work out the problems raised in the letters and also interpret our respective positions. The issues are drawn in the letters in ways which represent our thinking during 1972 and 1973 and also are not necessarily how they would be more widely formulated in the profession.

From *Journal of Economic Issues* 9 (March 1975): 15–38. Reprinted from the *Journal of Economic Issues* by permission of the copyright holder, the Association for Evolutionary Economics.

Among the issues raised and discussed in the correspondence are: the meaning of *positive* and *normative;* the role of antecedent specifications of property and other rights; the role of the status quo in positive science; the normative status of the status quo; the role of belief systems, social myths, and pretense in social science; the intrusion of additional normative premises into ostensibly positive analysis; the normative consequences of positive analysis; the attitude of the scholar to the world; the nature of liberal and conservative in economics; and, *inter alia,* what economics is all about. The most conspicuous substantive issue concerns the nature of public choice, specifically the economic role of government and how best to approach it as economists. While we both remain too ignorant in these fields, we have learned more about what each other, and ourselves, intends to accomplish therein.

The letters have been slightly edited, as indicated by ellipses, primarily to exclude material irrelevant to our primary discussions. Publication of the letters does present ideas in a somewhat novel or unusual format, and they were not written with publication in mind and do not have the gloss of analytical rigor and polish usually found in journal articles. Rather, they are informal and exploratory ventures by two economists with clearly different points of view and approaches to government who nevertheless respect and are willing to learn from each other.

The correspondence began with a letter from Buchanan accompanying the draft of his "Politics, Property, and the Law,"[1] written in response to Samuels's "Interrelations Between Legal and Economic Processes,"[2] and which elicited a "Defense" by Samuels.[3] The letters, therefore, ideally should be read in conjunction with these and other materials referred to in the correspondence.[4]

---

1. James M. Buchanan, "Politics, Property, and the Law: An Alternative Interpretation of *Miller et al. v. Schoene," Journal of Law and Economics* 15 (October 1972): 439–52.

2. Warren J. Samuels, "Interrelations Between Legal and Economic Processes," *Journal of Law and Economics* 14 (October 1971): 435–50.

3. Warren J. Samuels, "In Defense of a Positive Approach to Government as an Economic Variable," *Journal of Law and Economics* 15 (October 1972): 453–59.

4. James M. Buchanan, "The Limits of Liberty: Between Anarchy and Leviathan" (Chicago: University of Chicago Press, forthcoming). See also his "The Coase Theorem and the Theory of the State," *Natural Resources Journal* 13 (October 1973): 579–94. See Warren J. Samuels, "Welfare Economics, Power and Property," in *Perspectives of Property,* Gene Wunderlich and W. L. Gibson, Jr., eds. (University Park: Institute for Research on

Since the publication of the aforementioned articles, Buchanan has published his "Before Public Choice," in which he clarifies his position as follows:

Where does this leave us in trying to discuss criteria for "improvement" in rules, in assignments of rights, the initial question that was posed in this paper? I have argued that the contractarian or Paretian norm is relevant on the simple principle that "we start from here." But "here," the status quo, is the existing set of legal institutions and rules. Hence, how can we possibly distinguish genuine contractual changes in "law." . . . Can we really say which changes are defensible "exchanges" from an existing status quo position? This is what I am trying to answer, without full success, in my paper in response to Warren J. Samuels' discussion of the *Miller et al. v. Schoene* case. There I tried to argue that, to the extent that property rights are specified in advance, genuine "trades" can emerge, with mutual gains to all parties. However, to the extent that existing rights are held to be subject to continuous redefinition by the State, no one has an incentive to organize and to initiate trades or agreements. This amounts to saying that once the body politic begins to get overly concerned about the distribution of the pie under existing property-rights assignments and legal rules, once we begin to think either about the personal gains from lawbreaking, privately or publicly, or about the disparities between existing imputations and those estimated to be forthcoming under some idealized anarchy, we are necessarily precluding and forestalling the achievement of potential structural changes that might increase the size of the pie for *all.* Too much concern for "justice" acts to insure that "growth" will not take place, and for reasons much more basic than the familiar economic incentives arguments.[5]

Land and Water Resources, The Pennsylvania State University, 1972), 61–148; and "Public Utilities and the Theory of Power," in *Perspectives in Public Regulation,* Milton Russell, ed. (Carbondale: Southern Illinois University Press, 1973), 1–27. See also Warren Samuels, "The Coase Theorem and the Study of Law and Economics," *Natural Resources Journal* 14 (January 1974): 1–33; "Law and Economics: Introduction," *Journal of Economic Issues* 7 (December 1973): 535–41; *Pareto on Policy* (New York: American Elsevier, 1974); and "Some Notes on Government as an Economic Variable" and "Government in the History of Economics" (in manuscript).

5. Gordon Tullock, ed., *Explorations in the Theory of Anarchy* (Blacksburg, Va.: Center for Study of Public Choice, 1972), 36–37. Compare the review thereof by Samuels in *Public Choice* 16 (Fall 1973): 94–97.

On the other hand, Samuels, insensitive to neither the ethical limitations of assuming the propriety of the status quo system of working rules and rights assignments nor to the problem which Buchanan poses to orderly change and growth, prefers to analyze descriptively resource allocation as a function, proximately, of demand and supply, but more deeply as a function, in turn, of the power structure, rights, and the use of government. Samuels prefers to direct attention to such general interdependence dualisms as these: The power structure is a function of law *and* the use of government is a function of the power structure, and income and wealth distribution is a function of law *and* law is a function of income and wealth distribution. Samuels's interest is in the positive or objective comprehension of the interrelations between legal-political and economic (or nominally market) processes, in part for better understanding the chain of consequences of various government (and private) economic policies. As for the contractarian norm, Samuels finds it congenial but also finds a limited actual scope for Pareto-better adjustments and that such adjustments are always a function of the power structure as well as a wide range of non–Pareto optimal changes.[6]

In Buchanan's response to Samuels's initial article, in Samuels's defense, and in the early letters, the issue of positive versus normative, or of description versus prescription, was debated. The discussion quickly moved to various facets of the consequences of a positive analysis which posits the working rules of law and morals as contingent and subject to change and to concern with the consequences of an assumed propriety of the status quo system of power and use of government. We have somewhat different perceptions as to what order requires, as to what should be the "best" approach to the study of government as an economic variable (although neither would deny the other the opportunity to work as he pleases), and, *inter alia,* how these fundamental issues are to be reflected in the conduct of economic analysis. We agree with the Davenport-Samuelson principle that "there is no reason why theoretical economics should be a monopoly of the reactionaries,"[7] but we are quite far apart as to the nature of an economics (specifically the nature

6. Compare Samuels, "Welfare Economics," and "Some Notes on Government."

7. Paul A. Samuelson, "Maximum Principles in Analytical Economics," *American Economic Review* 62 (June 1972): 261.

of the analysis of the economic role of government) which will both contribute to a free and open society and have meaning as knowledge. Needless to add, neither Buchanan nor Samuels takes one position or another in pure black-and-white terms. But just where we stand and the impact thereof for the issues debated will have to be assessed by others as well as by ourselves. It is our hope that more economists will once again turn to these important issues.

18 May 1972

Dear Warren:

Thanks for sending me your draft response to my paper critical of your initial paper. I hope that Coase will decide to print it, since I think it does carry the discussion several stages along. And, after all, this is the purpose, to carry the discussion since neither of us would surely claim to have any of the final answers in these issues that have been discussed for centuries.

Let me make one or two more specific points by way of reaction. First, you protest too much your positivist stance. I agree that one can contrast a positivist and a normative stance, and I accept that my own is strictly normative in this context. But I submit that an unbiased reader of your piece would indeed read normative elements into it, and sometimes strong ones. And this through no necessary fault of your own. It is almost impossible to be purely positivist here, and, of necessity, we look at common facts through different windows, to use Nietzsche's term, and these windows are necessarily normative to a degree.

But, as I say, a good point can be made here.

I agree with many of the subcriticisms of my approach, which can be criticized on several grounds. I do not treat of property assignments, and this is what has been troubling me most this year. What can we say? I do not especially like the status quo defense that my methodology forces me into, but where can I go? I have been worrying about this for months now without much resolution or progress.

I should continue to insist that unanimity must remain the only acceptable rules for change, ideally, in any genuinely individualistic social order. And here is the problem. It is essential for social order, or a tolerable one at any rate, that men act as if and think as if the process works in a certain way even if, from another vision, the facts may seem so different. I do not really think that a viable social order that either of us would accept could exist if all men really looked on politics in the eyes of the elder Pareto, which sharply separated the rulers and the ruled. The basic and necessary myths of the free society. These are my main concern, and, admittedly, I have been partially concerned about my own little role in dispelling some of these. Once majority rule is shown to be the tattered relic that analysis must reveal it to be, what are we to think??? And of vital importance for our time (as surely is evidenced by the Wallace support) men must *not* see the judiciary as overtly legislating, even though, as scholars, we must recognize that judges do legislate and always have. But Earl Warren's tragic error was his failure to understand this.

These are but a few reactions. I should have more as I reread the paper and think about it more adequately.

Sincerely,
Jim

May 24, 1972

Dear Jim:

Thanks for your letter regarding my response to your paper.

Let me comment as follows:

I basically agree with you concerning the impossibility of a completely value-free positivism—but I think that the effort to generate as pure propositions as possible is desirable. People *will* read normative things from any positive proposition, but in reality they are adding their own normative premise and it is from that premise they draw their normative inferences. Thus, for example, my paper on government in the history of economics has made happy neither scholastic, libertarian, nor Marxist—but the central argument, despite its tautological element, remains intact!

Concerning the defense of status quo rights, the problem is that there is no agreement on the mechanism of change. Either we posit the status quo rights or some other structure of rights, or we posit some system for change. The problem has been discussed by Cardozo and Pound in books done years ago; see Cardozo's *The Growth of the Law, The Nature of the Judicial Process*, and, especially perhaps, *The Paradoxes of Legal Science*, and Pound's *Social Control Through Law*. The genius of the common law has been its gradualism, involving a balancing of continuity of rights against change of rights. The lawyers overdo the wisdom of their lady of the common law, but they have a point.

My own methodology forces me into allowing that an agnostic positive analysis opens the doors to change, to the lifting of the veil, so to speak. At the bottom of your first page, you say that, "It is essential for social order, or a tolerable one at any rate, that. . . ." Two points here: first, we must distinguish between seeing social order as a substantive attainment—i.e., as a set of particular relations—and seeing social order as a process of adjustment, including adjustment between continuity and change. Second, men (and women) do live by myths, but I dislike the game of pretending that things are otherwise than they are, that only safe things should be said in public, and so on. I dislike that with the admitted displeasure that there is only so much change that a society can put up with at one time or over a period of time. Here too we must distinguish between a particular structure and the process: in order for the pretense to have very much recommendatory forces, the status quo at stake must have some recommendatory force of its own—so that when I consider the function of pretense I try to examine it not only in the case of my own society but also in the case of societies of which I am not at all fond, e.g., the USSR, among others.

So there are dangers from an absolute and uncritical acceptance of the status quo *and* from an absolute and uncritical piercing of the veils and masks of society. This goes back, of course, to Plato versus Aristotle and their conflicting theories of the relation of knowledge to social action; to Mannheim on ideology and utopia; et al.

I think that this problem was the central problem which disturbed the late Frank Knight throughout his intellectual life. As for Pareto, what he said in the *Treatise on General Sociology* was said perversely but with much wisdom; but there has been much work done since then. . . .

A last word: perhaps you are right about Earl Warren's error, I do not know; what I do know is that if he was in error, so was the "conservative" court in the 1890s and 1920s and early 1930s in so clearly doing the same thing, namely, reading *their* vision of good economic policy, their vision of the proper resolution of class and other interest conflicts, into the Constitution. What I also know is that the Constitution is only a framework and it is inevitable that different world views will read and interpret it differently. I think that one role of the scholar here is to articulate how that has been done and not to mask it or to read his own interpretation of the clauses involved into his own analytical work. That is the value of a positivist approach, so far as it will take one. . . .

Yours sincerely,
Warren

16 August 1972

Dear Warren:

. . . As we both realize, our basic positions differ substantially. Despite this, however, I think that your efforts in this, and other pieces, are extremely useful. Economists need to be pulled up short on just what it is they are assuming when they talk about government, about the state. And your piece ["Government in the History of Economics"] certainly accomplishes this.

My difference with you lies, I think, in what you have called my essentially normative position, which I do not, in turn, quite accept as such. I think that there are positive elements that can enable us to distinguish among governmental forms. It seems to me that we can derive a logical basis for government of what you call the Lockean variety from the simple calculus of free men, and that no similar logical basis can be so derived from alternative forms. Descriptively, of course, I agree with you. We can always look on government as the agency through which some men exert power over others, Pareto's position. But we need to do more than sit outside, so to speak, and describe. We need to work within a philosophy, or so it seems to me. And there are differences among the alternatives. This is where I categorically disagree with you I think. The alternatives are not equally weighted. The despotic government is "worse" by objective standards, or quasi-objective standards, than the free government. Hitler was worse than Churchill. We can apply positive analysis to derive a constitutional structure, and this structure will have many elements of what you label as Lockean that merely support middle-class interests and property. But property, correctly interpreted, is nothing other than the way we define a man, his ability to do things. Hence, any government must defend property. You slip too readily into meaningless terms when you talk about defense of classes and groups.

All of this relates quite closely to what I have been working on all summer. I have been trying, with only partial success, to derive a concept or theory of government as it might have emerged out of Hobbesian anarchy. This involves first a description of this anarchy and then a discussion of the basic contract, with its emendations. From this I get into the role of government in its various forms. I plan to then use this derivation as the basis for diagnosing what is wrong now. We agree, I suspect, on the fact that there is utter chaos in our thinking about most of these matters. And this is where I come full circle. Your paper can be of benefit in forcing economists and other scholars to think more clearly.

Sincerely,

Jim

August 23, 1972

Dear Jim:

. . . Let me react to your letter as follows, all too briefly.

There are positive elements which *help* us to distinguish between forms of government; but is the differentiation to be normative or positive? You refer to objective standards and then qualify the argument by jumping to quasi-objective standards. Let's face it: whether you use logic or anything else, a logical basis for government of the Lockean variety is like any other normative, normative in its conception of what you call "the simple calculus of free men"—"free men," Jim, is too general, it avoids the problems arising when principles of freedom conflict and it avoids too specifying the underlying conception of "freedom." Furthermore, whatever the logic, as de Jouvenel put it (p. 249 of *Power*), "ideas get political meaning from the class which takes it over" (quote may not be exact; working from notes). But my main point is that your derivation of the logical basis of or for government will be normative. So that when you use this derivation (your last paragraph) as the basis for diagnosing what is wrong, you will be circular or tautological in that you will be applying the notion of wrong that is built into your logic or premises. You cannot derive an ought from an is alone and your analysis will not permit you to do so: you will be applying the ought built into your logical system or whatever you call it.

You cannot apply positive analysis to derive a constitutional structure *alone:* you need norms; implicit or explicit they are there, e.g., built into your concept of freedom or consent or what have you. I agree with you about the meaning of property but class is not entirely meaningless; you use it yourself three lines earlier.

I agree with you, too, about Hitler being worse than Churchill and about the need for working within a philosophy, and that there are differences—qualitative differences—between the alternatives. But: (1) there should not be an economic science built up pretending to be a science but which is only another ideology, and (2) there should be positive descriptive work (of my type) so that those who do want to construct normative systems will be better informed as to what is involved. Our norms are probably rather close; but we differ as to whether economics can be positive when it includes certain values which take on the luster of hard truth. I do not say that the alternatives are equally weighted; I am saying that we ought to know just what each one involves.

You earlier wrote me that your system favors established rights; when established rights are concentrated in relatively few hands, such concentration runs up against the notion of freedom involving a wide diffusion of rights and power; and it is exacerbated when the power holders use their power to further enhance their own capture of opportunities and inhibit the rise of the nonpowerful. The freedom for the few is wrong, just as the equality is wrong which is self-defeating in terms of the system.

Yours may well be an idealist position when mine, perhaps the realist position, says that you are trying to simulate with logic what is *in reality* a function of power, knowledge, and psychology. Or, whatever "the basic contract," it is only a framework within which power play etc. takes place.

Yours is the attractive but utopian position, I think! Or, to the same effect, so long as anarchy without social control is repugnant, the problem boils down to what (whose) system of social control.

The real gut issues, which cannot be resolved once and for all time, are: whose values; the balancing of freedom and control; the balancing of continuity and change; the balancing of hierarchy and equality. There is no simple calculus of free men—or none that does not ignore important facets (someone's important facets) of what it means to be free. Thus Hayek emphasized the rule of law, but as one of his own students (I believe) put it, there can be a foul law which we would not want all to be equally subject to. Moreover, the tragedy is that perhaps every institutional arrangement which perfects or cements freedom in one regard or for some people can be used to tyrannize others.

I repeat: I do not deny the existence of qualitative differences between alternatives, but (a) let's think clearly about government, and (b) let's see exactly what those differences are. Perhaps what I dislike the most (relevant to this discussion) is the pretense of those who would enjoin others' use of government while denying their own use of government, when the heart of the matter is which (whose) use of government. Knight would insist that my analysis does not make a good propaganda for economic freedom (his words, from his review of Robbins on the classicists) but I do not intend it to be—except in the sense that I believe that open and full and free discussion is necessary for a free society, in large part as a check on the cupidity of the powerful and on the foolishness of many others.

Perhaps the best historical way of putting this is in the terms I heard some years ago about the Chicago School: in their zest to defend the business system they defended anything that businessmen did (and against all others, save the consumer). Well, there is more to the business system than optimal market adjustments—as you have read in my paper on welfare economics, power, and property, and perhaps in the one on utilities and the theory of power.

Apropos the utility paper "Public Utilities and the Theory of Power," I hope to prepare an appendix dealing with responses to the paper while in draft stage. Among other responses, I have one which presumes what Gray called the old public utility concept (which he says has been corrupted) and concludes that I show the utility system to be corrupt etc.; and I have another which says that since that is the way the system is, anything the utilities do is fine. Needless to say, given that my analysis is positive description (and correct—which I do not want to argue, at least here), in order to reach either of those positions, one needs an additional normative premise—which I did not provide!

I have gone on much longer than I had planned; I hope I have not bored you.

Yours sincerely,
Warren

27 March 1973

Dear Warren:

Gordon Tullock has showed me a copy of your review of the anarchy volume. It is a fine and perceptive review, and I shall find it helpful in my own efforts toward completing the book I am half-way through in draft.

Your response to the JLE paper was, also, very good. One of my projects, to be completed when I get the time, is to write a new paper, not in response to you so much, but one stimulated directly by your accusation that my position is normative. I found this at first amusing, since I had just returned from a conference on property rights in San Francisco where I was, literally, read out of court because I was "positivist" in refusing to allow ethical norms to enter explicitly into the analysis. At the conference, I had read essentially the same paper as that which you discuss at length in the review and the first of my two in the anarchy book.

But, in a sense, you are quite correct. But we do use the word "normative" in two quite distinct ways that need to be carefully distinguished. My approach is not normative in any sense in which this term is most often used. I am not taking an advocacy position grounded on my own or anyone else's values. What I am doing, and explicitly, is to look at the universe of observations from a specific vision or window of social order, essentially the contractual one, in which men are free to trade. You are correct in that this way of looking at the world, either currently or historically as in the red cedar case, depends on my own private set of philosophical principles or tools. But most people would not call this normative, although it is personal, subjective, private. My main argument against you is that your position is, necessarily, also normative in this sense. At this level, positivism is impossible. You are, and you are of course allowed to do this, looking at essentially the same universe of observations, but with a different private, personal, subjective vision. You see different relationships because you look with different tools. Neither of us is normative, and both of us are positive, in the standard usage of these terms. But both of us are normative in the solipsist, subjective sense, as indeed all social science must by nature be.

I do bridle a bit at being labeled an establishmentarian. At a deep emotional level, I hate the "eastern establishment," far more, I am sure, than you do, and I suspect that, at base, I come much closer to the "revolutionary" than do you. One perceptive reader of our exchange in JLE interpreted you as defending the status quo, not me, and I think, correctly. In my vision, the status quo does have a unique place, for the simple reason that it exists, and hence offers the starting point for any peaceful (contractual) change. This is not properly labeled a defense of the status quo, as such. It seems to me that the establishmentarian would be one who defends the established way of doing things, which is far from my own position. We have gone far far away from the constitutional order that I should think essential, and my last chapter is, I hope, to be on "Prospects for Constitutional Revolution." I am, basically, a "constitutionalist" first of all, which is inherent in "individualism," terms that I gladly accept as descriptive of my position.

There is, at base, a faith here. If your "positivist" analysis of what we see is correct, and it may well be, then I simply cannot extrapolate this into a viable future social order at all. There will be collapse into anarchy, or tyranny, of one sort or another. I am by nature pessimist, but I must retain faith that what you describe is not basically descriptive, or at least need not be. I must hold onto the faith that individuals can live with one another, with at least the minimal respect for rights of others (minimal delineation of property rights) that makes society possible. My efforts are aimed at trying to analyze just how social order, to be viable at all, depends critically on a mutual willingness to accept individual rights, defined constitutionally, and enforced by the State. And how this might possibly be done without the State assuming powers of Leviathan. Perhaps you can call this a romantic attitude, perhaps it is. Your position, as I now interpret it, is closer to Hobbes than I had originally interpreted it. Incidentally, I was wrong in putting you in the "social welfare function" camp in the JLE piece, or at least I now think so.

But these are interesting issues, far more so than those with which most economists, or social scientists for that matter, deal. When and if I get my book in any sort of draft that I am ready to show to readers, I should greatly like to get your comments. I am shooting for September as the time for this, and I may send a copy along if my schedule is met.

Sincerely yours,
Jim

April 5, 1973

Dear Jim:

. . . On the normativism issue: yes, we are both subjective and we are both making methodological judgments (see Tarascio, *Journal of Economic Issues*, March 1971, 98–102). But you are deliberately building in—presuming the propriety of—the status quo whereas I am "only" providing for critical discussion of the status quo. Your specific vision builds in values on the most fundamental level; mine does not. If that is correct then the deepest normative element in my analysis is the provision I make for changing the status quo by building in the critical discussion of the status quo—but notice that this is open-ended, as no specific values are built in to guide change, only the door is opened. There is infinitely more implicit ethicizing in your approach than mine (selectively exercised, to be sure) as my paper on welfare economics, power, and property argues in regard to the ethical significance of the Pareto criterion. Further, I think that you are selective in what you accept from the status quo.

As for being establishmentarian: your writings seem to mix (a) the defense of the status quo and (b) an ideal system in which change comes from gains from contractual trade. Two points. First, it is hard to follow all this since you shift from a prejudice for existing rights to a desire to institute a new system of a particular genre. Part is against change and part is for change and the part that is for change is against all but contractual change thereafter. The second point has to do with your constitutionalism: whose constitution is it to be, since that will be of profound consequence in terms of results? Which rights will be protected and what provision for rights change in ways not loaded in favor of those in superior or advantageous positions in the status quo will be provided? I find, further, that in the real world of today you are more statist, Platonic, and authoritarian in your system than I am in mine: you want to establish a system whereas my analysis does not.

As for my own posture in re the status quo, I prepared a paper last summer on public utility regulation and power to which some responses had me convicting the utilities of social sins and others had me taking them off the hook. I urge that my analysis is strictly objective (given the subjectivity alluded to above) and that others' reactions involved *their* injection of an additional normative premise by which they read me as supporting or criticizing utilities, when all that I intended was to describe and nonnormatively interpret. My analysis, while it does open the door to critique of the status quo, does not presume its propriety nor does it abort any assumption of the propriety of any other system, including yours, insofar as it is normative. The reader of our exchange in JLE who saw me as defending the status quo either read certain normative elements into my analysis or juxtaposed my analysis to your proposed social order, a juxtaposition that was improper because my analysis is positive and not normative in regard to the status quo (and would be positive and not normative in interpreting your system if it existed) whereas yours is normative.

As for the problem of faith: you are, indeed, a pessimist by nature. I am not a pessimist by nature, though I am somewhat increasingly becoming a cynic. I always try to be an objective analyst—trying, whether optimistic or pessimistic about anything in particular. I do not see anarchy or tyranny, but much muddling through—though I must confess . . . that I dislike the state and the concentration of power via the war power. But I would guess that you elevate national security very highly and, while not in favor of the nation-state system, are prepared to live with it, with the war power of great moment necessarily. Also I would guess that while you may have second thoughts about the current administration and its corruption and arrogance (Watergate, ITT, etc.) you favor it versus a so-called liberal administration.

I would add that whatever the merits of your proposed system, and it has its attractions, its functional role in this world is to protect the status quo.

I am not sure, moreover, as to your meaning of "eastern establishment" and why you feel the way you do about it.

Also I would urge that society is comprised of more than property rights, that there are functional equivalents to property rights which your analysis neglects, e.g., regulation, because (at least in part) you prefer a once-and-for-all-time determination and assignment of rights by law. . . .

Yours sincerely,
Warren

August 8, 1973

Dear Warren:

. . . Now to your comments in the letter dated 5 April. The real issue concerns the place of the status quo in our respective scheme of things. I realize that my own position necessarily makes it seem that I am defending the status quo, and in a sense, I am doing so, not because I like it, I do not (and in this respect I am surely more radical than you are I think). But my defense of the status quo stems from my unwillingness, indeed inability, to discuss changes other than those that are contractual in nature. I can, of course, lay down my own notions and think about how God might listen to me and impose these changes on me, you, and on everyone else. This seems to me what most social scientists do all the time. But, to me, this is simply wasted effort. And explains much of the frustration. It seems to me that our task is really quite different, that of trying to find, locate, invent schemes that command unanimous or quasi-unanimous consent and propose them. Since persons disagree on so much, these schemes may be a very limited set, and this may suggest to you that few changes are possible. Hence, the status quo defended indirectly. The status quo has no propriety at all save for its existence, and it is all that exists. The point I always emphasize is that we start from here not from somewhere else. And as an economist, all I can do is to try to talk about and explain ways of changing that are conceptually contractual, nothing more.

This does allow me to take a limited step toward normative judgments or hypothesis, namely to suggest that the changes seem to be potentially agreeable to everyone, Pareto efficient changes, which must, of course, include compensations. The criterion in my scheme is agreement, and I cannot stress this too much. My approach is strictly Wicksellian here.

Having said all this, I realize that we are a long long way from ever defining properly just what is the status quo, and here I think my book goes a long way toward resolving some of your worries about my position. Given universal adult franchise, we had best start thinking in terms of just what this set of rights does via political process about the nominal claims to physical property that we talk about. "Ownership" is very fuzzy here, and needs clearing up, at least before we can so much as begin to suggest constitutional-legal changes.

Perhaps my own position is best summarized by a statement I made in the manuscript: viable society is impossible unless most people conceive political order in the consent paradigm. I am working always from this base.

Your position, as I now interpret it, is very close to Pareto, and I have much respect for it, and it holds continuing attraction for me, far more so than it does for the overwhelming majority of our colleagues in the profession. But aside from the necessary subjectivity in observation, which we both acknowledge, the positivist position is, at base, too cynical for me. As both Washington Irving and Joseph Conrad said, along with many others, it is nice to treat the world as if we were sitting in an observer's rocking chair and looking at its absurdities. But this is not enough. I think that I have, personally, some responsibility to do more than this.

As for your inferences about my current political attitudes, these are only partially correct. I do view the greatest danger to be Leviathan, the State, and I was strongly in Nixon's camp when he tried to make this the second-term theme, pre-Watergate disclosures. For these reasons, I tend to support whatever party or candidate that will promise to cut the size of government, central government in particular, down. I am not, as you infer, greatly interested in or concerned about national security issues. Perhaps I should be, but this is a point of continuing argument between Gordon Tullock and me.

My comments about the eastern establishment and my feelings toward it are based on a personal experience that has colored my attitudes. As a southerner, I was long ago explicitly and overtly subjected to discriminatory treatment of a particularly blatant sort. Hence, my broad sympathies with those who talk about the establishment. More soberly and rationally, I use the term pejoratively to refer to the dominant and pervasive attitude of the eastern-based media-intelligentsia axis. Exemplified now by the *Washington Post* treatment of Watergate. . . .

Sincerely yours,
Jim

September 1, 1973

Dear Jim:

. . . We apparently do not disagree as to the place of the status quo in your approach. Whether you defend the status quo for one reason or another it still has the position of being taken for granted. Moreover, you do more than say that it has to be reckoned with because it does exist; you go further and apply the unanimity or consent rule to any change from the status quo, thus giving it a preferred position normatively; it may not have any propriety at all save for its existence, as you put it, but the propriety which you give it because of its existence is all that is necessary. Change or continuity of the status quo *is* a normative matter and your approach builds in the continuity of the status quo.

You are quite right in stipulating (p. 2) that we are a long way from ever defining properly just what is the status quo. The status quo is selectively perceived and changed; it is differentially treated, depending upon the identification thereof. This is a point I made in my paper on welfare economics and power. The principle of selective perception, with regard to the status quo, freedom, coercion, government and so on, is very critical to the areas in which we are working.

You want only contractual changes from the status quo, i.e., consensual, unanimous (or quasi-unanimous) changes. But I find ubiquitous externalities produced by contractual changes. The Buchanan-Stubblebine Pareto-relevant and Pareto-irrelevant analysis obscures the importance of this (as I developed in the same paper). The problem with the consensus-unanimity-consent rule is that it neglects non-Pareto optimal changes through the market. It has a narrow identification of injury and of evidence of injury. The Pareto rule is thus itself applied only selectively and not to all changes or to all visitation of losses. The thrust of part of your analysis would also apply the consent rule unequally or selectively: only to government and not to market changes. The generalized externality problem is much greater, deeper, and more ineluctable, I fear, than you recognize.

Apropos the normative quality of your analysis, I reiterate my plea for a positive analysis of government and of public choice generally. The political economist, institutionalist or otherwise, must study more than choice from within opportunity sets (which is what the contractual model involves) and study the formation of the structure of opportunity sets, as they are in the real world. As you correctly perceive I am not trying to play God, only trying to study the legal-economic world as it is. It may shock you for me to say this but your endeavor to find or invent schemes that change through unanimous or quasi-unanimous consent is itself one form of playing God, Jim: for you are trying to reduce the set of change processes that are open to society, to subgroups within society, and to individuals. That the consent principle is attractive to me (whatever faults I find with it) does not obliterate that fact. Needless to say, I would not deny that the consequences of positive or descriptive, objective study of what is may have similar effects and that some of them may be untoward.

As for the status quo, it is not contractual and there is no justification for giving it such preeminent status simply because it is in existence and requiring contractual and only contractual (consensual, etc.) change from now on. Let me make a series of terse points about this:

1. Your approach to continuity versus change would very narrowly channel, indeed, very narrowly interpret, what Joe Spengler has called the problem of order. As a practical matter—not as a normative matter—I

think that Pareto knew better, that while he was clearly sympathetic to the Pareto rule he must be chuckling at the extent to which many people seem to think it empirically relevant. In a forthcoming book on Pareto one of the things I show is the extremely narrow empirical status of the Pareto rule according to Pareto himself. I also show his great realism as to how the world really is, as well as his own use of the rule in a conservative manner. Normative predilections do have to come up against the real world—though you may feel that I am here decidedly much less radical than you, perhaps even reactionary.

2. Your approach to public choice (which defends the status quo indirectly, as you put it) neglects the hard decision-making society faces with regard to difficult issues of the power structure (the balance of freedom or autonomy and control, as Spengler puts it); or, rather, predisposes both normative and positive analysis along the lines of one strained (I think) solution or resolution thereof. It allows the privileged in the status quo to hold out and perpetuate themselves by being able to withhold their consent. As attractive as the consent (unanimity) rule is, it places too much power in the hands of the already privileged, indeed cementing their mortgage upon the future; and it fails to comport with the experience and realities of public choice, and is evasive of the real problems of public choice—which Tullock and others did get to in the *Explorations* book. In other words, in part, it reenforces the power of the powerful in the status quo to produce non–Pareto optimal changes not subject to controls exogenous to themselves, and it does this by giving them a veto (as Arrow and Baumol have commented).

3. Your approach, then, or so it seems to me, completely avoids the distributional issues: distribution of income, wealth, power, and so on. It epitomizes the rationale of a contractual age to the neglect of status or distributional realities in the status quo and thereby to the neglect of private power play factors; to the neglect, that is, of the fact that power operates *through* the contractual market even ceteris paribus government.

4. As for government, your once and for all time legal property rights identification and assignment process (quite a mouthful but very important) denies opportunity for future generations to review the social structure—even incrementally—and to revise institutions, including the Constitution. It perpetuates the past, which is to say, it perpetuates the decisions

of those with power in the past (the status quo); it ignores non–Pareto optimal changes and their impact; it subjects the future to the system of the past. Continuity versus change *is* a problem and cannot readily be resolved through a unanimity rule; resolution through the market is only one narrow and incomplete solution.

5. I also must say that your disregard of the distributional issue takes for granted the existing pattern of interests which government has been used to support, whereas the rights identification and assignment process is a continuing one. There is something of fantasy here: a fantasy of a once and for all time rights identification and assignment process, a fantasy which parallels the fantasy (of the Coasian analysis) of ubiquitous markets for everything.

6. I would repeat the point which Al Schmid and I have repeatedly made: before Pareto efficient changes can be made, an antecedent determination of whose interests must be made. Your analysis seems to accept the status quo when it was not contractually produced or adopted, a major restriction upon your own principle.

7. I would add the point that you cannot derive an ought from an is: the fact that the status quo does exist does not mean that it ought to be defended by any rule like that of unanimity, does not mean that it should be given, even indirectly, preeminent status. History involves a subtle value clarification process in which values are exploratory and emergent, and the changing status quo must be subjected to valuational analysis— and your unanimity rule is not the only component thereof.

Continuing, with regard to your statement on p. 2 that "viable society is impossible unless most people conceive political order in the consent paradigm," I suggest that you must have a special meaning of "viable" that becomes tautological with the consent paradigm: e.g., given viability requiring consent, it follows that only consent produces viability.

Returning to my emphasis on the positive (your p. 2, paragraph 4): I emphasize knowledge (positive analysis) is a basis for action, thereby making choice and the art of the possible more informed, trying to minimize or at least identify any values that creep in. This is hardly a cynical position (though I do have considerable cynicism in regard to power play in reality). If we do not follow a positive approach with students then we tend to make of ourselves high priests in respect to our own values and, moreover, we obscure the scope and meaning of the actual "public choice" processes that exist in society. Before we try to change those processes (there I go again, becoming a reactionary!) we had better learn how they work—which is the message long insisted upon by conservatives. My objection, then, to your scheme is that it is unrealistic in those respects—I think that I called it utopian in the best tradition in my response to your paper reacting to my JL&E paper.

I come next to your desire to cut the size of government, to reduce the power of government. I make the following points:

1. The power of alpha is relative to that of beta; if one's power is reduced, the power of the other is increased. Whose power is enhanced if government power—central government power—is reduced? That is an empirical question, in part at least.

2. De Gaulle wanted to "reform" the French senate ostensibly to diffuse power back to the localities; the French saw through that, I think: they saw that this meant that only he would have real power at the center and that the ostensible diffusion of power really meant further concentration of power.

3. Nixon's new federalism similarly may be seen—you will find this offensive, I am sure—as an attempt to reduce the use of government (the central or federal government) by certain groups by diffusing the power of government—but this would only mean that certain other groups in control at the state level and lower would have power. This is not diffusion of government as much as it is a restructuring of the control of government. It may also mean that government would be controlled by more concentrated power than—paradoxically—when it was centered in Washington, i.e., government in the aggregate becoming less responsive to the larger numbers or wider range of interests than formerly.

4. So that I suggest that the mere invocation of one change in the power structure without study of the total power structure may not and probably would not permit perception of just what power-diffusion or power-concentration consequences will follow.

5. I guess that we may differ in your eyes this way: that you oppose concentrated government power and my analysis looks to all concentrated power and the two are different, government power being more malicious. That may be true to a point; but I would have you recall my argument that

it is not a question of government or no government but which government or which interests government is to support. If Howard Hughes were the nation's or the system's sole capitalist we would be just as socialized as if we had a traditional socialist regime.

Finally, apropos Watergate: Jim, de Tocqueville inquired as to where the principle of authority in our system resided and he found it in public opinion and, upon seeking further, located it in the press; that is to say, he saw a tension between the politicians and the press when there was no alliance between them, both competing at times to influence public opinion. In my view, the *Washington Post* was doing precisely what it would have been doing following de Tocqueville: serving as a check on government. The pity is that more papers were not so inquisitive and that the *Post* stumbled on it all by accident almost. The press is a major check on the emergence of tyrannical power in our world—it is this despite its seeming and perhaps actual arrogance. (Social control institutions are, after all, power players themselves; the answer is in pluralism, but that is another story.)

Your attitude, Jim, toward the *Post* seems to me to presume too much in favor of governmental authority. You seem to identify with authority here, perhaps because you would prefer to think of Nixon as safe, perhaps not. I think that there is in your mental structure a subtle admixture of emphasis upon freedom and emphasis upon tradition and authority (see the first three papers in Meyer, ed., *What is Conservatism?*). Nixon-Agnew is a disaster for the moral fibre of this country. Knight said that there is precious little freedom even in a free society; I hope that we have what little there is now in 1984. Orwell was no fool; I think he sensed that tyranny would come from the right in the West.

I think that I share your dislike of the nation-state system; at any rate, I thoroughly dislike the nation-state system. Yet I have great concerns and fears about national security in the existing nation-state system. We are surely entrapped in a Greek tragedy. But I also fear the abuse of national security by political groups on the make and by self-serving politicians, as well as by those enamoured of nationalism and the like. We are caught in a web of dysfunctional psychology, misconceived and misapplied definitions of reality, and the machinations of those who play the game of power in the nation-state. With your views about the *Post* and Watergate I can only infer that you would excuse the Administration because it is "safe" insofar as socio-economic policy is concerned. If that is too strong, please excuse me for jumping to conclusions.

As for the discrimination you have suffered as a southerner: I lived in the South for something like seventeen years in Miami, one year in Missouri, and one year in Georgia. I can understand, perhaps, your feelings and sympathize with them, though I do not know of my having been discriminated against, at least on that account. I hesitate to say this, Jim, but the reputation of the South (which is admittedly not that much worse than the North) is deserved in the matter of slavery and segregation. I know that both are "solutions" to the problem of heterogeneous populations, but I think that the valuational process of society can and has come up with better solutions. Still, two wrongs do not make a right. Incidentally, this is a good example of how social-structure and power-structure factors can inhibit and impinge upon and operate through the contractualist marketplace.

In sum, then, I would say the following. You are primarily normative and I am primarily positive in our respective endeavors; you are trying to indicate how things would go if they were organized in the manner you prefer (e.g., your interpretation of *Miller* v. *Schoene*) and I am trying to objectively describe (as objectively as I can at any rate) how things are going in the way they are presently organized. Curiously, you take the status quo for granted in your normative system and I take it only as the object of my positive study. Furthermore, with regard to your normative approach, while I am sympathetic I find problems with it, first, in juxtaposition to other normative considerations and, second, with regard to its feasibility in the world as I see it positively. Is this how you see our respective positions and relationship? . . .

Yours sincerely,
Warren

16 November 1973

Dear Warren:

. . . There is a basic philosophical difference between us; this we both acknowledge. There also remains some communication failure, but it seems unlikely that this can be cleared up in correspondence. The central point hinges around the discussion of the status quo, and about the humility required of the social scientist. Let me demonstrate by reference to one phrase in your letter of 1 September (bottom of page 2, middle of paragraph). You say that my position "places too much power in the hands of the already privileged." I accept this, and agree with it, as a value judgment. But who are you and I to impose our private values as criteria for social change. Each man's values are to count as any other's, at least in my conception, and what I am looking for are the implications of this genuinely "democratic" position for what we can, as social scientists, say about social change. This is the whole basis for the status quo and its uniqueness, and for the Wicksell-Pareto criterion for change. I can readily extend my conception to cover your worries about ubiquitousness of externality in market dealings. In an extremely abstract model, one in which the status quo is very well defined, and agreed on, all changes, in any form, must require unanimous consent, at least in the limit of rules.

Many of the points of disagreement will possibly be clarified, at least to the extent of knowing precisely where we disagree, when you get the opportunity to read my book, a manuscript of which I shall send you as soon as I get a copy available to send you. . . .

Sincerely,
Jim

December 13, 1973

Dear Jim:

. . . You are correct that we maintain our original differences but I think that now we are more informed about them. Perhaps there is communication failure also, I am not sure and tend to doubt it. Our differences are, first, over the valuational force of the status quo and, second, the role of positive and descriptive analysis.

I concur that the status quo is unique: it exists. But it is not humility to accept it: it is a valuational choice, a choice which constitutes the imposition of one's private values for (against) social change. Your private values (or mine, for that matter) with regard to the status of the status quo are no better than any change oriented one, notwithstanding that the status quo exists and has to be reckoned with.

The rationale that each man's values are to count as any other's is inaccurate and obscurantist in the context of any system of privilege. It presumes an equality that does not exist. There is coercion even in a market relying upon contracts; the problem is not coercion or no coercion but coercion within which institutional or power structure. The Wicksell-Pareto rule, as you call it, governs, but does not eliminate, the structure of coercion and sacrifice. Neither you nor Rothbard seems to want to recognize that structures of private privilege—particularly when ensconced in the Pareto criterion—can be just as damnable as government at its worst, especially when viewed from the perspective of those excluded from privilege. Moreover, the unanimous-consent-within-the-rules begs the substance of the rules as, say, imposed and/or administered by and in favor of the privileged.

Your position is clearly normative except in the context of a science (positivism) which studies the status quo only to cast luster on it, which gives effect to antecedent normative premises concerning the propriety of the status quo, in which case the normative character is present albeit not so clearly seen.

I find it hard to believe that you would have the Wicksell-Pareto criterion apply to any and all extant systems, to any status quo.

I also find that disciples of your position do not merely accept the status quo (and then proceed to exchange as the route to change) but only selective aspects of the status quo, e.g., accepting concentrations of power deemed hospitable to or consonant with capitalism but excluding others.

In short, I think you carry your acceptance of the status quo too far.

As for positive science, I still insist upon the possibilities of knowledge about legal-economic interrelations that can be gained from positive, objective descriptive analysis of the status quo, as in my original JL&E paper. I have further developed my ideas in the paper sent you earlier, comprising some notes on government as an economic variable.

Apropos the problems I find with your seemingly uncritical acceptance of the status quo, I find that positive study indicates that the world is an arena for struggling over continuity versus change and that the future, like the past, is made in the process. The reality is one of vast difficulties in adjusting the status quo to desired changes and that is an existential burden upon man, one not easily avoided by adopting the Pareto criterion.

Which brings me to Pareto himself: Pareto, in the *Treatise,* knew better, namely, that there is only a thin slice of social reality amenable to the Pareto criterion (as we have come to call it), and that most of the world is a matter of power play, the manipulation of derivations as vehicles for the manipulation of sentiments. My relation to you, in terms of principles, is much the same as the relation of Pareto's descriptive work to the Pareto criterion. Moreover, Pareto did not advocate the Pareto-rule as *the* criterion (as you do); he coupled it with the possibility of change in accordance with other decision rules based on values and/or sentiments; this notwithstanding that he strongly tended to conservatively apply the Pareto criterion himself.

In short, I think that we had best objectively analyze government as an economic variable, in part as an economic alternative. . . .

Yours sincerely,
Warren

January 1, 1974

Dear Warren:

Thanks for your letter dated 13 December. Let me respond once again to your remarks on my interpretation of the status quo. Apologies if I seem to be repeating what I have said before, but mayhaps we are coming closer to an understanding of each other's position.

The key remark that you make, to me, is "in the context of any system of privilege." This implies that you, somehow, have already introduced some standard, some external criterion, to determine whether or not privilege exists. My approach requires, and allows, no such external criterion to be introduced. I say that I observe persons, as they exist, and as they are defined by the rights they possess. I do not place evaluation on relative positions, since, conceptually, I cannot know what relative positions should be in some normative sense. Note that I do not, repeat not, imply that persons are *entitled* to what they possess. (I use this word here because just yesterday I read Nozick's long piece on "Distributive Justice" in the new issue of *Philosophy and Public Affairs;* presumably a chapter from his forthcoming book *Anarchy, Utopia, and the State.* Nozick does, in contrast to me, present an entitlement theory of justice.)

Persons possess rights, vis-à-vis each other in an observed social order of sorts. What is my role, as a specialist in *contract* here? Is it not to try to point out ranges of mutual gains from exchange, from trade, in whatever form? This is what I mean by humility, an unwillingness to go beyond the contractual limits imposed by the disciplinary specialization of economics.

By comparison, if I were a specialist in power relations among persons, I should look at the same set of interactions and try to suggest ways in which some persons may gain more power over others or may prevent others gaining power over them.

I do not see that these two roles need intersect in the same diagnosis or that the prescriptions be the same at all. Nor do I see that either approach necessarily involves evaluation in the sense that you suggest.

Consider the following mental experiment. You are allowed to observe, but not to be a participant in life on another planet. You observe two beings, which seem to be of different species, interacting one with another. You have no external criterion to tell you whether or not the observed interaction is imbedded in a system of privilege since you have no way of knowing much about alternative systems. As an economist, you observe what seem to be potential improvements, defined in the Pareto sense as providing more of everything to both parties. Your contribution lies in pointing this out, in explaining these possibilities.

I agree that, in a separate and distinct role, you may also make positive contributions, in the purely descriptive sense, in working out uniformities in the relationships that you observe, in delineating the structure of power. And, in offering some understanding of this set of relationships, you can be of assistance in the former and different role. Also your work may be of major help to the party whose power may be enhanced by greater understanding. (The Prince who followed Machiavelli's precepts surely fared better than the one who did not. But this did not imply that Machiavelli, himself, placed any normative evaluation on the role of one prince or the other.)

My distance from Pareto, or from you, is not nearly so far as you imply. Descriptively, most of what I see is explained precisely as you suggest Pareto explained most of what he saw. But this wholly detached role is simply not a responsible one until and unless one does something else. I go beyond this purely descriptive role in trying to find contractual improvements; that is all. You too, go beyond this role in talking about systems of privilege, etc. Pareto, in his old age anyway, more or less opted out, in my sense became irresponsible. Is this the ideal role you seek to play? I can respect this, but, if so, you need to rid yourself of evaluations, to quit talking about systems of privilege and the like, and to sit back, literally, in the scholar's rocking chair and do nothing but observe the world that you see. . . .

Sincerely,
Jim

January 7, 1974

Dear Jim:

. . . Perhaps we are coming closer to mutual understanding notwithstanding repetition.

Certainly I disagree with your view that specification of the power structure—say, system of privilege—requires a standard, some external criterion. I admit that it is a difficult task but positive (descriptive) and normative definitions or specifications of status quo power structures can be differentiated; one does not pass judgment, necessarily, upon a power structure by identifying it. As I perceive your position on this, it easily becomes useful as a stratagem to mask the existing system of privilege, to obscure it, or to permit selective alternation of it. Needless to say, the high priest function is repugnant to me, although I do acknowledge its function in legitimizing this or that system or subsystem.

I certainly do not totally object to seeking contractual solutions; but I do think that they cannot be projected in a vacuum which allows the status quo power structure to go unspecified and unexamined. As for economics as a discipline, I do not feel that the disciplinary specialization of the field mandates contractual limits. Economics does serve the high priest function (some economists perform very well at it) but I prefer to see economics as the objective study of the factors and forces governing resource allocation, income distribution, level-of-income determination, and the organization and control of the economic system. I do not feel that disciplinary specialization requires that I preach or preach only certain things—or study only certain things. As someone interested in power relations, furthermore, I am interested in description and not the advisory role.

With regard to your extra-terrestrial example, your argument rests upon ignorance by the observer, which further study can tend to correct; this same ignorance must tend to distort the substance and decrease the usefulness of any perceived potential improvements. Nothing wrong with making such suggestions, of course; but that is different from descriptive analysis. I question how wholly detached is the role you assume. I have in mind here not only that it takes the status quo power structure as given and operates to give it normative stature or propriety, but that as the position is usually employed it resonates with and serves to reenforce traditionalist or conservative arguments. Witness your dismay at liberalism, so-called, which I interpret as objection to certain uses of the state and not others. Your reliance upon the Pareto rule resonates very well with other anti-liberal or conservative arguments.

Upon reflection I find it interesting that you find my analysis of power to necessarily contain evaluations and I find your use of the Pareto or contractarian formula to necessarily contain evaluations. Your position is based upon the value-status of the contractarian principle—which I find admirable but capable of severe abuse—and my position is based upon the value-status of positive, neutral description—which you find, I think, acceptable but capable of severe abuse.

Perhaps we are each following a different strand of Knight's reasoning. You are concerned with order in the sense of stability, continuity, and reliance upon the market, as well as "minimizing" the economic role of government; and I am concerned with description on as fundamental a level as I can get to and master. Thus Knight could argue that there is precious little freedom even in a so-called free society and that religion is not only the opiate of the masses but the sedative of the classes.

(Apropos the last clause of the preceding sentence, I think that you would agree with me that Knight was not introducing external criteria when he recognized the existence of classes [however much they are difficult to precisely identify], that his was a most penetrating analysis of what I would call power.)

When you get a chance to read and reflect upon my paper on some notes concerning government as an economic variable I would appreciate your reactions, particularly as to how I handle the role of government as both a dependent and independent variable, but also the descriptive quality of the analysis given its level of generality.

Rereading your paper once again induces the following, though it is somewhat repetitive of an earlier letter of mine. On page one, paragraph three, you reiterate the humility argument; but on page two, paragraph three, you chastise me for taking a detached view which is not a responsible role (I extend your criticism of Pareto in his old age to me). The argument is—I think—contorted by introducing your perception of my need to rid myself of evaluations (see above); but you would have me not opt out. Two points here: first, I hardly think that an attempt at positive description is really opting out (though I do confess that it makes taking extreme positions for partisan purposes more difficult), rather it seems to me to perform one of the social roles of science; and second, it is not humility to be responsible according to your usage but activism—and an activism that, insofar as the Pareto rule is followed, gives effect to the interests of those with already dominant positions of power. Thus we have come back to where your letter starts, namely, with my interpretation of your posture with regard to the status quo! . . .

Yours sincerely,
Warren

23 January 1974

Dear Warren:

. . . Incidentally, our own extensive correspondence has been helpful, for I found very little to criticize in your last long letter to me, dated 7 January

1974. This seemed to me to be a good statement of our differences. With respect to the last paragraph of your letter, concerning my associating you with the aging Pareto's position, and with my own worries about this position, you will be perhaps amused to learn that the major criticism I got from Chicago Press referees was on my refusal to take an activist-partisan role and propose explicit reforms. If I had tried to stay all the way over to the position that you take, I should have brought down the house. Let us face it. People demand saviors, and they want all of us to show them the way. One of the readers for my book even said "he has showed us the way to the golden doors but he refuses to show us how to open them." So it goes.

Sincerely,
Jim

Economic Analogues to the Generalization Argument

James M. Buchanan and Gordon Tullock

This note aims to provide independent logical support for the position advanced by Neil A. Dorman in his recent paper refuting the generalization argument.[1] An example will be introduced to suggest a situation not treated by Dorman, one that lends additional support to his basic argument. Three complementary purposes will also be accomplished. First, current discussion in the theory of economics will be related directly to the analogous discussion in the theory of ethics. Second, the argument will be shifted from a normative to a predictive framework, which will possibly make for readier acceptance in the minds of some scholars. Finally, an extending qualification will be introduced which applies to the economic analogue as well as to Dorman's modified generalization argument.

To the welfare economist, when a person's actions generate effects on others than himself and the direct parties to exchange with him, these actions are said to involve "externalities." If the effects are beneficial, they are called "external economies"; if they are harmful, they are called "external diseconomies." Consider a simple example of external economies, that of getting inoculated for protection against a communicable disease. A person who gets inoculated not only protects himself; by reducing the potential agents of

From *Ethics* 74 (July 1964): 300–301. Copyright 1964 by The University of Chicago. All rights reserved. Reprinted by permission of the University of Chicago Press, publisher.

1. Neil A. Dorman, "The Refutation of the Generalization Argument," *Ethics,* 74 (January, 1964), 150–54.

contagion, he also benefits others. On the other hand, immunization uses up resources, and the optimal proportion of the population immunized will not normally be 100 per cent. As a simple, if extreme, illustrative proof, consider the situation where all but one person in a closed group have been inoculated; here the inoculation of the last person would clearly waste resources since there is no remaining source of contagion. In realistic cases, the optimal percentage of the population to be immunized may fall far short of 100 per cent.[2]

Singer's generalization, as cited by Dorman, clearly gives peculiar results in this example. The consequences for all members of the group are "undesirable" both when no one person gets inoculated and when all persons get inoculated. Under either Singer's (GA) or (GP) no one has a "right" to be inoculated or to refrain from being inoculated. Dorman's position, by comparison, fits the situation neatly. The desirability of having a rule is not directly affected by the fact that the particulars of the rule specify some non-uniformity in treatment among persons. There would, of course, be required some subsidiary rule that determines how the appropriate discriminations shall be made, but this, in itself, raises no conceptual difficulties. The obligation to abide by the general rule would not be affected by the fact that, as the rule works out, two or more sorts of behavior would be specified.

To the economist, however, the question is not really the normative one posed in the theory of ethics. The economist, as such, is not concerned with whether a person "should" or "should not" take action. Instead, he is concerned with determining the conditions under which a person will or will not take action; he is concerned with predicting behavior (and, perhaps, with advising), but not with prescribing. In the example, will a single person, any person, get inoculated or not? If all of the persons in the relevant group are substantially similar, and if they all act simultaneously, then either all of them or none of them would get inoculated. Here we are in a strict analogue to a game situation that contains no saddle point; there is no solution. And the apparent result is surprisingly akin to the unmodified generalization dilemma.

2. We have introduced this example in a recent paper. See our "Public and Private Interaction under Reciprocal Externality" (prepared for Conference on Urban Expenditure Decisions, February 22 and 23, 1964, and to be published in Conference papers, by Resources for the Future).

The problem is changed, however, by making the wholly plausible assumption that "someone acts first." In this case, some persons initiate action by getting inoculated, and, as they do, other persons in the group take this immunization into account in making their own decisions. The final outcome, the "equilibrium" solution that private interaction of individuals produces, will involve some of the individuals getting inoculated and some of them remaining not inoculated. In this private-adjustment equilibrium, each person, whether he gets immunized or not, is bearing roughly the same total cost, either in the form of the outlay on getting inoculated, or in the form of some expected value of his chances of contracting the communicable disease. This equality between these two costs is the device which produces the private-adjustment equilibrium in the first place.

Purely private behavior will not, however, produce the socially optimal results, at least in the normal case independently considered. The equilibrium will not be "Pareto-optimal," to introduce here another specialized term from theoretical welfare economics. There will normally exist some other position which could be achieved where at least one person in the group is made better off and no one worse off than in the private-adjustment solution. In the external economies model, this optimal solution normally involves some greater amount of activity, in total, than that which private behavior produces. Here then, almost by definition, there will be some change from the private-adjustment position that can be agreed on by *all* members of the group, provided only that they combine forces and act *collectively,* rather than *independently;* that is to say, provided only they consider the introduction of a *general rule* for behavior. Again, the attention of the economist is focused, not on whether or not all persons in the group should, on ethical grounds, agree to make the change, but instead on whether or not all persons have something to gain by agreeing.

This process of reaching agreement on the change from a position of private-adjustment equilibrium to a position that is Pareto-optimal is the economic analogue to the modified generalization argument (MGA) presented by Dorman. If the consequences of allowing unrestrained private behavior in immunization against the communicable disease are non-optimal, the members of the group will tend to reach agreement on some political or collective "solution" that will guarantee removal of the undesirable consequences. Dorman's "there ought to be a rule" is replaced here by "there will be forces tending to the establishment of a rule."

There are, however, complications that this elementary formulation neglects, in both the ethical and the economic models. Whereas the shift to some optimal position will be beneficial to all persons in the group, if agreement can be reached costlessly, the shift may not be made if the costs of reaching agreement itself prove to be high. And if there are inframarginal gains to be exploited in making the change, individuals will be led to invest resources in strategy. In some cases, the probability of such costs may be such that, at this more complex level of consideration, the initially attained private solution is adjudged to be "optimal." Again there is an analogue in Dorman's (MGA): "If the consequences of not having a rule against X would be undesirable, then there ought to be a rule against X." But this holds only if the costs of reaching agreement on a particular rule are neglected. If, in fact, there are several possible rules that will remove the undesirable consequences of X, and if there are differential gains to be secured from the particular rule adopted, then the undesirable consequences of X may be more than offset by the costs of agreeing on a rule that will eliminate X.

Monetary Research, Monetary Rules, and Monetary Regimes

I want to raise some general points in the whole rules-versus-authority set of issues. And, since comments are supposed to be critical, let me start by stating that Carl Christ joins many of his economist peers in what I have long considered to be a major error in the whole discussion, although, to his credit, he does acknowledge the problem. The error lies in using empirical data accumulated in a history when there existed no policy rule as evidence for or against the efficiency of such a rule, had such a rule been in existence.

Do we really want to assume that individual behavior in monetary matters would remain invariant as between two quite distinct monetary regimes? For example, Christ referred to the historical record over the period 1929–33 to suggest that a growth rule tied to the monetary base would not have worked well because the base moderately increased over the period while M1 fell dramatically. But would this relationship have been observed under a rule tied to the base? The fact is that there was no such rule then in existence; there was basic uncertainty about policy, as it was implemented by the authorities. There was a wholly different monetary constitution or regime from one that would have embodied an effective monetary rule, whether tied to the base or anything else.

If we do assume that behavior would have been invariant, it is always possible to demonstrate that no rule could possibly have worked so well as an ideally omniscient authority. Further, it is also always possible to use the data in the historical record to construct, *ex post,* a complex rule that would have

From *Cato Journal* 3 (Spring 1983): 143–46. Reprinted by permission of the publisher.

worked better than any simpler rule. I am not sure here just what limit those who play such games would want to place on the mathematical order of the fitted "optimal" rule.

My criticism is, of course, a simple and obvious one. Presumably, the error continues to be made because the only data we have are historical, and we really do not have much history of rule-oriented regimes. Further, modern economists do not really feel "with it" unless they can refer to data somehow.

My second main point is not primarily directed at Carl Christ, although I think that he, too, may fall within its targets. I think that the debate-discussion is prematurely joined when we start referring to the advantages and disadvantages of this rule or that rule, this regime or that regime, all within the set of regimes that are alternatives to that which is in existence. I agree, of course, that any monetary reform must ultimately replace the existing regime with *one* alternative that has, in the process of the dialogue, emerged as "winner." Debates about which of the alternative regimes is to be preferred must take place. But prior to this discussion, we should try to attain consensus on the need for *some* alternative regimes that will embody greater predictability than the unconstrained monetary authority that exists. The familiar analogy is with traffic chaos that would exist if there were no rules. The first requirement is that there be rules of the road. Whether or not these rules require driving on the left or the right is of secondary importance to the requirement that there be a rule.

In our monograph *Monopoly in Money and Inflation* (London: Institute for Economic Affairs, 1980), Geoffrey Brennan and I distinguished among three stages or levels of monetary argument. First, debate about the appropriate direction for policy under an existing regime is, of course, where most attention has been centered until very recently. (In this respect I am quite pleased with the organization of this conference, which does represent an attempt to shift beyond this first level of discussion.) Second, there are or should be debates about whether or not the unconstrained monetary regime works as well as alternatives that would embody more predictability. In other words, the debate at this level is over whether there should or should not be a shift in regimes. Here the debate is properly joined between the nonconstitutionalist (the supporter of continued discretionary authority) and the constitutionalist (the supporter of some alternative regime). Third, there are the debates already mentioned, between the supporters of this or that option among the set of alternatives to the existing regime.

There seems to be continuing confusion and shifting between the second and third levels of discussion. Careful distinction would allow the supporters of Friedman-like money growth rules, commodity-based monetary arrangements, and competitive currencies to join in arguments against those who support unconstrained discretionary monopoly. In other words, the central issue is not one of "rules versus authority"; the central issue is one of "alternative monetary constitutional regimes versus unconstrained monopoly." Let us first agree that genuine constitutional reform is needed before wasting our energies in arguing with each other as to merits of this or that regime.

Having been critical, either directly or indirectly, in my comments on this point, let me support Carl Christ's emphasis on the effects of the foreshortened political time horizon in generating the modern stagflation dilemma. We are in a classic dilemma here, as the events of the last two years have indicated. Attempts to reduce the rate of inflation generate unemployment that is not acceptable politically; the short-run Phillips curve is too flat. Yet we all recognize that there is no advantage whatever, while there are major disadvantages, in sustaining inflation at rates of the 1970s. We were politically motivated by the prospects of moving up short-run Phillips curves, and we kept doing so even as these curves shifted successively upward and outward. We may have reached some sort of political equilibrium in the 1979–80 period, as analyzed by Kydland-Prescott, Barro-Gordon, and others.

I do not think that ordinary politics, whether at the level of the existing monetary authorities, the Congress, or the Presidency, can get us out of the dilemma. And this conviction becomes, for me, the strongest of all arguments for genuinely *constitutional* change, for a change in regimes. I am referring here to reform that must extend beyond any announced adoption of a rule by the monetary authority and also beyond any mere congressional instruction to this authority. I am referring to a change in the constitutional setting for monetary institutions.

Prospects for dramatic constitutional change may seem dim in the political climate of 1983. But it is possible that some such reform might even find support from the central bankers themselves. We suffer now from the absence of credibility in the pious pronouncements of policy direction. Credibility can be restored only if the monetary authorities are bound constitutionally. And should not these very authorities, like Ulysses, agree to be so bound in their own long-term interests?

Unless we can get an effective change in regimes, we cannot expect our politicians or our central bankers to resolve the stagflation dilemma. Until and unless we begin to take the long-term perspective in our private and in our public capacities, including the adoption of new and binding constitutional constraints on the fiscal and monetary powers of government, we are doomed to remain mired in the muck of modern politics.

PART TWO

Belief and Consequence

The Potential for Tyranny in
Politics as Science[1]

I. Introduction

My title may be extended to the positive statement: There is a potential for tyranny if the enterprise of politics is interpreted as being analogous to that of science. I am not directly concerned with an empirical description of the scientific process itself, a description that may be widely at variance with the representation of this process by those who concern themselves with the workings of politics. I hope that this proviso will forestall potential mis-directed criticism from those who might consider my effort to fall within the philosophy of science, even broadly conceived. My subject matter is *politics,* not science, and concerns the illegitimate juxtaposition of two categorically

From *Liberty, Market and State: Political Economy in the 1980s* (Brighton, England: Wheatsheaf Books, 1986), 40–54. Copyright 1986 by James M. Buchanan. First published in Great Britain in 1986 by Wheatsheaf Books Ltd, Brighton, Sussex. Reprinted by permission of Pearson Education Limited.

1. In 1967, I published a paper, "Politics and Science," *Ethics,* 77 (July 1967), 303–10; reprinted in my book, *Freedom in Constitutional Contract* (College Station: Texas A&M University Press, 1978), 64–80. In that paper I attempted to clarify issues in an unresolved conflict of views between Frank H. Knight and Michael Polanyi. This earlier paper differs substantially in content from this chapter, but the overlap in subject matter should be acknowledged.

This chapter was initially presented at a Liberty Fund Conference on George Orwell in Cambridge, England, in August 1984. I am grateful to Dr Shirley Letwin, who organized the conference, and to Liberty Fund for permission to reprint the paper here.

I am indebted to Geoffrey Brennan, Paul Heyne, David Levy, Karen Vaughn, and Viktor Vanberg for comments on earlier drafts.

distinct types of social interaction, along with the implications of this juxta-position for politics. Quite a different, and possibly equally interesting, paper might be written on the implications for science that would emerge from its being modelled as politics. In jargon that George Orwell would have de-spised, my concern is "scientized politics" not "politicized science."

In its common representation, science is a process in which conflicts about truth are resolved. Those who participate in the process acknowledge the existence of a reality that is itself independent of any belief about it. The scientific enterprise is necessarily teleological, even when the provisional na-ture of any established truth is recognized. By comparison and contrast, poli-tics is a process in which conflicts among individual interests are settled.[2] In this enterprise there is no independently existing "interest" analogue to truth, towards which an interaction process converges. The end-states emer-gent in the two processes remain categorically different.

When politics is wrongly interpreted as being analogous to science, as a truth-discovery process, coercion may find moral legitimization for those who claim enlightenment. By contrast, when politics is rightly interpreted as a process for settling conflicts among interests, which are acknowledged to be individually derived, those who seek to impose preferred solutions do so without claim to moral superiority.

So much for a summary statement of the argument, one that seems al-most self-evident to me but which has proved to be highly objectionable to critics whose views I otherwise respect highly. Their reactions suggest that an attempt to restate the argument in some detail may be warranted.

---

2. In a 1983 draft paper "Science and Politics" I stated that politics is the process through which "conflicts about values are settled." This statement aroused such criticism, particularly on the part of Geoffrey Brennan and Paul Heyne, that I have now substituted "interests" for "values" in some parts of the text. For my central argument, this change in terminology is not important. It is "politics as truth-seeking" that I am directly concerned with, and not the possibility of there being "truth in values," moral or otherwise. To the extent that the moral absolutist extends the discovery process to politics, my strictures, of course, apply. But I should recognize the position of someone who simultaneously re-stricts politics to conflicts of interests and engages in a non-political, non-scientific enter-prise described as a search for moral absolutes. Nonetheless, the temptation facing the moral absolutist must remain omnipresent. Why not impose that which is true?

II. Belief, Science, and Truth

Individuals confront the world of reality with a set of beliefs about that which their senses perceive. They conduct personal experiments and, in the process, continually revise their earlier beliefs. They engage with others, directly and/or indirectly, in the discovery enterprise. The boundaries of the "understood" are continually pushed outwards; the discovery process is never-ending. The "truths" that are filed away in the category of the "accepted and understood" are not totally frozen; these remain, at best, "relatively absolute absolutes," always subject to challenge, exhumation, autopsy, and reversal.

In the scientific quest so interpreted, agreement among informed persons offers a test for the validity of a proffered truth, but agreement, in itself, does not intrinsically validate that which it seeks to establish. Agreement is a stage in the process of moving from personal belief to truth, and agreement signals a resolution of conflict among separate personal beliefs that were earlier advanced. Upon agreement, that proposition which is "true" can be put away, as if in a filing cabinet or computer memory, and scientific inquiry may be shifted to territory that remains unexplored (Polanyi's metaphor of science as the "society of explorers" is apt here). It is precisely because agreement does not intrinsically validate a proposition, however, that the possibility for re-examination always stands open. Much of what we accept as truth today, and which does command requisite agreement, will surely become error at some later date. Science does indeed make progress; genuine discovery does take place.

I want to concentrate attention on the position of the individual, any individual, in the discovery enterprise, so interpreted. Regardless of the state of his information, the individual confronts reality with a set of beliefs that enable him to exist and to function. But the individual does not consider these beliefs to be applicable uniquely to him as an individual member of the human species, or even to the species itself. He believes, and accepts as fact, that he cannot walk through the wall. But he also believes, and accepts as fact, that no other person can walk through the wall. That is to say, the individual's beliefs about reality are general in their potential extension. They describe a reality that the individual presumes to exist for everyone. They are not descriptive of a reality that is private and personal and, hence, unique to the person who holds them.

Recognition of this generalization of belief about the reality that exists does not involve imputing to the individual any commitment to Platonic ontological precepts. The individual may acknowledge that the physical theory of atomic structure may not describe the world as it might "really exist." The theory, instead, may be acknowledged to do nothing more than allow predictions that have not, as yet, been falsified. My concern here is not with correspondence between the theory of reality that the individual accepts and the underlying reality itself, in some deeper ontological sense.[3] My point is that, quite apart from the presence or absence of such correspondence, the individual extends his working hypotheses about reality to others than himself. It simply makes no sense for a person to believe that he, personally, confronts a reality that is different from that confronted by others than himself.

Important implications seem to follow from this generalization of beliefs. Because the individual lives in the same world as other persons, he may be willing to learn from others. The individual may recognize that his own personal, subjectively experienced set of beliefs about reality remains always incomplete and that this set does not facilitate an understanding of that which he may observe as well as a competing set held by others. To refuse to learn, to hold onto privately generated beliefs in the face of evidence that better explanations are available would reflect abnormality and would be taken as such.

The correction of error in beliefs previously held is so commonplace an event in all our lives that it is often not discussed at all. The farmer counts the number of cows in his herd; someone alongside counts the same herd and comes up with a different number. The farmer corrects the initial error and attributes it to earlier misperception. In the adjustment he may feel a minor psychological disappointment, but he has not compromised either his virtue or his honour. He simply acknowledges the error and goes on his way.

Much the same thing occurs when a person is shown that he has erred in the logical analyses that are employed to support a particular set of beliefs that are held. If the analytical errors are pointed out, the individual will

---

3. For a discussion of some of the issues here, see Colin McGinn's review of Hilary Putnam, *Realism and Reasons* (Cambridge: Cambridge University Press, 1983) in *Times Literary Supplement*, 25 Nov. 1983, 1307.

change the emergent beliefs, and without undue psychological embarrassment. In the broadest definitional sense, as here interpreted, science is the process through which individual beliefs about reality are continually corrected, and a process within which individuals are brought into agreement about that which is, at least in the provisional filing cabinet, relatively absolute absolutes sense previously noted. The activity of "science," more narrowly defined, takes place along the margins of established truths and is, of course, carried on by specialists in inquiry. For the overwhelming majority of persons, and for almost all of those elements of reality they confront, there are truths that remain unchallenged. And it is these truths and their generalization that persons utilize in their daily lives.

The social function of "science," the activity of the specialists, is that of shutting off dialogue and discourse, of resolving conflicts among competing explanations of physical reality, and of allowing provisional truths to be put to everyday usage, at least until more acceptable alternatives emerge. Agreement among the specialists in inquiry, along with the subsequent acceptance by non-specialists, signals the end of scientific conflict and the establishment of peace among the contending parties. The nature of this resolution is my point of emphasis here. Conflict is not settled by compromise. Conflict comes to be resolved by a "victory" of sorts; those who give up a previously contending view of, or belief about, reality do so because they have been led to "see the light." They are genuinely "converted" to the alternative vision that the now agreed-upon explanation offers. Agreement comes about when one protagonist gives up a competing set of beliefs and takes on another. (The farmer does not count twenty cows and his wife twenty-one on the way to a compromise agreement on twenty and one-half as the settled number.)

In the enterprise of science it would be folly to think of agreement among competing specialists as being settled by compromise, with some mixture of competing elements counterposed, one to another in the final terms. Truth tends to be mutually exclusive; agreement settles on the "either" or the "or." Two competing and mutually contradictory explanations of reality cannot be simultaneously held, nor can two explanations be held by different persons and both deemed to be "correct" in any meaningful scientific sense.[4]

4. I am not, of course, rejecting the proposition that each of several alternative models or theories of reality may add explanatory value in the search for a general or inclusive

The scientist who challenges a proposition in the widely prevailing structure of agreement does so as a genuine revolutionary. He seeks to overthrow the existing scientific regime on the point in question and to set up his own competing hypothesis as a new truth, to which all must eventually come to pay homage through their ultimate acceptance and agreement. Note that in the process of accomplishing this result, the individual scientist is not trying to get his hypothesis accorded equal weight with those that might be advanced by competitors on the subject matter of concern.

There is something profoundly misleading in the familiar metaphor of "the free market of ideas." Organizationally, the scientific enterprise may operate in ways similar to a competitive market. But there remains a categorical difference. In the market, each participant pursues *his own* ends, purposes, or values. In science, each participant advances *his own claim* to truth that must ultimately be accepted by all. Each scientist is dedicated to the advance of the frontiers of "truth" against "falsehood"; each is seeking to impose his own emergently correct vision of reality on the great unwashed. In this sense, science is more akin to a war of annihilation than it is to a market process. It is improper, even metaphorically, to conceptualize scientists as "trading," either with other scientists or with persons outside the scientific community. As many have recognized, science as an activity is much more analogous to religion than to trade, and the liberty of individual scientists to present their own hypotheses is analogous to the liberty of persons to promulgate their own faiths and to seek the conversion of others. The activity of trade, by contrast, in which one person attempts to demonstrate to another an advantage of interest rather than a path to the light is at the opposite pole of human interaction from that of science or religion.

The analogy between science and religion is helpful when we consider the attitudes that persons adopt towards one another. Consider a person who

---

explanation. For example, the *Homo economicus* model of man's behaviour, defined in operationally meaningful terms, explains some aspects of observed behaviour in almost all interaction settings. At the same time, an altruistic model of behaviour, again defined operationally, might be acknowledged to yield further explanatory insights. It is possible that these competing models be simultaneously used, each considered as partially explanatory. The statement to the effect that two competing explanations cannot simultaneously exist would arise in this example only if someone claimed that the *Homo economicus* model fully explains human behaviour while, at the same time, holding to the view that the altruistic model explains any or all of the same behaviour.

has "seen the light," for example, as a born-again or evangelical Christian. To such a person, others who have not experienced conversion continue to live in sin. They are to be pitied, persuaded, perhaps tolerated, and possibly persecuted. But their views can never be respected in the sense that embodies granting them equal weight with those of the person who possesses the inner light. A person cannot, by nature of his belief, treat someone who holds a contrary belief with mutual respect if this treatment requires that both beliefs be acknowledged as being equal claimants to "the truth." To accord such respect to others in matters of belief would amount to a sacrifice of one's own, or rather to an acknowledgement that one's own beliefs, as such, are not generalizable.

How different is the activity of the scientific enterprise, broadly defined? The scientist who has discovered, or who has been convinced by the discoveries of others, that the world is curved rather than flat must hold all flat-earthers to be "living in error," persons who may be pitied in their ignorance, persuaded so that they too can become enlightened, and possibly even to be persecuted if they remain too stubborn. The flat-earthers' claim to truth cannot be respected in any mutual or reciprocal interpretation of this term. The scientist who now sees the earth as spherical cannot respect the belief of the flat-earther as deserving of equal weight with his own in some measuring of "truth."

III. Interests, Politics, and Order

My purpose in this chapter is not to make any direct contribution to the interpretation of science (or religion). As previously noted, my description is intended to convey the representation of the scientific enterprise as it is broadly interpreted by those who would extend its workings, at least by analogy, to politics, an extension that is both inappropriate and potentially dangerous for the preservation of individual liberties.

In the preceding section I commenced with the statement that individuals confront the world of reality with a set of beliefs. They also confront this world of reality, which includes other persons, with a set of evaluations over and above, and categorically different from, the set of beliefs. For my purposes here, I do not need to identify with any precision the sources of individuals' interests or to assign weights to differing components in what might be called an evaluation vector. Further, I need not express direct concern about the possible malleability of individual interests. My argument depends only on acceptance of the restricted proposition to the effect that an individual can be modelled as possessing (at any given moment) an evaluation or utility function reflecting interests or preferences and a set of beliefs and that these two ultimate determinants of action are logically distinguishable.[5]

The set of beliefs that an individual holds is, in one sense, necessarily prior to the evaluations that reflect his interests and which become relevant only within those beliefs. Indeed, it would be difficult to imagine a person expressing a preference for, an interest in, or value of, something that he did not believe to exist, actually or potentially. Or, to put the point differently, those interests that are potentially relevant must be those that are constrained by beliefs about reality; the values that emerge only in daydreams or fantasies are irrelevant.

Beliefs and evaluations exist simultaneously in the mind of the individual, but they serve totally different functions. Beliefs enable a person to understand reality, to impose a mental order on that which he observes, quite independent of any participation in that order. By comparison and by contrast, evaluations become conceptually necessary for participation in the order that a person's beliefs define as existing. A person totally without values or preferences would have no ability to choose. But, of course, the existence of such preferences is not sufficient to insure a power of choice, since actions may be totally constrained.

As in the discussion of section II above, my primary concern is about the individual's attitude towards his own values or interests and about his attitude towards the values expressed by others, and especially as these attitudes are compared and contrasted with those accorded to beliefs. At some fundamental level the individual must acknowledge that interests (values, pref-

5. In economic theory there is a distinction between preferences and constraints. Preferences are the same as interests in my terminology here, but note that the very definition of constraints presupposes agreement on a set of beliefs. (To use the earlier example, my interests or preferences may be to walk through the wall, but I am physically constrained from being able to do so and act within this constraint because I hold the belief that I could not carry out my preferences, even if I tried to do so.)

erences) are individually derived and privately held, an acknowledgement that is not extended to beliefs, as previously noted. This distinction is important for my argument, and it deserves detailed discussion.

Consider an example. A person faces a wall with a door in it. His set of beliefs suggests that he cannot walk through the wall but that he can walk through the open door. These beliefs are generalizable to other persons; they, too, must walk through the door to get to the other room. The individual whose calculus we examine, however, also has a set of preferences, values, or interests, which include some comparative evaluation of the two locations. Suppose that the person places a higher value on being in the room beyond the door than on staying put. This will provide the motivation for walking through the door. But the individual who acts in this way need not, and indeed does not, generalize this evaluation to others in any manner at all analogous to the generalization of beliefs as previously discussed. The individual may acknowledge that his own comparative evaluation of the two locations is different from, or can be different from, the comparative evaluation of another person who stands alongside him in the initial location.

Once this elementary distinction is made, however, it becomes evident that there will exist a categorically different relationship between the individual and the other person who holds contrasting or dissimilar evaluations and the relationship between the individual and the person who holds contrasting or dissimilar beliefs. The individual need feel no intellectual or moral superiority over the person who simply values the alternatives differently. In the example, the person who initially stands alongside and who chooses not to go into the room beyond is judged to be neither "in error" nor "in sin." Such a person is acknowledged to have a different utility function, which carries the further and important implication that *differing values can coexist* with no relegation of any one set to a status of inferiority. The implication that is important for my purposes is that the individual, who may be quite secure in his own values, can accord respect to the values of others, respect that can embody the recognition that one person's values count for as much as another's and that, ultimately, each person's values can be assigned equal weight in social order. In summary, a "democratic" attitude is possible with reference to individual values; a "democratic" attitude is impossible with reference to individual beliefs.

The elementary distinction I have drawn here is applied by each of us in everyday life. We treat the person who claims that two plus two makes five as a fool; we treat the person who prefers coffee to tea to be entitled to his own preferences.[6]

In the introduction to this chapter, I defined politics as the process through which conflicts among separate individuals' interests are resolved or settled. As the above discussion makes clear, however, conflicts among individuals' separate interests need not arise at all in many settings of human interaction. In the example, each of the two persons can choose his preferred location, each can exercise his own choices. Freedom is possible because the spaces do not necessarily intersect. By contrast, conflicts over beliefs must always arise because of the mutually exclusive nature of "truth" itself. Persons act as if "that which is out there" is independent and apart from their own interpretations of it. We do not behave as if each of us lives in his own personal world, with our privately imagined models of reality. Potential conflicts over beliefs cannot be confined only to the intersections among "private spaces," as is the case with interests or values.

Politics, in my definition, should be limited to that set of interactions where "private value or interest spaces" come into potential conflict. The range of politics is, then, determined by the technology of interaction itself, including behavioural and institutional elements as well as those more normally considered. Values or interests come into potential conflict only at the edges, so to speak, of the behavioural spheres of action pursued by persons seeking their own purposes. Conflict arises when an individual's action, motivated by his interests, affects the interests of another person. That which one person does may invade the claimed domain of someone else. When such a conflict arises, there is nothing akin to the scientific enterprise that may be called on to suggest means of resolving the issues. You do not become

6. Critics of an earlier draft have, at this point, raised the problem of aesthetic as compared with moral or intellectual superiority. They have suggested that a person may adjudge his colleague who has "bad taste" comparably to the colleague who is "in error" or who "has not seen the light." My argument with such critics can be resolved only empirically. The implicit hypothesis of this chapter, which reflects my general position, is that persons tolerate wide divergencies in tastes or preferences much more readily than divergencies in beliefs.

my slave because I succeed in converting you to a new vision of the world, at least not in normal settings.[7]

In its most general sense, one of the functions of politics is the establishment of "rules of the road" which enable individuals and groups with differing sets of interests to pursue widely divergent objectives without the emergence of overt conflict.[8] Politics in its constitutional, or rule-making, function resolves potential conflicts among individual interests by setting boundaries for private spaces, which, if respected, allow persons to pursue their own ends without interpersonal conflict. One interpretation that may be placed on the working of politics at this level is that the rules themselves can become elements in the belief structure of persons, despite the artifactual origins. That is to say, individuals may accept, as a part of the reality they live in, the existence of quasi-permanent rules that define the private spaces within which individuals may operate without overt conflict. In terms of our simple example, the individual who walks through the door may also prefer that his counterpart in the initial location also walk into the adjoining room. But if the other person does not share this value, potential conflict may be forestalled because the reference person may also accept, as a part of his structure of reality, the legal rules that allow persons to choose their own locations. In this setting there is a shared acquiescence in the possession and retention of differing values.

In this function of rule-making, politics may sublimate conflicts among interests and values by making explicit the appropriate limits within which individuals can act so as to secure their objectives. A set of property rights may be defined, and contracts among persons in exchanges of these rights may be enforced. Within this defined structure of rights, persons may promote their own privately generated values without running afoul of other persons. The interests of the individuals are different in market-exchange interactions, but these interests do not come into overt conflict because the structure of legal rights does not allow non-voluntary boundary crossings without penalty.

---

7. The behaviour of leaders and followers within cult relationships, where something like slavery emerges from a conversion process, is considered to be abnormal and even bizarre. The general public attitude towards such cults corroborates my central theme.

8. For a general discussion of this point, see Geoffrey Brennan and James Buchanan, *The Reason of Rules* (Cambridge University Press, forthcoming), Ch. 1.

There may be near-universal agreement on many elements in a structure of legal rights. Laws against murder, rape, assault, and theft may command almost unanimous consent. Such laws represent the translation into politics of widely held and commonly shared moral values. In many respects such values seem analogous to truths of science. In the critical sense emphasized here, however, values, even if commonly shared, remain categorically different from truths because they emerge only from individuals and do not exist independently. There may be universal agreement that murder is wrong, but there is a distinction between this commonly shared value and a truth that is universally acknowledged to be non-falsifiable.

There may be types of personal interaction, however, where no structure of rules, no assignment of rights, can succeed in eliminating conflicts among individual values and interests. In our simple example, suppose that the two persons in the room should be Siamese twins. In the language of modern economics, the relationships among persons may involve elements of "publicness"; either technological features of jointness efficiency and/or non-exclusivity make conflicts among interests inevitable. No arrangement or redefinition of individual rights can resolve the conflicts that may arise in such instances.

Consider a familiar classroom example. There are three persons in a room, A, B, and C. Each desires a differing ideal value for the thermostat setting, say, 60, 65, and 70 degrees Fahrenheit, respectively. There will be a range of conflict over the setting, which, because of technological necessity, must be the same for all three persons. In its ordinary function, post-constitutionally, politics is a process of settling such conflicts through institutionalized procedures that take the form of agreed-upon decision rules, at least in nominally democratic politics, rules that take individual evaluation as inputs and then generate results that are applied to all parties. The way such instruments work is the central subject matter, positive public choice—a subject matter that is not germane to my purposes here. My stress is on the nature of the results or outcomes that are generated by the instruments or institutions of ordinary politics and, importantly, on the interpretation of these results or outcomes by those who are affected by and who are specialists in inquiry.

Let us stay with the thermostat example. If the preferences or interests of the persons are plausibly single-peaked, simple majority decision will produce the median-value outcome, or the 65-degree setting. This outcome is, in genuine respects, a *compromise*, a plausibly acceptable reconciliation of the conflicting values (interests, preferences) and *nothing more*. This outcome does not represent the "community's value" or the "society's interest," merely because it emerges from the decision rule that has, by presumption, been agreed on at some constitutional stage of rule-making for politics. Nor does this outcome, which in the example comes close to the ideal for the middle or median person in the group, have any claim at all to "truth." The persons whose preferred settings are not chosen in the process, A and C, are not, thereby, proven to be "wrong." They are not expected to modify their own value or preference orderings over the alternatives because the median result emerges from the operation of the decision rule.

There cannot, of course, be two thermostat settings; the alternatives for choice are mutually exclusive. But this feature is technologically rather than ontologically determined. There is no unique "true" value for the room temperature that politics somehow mysteriously discovers and which comes to be established in the working out of history. Agreement may emerge in politics, either among all persons at the rule-making stage (where all may agree on laws against murder) or among only a required subset of persons at the post-rule stage of ordinary politics (where a simple majority may agree on the size of the education budget). But this sort of agreement is not at all analogous to that which occurs in science and the scientific enterprise. Agreement in politics reflects concurrence in individual interests, values, or preferences. At the rule-making or constitutional stage of deliberation, agreement may emerge among all or nearly all prospective participants in collective interaction if they are placed behind a sufficiently thick veil of ignorance and/or uncertainty so that their own interests, post-constitutionally, cannot be accurately predicted.[9] Or, at the post-constitutional stage of ordinary politics, agreement may emerge from a concurrence of individual interests or from a set of trades among members of the requisite coalition. In neither case does observed agreement among all persons or among the required subset provide a proximate way-station toward "truth," as is the case in science. There is simply nothing analogous to truth in politics at all. There

9. See John Rawls, *A Theory of Justice* (Cambridge, Mass.: Harvard University Press, 1971); James M. Buchanan and Gordon Tullock, *The Calculus of Consent* (Ann Arbor: University of Michigan Press, 1962).

is no unique value "out there" that exists, or that should be thought to exist, apart from the individual valuations. The individual participant in politics is not engaged in a discovery enterprise. His position is much closer to the role of the trader in the market-place. He expresses his own interests through the instruments available to him, and he accepts the outcome that emerges from the process. Politics is a "market in interests or values" much as the ordinary exchange process. Its difference from the market lies in its more inclusive range. Politics has the functional task of setting conflicts among individual interests and values at several levels simultaneously, and not only within well-defined legal structures, which themselves emerge from politics in its rule-making stage.

A somewhat different way of emphasizing the relationship between economics and politics, as social processes, is to say that in the formulation here "economics" is fully incorporated within "politics." Economics is one particular process through which potential conflicts among separate individual interests are settled. As noted earlier, at the rule-making or constitutional stage, politics may assign to the market the task of facilitating social interaction without overt conflict over a wide range of activities.

The central institution of the economic process, that of exchange, points up the distinction between interests and beliefs. In an ordinary exchange setting, traders possess initially differing endowments and they have initially differing preferences. So long as prospects for mutual gain exist, there are motivations for engaging in exchange or trade. The initially divergent valuations are resolved; at the relevant margins the relative evaluations are brought into equality. But the equality in marginal valuations does not, in any sense, imply that there is something intrinsically determinant in the outcome that is akin to the truth of a proposition, even provisionally interpreted. The agreement between traders does not signal the bringing of separate values into line with something that exists over and beyond the traders themselves. Traders are not "converted" by the trading process into some modified version of the world of economic reality. The valuations or preferences over alternatives remain internal to the individuals who engage in trade, and there is no convergence to anything that exists over and beyond internal evaluations. Individuals, through trade, are enabled to maximize that which they seek to maximize, given the instruments that they are presented with and in accordance with the constraints that they face. The exchange process allows traders to realize the most from values that are internally based; the process may, in one sense, involve internal discovery of one's own values, but it does not involve exploration of anything beyond the individuals themselves.[10]

Economists have themselves been responsible for confusion at this point, in their definition of "efficiency" in resource allocation. They have often talked as if "an efficient allocation" exists quite independent of the process through which the outcomes of market exchange are generated. In a very real sense, therefore, many economists have putatively tested market or exchange institutions against an idealized criterion of "efficiency" in a manner that has elements similar to the truth test of the scientist. Fortunately, this ultimate absurdity in economic method seems on the way to intellectual oblivion.

IV. Provisional Truth and Absolute Value

I have deliberately counterposed the processes of science and politics in extreme terms. The scientific enterprise that embodies the search for, and discovery of, truth, including the process through which truth comes to be established, has been sharply distinguished from the enterprise of politics, which embodies institutional means of resolving conflicts among individual values or interests. It should be clear, however, that to the extent that the "truth" established by science and in science is, itself, acknowledged to be provisional (as implied in the discussion in section II above) and subject always to falsification by yet unknown explanatory hypotheses, there may be considerably less danger from modelling politics as science than would be the case were science to be interpreted in pre-Popperian terms. The developments in the philosophy of science in this century which have had the effect of removing scientific truth from the realm of the sacred could have

---

10. My reference here is to individuals who participate in ordinary markets as they confront exchange opportunities. If we extend the interaction examined to include the activities of entrepreneurs, who can be described as seeking out potential exchange opportunities that have not been previously foreseen, the model of the scientist becomes more acceptable. In this context the reality sought is the valuations of persons, and the generalization of beliefs about such reality is reflected in the tendency for any newly discovered profit opportunities to be dissipated quickly.

For a discussion of the entrepreneurial role, see Israel Kirzner, *Competition and Entrepreneurship* (Chicago: University of Chicago Press, 1973).

had only salutary effects on the interpretation of political reality. The moral force of provisional truth is necessarily less than that of truth established as dogma. I should argue, nonetheless, that the moral force even of provisional truth, acknowledged to remain at best a relatively absolute absolute, remains categorically distinct from that of value, so long as value is acknowledged to be derivable only from sources within the individual psyche.

Conversely, of course, to the extent that values are themselves held to be independently determinate, and hence outside of and beyond individual scalar orderings over alternatives, there may be relatively little difference between modelling "politics as science" and politics as the process for resolving "conflicts among values." Indeed, in some circumstances the direction of argument may be reversed. If values are deemed to exist "on their own" and quite apart from human minds, and, further, if these values are deemed to be universal in application, over persons, places, and times, then the moral force claimed for such values may well exceed those which could ever be claimed for the provisional truth of modern science. In such extreme cases, value is treated as some higher form of truth, revealed only to those who hold the sacred keys and hence undiscoverable and unchallengeable, even to those who might qualify as scientists. In these circumstances, those who suggest the appropriateness of modelling politics as science rather than as theology may actually exert an influence towards a less coercive social order. To the leaders of the Inquisition or to the Khomeinis of today, any move towards treating politics as Popperian science might indeed serve to reduce human suffering.

V. Conclusions

In modern Western countries, however, the balance seems surely to be tilted in the manner that my argument has presupposed. Values are widely acknowledged to be derived from individuals, and there are no absolutes. God has been dead for a century, and attempts to revive him are likely to founder. The moral relativism of modern times may be, and has been, assigned a share in the responsibility for the social ills of this century.[11] And we might all agree that politics, modelled as a resolution of conflicts among competing

---

11. See, for example, Paul Johnson, *Modern Times* (New York: Harper & Row, 1983).

individual values and interests, might have been quite different if a world of absolutes in ethics should have continued to exist. But is such a world of moral absolutes that which the Enlightenment promised? Must we sacrifice our nature as individual sources of valuation to insure our survival in viable social order?

The thrust of my own argument, in this chapter and elsewhere, runs counter to that which calls for a return to absolute values in ethics, if such were possible. There is a positive side to value relativism that is too easily overlooked. Because values are relative, and because the individual recognizes that his values are indeed his own, it becomes possible for man to model an existence in social interaction with other persons that does not involve acquiescence in a single-value norm. This essential vision of the great eighteenth-century social philosophers was somehow lost to the mind of this century. Without this vision, and in the face of earlier moral absolutes, it was perhaps natural that scholars should have promoted "salvation by science," even in extension to the political enterprise itself.[12]

The social engineer would never have dared base his argument for constructive (destructive) change on his own, personal, and private preferences "for society," which he would be forced to acknowledge as relative. He turned instead to science for intellectual and moral support and justification. He advanced the claim, directly and/or indirectly, and often in a confused way, that politics, like science, involves a search for truth. And truth, once discovered, carries its own moral justification. Those who do not "see" must be "shown the light," perhaps preferably by persuasion but, if necessary, by coercion.

Value is relative, truth is not, at least within the realm of ordinary discourse. To introduce the fallibility of post-Popperian science as a helpmate in the philosophy of politics seems to me to be misguided and ultimately to be dangerous.[13] It is not the recognition of fallibility in scientific truths

---

12. "Salvation by Science" was the title of one of the most devastating of Frank Knight's review articles. See Frank H. Knight, "Salvation by Science: The Gospel According to Professor Lundberg," *Journal of Political Economy*, 55 (Dec. 1947); reprinted in Frank H. Knight, *On the History and Method of Economics* (Chicago: University of Chicago Press, Phoenix Books, 1956), 227–50.

13. See T. W. Hutchison, *The Politics and Philosophy of Economics* (Oxford: Blackwell, 1981), vii.

that facilitates man's understanding of his social order and that renders him tolerant of dissent. It is, indeed, the recognition of the necessary relativism and *individualism* of values, along with the modelling of politics as the enterprise of resolving conflict among such values, that makes the libertarian social order meaningful.

Belief, Choice and Consequences
Reflections on Economics,
Science and Religion

I. Introduction

In an essay written in early 1984, I stated:

> Beliefs and evaluations exist simultaneously in the mind of the individual, but they serve totally different functions. Beliefs enable a person to understand reality, to impose a mental order on that which he observes, *quite independent of any participation in that order*. By comparison and by contrast, evaluations become conceptually necessary for participation in the order that a person's beliefs define as existing. A person totally without values or preferences would have no ability to choose. (Italics supplied.)[1]

Let me draw attention to two separate implications that might be drawn from the above statement. First, the statement seems to allow for skepticism, a suspension of belief on those aspects of reality about which the individual has insufficient evidence upon which to form a judgment. Secondly, the circumstances in which individual choices are made are not directly related to the status of belief, although it may be inferred that a condition of skepticism

From *Wege der Vernunft: Festschrift zum siebzigsten Geburtstag von Hans Albert*, ed. Alfred Bohnen and Alan Musgrave (Tübingen: J. C. B. Mohr [Paul Siebeck], 1991), 151–63. Reprinted by permission of the publisher.

1. "Potential for Tyranny in Politics as Science," in *Liberty, Market and State* (Brighton: Wheatsheaf Books, 1986), 45.

could preclude the evaluation that might be required in order for choice to be made.

My purpose in this essay is to explore these implications further, and particularly as they may apply to economic models of choice, to scientific hypotheses and to religious belief. I propose to examine in some detail the evaluation of scientific and religious alternatives that precede relevant "choices" made by individuals in these domains. My reflections are stimulated by two quite unrelated sources: first, by a re-reading and subsequent re-thinking of G. L. S. Shackle's conception of choice, and, secondly, by a reading of Gerald E. Myers' discussion of William James' criticism of religious skepticism.[2]

II. Why Is Choice Necessary?
When Is Choice Necessary?

Economists have concentrated much of their analytical attention on choice, defined as the selection among alternatives that are available within exogenously determined constraints. But they have almost totally neglected the questions: Why is choice necessary? When is choice necessary? The individual is presumably described by a utility function or preference ordering that defines the underlying motivation for action, a motivation that does not require explicit consideration. As driven by the desire to maximize utility and as described by the relative evaluations of alternatives contained in the utility function, evaluations that must, in turn, be dependent on a set of beliefs concerning the efficacy of alternative end-objects in generating utility, the choice behavior of the individual in this economist's model seems to be completely explained.

But what happens if the individual lacks the evidence required to translate choosable end-objects or actions into utility increments? What happens when the individual simply does not know the relative utility values of the alternatives among which he is enabled to choose? The economist has an answer ready in hand. The individual is acknowledged to choose in situations involving uncertainty along several dimensions, including the po-

---

2. See G. L. S. Shackle, *Business, Time, and Thought* (New York: New York University Press, 1988); Gerald E. Myers, *William James: His Life and Thought* (New Haven: Yale University Press, 1986), especially Chapter 14.

tential utility-enhancing content of the alternatives confronted. But within any given set of limits on his beliefs in this respect, the individual is still presumed to be able to carry out some subjective calculus of probability and, finally, to make choices that maximize anticipated or expected utility.

Note that the individual is not allowed to hold off, or to suspend, choice in the event that the evidence concerning the empirical qualities of alternatives, as these relate to the potentials for generating utility, is lacking. Choice is presumed to be *necessary* in this economist's model of behavior. But why is choice necessary? What is it in this model that precludes the withholding or abstention from choice?

These questions may be made to seem irrelevant if the choice alternatives are defined inclusively enough to allow the no-choice option in the set. It is clear, however, that economists do not model choice behavior in this way. Their models examine choices among apples, oranges and bananas; they do not examine choices among apples, oranges, bananas and "none of the above."

A more satisfactory response to the questions posed is to suggest that choices are dictated, in some ultimate or final sense, by the requirements of physical or biological survival. The chooser is a living being who must choose to continue living. Buridan's ass starves because it cannot decide which bale of straw to choose. Unless economic man chooses to undergo the disutility of effort to earn income, he, too, must face hunger. And, in a money economy, unless choices are made as among the uses to which income may be put, survival is jeopardized. And so on to the chooser among end-items that meet differing categories of physical needs: food, clothing, shelter, etc.

This response adduces physical survival as the ultimate explanation for the necessity of economic choice, with survival *through time* recognized to be a basic motivation for living beings. The temporal dimension becomes relevant when we compare economic choice with scientific "choice" later in this essay. The individual, as an economic chooser, cannot stop the world and get off while he postpones making choice commitments, regardless of his state of ignorance concerning the utility-enhancing efficacy of the choice alternatives.

Consider the following straightforward example. A young person, at twenty-two years of age, must choose whether or not to undertake graduate study. This person may not possess sufficient evidence upon which to make even a tolerably well informed judgment as to which of these two choice options will prove ultimately more productive of utility. Despite this epistemic limit, however, the person cannot adopt the stance of the skeptic who simply refuses to choose. By not entering graduate school at twenty-three, an opportunity is foreclosed that can never be opened. Either of the choices must set in motion a sequence of events that would never emerge in the scenario consequent upon selection of the other alternative.

To summarize the argument to this point, the whole analysis of choice, as conducted by the economist, presupposes that the individual is continually confronted with the necessity of choosing among the alternatives presented to him, either by external circumstances, by the choices of others or even by his own creation, quite independent of the information possessed concerning the nature of the choice alternatives. The individual's beliefs about these alternatives may be accurate or inaccurate, complete or incomplete, biased or unbiased. But there is nothing in the characteristics of beliefs that obviates the necessity of choice itself.

III. The Atemporality of Scientific "Choice"

In carrying on their ordinary affairs, professional scientists make choices that can be analyzed by the economist's model; in this ordinary behavior, scientists are like everyone else. But, in their capacities as scientists, they enter into a different realm of "choice," and one that must be categorically distinguished from that which commands the attention of economists. Science is about resolving conflicts among competing beliefs about reality. The choice, if we call it such, faced by a scientist is, then, a choice among *competing beliefs.* But beliefs, as such, are not convertible, either directly or indirectly, into end-objects that ultimately yield utility or satisfaction to the chooser. The scientific effort, which may be said to embody choices among beliefs, cannot be modelled or described as being motivated by a desire to enhance utility, at least not in any sense analogous to the economic effort previously discussed. The scientist selects among competing beliefs (explanations) in accordance with the unique criterion of truth which is generalizable over all scientists and over the whole domain of the scientific enterprise. There is no personalized or individualized evaluation process involved here, in which the individual who chooses assigns prospective utility values to each of the choice options confronted.

The scientist's participation is limited to a generalized discovery process, out of which there emerges agreement on what reality is, or, more carefully stated, on models of reality that allow falsifiable experiments to be carried out. In all this effort, there is no necessity that the individual scientist choose at all in the absence of evidence that convinces him of the truth of one of the alternative explanations advanced. There is no temporally measured opportunity cost stemming from a withholding of selection among competing beliefs. From this it follows directly that skepticism in the face of unconvincing evidence, in favor of or against any one of the proffered hypotheses about reality, is not only a possible stance, but, in many cases, is the indicated stance of the scientist who is driven only by the pursuit of truth. What is there to dictate choice when choice is not necessary?

The introduction of some calculus of subjective probability seems unwarranted here, so long as we remain within the pure scientific enterprise and do not extend analysis to the utilization of scientific findings in making ordinary choices. Suppose that there are two competing hypotheses, two opposing beliefs about reality. The scientist may legitimately refuse to accept either hypothesis and withhold judgment until further evidence is generated. He gains nothing, as a scientist, in trying to arrive at some certainty equivalent through usage of a subjective probability calculus.

In scientific selection among competing alternatives, there is no opportunity cost of refraining from such selection that carries a temporal dimension. If, in ordinary choice, Mrs. Jones refuses to spend food dollars on bread or meat, her family goes hungry during the period that she hesitates; there is an anticipated utility loss through time that will be consequent on her refusal to choose. Contrast this situation with that of the physicist of mid-century who refused to accept either the continuous creation or the big bang theory of the formation of the universe. For such a physicist, there was nothing directly analogous to "going hungry" for the Jones family in the example. For pure scientific "choice," the argument implies that the selection among beliefs, as such, *has no consequences*. The selection of one belief over another does not set off a sequence of events, either for the person who chooses or for others. Choices made by individuals in their capacities as pure scientists are mental events and without direct external effects.

Viewed in this perspective, it seems questionable whether choice is at all the appropriate term to apply to the scientist's act of selecting among beliefs, among alternative explanations, among competing hypotheses. In the

Shackle definition, the scientist does not "choose," at least in any manner analogous to the person who chooses in ordinary situations. There is also a deeper sense in which "choice" may be semantically inappropriate to describe that which the scientist does in selecting beliefs. Choice, as such, implies that alternatives can be rejected, that the individual has within himself a control over which sequence of events will be set in motion by his action. Does the scientist have free will of the sort that is presumed in any analysis of ordinary choice? Or is the scientist's selection among competing hypotheses beyond his own control? Is this selection necessarily determined by the objective reality that exists quite independent of the scientist and by the perceptual-mental apparatus that the scientist brings to that reality along with the pre-commitment to the generalizable criterion of truth?

My concern here is not, however, with any detailed analysis of the scientist's behavior in selecting among beliefs or hypotheses. My emphasis is limited to the central point that, in the pure scientific enterprise, there is no opportunity cost involved in the maintenance of the skeptical stance, in the continuing refusal to select among alternative explanations of relevant portions of reality. By contrast with the ordinary choices analyzed by economists, in science it is not necessary to choose until and unless the evidence is found to be convincing.

IV. Religion and the Necessity to Choose

As noted earlier, this essay was stimulated, in part, by reading Gerald E. Myers' discussion of William James' attack on religious skepticism. I propose, in this Section, to interpret James' discussion in terms of the earlier comparison and contrast between ordinary choice, as analyzed by economists, and scientific choice, as examined in the preceding Section.

For more than two centuries, and certainly since David Hume, religious "choice" has been generally conceived to be fully analogous to scientific choice rather than to ordinary choice, as analyzed here. That is to say, an individual's selection among competing sides of the basic or central religious questions has been intellectually modelled as a choice among beliefs, faiths or convictions. The fundamental issue has been treated as one of truth or falsity rather than as one of relative evaluations or interests in alternatives for choice. An individual's acceptance of the existence of God, or of any extra-individual being or force, has been deemed to be based on some accumulation of sufficient evidence to warrant the reaching of "God exists" as a truth judgment. In this familiar interpretation, God is "discovered" by the individual in a manner that seems precisely equivalent to the discovery made by the practicing scientist, who perceives a previously unrecognized aspect of an objective reality.

It is not all surprising that, if religious "choice" is conceived in this scientific, post-Enlightenment mind-set, the evidence suggests that skepticism is the position indicated for many persons. A suspension of belief, the essential stance of the religious agnostic, probably describes the attitude toward the central religious issues that is taken by most persons who are scientists in their mode of thought, whether or not they qualify as professionals. Recall from our earlier discussion, however, that this stance, for science propositions, involves no opportunity cost measurable in a temporal dimension. By weighing the evidence for the hypothesis that God exists, the person-cum-scientist adjudges such evidence to be insufficient. The hypothesis remains unconvincing; it is adjudged neither to be accepted nor to be categorically rejected. Skepticism seems to be indicated. This "non-choice" does not, in this scientific mind-set, have consequences, either for the individual who chooses or for the objective reality that remains to be discovered ultimately in the never-ending search.

As I interpret Myers' reading-understanding of the arguments advanced by William James, the focal point of James' attack on religious skepticism lies precisely in his rejection of the scientific mind-set. James seems to suggest, directly, that there are opportunity costs of religious skepticism that are measured in utility losses through time. James seems, in other words, to model the choice among religious beliefs analogously to what I have here classified to be ordinary choice rather than scientific choice.

Consider the following statement:

We cannot escape the issue by remaining skeptical and waiting for more light, because, although we avoid error in that way *if religion be untrue,* we lose the good, *if it be true,* just as certainly as if we positively chose to disbelieve. It is as if a man should hesitate indefinitely to ask a certain woman to marry him because he was not perfectly sure that she would prove an angel after he brought her home. Would he not cut himself off from that

particular angel-possibility as decisively as if he went and married someone else? Skepticism, then, is not avoidance of option; it is option of a
certain particular kind of risk. *Better risk loss of truth than chance of
error*—that is your faith-vetoer's exact position. (Italics in original.)[3]

As Myers suggests, this statement, taken independently, is confusing.
James conflates the two categorically separate types of choice previously
discussed here. But we can impose an order, of sorts, on the James position
here by concentrating on the marriage choice analogy. Despite the reference
to risk that makes the argument seem to be a version of Pascal's wager, note
that the opportunity cost is measured by utility loss that is to be suffered during the period of indecision. If all utility gains as well as all utility losses are
expected to occur only in some final achievement of bliss, there would be no
utility lost in postponing the angel possibility, so long as a decision is made
before such a moment of final bliss has passed. But James clearly is referring
to a wholly different dimension of a life experience here. His example fits
perfectly into our model of ordinary choice. By postponing marriage, the
individual anticipates that he will suffer emotional and sexual starvation;
choice becomes necessary to avoid the sequence of events that indecision
guarantees.

The religious application becomes straightforward. In the suspension of
belief that skepticism represents, the individual suffers spiritual hunger, a
consequence that can be avoided only on a positive choice of belief. Such
"choice" is necessary if the suffering is to be alleviated; religious skepticism
is not maintained without anticipated utility loss. Whether or not there is
some intrinsic human "need" for spiritual sustenance that is generalizable
for all persons remains an empirical question that James does not try to answer. His argument refers strictly to his own acceptance of a positive belief in
God's existence. James was, apparently, willing to allow for differences
among individuals in the religious aspects of their life experiences. Again,
this view would be quite consistent with the model of ordinary choice in
which individuals are allowed to evaluate end-objects of choice differently,
by contrast with scientific choice, where there is no room for individual di-

---

3. William James, *The Will to Believe* (New York: Dover, 1956), 26, as cited in Gerald
Myers, op. cit., 451–52.

vergencies once a truth judgment is reached. The religious tolerance of William James would seem incoherent in an interpretation that makes religious choice analogous to scientific choice.[4]

We may go somewhat further with our interpretation of James' attitude toward the choice of belief in the existence of God. If we model this choice analogously with ordinary choice, as suggested, what does the individual choose? Note that he is *not* making a truth judgment to the effect that "God exists." Nor is he making a positive commitment to "act as if God exists." The individual is, instead, making a choice "to believe that God exists." The end-object chosen is "to believe," not the existence of God, as such. A life plan that includes such belief as an end-object is expected to yield a flow of benefits over the whole period subsequent to the decision. The anticipated utility gains from holding positive belief in God's existence may, but surely need not, include some discounted value of expectations concerning some afterlife personal existence.

The attitude that I have attributed to William James here suggests that a positive choice to believe may be made independent of the closely related but still categorically different scientific "choice" or truth judgment on the existence of God. Can an individual choose "to believe" that God exists unless, at the same time, he makes a truth judgment in the full scientific sense? In other words, is it possible for the genuine skeptic to heed James' advice?

The absence of any psychologically devastating contradiction in this respect is suggested by reference to the necessary imaginative leap that is required to enjoy fiction, as represented in theatrical or film production or in published stories. At one level of consciousness, the viewer-reader recognizes the unreality of the characters and events depicted before him. But, at another level of participation, by the very act of viewing or reading, the individual is choosing to believe that the fictional world is real. Unless he does this, it becomes impossible to enjoy the spectacle, save in some detached, quasi-scientific observational stance.

I should emphasize that this reference to the enjoyment of fiction is *not* aimed to imply that a choice to believe in the existence of God is analogous to the imaginative leap into a fictional world, and that it is recognized to be

4. For further discussion of this point, see my paper "The Potential for Tyranny in Politics as Science," op. cit.

such. The reference is aimed, instead, to suggest [that] if a person can secure utility gains from a deliberative choice to believe that which, at yet another level of consciousness, is known to be false, then it is surely the case that a person can secure utility value from a choice to believe in settings where the empirical-logical evidence remains, at best, ambiguous.

I have interpreted William James to suggest that the individual may suffer "spiritual hunger pangs" unless he chooses to believe in God's existence. But why could such explanations not be extended to quite arbitrary, and wholly unreal, beliefs? Perhaps someone might expect to secure utility gains from choosing to believe that he can walk on water. The effective limits of such beliefs are set by the potential falsifiability of that which is contained in the empirically defined spheres of the individual's personal experience. The individual who chooses to believe that he can walk on water finds such belief non-sustainable when he makes the attempt to test it. If, however, the belief in question remains non-falsifiable, there is no empirical feedback from the objective reality of the natural order of things to the status of belief. The individual may remain secure in his *chosen* non-falsifiable belief.

God's existence is a non-falsifiable hypothesis. At this point, Sir Karl Popper's distinction between corroboration and non-falsification of hypotheses is helpful. The religious skeptic holds that the hypothesis of God's existence is not corroborated by the evidence available. William James might respond by stating that the hypothesis has not been falsified and, further, cannot be falsified. Hence, if there is an opportunity cost in holding to the skeptical position and a utility gain from choosing to believe, the indicated behavior is to make such a positive choice.

Nietzsche once said that "faith means not wanting to know what is true."[5] William James might have responded as follows: "Faith means choosing to believe in a setting where it will remain impossible to know the truth." If, however, we put the James position in this way, its weakness is most clearly exposed. Who is to draw the relevant distinction between falsifiable and non-falsifiable hypotheses? And if it is necessary to choose in the second of these domains, will not choice, in itself, shut off efforts to expand the first set? Again James might respond by drawing a categorical distinction between choosing to believe a non-falsifiable hypothesis and choosing to believe a

5. F. Nietzsche in *Antichrist,* as cited by Walter Kaufmann, *The Owl and the Nightingale* (London: Faber and Faber, 1959), 173.

potentially falsifiable hypothesis that has not been yet falsified. In the second case, truth has been provisionally established, and, with such establishment, there comes the implicit dogma of scientific validity. Intolerance toward those who would challenge the authority of established truth becomes appropriate, within the limits of open exploration. In the first case, however, where an individual, or a collection of individuals, chooses to believe an hypothesis that is acknowledged to be non-falsifiable, there is no accompanying aura of scientific authority. There is no foundation for the dogma inherent in provisionally established truth. Tolerance, rather than intolerance, is a necessary consequence of beliefs that must remain in the domain of non-falsifiability.

It is perhaps worth noting that a non-falsifiable proposition is not equivalent to an illusion precisely because of the ultimate non-falsifiability. The perception that the lake lies just ahead in the desert is falsified as the thirsty traveler proceeds and finds no lake at all. The religious "traveler" who chooses to believe that God exists encounters no possibly comparable disproof of his belief. In an explanatory-predictive sense a non-falsifiable proposition is of no value. But this familiar dismissal of such a proposition depends on an implicit and prior acceptance of the scientific mind-set. As interpreted here, a non-falsifiable proposition may, if a person chooses to believe it, yield a direct utility value. It offers the believer a flow of utility that meets basic needs in a manner fully comparable to the utility flows provided by ordinary consumables. William James clearly had such a personal conception of his own religious belief when he stated:

> . . . had I not clung to the scripture-texts like "The external God is my refuge," etc., "Come unto me, all ye that labor and are heavy-laden," etc., "I am the resurrection and the life," etc., I think I should have grown really insane.[6]

V. Shackle and the Nature of Choice

I noted earlier that this essay was stimulated by a serendipitous juxtaposition of Myers' account of William James' attitudes toward religion and a re-

---

6. William James, *Varieties of Religious Experience* (New York: Modern Library Ed.), 157. As cited in Myers, op. cit., 468.

reading and re-thinking of G. L. S. Shackle's conception of the nature of choice. It will be useful to review Shackle's views on choice in a specific application to the arguments that I have advanced in preceding Sections.

To Shackle, the individual chooses among alternative "future possibles": no one of which comes into existence in the absence of choice. The *originative* element is central to the nature of choice itself, which is necessarily made under conditions of uncertainty. That which does not yet exist cannot be known, and the sequence of events that is to come into being is determined only upon the act of choice itself. It is evident that, in Shackle's conception, the epistemic standing of the alternatives in the mind of the chooser cannot be directly relevant to the act of choice itself.

Although, to my knowledge, Shackle does not specifically discuss the point, his whole analysis depends on the presence of the continuing necessity that the individual actually choose among the "future possibles" that are available to him. Choices have consequences; one sequence of events takes place; other sequences are forever foreclosed. The temporal dimensionality of the utility flows that enter into the calculus of opportunity costs seems implicit in the whole Shackle framework.

As I noted earlier, the very word "choice," as used by Shackle, could not apply to the stylized scientific selection among alternative beliefs or hypotheses. To call the making of a truth judgment about objective reality a "choice" would run counter to Shackle's relationship of choices with consequences. A "choice" among beliefs, as such, is a pure mental event, from which nothing follows. There is no sequence of events that is set in motion.

By contrast, in Shackle's formulation, choice necessarily sets off a sequence of events that would not come into being had the particular choice not been made. The 12th-century scientist who chose to believe that the earth was flat did not relate his acceptance or rejection of this hypothesis with the flatness or roundness of the earth in any modern falsifiability sense. Such a scientist would have acknowledged, along with those who held opposing views, that the pure selection among beliefs had no consequences for the reality that remained "out there" in the non-discoverable. Nor did the selections among beliefs have consequences for either the overt behavior of the scientist (in a stylized setting detached from any navigational experimentation) or the utility flow enjoyed in going about the ordinary affairs of life.

Such a selection among competing beliefs can be converted into genuine

Shacklean choice if we allow for consequences along any of several dimensions. Consider, again, the "God exists" proposition. Presumably, few individuals would be arrogant enough to think that their own choice behavior could bring God into existence from nothingness. Along this dimension, the choice of belief in this hypothesis does not meet Shackle's criterion. The choice of belief may, however, have consequences along other dimensions.

It is useful to distinguish between behavioral and utilitarian consequences of choice. In ordinary choice, as modelled by economists, these separated dimensions are closely related. A person chooses one alternative from among a set of possibles because he expects his utility flow to be enhanced; that is to say, choice is motivated by its consequences for personal utility. At the same time, however, and as Shackle stresses, there are behavioral consequences of choice that bring the anticipated utility consequences into being.

Consider, again, the choice of the belief in God's existence. In the stylized scientific conception, this "choice" remains a pure mental event, nothing more. There are neither utility nor behavioral consequences. As we move beyond this pure truth-judgment characterization of the choice of belief, however, consequences follow choices in one or both of the relevant dimensions. In Pascal's setting, the choice of belief in itself is presumed sufficient to determine consequences in some afterlife personal existence, but belief also carries consequences for the individual's behavior within the life experience. In William James' conception of the choice of belief, as I have noted, there are both utility and behavioral consequences. The person who chooses to believe finds his life enriched, or, in economists' terms, finds his flow of utility enhanced while, presumably, he modifies his current behavior toward some measure of coherence with the belief. The effect in some imagined afterlife need not enter into the choice calculus at all.

VI. Generalizations

I have suggested that stylized scientific "choice" among competing explanations of a presumed objective and existing reality does not meet Shackle's criterion for genuine choice because no consequences follow. I have suggested that the scientific mind-set has treated the choice of religious belief as if it is equivalent to stylized scientific "choice," or to the making of a judgment as to the truth or falsity of the central hypothesis concerning God's existence. I have suggested, however, that the William James attitude toward the choice of religious belief removes the scientific mind-set and shifts the choice of religious belief into the domain of genuine choice, defined strictly in the consequentialist manner of G. L. S. Shackle.

I have interpreted the "God exists" belief as a non-falsifiable hypothesis, but I have stressed that non-falsifiability, as such, need not imply the absence of consequences of such belief for the utility flows anticipated by the individual who chooses. As James clearly suggested, an individual's life experience may be made more tolerable by the acceptance of a belief that he recognizes to be non-falsifiable in any strict scientific sense. There are no bases, however, for generalizing the utility consequences of positive belief over all individuals, even in a single cultural grouping. Those persons who feel no need for a positive belief in a supreme being or supra-individual force are in a position analogous to those persons who feel no need to consume ordinary goods that may be desired by others. For such persons, religious skepticism involves none of the opportunity cost that James emphasized.

Before those of us who may classify ourselves to be in such a group, that is, without a felt need for religious belief, are allowed to assume a stance of intellectual-scientific arrogance and superiority, we should shift the discussion beyond the confines of religious belief, as such. Do we not find our own utility enhanced by choosing to believe non-falsifiable hypotheses, even if these are not those concerned with God's existence? What about the modern liberal humanist who chooses to believe in the inherent goodness of natural man? Does such a person not "feel better" by living with his own non-falsifiable proposition? Or to bring the issue closer to my own sphere of research interest, what about the individualist-contractarian who chooses to believe in the ultimate rationality of individual members of the human species? What evidence could be adduced to cause one to modify this organizing belief? And would such a shift away from this belief amount to a dramatic utility loss that we are simply unwilling to contemplate?

PART THREE

Moral Community
and Moral Order

Moral Community, Moral Order, or Moral Anarchy

I. Introduction

In this lecture I shall discuss the "ties that bind" persons with each other in society, and the instruments and attitudes that may break those ties that exist. I am concerned with the ways that persons act and feel toward one another. For this reason, I have inserted the adjective "moral" before each of the nouns in my title. "Community, Order, or Anarchy," standing alone, would not convey my desired emphasis on personal interaction. To forestall misunderstanding at the outset, however, I should note that there is no explicitly moral content in the lecture, if the word "moral" is interpreted in some normative sense.

My diagnosis of American society is informed by the notion that we are living during a period of erosion of the "social capital" that provides the basic framework for our culture, our economy, and our polity, a framework within which the "free society" in the classically liberal ideal perhaps came closest to realization in all of history. My efforts have been directed at trying to identify and to isolate the failures and breakdowns in institutions that are responsible for this erosion.[1]

The Abbott Memorial Lecture no. 17 (Colorado Springs: Colorado College, 1981). Reprinted by permission of the publisher.

1. For earlier works that provide some indication of the development of the ideas presented in this lecture, see *The Limits of Liberty* (Chicago: University of Chicago Press, 1975); "Markets, States, and the Extent of Morals," *American Economic Review*, 68 (May, 1978), 364–68; "The Limits of Moral Community," to be published in *Ethics and Animals*,

My discussion here will be exclusively conducted in terms of the three abstract models or forms of interaction listed in my title: (1) moral community, (2) moral order, and (3) moral anarchy. Any society may be described empirically as embodying some mix among these three forms or elements. A society is held together by some combination of moral community and moral order. Its cohesion is reduced by the extent to which moral anarchy exists among its members. The precise mix among the three forms or elements will, therefore, determine the observed "orderliness" of any society, along with the degree of governmental coercion reflected in the pattern that is observed to exist. The need for governance as well as the difficulty of governing are directly related to the mix among the three elements.

II. Moral Community

I shall commence by defining the three abstract models or forms of interaction. A *moral community* exists among a set of persons to the extent that individual members of the group identify with a collective unit, a community, rather than conceive themselves to be independent, isolated individuals. In one sense, of course, moral community always exists. No person is totally autonomous, and no one really thinks exclusively of himself as a solitary unit of consciousness. Each person will, to some extent, identify with some community (or communities) whether this be with the nuclear family, the extended family, the clan or tribe, a set of locational, ethnic, racial, or religious cohorts, the trade union, the business firm, the social class, or, finally, with the nation-state. Most persons will identify simultaneously and with varying degrees of loyalties with several communities of varying sizes, types, and sources of valuation. The set of communities and the value or loyalty weights assigned to the members of the set will, of course, differ from person to person. I suggest, however, that it is possible to characterize different societies in terms of the relative importance of *moral community* as an element of social cohesion among persons within those societies. It is possible to classify societies as more or less communitarian (collectivistic), as less or more individualistic.

---

forthcoming under the editorship of Harlan Miller and W. Williams; "A Governable Country," in *Japan Speaks 1981* (Osaka, Japan: Suntory Foundation, 1981), 3, 1–12.

III. Moral Order

A *moral order* exists when participants in social interaction treat each other as moral reciprocals, but do so without any sense of shared loyalties to a group or community. Each person treats other persons with moral indifference, but at the same time respects their equal freedoms with his own. Mutual respect, which is an alternative way of stating the relationship here, does not require moral community in any sense of personal identification with a collectivity or community. Each person thinks about and acts toward other persons as if they are autonomous individuals, independent of who they might be in terms of some group or community classification scheme. In a moral order, it is possible for a person to deal with other persons who are not members of his own community if both persons have agreed, explicitly or implicitly, to abide by the behavioral precepts required for reciprocal trust and confidence.

The emergence of the abstract rules of behavior describing moral order had the effect of expanding dramatically the range of possible interpersonal dealings. Once rules embodying reciprocal trust came to be established, it was no longer necessary that both parties to a contract identify themselves with the same moral community of shared values and loyalties. There was no longer any requirement that trading partners claim membership in the same kinship group.[2] Under the rules of a moral order, it is conceptually possible for a genuinely autonomous individual to remain a viable entity, whereas no such existence would be possible in a structure characterized solely by moral community.

I suggest that different societies may be classified in terms of the relative importance of the rules of moral order in describing the observed relationships among the persons within each society. These rules may either supplement the sense of moral community as a source of social cohesion where the

2. Professor F. A. Hayek, particularly in his most recent writings, has stressed the emergence of these abstract rules of behavior through some process of cultural evolution: rules that man does not and cannot understand and which run counter to those instinctual bases of behavior which find their sources in the primitive sense of moral community. See F. A. Hayek, *Law, Legislation and Liberty,* Vol. 3, *The Political Order of a Free People* (Chicago: University of Chicago Press, 1979), especially "Epilogue," pp. 153–76.

latter exists, or these rules may substitute for moral community to the extent of rendering it unnecessary.

IV. Moral Anarchy

Moral anarchy exists in a society (if it can remain a society) when individuals do not consider other persons to be within their moral communities and when they do not accept the minimal requirements for behavior in a moral order. In moral anarchy, each person treats other persons exclusively as means to further his own ends or objectives. He does not consider other persons to be his fellows (brothers) in some community of shared purpose (as would be the case in moral community), or to be deserving of reciprocal mutual respect and trust as autonomous individuals (as would be the case in moral order).

In a real sense, moral anarchy becomes the negation of both moral community and moral order. It is a setting within which persons violate the basic Kantian moral precept that human beings are to be treated only as ends not as means. It is perhaps more difficult to conceptualize moral anarchy as a general model of human interaction than the two alternative models already discussed. Moral anarchy seems somehow less descriptive of the behavior that we observe around us. For my purposes, however, I want to employ the model in the same way as the others. I suggest that it is possible to classify different societies in terms of the relative significance of moral anarchy in describing the attitudes and behavior of their members, one to another.

V. Implications for Social Stability
and Governability: Moral Anarchy

I shall now employ the three basic models or elements of interaction in order to discuss problems of social viability and, indirectly, problems of governability in a society. It will be useful to take extreme examples in which one of the three models is primarily descriptive rather than some undefined mix among the three. It will also be useful to change the order of discussion from that which was used in defining the three elements. I shall first take up moral anarchy, then moral order, and, finally, moral community.

Consider first, then, a setting in which many persons behave as moral anarchists. In this setting, life for the individual is "poore, nasty, brutish, and short," to employ the colorful language of Thomas Hobbes. Men who neither feel a sense of community with others, nor respect others as individuals in their own right, must be ruled. Individuals will sacrifice their liberties to the coercive sovereign government that can effectively insure order and personal security. But those persons who act on behalf of the sovereign government may themselves also be moral anarchists. There would seem to be no reason to anticipate that persons who secure powers of governance would be less likely to behave as moral anarchists than their fellows; indeed, the opposite conclusion seems the more plausible here. Social stability is purchased by individuals at the price of a coercive state regime. Repressive government may emerge as a necessary condition in a society with many moral anarchists.

VI. Implications for Social Stability and Governability: Moral Order

In sharp contrast with the setting discussed above, now consider a setting where many persons adhere to the precepts and behavioral rules of a moral order. Each individual treats other persons as deserving of mutual respect and tolerance, even though there exists no necessary sense of belonging to a community or collectivity of shared values and loyalties. In this setting, individuals may be secure in their persons and property, social stability may exist, and the needs for governance may be minimized. Correspondingly, the liberties of individuals are maximized.

In the extreme case where, literally, all persons behave in accordance with the rules of moral order, there would be no need for government at all. "Orderly anarchy" would be produced by the universalized adherence to rules of mutual respect among persons. In a more plausibly realistic setting, where most but not necessarily all persons are expected to follow the precepts of moral order, government as such may be restricted to a minimal, night-watchman, or protective state role.[3] The government need only protect per-

---

3. The term "minimal state" is used by Robert Nozick in *Anarchy, State, and Utopia* (New York: Basic Books, 1974). I used the term "protective state" in *The Limits of Liberty*, op. cit. The nineteenth-century writers often used the term "night-watchman state."

sonal and property rights and enforce contracts among persons. In more general terms, the government may be limited to enforcing the laws. It need not do more. In one sense, there is no need for "governing" as such.

VII. Implications for Social Stability and Governability: Moral Community

I have relegated moral community to third position here because this model is much the most difficult of the three to discuss in terms of the implications for overall social stability and for the needs for governance. The difficulties arise because of the many possible moral communities that may exist within a single society simultaneously, communities that may carry with them quite differing implications for the viability of social order. At one limit, if all persons should identify with the community that is coincident in membership with the inclusive political unit, the nation-state, the implications are relatively straightforward. In such a setting as this, all persons act as if they share the same objectives, as members of the national collectivity, including those persons who act on behalf of the government. Vis-à-vis other nations, this model of society might be a source of nationalistic adventure. Or to put the same point in a different perspective, when the national unit is threatened by external enemies, the sense of national community is more likely to emerge as a real force. Since all persons tend to share the same objectives, governance becomes easy. Persons "obey" the sovereign because they feel themselves to be part of the larger unit; conversely, the sovereign also behaves as persons would have it behave. Persons ruled or rulers do not behave toward each other as separate interacting individuals. They do not really consider themselves to be autonomous units.

At the other limit, there may exist no sense of moral community, no shared values, over the whole membership of the inclusive political unit, the nation-state, while at the same time, all or substantially all persons may express and act upon loyalties to collective units, subnationally classified. Persons may identify with specific communities (ethnic, racial, religious, regional, occupational, employment, class, etc.) while sensing no identification with or loyalty to the national unit. This sort of society will have some of the characteristics of that which contains only moral anarchists, discussed above. The difference here is that the relevant entities are themselves collectives rather than individuals. Persons may, in this society, exhibit sharply divergent behavior patterns as between treatment of members of the relevant community and persons who do not qualify for membership. Social conflict will tend to emerge between the relevant communities or between persons who are members of differing communities. Because of the prevalence of such conflicts, there will be a need for governance, and possibly by a coercive sovereign. Without such force, the Hobbesian war of each against all may apply to the separate collectivities rather than to individuals.

In effect, moral community as a concept can satisfactorily be discussed only in two-dimensional terms. The first dimension involves the general individualism-communitarianism spectrum, discussed initially. The second dimension involves what we may call the nationalized-localized spectrum, described in the two examples immediately above. A simple, two-dimensional diagram (Figure 1) will be helpful here. A society located at Point 1 of the diagram is largely individualistic, with little sense of moral community but with what there is limited to localized groupings (perhaps family or firm ties). A society located at Point 2 would be, in contrast, largely communitarian, but also with the loyalties of persons largely limited to localized collectivities, and with little or no sense of national community. A society at Point 3 would remain largely individualistic, like that at Point 1, but in this society there does exist some sense of national community. At Point 4, the society is largely communitarian, but also, the personal loyalties are largely concentrated on the national collectivity; there is little sense of localized community.

If we restrict analysis to the more basic concept, moral community, with-

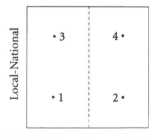

Individualism-Communitarianism

Figure 1

out reference to the national-local dimension, we can classify societies along the left-right dimension only. Any society classified to fall on the right side of the matrix would exhibit moral community as a relatively predominant characteristic.

VIII. Moral Community, Moral Order, and the Range and Scope for Governmental Action

In this section, I shall compare the two forces for potential social cohesion, moral community and moral order, in terms of the specific implications for the range and scope for governmental actions. I shall largely ignore the considerations raised in Section VII concerning the existence of moral communities of subnational memberships. I shall restrict discussion to the sense of moral community that exists among all members of a polity. As noted, in such a setting persons share the same national objectives and need not be "directed," as such, by the state. In a moral order, as noted above, persons further their own objectives within a legal framework that requires no active interference by government.

As we part from the idealizations of these two models, however, and as we allow for a potential threat of moral anarchy in each case, important differences emerge. The necessary conditions required for the maintenance of tolerably effective social stability are considerably more constrained in moral order than in moral community. The difference to be emphasized here lies in that between the individualized basis of any effective moral order and the nonindividualistic or collectivist basis of any effective moral community. In the former, individuals are bound together in adherence to a set of abstract rules or laws which are fundamentally impersonal and which are grounded in the generalized recognition that all persons are cooperating moral equals. The moral requirements placed on persons in such an order are minimal. The individual need not feel himself to be part of some inclusive collectivity. He need not exhibit feelings of benevolence or altruism toward any other persons, whether these be his neighbors or strangers. On the other hand, if he is expected to abide by the minimal behavioral precepts for such an order, to refrain from lapsing into the role of moral anarchist, he must think that the framework rules of the legal-political order are themselves "fair" in the sense that all persons are effectively required to play by the same rules.

In an effective moral order, a government that discriminates among persons in its treatment, that violates elementary precepts for fairness in dealing with separate individuals, will immediately face resentment and must ultimately expect rebellion. This predicted reaction follows from the very autonomy of individuals; each person remains a person and, as such, can claim entitlement to uniform treatment by those who administer the law. There exists no overriding "community interest" within which individual interests are subsumed.

This setting may be contrasted with one properly described as moral community coincident in membership with the national political unit. Here government may discriminate among persons without necessarily generating negative feedbacks in citizen discontent provided only that the discrimination is justified, explained, or legitimized in terms of the wider interest of the inclusive national community, an interest that exists by definition of the community, as such, and which is, also by definition, shared by everyone. Since the individual person in such a setting thinks of himself as a member of this community rather than as an individual, he will more readily acquiesce in what would seem overtly unfair treatment under a moral order. In the setting best described as moral community, therefore, the whole set of issues involving "justice" or "fairness" in governmental dealings with separate persons does not arise with nearly the same degree of intensity as it would in a moral order. It follows that government in a society described by national moral community will possess a wider range of options in taking actions than would government operating within a comparable moral order.

The range and scope for governmental action is more limited in a society that locates its source of social cohesion largely in moral order rather than moral community. At the same time, however, such a society (one based on moral order) can allow for greater flexibility and change in the attitudes and behavior of its individual members. As noted, in an effective moral order individuals need not share common purposes; they need only respect each other as individuals. From this it follows that individual attitudes and behavior may be widely varying, and may accordingly change within wide limits, but still be within the minimal requirement for productive interpersonal interchanges. In a very meaningful sense, individuals are free to select their own private purposes in this setting, a freedom that is necessarily absent in moral community.

The range and scope for governmental action is more extensive in a society that locates its sources of social cohesion in moral community rather than in adherence to the rules of moral order. On the other hand, the society largely held together by moral community is necessarily more vulnerable to shifts in the attitudes and the behavior patterns that might reflect individual departures from the shared purposes of the community. Persons are tied, one to another, by their common identification with the collective, with their shared sense of nationhood, race, class, or ideology. The loss of this identification may involve an unavoidable plunge into moral anarchy. Persons are not free to "do their own thing," within limits, as they might be in a society organized on the principles of moral order, principles that are mutually acknowledged to generate general benefits to all adherents.

IX. The United States in the 1980s

To this point, my discussion has been confined to a generalized analysis of the three abstract models or forms of social interaction: moral community, moral order, and moral anarchy. Any historically observed society will embody elements of each one of these models. Nonetheless, the mix may vary significantly among separate societies, and these differences may be important. In the next two sections, I shall apply the analysis to real-world societies. In this section, I shall discuss the United States in the 1980s in terms of the three models of interaction. In Section X, I shall briefly discuss modern Japan for purposes of comparison and contrast with the United States.

In the United States of the 1980s there is little moral community that extends to the limits of the inclusive national unit, the nation-state, as such, and which embodies the central instrument of the polity, the federal government in all of its arms and agencies. There is relatively little sense of shared purpose among the two hundred twenty-five millions of persons in the nation. Individuals tend, instead, to relate to and to identify with communities larger than themselves and their immediate families, but these communities tend to be of subnational sizes of membership, both geographically and numerically. The central government, therefore, is unable to call upon or to exploit a strong sense of genuine "national interest" or "national purpose," although, of course, such an "interest" might be called into being in the face of a demonstrated and well-understood external threat. Further, and importantly, those persons who themselves serve as "governors" possess little sense of "national interest," and they are not seen to possess such interest by those who are "governed." Those persons in positions of political power, like their cohorts who are outside governmental office, identify with various subnational groupings if, indeed, they adhere to moral community at all in any relevant way.

The United States, as a single society, does not depend primarily or critically on the presence of national moral community among its citizens. By historical tradition, the society has been made viable because its citizens have adhered behaviorally to the precepts of a moral order. There has existed a tradition of respect for adherence to the rule of law, for general rules, for promise keeping, for honesty in trading even of the most complex types. Voluntary adherence to the rules and regulations laid down by government remains widespread, including the voluntary payment of income taxes. With relatively few exceptions, government has not needed to become repressive.

For several decades, however, our moral order has been in the process of erosion. Larger and larger numbers of persons seem to become moral anarchists; they seem to be losing a sense of mutual respect one for another along with any feeling of obligation to abide by generalizable rules and codes of conduct. To the extent that such erosion continues and/or accelerates, the internal social stability of the United States must deteriorate. If confronted with this apparent breakdown in the internal cohesion of the social structure, more and more persons who are not themselves moral anarchists will turn to the arms and agencies of government for more direct protection than seems to be currently provided. The problem is explicitly exemplified in observed increases in criminal activity, which must, after some time lag, result in an increase in governmental coercion on all persons, the lawful and the unlawful alike. The voluntary limits on behavior that have worked in the past but which now seem to fail must be replaced by governmentally imposed restrictions. Government necessarily will move toward repression in the society as moral anarchy becomes more and more descriptive of the relationships among persons.

Government itself is partially responsible for the erosion of the traditional moral order in America. As the national government sought to take on a more comprehensive role in this century, and a role that is necessarily coincident with the presence or presumed presence of some "national interest," it has been unable to find moral support in the communitarian sense discussed above. Those who have promoted the extension of government's role under the folly that some national interest exists have, perhaps unwittingly, aided in the breakdown of effective moral order. As laws and regulations have multiplied, competing group interests have been promoted. And persons selected for governmental office have exploited their positions to advance their own private interests under the guise of nonexistent "national purpose." Observing this, citizens have become more disillusioned with governmental processes, and are more and more attracted to assume roles as moral anarchists. Confronted with a government that imposes rules that seem to command little or no respect, individuals quite naturally come to question other long-standing rules that have traditionally solicited voluntary adherence. Restoration of moral order, or even a stop to the erosion process, requires a roll-back of governmental intrusions into the lives of citizens, while at the same time, the growth in moral anarchy suggests, for the reasons noted above, an expanded governmental role in maintaining social stability.

Somewhat paradoxically, as our traditional moral order loses its ability to insure social stability, the United States becomes increasingly ungovernable even while the share of resources commanded politically continues to increase and as governmental interferences with the lives of ordinary citizens expand.

X. Japan: Comparison and Contrast

I shall now discuss modern Japanese society for purposes of drawing comparisons and contrasts with the United States. I do this not because I claim any expert knowledge of Japan and its people, but because my initial reflections on the subject matter of this lecture were prompted by an assignment to examine the "governability" of the Japanese.

There is widespread agreement, both among modern Japanese themselves and among external observers, that there is a relatively strong sense of identification of persons with moral communities beyond themselves, or, in terms of my three models, that Japan is clearly less individualistic and more communitarian than the United States. Disputes may arise concerning the relative importance of national and localized moral communities in modern Japan. To a degree, of course, the communitarian sense is limited to subnational groups, and notably to the employing firms. But nonetheless, for many reasons, it remains evident that there does also exist a relevant national moral community. The Japanese, as Japanese, share a set of values that affects their behavior as individuals. There is genuine meaning in the term "Japan, Incorporated."

As I have noted, this relationship between the individual and his fellow citizens in the inclusive national community allows the Japanese government greater freedom in the formulation and administration of laws and regulations than would be the case in a society more critically dependent on moral order. However, and also for the reasons discussed above, the continuing stability of the society may be dependent on the maintenance of the shared loyalties that now exist. From this it seems to follow that Japan may possibly be more vulnerable to shifts in attitudes and behavior patterns on the part of individuals and groups who somehow lose their identification with the nation. If such identification should be lost, such individuals may lapse directly into roles of moral anarchists.

If this scenario should unfold, there might exist no apparent means through which Japan could recapture its sense of national moral community short of possible international adventure. If my diagnosis is at all suggestive here, the question that emerges is whether or not a nation like Japan, faced with a possible erosion in its shared sense of moral community, could adopt essentially Western notions of moral order before moral anarchy assumes predominant importance and generates a breakdown in social structure. Can the Japanese citizen, circa the year 2000 or 2050, who may have lost his identity with the nation as a community, as an entity that commands his loyalty and respect, can he come to understand, appreciate, and live by the behavioral precepts of moral order, precepts that require him to grant fellow citizens mutual respect as moral equivalents and which give him criteria for evaluating governmental rules in some personal and noncommunitarian way? Can Japanese governments, in their own right, keep within the limits of power that will allow a functioning moral order to evolve, and further, can Japanese governments hold this stance as Western nations themselves are observed to sink further into the collectively dominated moral anarchy that now seems their fate?

XI. Prospects for Constructive Reform

In his recent writings, Professor F. A. Hayek has stressed that modern man's behavioral instincts are those that characterize what I have here called moral community and which evolved over the ages in essentially tribal settings. He suggests that Western man very slowly evolved patterns of adherence to abstract rules that he does not understand, the rules of moral order, and which really run counter to his instinctual proclivities.[4] Professor Hayek's response to the first question posed for the Japanese society above would, presumably, be negative. The behavioral rules of effective moral order cannot be "laid on"; cultural evolution cannot be directed. I am somewhat less evolutionist and more constructivist than Professor Hayek, but my concern here is not primarily with what the Japanese society may face in future decades. My concern is with the prospects for constructive reform in the social order of the United States, and I should stress that reform need not depend exclusively on changes in rules for behavior.

I have suggested that those who have promoted the extension of Western national governments have done so in their failure to recognize that the moral order, described by voluntary adherence to abstract rules of behavior, carries implications for the reach of governance. Accordingly, these governments have been allowed to grow far beyond the limits that might sustain and reinforce effective moral order, while at the same time, they have failed to generate effective moral community as a replacement force that might, in turn, legitimate such extended governance. Indeed, the moral anarchists among us have used the instruments of governance to subvert both moral community and moral order as necessary to advance their own ends.

Even in the 1980s, however, relatively few Americans are moral anarchists; most Americans continue to treat their fellows with mutual respect and abide by the rules of moral order. Most Americans also maintain a limited sense of moral community, a sense that could be maximally exploited with appropriate devolution and decentralization of governmental authority. Constructive reform is possible provided that the institutions of social order are so modified as to make them consistent with the *empirical realities* of modern man as he

4. See Hayek, op. cit.

is, rather than man as the naive reformers of decades past have hoped he might become.

Institutional and constitutional reforms are not equivalent to behavioral reforms, and they need not depend critically on changing "man's nature." In economists' terminology, institutional-constitutional change operates upon the constraints within which persons maximize their own utilities; such change does not require that there be major shifts in the utility functions themselves.

Moral Community
and Moral Order
The Intensive and Extensive
Limits of Interaction

In an earlier paper, I argued that human moral capacity, defined as the potential outreach of one's moralistic behavior toward others of the species, is stretched beyond tolerance limits in modern political settings.[1] Humans are called upon to "care about" unknown persons with whom they have no means of identification, and with whom they share no common loyalty to external symbolic entities capable of stirring emotions. Thrust involuntarily into such settings, modern people necessarily behave so as to further their own narrowly defined self-interest. I inferred from this essentially empirical hypothesis that the moral potential of humankind could be exploited only if the institutions of political interaction were to be reconstructed so as to correspond more closely with the limits of the human moral "community."

In this paper, I want to build upon the earlier analysis and, in particular, to examine the position of animals in that human moral community. I now realize, however, that I failed in my earlier paper to make a necessary and categorical distinction between moral "community" and what I shall here call a "moral order." I shall argue that animals may be treated as members of

From *Ethics and Animals,* ed. Harlan B. Miller and William H. Williams (Clifton, N.J.: Humana Press, 1983), 95–102. Reprinted by permission of the publisher.

1. *Moral Community, Moral Order, and Moral Anarchy,* The Abbott Memorial Lecture No. 17 (Colorado Springs: Colorado College, 1981).

the human moral community, but that they have no place in the human "moral order," as the latter is distinguished from "community."

Membership in Moral Community

I want to discuss the question of membership in a moral community empirically. I want to discuss the behavior of persons precisely as we may, conceptually or actually, observe it, rather than how such behavior ought or ought not to be. In this context, I hypothesize that persons do include animals (more generally, nonhuman animals) in their moral communities, defined as relevant for behavior, and, further, that persons exclude *some* humans from such communities. In saying this, I am not, of course, advancing anything at all new or novel. Nonetheless, it does continue to surprise me to find how scarce are discussions of the implications of this simple hypothesis, or at least as I have found them. Discussions in morals and ethics concentrate on how, why, and when a person does or should "love my neighbor," without paying much attention to the more important question: Who is to count as "my neighbor"?

Human beings have within them instincts and drives that were developed, that evolved, from thousands of years of living in essentially tribal groupings. These instincts and drives presumably are related to those behavior patterns that enhance the survival characteristics of the tribal group. Such groups probably numbered between fifty and one hundred persons, and the human instinctual structure is presumably related to behavioral traits consistent with the survival of the tribe as a unit or entity. I am not concerned here with the problem of distinguishing that portion of these instinctive behavior patterns that may be genetic in origin from those that may have evolved culturally as a set of rules or codes of conduct. I want to postulate here only that human beings have within them such instincts that they do not, indeed cannot, understand and explain rationally in any scientific sense.[2]

---

2. In this postulate, and in much of the discussion of this whole paper, I should acknowledge my indebtedness to Professor F. A. Hayek, who has, especially in his most recent, and unpublished, works, largely in the form of lectures, stressed the importance of the potential conflicts between human tribal instincts and the social settings that humans confront.

In the tribal setting, the rules of conduct, or behavior patterns, would have led a modern external observer to attribute "morality" to persons, and to define readily the limits to the moral community of a particular person. Toward members of the tribe, behavior would appear to be "moral." Toward persons outside the tribal membership, no such behavior would be observed.

In such a conjectural setting, what can we postulate about human behavior toward animals? Clearly, to the extent that animals are essential elements in the tribal life-chain, behavior toward them would have attributes of "morality" little if any different from those directed toward human members. For animals beyond the needs of the tribal life-chain, behavior directed toward them would be akin to that directed toward human "outsiders."

Human beings have, of course, moved far beyond their tribal heritage, but carry within themselves the basic patterns evolved within the tribal setting. Civilization as such is simply too brief a span of history to have exerted important effects on basic genetic or culturally evolved human traits or proclivities.

As humans shifted from a tribal setting, where they were instinctively "at home," they faced challenging problems of behavioral adjustment. Basic instincts failed as soon as they found that they could not identify tribally with persons they confronted in any sort of personal interaction. There are essentially two separate and distinct socio-institutional responses to humankind's "dilemma of civil order," to the behavioral dilemma that humans in a nontribal setting have confronted, and continued to confront, since they emerged as civilized beings. Perhaps I should not refer to these as responses since, instead, they may be considered to be preconditions that allowed humans to supersede tribal organization in the first place. I shall discuss the two "attempts" or "responses" or "institutions" in the two following sections. At this point, however, I want to stress that the innate *moral* behavior of humans, that which is motivated by genuine "fellow-feeling" in an unthinking, unrationalized sense, remains tribal in its extent. Human beings react instinctively toward members of their "tribe" in a way that we might classify as "moral"; they do not extend such "morality" to those outside the tribal membership, whether the units encountered be human or nonhuman.

Extending the Intensive Limits
of Moral Community

In order to behave toward persons (and/or animals) beyond tribal boundaries in a manner that might be considered moral; that is, in order to behave
as if motivated by genuine concern for the well-being and the survival of
what we might call nonnatural members, *artificial* or *artifactual* criteria had
to be established that would allow persons to extend the insider group beyond its natural limits. And rules of conduct based on these essentially
arbitrary (noninstinctive) criteria had to be established and generally acknowledged.

The great religions can be interpreted as having been born in response to
such a set of requirements, and the treatment of persons beyond the pale reflects the straightforward extension (and aberration) of the categorical moral
differentiation between tribal members and outsiders. As tribal interbreed-
ing took place, but within narrowly defined groupings, something akin to
race emerged to offer yet a further correlate criterion for arbitrary moral differentiation. As communication was developed and politics established, geo-
graphical differentiation reflected in manners, in speech, in dress, provided
still further grounds for moral classification. In each case, however, the basically artificial nature of the rules for morality must be stressed. And those
humans who remained outside the new moral community were "heathens,"
to whom no moral rules of behavior were to be applied, and to whom no
sense of deservingness was owed. In this setting, then and now, animals
(nonhuman) and "heathens" were not treated differently in any moral sense.
Some of the great religions included the treatment of animals within their
artificially derived rules of conduct; some did not. In any case, however, the
membership of some animals within the instinctively based moral community of the tribe remained as a behavioral force.

Some of the religions were "open" in the sense that all persons might
qualify for membership, and hence for a status of moral equality, but the
moral differentiation between members and nonmembers carries over
throughout almost all religious history. Humanism, considered as a great
religion, may offer an exception to this generalization, but it never seems
to have exerted an influence comparable to the more discriminatory cults

that do, indeed, promise members better treatment on earth and/or elsewhere.

Have the great religions, inclusively defined to embody racial mythologies, nationalisms, and other symbolic bases for classification, been successful in pushing human moral capacities beyond tribal limits? A dual response is indicated here. As human interaction extended beyond the tribal limits, "the tribe," in any determinate sense, disappeared. Individual family units were left, more or less as floating islands, without a "tribal home." They found it almost necessary to adopt, in one form or another, the arbitrary schemata suggested to them by the religions. At one and the same time, however, individual human beings retained tribal instincts that did not allow them to behave morally toward arbitrarily defined and nonidentified humans. There remain distinct limits to human "moral capacities," the point that I discussed in my earlier paper. Humankind is thus caught up in the moral dilemma; it can and does have genuine fellow-feeling for a potentially limited set of others of its species, and for some animals. But it cannot, *naturally,* possess comparable fellow-feeling for a potentially unlimited set extending to the whole of humankind and, beyond, to all of life itself. Tribal constraints prohibit this extension of moral community. Those persons who exhibit such generality of moral concern are those who have most successfully sublimated or superseded the tribal constraints.

The conjectural "history" that I have sketched here may be open to criticism on many grounds. I have played fast and loose with subject matter from many disciplines: anthropology, history, psychology, genetics, theology, ethics, and others, in none of which do I claim any expertise. But I emphasize again that my central hypothesis is subject to empirical test and to refutation. I present it as such, and I use conjectural history in the 18th-century sense of offering an interesting story that you may or may not take as plausible. In a more formal variation, I should suggest only that human moral attitudes, as reflected in potentially observable behavior, may be depicted in the shape of a curve such as that drawn in Fig. 1, where the ordinate reflects the value an individual places on a life other than his own, and the abscissa represents an array of other lives (human and animal) in descending order of such evaluation. My hypothesis is summarized in the relatively sharp inflection points reached beyond members of the individual's family and beyond plausible limits of his localized community. I am

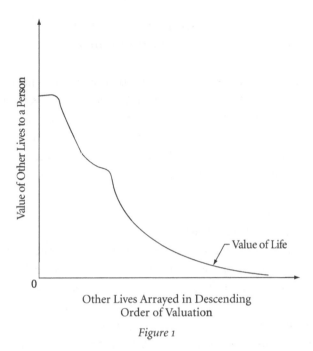

Figure 1

not suggesting, of course, that *all* persons are identical in their moral communities, far from it. There may well exist saints whose appropriate curve would be horizontal out to the limits of existence. As regards ordinary people, however, I am hypothesizing the generalized shape of the curve in Fig. 1, and, further, I am suggesting that for some people some animals fall in the array well above the limits where the human species is exhausted.[3]

---

3. Economists have discussed in some detail the interesting problems that emerge in placing values on human lives. Almost exclusively, however, the focus of their discussion has been on the question of valuation of his *own* life by the individual, or at least on the question of how such conceptual evaluation should be entered into a social policy benefit-cost comparison. There has been little explicit discussion of the equally interesting set of questions raised here. How do individuals value other lives than their own? A probabilistic approach to behavior similar to that used in the other analysis should yield clearly testable hypotheses. Casual empiricism suggests that in some cases, e.g., children, individuals may well place a *higher* value on lives other than their own. That is, a person may pay more for an extra margin of safety for his children than for himself.

The Extensive Limits of "Moral Order" as a Means of Effectively Superseding Moral Community

I now want to discuss the second response to humankind's challenge when it moved beyond tribal limits, a response that does not require an extension of its moral community, as this term might be ordinarily interpreted. That is to say, this second response does not require that humans extend, at least directly, their sense of concern for the well-being of others. The second response involves the generation of a "moral order," as opposed to "moral community," an order in which behavior may be constrained by rules that, in themselves, seem basically *amoral*. Indeed, I should argue that it is through the development of the rules of such a "moral order" that humans have successfully confronted the challenge of civilization. The moral order that allows humankind to supersede the effective limits of its expressly revealed moral community is best described as the order of *law*, in which persons abide by abstract rules of law that lay down rights of separate persons and that provide bases for mutual respect, tolerance, and, most importantly, for trade and exchange that, in turn, greatly enhances the level of personal well-being for all participants.

It is important to clarify the distinction between the explicitly *moral* behavior extended to members of a person's appropriately defined moral community and the sort of behavior toward others, which is basically *amoral*, that characterizes relationships in the market. An example may be helpful. A beggar will starve without bread; a person who recognizes the beggar as a member of his or her moral community and gives that beggar bread is behaving *morally* in the standard usage of this term. The donor carries out a moral act, motivated by a sense of concern for the beggar's well-being, directly or indirectly experienced. Let us now modify the example only slightly. A second beggar is observed to possess a loaf of bread, without which the indigent will starve. A person who refrains from stealing the bread from that beggar is not carrying out a moral act; such behavior is, in my terminology, or may be, *amoral*. To steal the bread would be *immoral*, but to refrain from stealing implies neither concern nor lack of concern for the beggar's well-being. Similarly, in the first example, to refrain from giving bread to the starving beggar cannot, in itself, be classified as immoral action. To refrain from giving bread in this case and to refrain from stealing bread in the second case both reflect amoral behavior, but behavior that is still in accordance with abstract rules consistent with a moral order of law, characterized by mutual tolerance of other persons and mutual respect for other persons' rights.

I hope that this example clarifies the distinction that I am trying to develop here. If there exists no moral order of law, the treatment of the beggars would, in each case, depend strictly on whether or not the other person, the potential donor or potential thief, did or did not accept the beggar as a member of his or her own moral community. There would, in this setting, be no distinction to be made between giving bread on the one hand and refraining from stealing on the other, or, conversely, between refusing to give bread and stealing in the second case. The relatively narrow limits of human interaction that could take place under such restrictions should be clear. General adherence to the moral order of law, however, and to the distinct rules of behavior that such an order embodies, allows persons to interact one with another independent of membership in expressly defined moral community one with another. This extremely simple point should never be overlooked, nor its importance neglected. A personal example may illustrate.

I wrote the initial draft of this paper during a period of several weeks in Vienna in early 1979. My conversational German is almost nonexistent, and my knowledge of Vienna's history and culture is limited. Yet I was able to function, very satisfactorily, in this community of "foreigners," or "aliens," to me, who were not, I am sure, in the least concerned for my own private welfare. I did not qualify for membership in the Viennese or Austrian moral community at all. But I was able to survive well by a knowledge of and adherence to a system of rules that involved a mutuality of respect for the rights of property, that of my own and those persons with whom I had dealings! It is easy to imagine the difficulties I might have encountered in a genuinely "foreign" land that was not characterized by such agreed-on rules of behavior and in which, quite literally, I should have been required to depend on the genuine "morality" of others to survive. And is not this precisely the distinguishing difference between "civil order" and "anarchy"?

The example is helpful also in suggesting that human behavior in the moral order of law is and must be unique to humans, or to that subset of the human species that abides by the appropriate abstract rules. In a "society" of animals outside such a subset, whether the animals be human or nonhuman, there is no way that a person might know what rules of conduct to follow if any at all were appropriate. My professor, Frank Knight, used to say that humans are, or may be, law-abiding animals, which is about all I am really saying here.

Conclusions

To bring my discussion back somewhat more closely to the subject matter of this conference, my discussion implies that the "moral treatment of animals" simply does not arise in an evaluation of human behavior toward fellow humans in the moral order of law. The moral treatment of animals does arise when the whole issue of limits to humankind's expressly moral community is raised. My emphasis on the necessary distinction between this moral community and the moral order that describes the potential for extending relationships far beyond those that may otherwise be possible reflects the disciplinary perspective or bias from which I commenced my inquiries. As stated at the outset, my hypothesis is that some animals are normally within the human moral community. I am relatively uninterested in the normative question whether any, some, or all life *should* be contained within such moral limits. This absence of interest in the normative question does not imply that I claim to be a "positive" scientist who remains aloof from the "should" or "ought" questions. Far from it. The normative issues that excite my interest are, however, the different ones that involve the proven values of maintaining and extending the moral order of law, within which humans become less dependent on the presence or absence of personal morality in the community sense. Modern politics, with its overreaching and apparently insatiable appetite for further and further intrusion into human behavior, tends to confuse the distinction that I have tried to stress here.

A Two-Country Parable

Consider a conceptual experiment. There are two physically separated locational units (call them "countries") that are descriptively identical and also are inhabited initially by equal numbers of humans, who are possessed of identical potential capacities. Throughout the historical period to be considered, there is no economic relationship between inhabitants of the two countries that extends across boundaries. Each unit exists in autarky.

Over some period of time, one of the two countries, call it A, either through an evolutionary process not well understood or through deliberative design and construction of constitutional constraints, comes to be organized in such a fashion that facilitates the production (and potential consumption) of a relatively high level of economic value (as determined by the preferences of inhabitants) and also facilitates relatively high increases in this level of value through time. By comparison, the other country, call it B, although initially equally endowed, does not experience a similar evolution and/or does not undergo a process of successful design and construction of constitutional parameters, effective as measured by the potential for facilitating the generation and growth of economic value. As a result of these disparate histories, the economy of country B produces a relatively low level of value, as measured by the preferences of its inhabitants, and this level increases relatively slowly through time, if at all.

In simpler terms, no matter where he or she is situated positionally within

From *Justice in Immigration,* ed. Warren F. Schwartz, *Cambridge Studies in Philosophy and Law* (New York: Cambridge University Press, 1995), 63–66. Reprinted by permission of the publisher.

This essay is a commentary on Chapter 2 of this volume, by Coleman and Harding. It has proved the most difficult I have ever tried to write. The argument presented here is the third in a series of efforts. My only consolation is that the authors of the main essay seem to have had comparable difficulties.

a country, the life of an inhabitant differs substantially between the two separated countries. Persons are relatively "rich" in one setting, A, and relatively "poor" in the other, B. In this situation, many of the inhabitants of country B will desire to migrate to country A if given any opportunity to do so. The question at issue here is: Do those who find themselves to be inhabitants (citizens) of A have any obligation, grounded in principles of justice, to allow those who seek entry to become members?

I suggest that the conceptual experiment constructed here offers the appropriate framework for addressing the issues. It seems inappropriate to postulate the existence of some "glob" of potential economic value in the world, a "glob" that emerges independent of productive effort on the part of persons and, in particular, emerges independent of organizational-institutional constraints within which persons act to produce value.

To separate the issues from those that might be based on measured economic interests, I postulate that in-migration, within reasonable limits, will neither increase nor decrease the economic well-being of those persons who initially inhabit the "rich" polity. We may think of a situation in which the effect of increasing returns from an expanded network of production and exchange (which allows for an extended division and specialization of labor) is precisely offset by the decreasing returns that arise from congestibility of fixed environmental parameters, including physical space itself. Possible economic effects on those inhabitants who might remain in the "poor" country after others have emigrated may also be made irrelevant by assuming that the two forces mentioned offset each other in directions that run counter to those in the "rich" country.

Under these highly abstracted conditions, immigrants do not impose either costs or benefits on previously existing inhabitants of the country A or on those inhabitants of country B who might remain after emigrants have departed. The situation, as described, would seem to offer the most favorable set of circumstances under which potential immigrants might advance claims for relocation based on principles of justice.

I suggest, however, that even in this idealized setting, no such claim can be supported. Let me attempt to justify my argument by examining more carefully just what immigration involves. The entry of an immigrant into an ongoing social-political-legal-economic order with a defined membership, an experienced history, and a set of informal conventions necessarily modifies the structure of "the game" itself, the complex and ill-understood set of interpersonal and intergroup relationships that generates the pattern of results that are observed by participants. I have postulated that there is no net effect on other persons that results from the addition of a person to the economic network. But this economic assumption is not itself sufficient to ensure an absence of effects from the addition of a full member to the existing group of inhabitants. Membership involves more than a joining of the economic interchange network. Membership carries with it power and authority, even if small, to modify the political-legal-constitutional parameters within which the ongoing economic game is played. The logic of partial derivation, which may be helpful in evaluating the measured economic effects of changes in the size of the interacting network, loses explanatory power to the extent that we allow persons to exercise genuine choices in their participation as ultimate sovereigns in the choices among the rules within which they carry out their relationships, one with another.

The argument here suggests that there is a direct relationship between the "democratization" of the parametric structure for sociopolitical interaction and the tolerance for immigration. An order that is described by constitutional stability that is based on continuing consensus that is, in turn, based on a genuine understanding of the difference between choice within rules and choice among rules may be much more tolerant toward entry of new members than an order that is described by continuous constitutional change emerging from shifting political coalitions. As my colleague Jennifer Roback has argued in connection with secession and territorial expansion, the coalitional politics of modern democracies make for major shifts in the evaluation of any alternatives that involve shifts in membership size.[1]

The argument is not intended to imply that immigration barriers should be established in any and all polities unless there are dominating, strictly economic reasons for allowing the entry of new members. The argument is intended to suggest, instead, that the effects of adding new members extend well beyond those that might be measured in economic terms and that they

1. Jennifer Roback, "Expansion, Secession and Lawlessness: A Contractarian Constitutional Approach" (George Mason University: Center for Study of Public Choice, March 18, 1992), paper presented at a meeting of the American Philosophical Association, Portland, Oregon.

become especially important in modern democratic states. The institutional parameters that have made some of these states relatively "rich" are often not understood, and the fragility of these parameters in the face of noninformed politicization must be incorporated in any calculus of evaluation. Action toward potential immigrants that may seem motivated by considerations of justice or compassion may generate results that are directionally reversed from those initially anticipated.

Finally, my argument does not carry with it any putative claim that those who happen to be current inhabitants of "rich" countries have other than purely existential rights to the positions they occupy. These persons may have had little or no part in the selection and maintenance of the institutional-constitutional structure that has allowed for the creation of relatively high levels of value. But in all such discussions, it is necessary to recognize that the starting point is the here and now. That which might have been will never be.

The argument that I have advanced suggests that there is a logical basis for differentiation between the entry of full members in an ongoing political community and the entry of persons into relationships that exclude direct political participation. Under the abstract conditions postulated for the example, persons from B might be allowed entry into A as "guest workers," since they impose no net economic harms on other persons in A or B, while themselves securing major benefits. Compassion alone might dictate this result. And, of course, an even stronger argument might be made for opening up markets in A, which may serve as a substitute for immigration.

Economic Origins
of Ethical Constraints

Christian churchism (teaches that) thou shalt attend to thy neighbor's business before thou attendest to thine own.

— Ezra Pound

The basic relationships between formal or legal constraints and ethical constraints on human behavior are widely recognized, both in theory and in
practice. To the extent that persons in social interaction, one with another,
behave in accordance with commonly shared ethical precepts, any rationally
based contractual justification for generalized legal constraints becomes
weaker. Common public awareness tells us that if relatively few persons steal,
and/or if these few steal relatively little, fewer and less restrictive laws against
stealing are needed, along with fewer policemen.

It is relatively straightforward to locate the logical origins of formal constraints in a calculus of individual self-interest.[1] To my knowledge, there exists no comparable explanatory exercise with respect to the origins of ethical
constraints. This chapter is a preliminary attempt to fill this gap.[2]

From *The Economics and the Ethics of Constitutional Order* (Ann Arbor: University of
Michigan Press, 1991), 179–93. Copyright 1991 by The University of Michigan. Reprinted
by permission of the publisher.

1. James M. Buchanan, *The Limits of Liberty: Between Anarchy and Leviathan* (Chicago:
University of Chicago Press, 1975).

2. For a more extended treatment that emerged from discussions of a preliminary
draft of this chapter, see Hartmut Kliemt, "Moral Externalities," in *Papers on Buchanan
and Related Subjects* (Munich: Accedo Verlagsgesellschaft, 1990), 37–60.

From an individualist perspective, a person involved in social interaction seeks to constrain the behavior of others, either through contractually derived legal rules or through the nonformal operation of ethical norms, only if and when nonconstrained behavior is predicted to impose damages, as measured in anticipated utility losses, at least in some opportunity cost sense. The existence of *externality* is necessary for the initiation of any effort aimed at constraining behavior. And, in this setting, legal and ethical constraints become alternative institutions of internalization.

Section 1 sets out the analytical framework through the introduction of familiar two-by-two matrix illustrations, which are, in each case, generalizable to the many-person setting by designating one player to be "all others." Emphasis is placed on the distinction between economic and ethical interdependence. Section 2 identifies the direct relationship between economic self-interest and investment in the ethical internalization of externalities. Section 3 examines the productivity of investments in persuasion. Section 4 extends the analysis and addresses the issues of comparability under modified preference orderings. In section 5, the discussion is related to the Hayekian theory of the evolution of moral order. The analysis is then summarized in section 6 through a comparison of the ethical constraints derived here with both legal-formal constraints and ethical constraints derived in alternative constructions.

I advance no claim of explanatory inclusiveness here; I suggest only that an understanding and appreciation of the economic origins of the ethical constraints on behavior move us somewhat closer to a match between our models of behavior and observed empirical reality. That is to say, the analysis here adds a hitherto missing element in our general understanding of why persons behave as they are observed to behave in social interaction.

1. Relevance and Irrelevance in Contractual (Economic) and Ethical Internalization of Externalities

The simple two-by-two matrix illustration in figure 15.1 will be readily identified by the cognoscenti as the standard Prisoners' Dilemma, with the numerical payoffs representing ordinal utility indicators for the two players. Almost all of the analysis and discussion in modern social contract theory, inclusively defined to cover applications that range from the origins of private property

B

		b₁	b₂
	a₁	I 3, 3	II 1, 4
A			
	a₂	III 4, 1	IV 2, 2

Figure 15.1

and the state, to public goods, environmental cleanups, through to matters of social etiquette have been (or could have been) put in this highly abstracted setting. The central result leaps out upon elementary observation. The self-interested, own-utility maximizing behavior of each of the two players generates a result or outcome that neither desires or would have independently chosen. The choice setting is such that separate and noncoordinated behavior on the part of each player produces a solution that violates the Pareto criterion for efficiency or optimality. Both players could be made better off, as measured by each player's own-utility indicator, in an alternative cell in the matrix, a cell that would reflect a different pattern of behavior but one that remains within the set of feasible options.

Attention is immediately focused on prospects for a coordinated or cooperative strategy, one that would represent agreement by the actors on a jointly chosen, two-element behavioral set that would shift the outcome to cell I, which would be preferred by each player to the noncoordinated outcome in cell IV. In the terminology of welfare economics, cell I is Pareto-preferred to cell IV. The indicated joint or cooperative behavior becomes possible, however, only if a binding agreement or enforceable contract between the players is possible. And an institutional change that would be represented by such a contract would act to modify the utility payoffs faced by each player.

In such a potential contract, note that each player trades or exchanges his or her own freedom to act independently for the reciprocal constraint accepted by his or her partner to the deal. Each player agrees to bind himself, not for the purpose of placing limits on his or her own behavior for his or her own benefit (not for self-control, à la Ulysses) but because only an acceptance of such constraint can secure the reciprocal constraint on the behavior of another party or parties to the agreement. And such an agreement-contract becomes possible without any requirement that either of the parties express concern for the well-being or utility of the other person or persons in the nexus.

In the setting depicted in figure 15.1, the two players are economically interdependent. Neither person, acting on his or her own and independently, can do as well as he or she could do by engaging the other in exchange or trade. This interdependence is reflected in the relative utility payoffs in cells I and IV. But note that the two players are also ethically interdependent. The separate behavior of one person outside or apart from any agreement on a coordinated strategy, affects the utility of the other person unilaterally. This sort of interdependence is reflected in the relationship between the ordinal utility payoffs in cell IV (the independent adjustment solution) and either cell II or cell III, each of which would represent a shift to cooperative behavior by only one of the two actors.

In the restricted setting of figure 15.1, the contractual and the ethical means toward internalization of the reciprocal externality are substitutes in a straightforward sense. If both parties can be converted to behave in accordance with an ethical precept that dictates cooperation (a_1 and b_1 in fig. 15.1), there is no need for an explicit contractual agreement.

In a paper written jointly with W. C. Stubblebine three decades ago,[3] we introduced the distinction between Pareto-relevant and Pareto-irrelevant externalities. A Pareto-relevant externality exists when the behavior of one or both parties in an interaction affects the utility levels of other parties, *and* there exist potential arrangements through which the behavior can be modified to the benefit of *all* parties. That is to say, Pareto-superior corrective changes are possible, by definition, when Pareto-relevant externalities exist. In the standard Prisoners' Dilemma case depicted in figure 15.1, the reciprocal externality is clearly Pareto relevant. Either contractual or ethical internalization can shift the solution to the Pareto-preferred cell I.

An externality is defined to be Pareto irrelevant if the behavior of one or all parties to the interaction continues to affect the utility levels of other par-

3. James M. Buchanan and W. C. Stubblebine, "Externality," *Economica* 29 (November 1962): 371–84.

ties but there exist no alternative arrangements through which this behavior can be modified to the expressed mutual benefit of all parties. The payoff matrix of figure 15.2 illustrates this case, again under the symmetry assumptions consequent on the use of ordinal utility indicators.

The economist will directly observe that, despite the continued presence of row and column dominance that describes the payoff matrix, no potential for corrective adjustment appears. In the choice setting depicted in figure 15.2, independent behavior on the part of each of the two players will generate the cell IV solution, as before, but this solution is now Pareto optimal. No further gains from trade, no matter how complex, are possible. Hence, the economist, who concentrates his or her attention almost exclusively on trade, exchange, and contract, will not be concerned with such interactions. There is no economic interdependence that remains for further exploitation in the independent adjustment solution in figure 15.2.

Note, however, that the reciprocal externality relationship remains. The two persons remain ethically interdependent in the sense used earlier, in that each person's utility can be affected by a unilateral shift in the behavior of the other. To the economist, the externality that remains is Pareto irrelevant.

What, precisely, does Pareto irrelevance mean in this setting? The shift on the part of A from the a_2 to the a_1 strategy will, as in figure 15.1, exert spillover benefits on B (and vice versa for a behavioral shift by B in affecting A). But B remains unwilling to accept constraints on his or her own behavior that require a shift from b_2 to b_1, if this should be required. The spillover benefits to B, from A's shift from a_2 to a_1, are less than the internal utility loss that B expects to suffer in modifying his or her own behavior from b_2 to b_1. The potential losses from the potential behavioral "exchange" exceed the gains; hence, the reciprocal externality, though it remains, is Pareto irrelevant.

B

		b_1	b_2
A	a_1	2, 2	1, 4
	a_2	4, 1	3, 3

Figure 15.2

As a simple comparison suggests, there is a categorical difference in the *economic* characteristics of the two choice settings depicted in figures 15.1 and 15.2. However, the comparison also reveals that there is essentially no difference in the *ethical* content of the interaction. That is to say, the distinction between the Pareto-relevant reciprocal externality (fig. 15.1) and the Pareto-irrelevant reciprocal externality (fig. 15.2) does not, in itself, carry ethical implications.

This result is not, of course, surprising when it is recognized that the utility dimension is not the same in the economic and the ethical relationship. Any economic evaluation of a choice setting involves some assessment of the potential gains and losses from a change for *both* (or all) parties. Exchange is necessarily reciprocal; each trader gives up something of value in exchange for something of value given up by the other trader. In the universe of social interactions, it seems clear that the set of possible mutually beneficial exchanges will be small relative to the set of unilaterally beneficial gifts. (The Christmas tie would never have been purchased; yet it remains undiscarded on the tie rack in the closet.)

2. Ethics and Economic Self-Interest

The absence of an ethical distinction between the two types of interaction analyzed in section 1 suggests that the motivation behind efforts to seek out ethical internalization is more general than that behind efforts to organize trades or contractual agreements. As a glance at figures 15.1 and 15.2 indicates, each party will, in either setting, place a value on unilateral action by the other party that is higher than that placed on any two-party behavioral shift. Each person, in each setting, will find it advantageous that the other person in the interaction choose a cooperative strategy on the basis of ethical or moral principle. The "ideal" arrangement for any person is located when he or she remains at liberty to act as his or her raw utility indicator dictates while the other party acts cooperatively.[4]

---

4. See James M. Buchanan, "Ethical Rules, Expected Values, and Large Numbers," *Ethics* 76 (October 1965): 1–13; reprinted in idem, *Freedom in Constitutional Contract: Perspectives of a Political Economist* (College Station: Texas A&M University Press, 1978), 151–68.

In either of the two settings depicted, each person has a direct economic interest in the ethical or moral characteristics of the behavior of the other. Hence, unless this latter behavior is assumed to be wholly beyond the possibility of change, each person finds it privately rational to invest at least some resources in efforts to modify the behavior of the other unilaterally in the direction of enhanced cooperation. If, at the same time, the technology involved in "producing" any such desired behavioral shift embodies publicness of the classical variety, the result is that generalized investment in the promulgation of moral norms will be observed, with all parties being subjected to essays in persuasion carried out by specialists, whom we may call "the preachers."

Note that this result is described by the provision of privately costly inputs by all parties, but with this provision being accompanied by no conscious sense that any explicit exchange of inputs is taking place. Each party considers the return on his or her investment to be measured by the potential change in the behavior of the other party (parties). Each party gives up some valued resource in exchange for some prospect of a change in the other party's behavior. But there is no agreement, either explicit or implicit, that involves either party's willingness to constrain his or her own behavior, which represents potential value loss, in exchange for reciprocal constraints.

It is helpful to compare and/or contrast the economic analysis approach to ethics advanced here with its familiar alternatives. In each of these, the origin of the constraint that is expected to modify individual behavior is *internal* to the calculus of the actor. Attention is exclusively focused on answering the question: *Why* might the choosing-acting person behave cooperatively, when opportunistic utility maximization indicates noncooperation? The first, and most familiar, alternative invokes the dominance of learned and self-imposed moral norms, which are quite consciously allowed to supervene a sensed loss of utility in directing behavior. The individual follows the moral norm in an expressed departure from that course of action that would maximize his or her expected utility. The second alternative simply redefines utility maximization in such a way that the acting-choosing individual fully takes into account the long-range consequences of his or her behavior, and particularly as it may motivate, at least probabilistically, reciprocating behavior on the part of others in the relevant social interaction. The third, and closely related, alternative incorporates a disposition to cooperate more directly into the meaning of rationality and does not require reckoning of long-range consequences.[5] In one sense, of course, the second and third alternatives here do not seek to explain the origins of ethical constraints; instead, these approaches involve attempted demonstrations that behavior normally considered to be ethical or moral follows from properly conceived self-interest on the part of persons caught in dilemma-type interactions, one with another.

By contrast with these alternative means of incorporating something like cooperative behavior internally into the individual's choice calculus, the model presented here does not require either that moral norms override utility maximization or that utility maximization be reinterpreted to generate behavior that looks like it is motivated by moral concerns. My approach in this chapter does not seek an *internal* origin for the modified set of constraints that may be required to resolve, in whole or in part, the generalized social dilemma. Note that in the settings depicted in figures 15.1 and 15.2, I have emphasized only that parties in the interactions retain an economic self-interest in modifying the behavior of others, and that they will seek to further this interest by investment in "behavior modification" if this prospect is technically feasible. To the extent that the result of such investment embodies more cooperative behavior on the part of one, or all, parties, the origins of the behavioral changes are *external* to the choosing-acting participants. Neither some self-imposed ethical limit nor some heightened awareness of "true" self-interest is called on to generate the escape, partial or total, from the utility losses produced by ethical interdependencies.

3. The Productivity of Preachers

As noted, straightforward utility maximization on the part of persons who recognize the existence of ethical interdependency dictates some investment of resources in efforts to secure unilateral behavioral changes by others in the social interaction, provided only that such an investment, over some range, yields a return over and above opportunity costs. And, of course, rationality norms would suggest that the extent of such an investment would

5. David Gauthier, *Morals by Agreement* (Oxford: Oxford University Press, 1985).

be determined when expected marginal yield here is equalized with other investments.

Economists, in particular, have tended to neglect analysis of this sort of investment because their disciplinary tool kit embodies the fixity of utility or preference functions. If individuals' preferences are indeed rigid, and hence immune to change, any investment in efforts aimed to modify behavior through inducing preference shifts must remain totally unproductive. In this setting, persons who recognize the presence of ethical interdependence have no recourse other than exchange or contract, which is, as indicated above, viable only for the Pareto-relevant subset.

For many purposes, the economists' working hypothesis of fixed preferences is useful, but surely any rigid advocacy of this hypothesis as descriptive of behavioral reality makes the economic enterprise vulnerable to the familiar communitarian criticism which is then extended to any and all efforts to derive characteristics of social interaction from individual choices. The methodological individualist must, it seems to me, acknowledge the relationships between individual utility functions and the socioeconomic-legal-political-cultural setting within which evaluations are made. But such acknowledgment carries with it, almost as a matter of course, the possible productivity of investment in the promulgation of moral norms. The relative efficacy of such investment will, of course, vary among the several targets of effort. Persons who are hardwired into the set of preferences that dictate strictly opportunistic behavior, as defined by the observing economist, will represent less productive yields to the "preachers" than the persons whose preferences are less firmly anchored.

To be productive, investments in the promulgation of moral norms must change behavior through a shift in utility functions. But return to the internal-external distinction emphasized earlier. The analysis here does not require that persons seek to change *their own* preferences. While it may be empirically descriptive to say, with Frank Knight, that persons really "want better wants," we do not need to take this additional step here. We need no such bootstrap ethics. Individuals may or may not seek to modify their own preferences. My model suggests, much more restrictively, that persons rationally will "want others to want better wants," or, specifically, that others behave more cooperatively toward themselves in social intercourse.

4. Internalization by Ethics

The next stage in the argument is to demonstrate precisely how ethical inter-dependence is internalized by rationally selected, and, hence, successful in-vestment in the promulgation of moral norms. As the simple two-by-two matrices of figures 15.1 and 15.2 indicate, each person faces a rational incen-tive to undertake an investment in modifying the preference ordering of the other. Let us suppose that, for the discrete, two-element behavioral set of each person, the investment of each participant is successful in changing the behavior of the other. As mentioned, however, this result can take place only if preference orderings over the relevant outcomes are shifted. If we remain within the discrete two-by-two matrices, successful two-way promulgation of the cooperative behavioral norm must modify the preference orderings to those embodied in figure 15.3.

The combined orderings in figure 15.3 continue to exhibit both row and column dominance for players in their choices. The solution in cell 1 is pre-ferred by both parties to any other outcome that is attainable by either indi-vidual or joint action. Note that the presumed successful effort on the part of each party to modify the preference ordering of the other internalizes the

		B	
		b_1	b_2
A	a_1	4, 4	2, 3
	a_2	3, 2	1, 1

or

		B	
		b_1	b_2
A	a_1	4, 4	3, 2
	a_2	2, 3	1, 1

Figure 15.3

externalities that were present in the settings of both figures 15.1 and 15.2. There is no problem with the dilemma-type setting of figure 15.1; the shift in utility functions has been such as to enable the interacting parties to shift to the cooperative solution, which is Pareto optimal, under *either* configuration of preferences.

But what conclusion can be drawn when we compare figure 15.3 to figure 15.2? By having their preference orderings modified so as to induce cooperative behavior, a solution in cell I is insured. But this outcome is not Pareto optimal if evaluation is carried out in terms of the nonmodified, or "raw," preference orderings of figure 15.2. Does the internalization of the externality represent an improvement in the well-being of the parties in this case, or the reverse? Or is there, here, a welfare theory example of an index number problem?

In one sense, of course, the two solutions remain noncomparable, since for analytical purposes we define an individual by a preference ordering over alternative outcomes. Hence, a shift in the ordering redefines the person; evaluative comparisons become empty. But we may, to some extent at least, overcome this personal identity problem (so dear to philosophers) by looking more carefully at the payoff matrices of figures 15.2 and 15.3. The independent adjustment, or Nash equilibrium, in each of these cases is Pareto optimal if evaluated in terms of the preference orderings that generated the equilibrium. But there is an element of social stability present in the equilibrium of figure 15.3 that is absent in that of figure 15.2. As previously noted, in the cell IV solution of figure 15.2, each party continues to have an incentive to invest in changing the behavior of the other in the direction of inducing more cooperation. And, as discussed above, if these investments succeed, a shift of orderings to those shown in figure 15.3 becomes possible. In the solution of figure 15.3, however, no comparable externality remains. Each party now has an incentive to insure that the other party's behavior remains unchanged, and, hence, that there be no shift in utility functions. To the extent that some slacking off of the morally induced behavioral pattern is anticipated, investment in moral suasion may continue, but now this investment will be directed toward maintenance of the ethical status quo. The solution in figure 15.3 can be described as an *ethical equilibrium* as well as an exchange or economic equilibrium. The second characterization tells us that players have no further incentive to initiate trades, contracts, or agreements. The first tells us that the players have no incentive to initiate efforts to change the behavior of others, a feature that is absent from the equilibrium of figure 15.2.

The highly simplified and abstracted models introduced here are useful in allowing the central features of personal interaction to be identified, but the possible extension to more complex interaction settings would be recognized. The two-element behavioral set of alternatives faced by each player (cooperate-defect) can, of course, be replaced by a multielement set which might approach continuous variation in some limit. And the symmetry between players emerges from the use of ordinal utility indicators and need not be a condition of interaction. More importantly, the two-person interaction can be generalized to cover individual behavior in n-person settings, where each player confronts "all others" in some relevant sense. While this change in the models leaves the logical structure of the analysis in place, it does reduce the possible direct incentive that each person has to invest privately in the promulgation of moral norms designed to affect the behavior of others. The results of such investment become genuinely public goods in large-number settings, and each individual will have familiar free-rider incentives to hold back on his or her own contribution. Collective organization of the moral persuasion enterprise may be necessary. These free-rider difficulties are, of course, equally severe in securing support for enforcement outlays required for contractually agreed schemes of cooperation, that is, for ordinary laws against defection. Since, however, contractually agreed schemes are, ideally, limited to those interactions that exhibit potential economic interdependence when uncorrected, while ethical interdependencies are more inclusive, we should predict that there will exist an inverse relationship between the size of the relevant interacting community and the amount of investment (per person) in the promulgation, transmission, and maintenance of moral norms.

5. The Evolution of Moral Order

F. A. Hayek, particularly in his later works,[6] has emphasized the cultural evolution of the norms of a moral order, norms that are quite distinct from

---

6. F. A. Hayek, *The Political Order of a Free People*, vol. 3 of *Law, Legislation and Liberty* (Chicago: University of Chicago Press, 1979).

those of a moral community, and he has persuasively argued that some emergence of culturally evolved norms was a necessary condition for the modern leap into what he calls the "great society," where social interaction is extended to include persons who do not share membership in genetically derived groupings, those that describe moral communities.[7] Hayek has stressed that individuals who behave in accordance with the norms of a moral order are not conscious of, and do not understand, the origins of such norms.

For my purposes, it is noteworthy that the norms stressed by Hayek are roughly those that we have concentrated on in the game-theoretic settings of this chapter. These norms do not, in any case, require explicit concern for the utility of others; altruism does not enter the calculus. They include, instead, such moral precepts as promise keeping and respect for personal and property rights. Again roughly, the ethics is that which is appropriate for sportsmanship; the norms embody playing by the rules; they exclude cheating.

The analysis in this chapter offers a possible understanding of *why* the behavioral rules necessary for the functioning of a moral order emerged. By drawing attention to the economic interest that each person has in the behavior of others with whom he or she interacts, or may interact, we have located a source for efforts directed toward a modification of preference orderings that may, ultimately, generate the behavioral changes desired. We need add only the presumption that such investment is, to some extent and over some range, productive in order to "explain" the process through which preference orderings, generally, come to be changed.

The emergence of the minimally cooperative norms that are necessary for the effective functioning of the extended economic nexus offers a good example of "order without design," again stressed by Hayek and attributed to the insights of the eighteenth-century Scots moral philosophers. In the scenario suggested here, each individual who anticipates participation in social interaction with others will have a direct, and continuing, incentive to take action to insure that others with whom he or she may interact "play by the

---

7. I have elaborated the differences between membership in, and individual behavior within, moral community and a moral order in James M. Buchanan, *Moral Community, Moral Order, or Moral Anarchy,* Abbott Memorial Lecture Monograph no. 17 (Colorado Springs: Colorado College, 1981); reprinted in idem, *Liberty, Market and State: Political Economy in the 1980s* (Great Britain: Wheatsheaf Books, 1986), 108–20.

rules." There need be no consciousness of the generalized importance of an inclusive economic-political-legal nexus characterized by such behavior, and there is no sense of submission, personally, to some agreed upon set of rule following constraints. Because, however, all participants are roughly symmetrical, or may be, in their incentives here, persons will necessarily find themselves subjected to external persuasive pressures that may succeed in modifying their own orderings, with no internally generated conscious shift. Ultimately, all participants may find themselves "wanting to play by the rules," even if they have no sense of being coerced to choose and act other than in their own interests, while, at the same time, they do not trust others to behave similarly without continued efforts at persuasion.

6. Summary and Comparison

Why do individuals in socioeconomic relationships, one with another, behave in ways that seem to be contrary to their own economic interest, as such interest may be assessed by an external observer? This question is of especial importance to the economist because the empirical evidence seems to place limits on the explanatory range of his or her basic behavioral hypothesis, despite the empirical support for this hypothesis over an extensive domain of human action. How can the economist draw the distinction between these choice settings in which operationally meaningful utility maximization hypotheses apply and those settings in which some emendation of these hypotheses are required for explaining the choice behavior that is observed?

Let me be more specific. Why do individuals play by the rules of the socioeconomic game? Why do they often seem to shun and to pass by opportunities that would, if expediently seized, further their own apparent self-interest? The argument that I have developed in this chapter can be adequately summarized in a comparison with different responses to these questions.

THE COSTS OF VIOLATING RULES

The standard economists' response to the question invokes the presence of collectively enforced rules that insure the imposition of costs on violators sufficient to change the ordinal payoffs from those that describe the no-rule setting. In this model, individuals act always to maximize measured self-interest, and they would not refrain from cheating in the absence of formal rules when such behavior is anticipated to advance their interests. The dilemma-type choice settings of figure 15.1 are used to justify contractual-collective agreements that effectively enforce cooperative behavior on the part of all parties. The agreement itself, "the law," will and must include penalties sufficient to shift the original utility payoffs to those of figure 15.3.

This model leaves no space for that realm of social intercourse that is ordered voluntarily by nonopportunistic behavior. Simple empirical observation suggests that this realm of "orderly anarchy" may be large, relative to that which is described by the existence of formal rules. The economists' response must be judged incomplete.

OVERRIDING TRANSCENDENTAL NORMS

The responses that depend on some internally generated motivation of behavior that departs from the strictly interpreted *Homo economicus* hypothesis have been already introduced in section 2 and may be briefly summarized here. In the most traditional of these models, advanced by ethical philosophers through the ages, "higher values" derived from sources external to the individual are allowed to become compelling in some choice settings, even when they conflict with the actor's preference orderings. "Values" trump "tastes." The opportunity cost, measured in utility sacrificed, from behaving in accordance with moral precepts is acutely sensed by the chooser-actor.

The problem with this essentially Augustinian model lies, first, in locating the source of the external values, and, second, in the articulation of a choice calculus that would require action contrary to preference.

ENLIGHTENED SELF-INTEREST

David Hume's response relies on a redefinition of individual self-interest rather than on any behavioral departure from utility maximization.[8] An individual's interest, properly defined, embodies predictions about the generalized consequences of departures from broadly cooperative interactive

8. For modern variants of Hume's argument, see Robert Axelrod, *The Evolution of Cooperation* (New York: Basic Books, 1984); and Robert Sugden, *The Economics of Rights, Cooperation, and Welfare* (Oxford: Basil Blackwell, 1986).

strategies, especially in settings characterized by repeated or continuous dealings. An individual's choice to play beyond, or in violation of, established rules, that is to cheat, even when it may seem expedient to do so, must reckon on the potential for reciprocating behavior on the part of others in subsequent rounds of play. Full recognition of such feedback effects may, for many choice settings, suggest that rule following remains privately rational.

The limits of the Humean argument are evident. There remain many choice settings in which individual defection or violation promises to yield utility gains with little or no prospect for subsequent losses.

EXTENDED RATIONALITY

David Gauthier has mounted a valiant modern effort to extend the very meaning of rational choice to include cooperative, rather than noncooperative, behavior in all dilemma-like settings.[9] If the individual recognizes the mutual destructiveness involved in following straightforward utility maximization strategies, he or she will find it rational to take on a "disposition to cooperate" when he or she identifies others like himself or herself in social interaction. Morality in the form of cooperative behavior will emerge from the implicit agreement of the parties, and need not call on anticipations of repeated encounters or on transcendental norms. The Gauthier enterprise, like the others, requires that the individual choose and act, at least on occasion, contrary to the predictions implicit in preference functions.[10]

ECONOMICALLY MOTIVATED PRODUCTION SHIFTS

In one sense, the analysis developed in this chapter is simpler and more straightforward than any of the alternatives sketched out above. Individuals behave in accordance with norms of cooperation in social interaction because of the dictates of their preference orderings. They "do not want to steal," even when opportunities exist. This behavior is differently motivated from that which relies on expected losses upon probable apprehension and

9. David Gauthier, *Morals by Agreement*.
10. For an extended treatment, see chap. 16.

punishment for formal rules violations, from that which expresses the over-riding of temptation by a conscious inner morality, from that which represents generalized adherence to the furtherance of enlightened self-interest, and from that reflecting acceptance of the extended rationality of provisional cooperative dispositions.

The construction here does not require that the individual sense that he or she behaves differently than he or she might have behaved if the investment of others had not been successful in shifting his or her preference ordering toward cooperation. There is no consciousness of coercion, whether legal or ethical; there is no psychological tension of the sort that is present in any of the other models.

The analysis is consistent with the sociologists' criticism of the economists' hypothesis of operationally meaningful utility maximization. The preference orderings of individuals are subject to change brought about by the sociocultural environment within which choices are made and action taken. "Social norms" do, indeed, determine individual choice behavior, at least within limits. But the model supplies operational content to the sociologists' criticism; the origin of and the direction of the effects of social norms are themselves grounded in a calculus of self-interest.

As suggested initially, I do not claim inclusive explanatory power for the model of economically motivated, externally influenced shifts in preference orderings. Each of the several alternatives, including, perhaps, others than those discussed briefly above, may be helpful in explaining behavioral departures from opportunistically calculated self-interest in social intercourse. I suggest only that a person does not steal, in part, simply because he or she does not want to steal, and that the preference ordering that reflects this stance may have been, again in part, "produced" by the moral suasion undertaken by others, in furtherance of their own economic self-interest.

PART FOUR

Moral Science, Equality, and Justice

Political Economy
and Social Philosophy

I. Introduction

Scientific economics was born as a by-product of social philosophy. Adam Smith found it necessary to explain how markets work in order to carry his argument for the dismantling of the mercantilist regulatory apparatus. Some of Smith's followers in classical political economy overextended his teaching, and treated their subject as an inflexible "natural" science. Whereas the mercantilists had failed to understand how free markets generate order, the extremists among the classical economists failed to understand that the institutions of markets were not themselves immutable. The socialist impetus of the late 19th and 20th centuries was, in part, however, provided by a false rather than a true comparison of market institutions and practicable political alternatives. Only in the last part of this century did "political economy" potentially emerge into its current status as a continuing and necessary element in the philosophical evaluation and comparison of *attainable* institutional structures. Modern public choice theory provided insights into the working of politics much as Adam Smith offered initial insights into the working of markets. We now know that neither market nor political institutions match up to the performance of their conceptually idealized models, a simple truth of course, but one that social scientists and philosophers have so often failed to recognize.

From *Economics and Philosophy,* ed. Peter Koslowski (Tübingen: J. C. B. Mohr [Paul Siebeck], 1985), 19–36. Reprinted by permission of the publisher.

I am indebted to Viktor Vanberg for comments on an earlier draft.

The ultimate question in social philosophy remains: How should we organize ourselves, one with another, so as to secure peace, freedom, and prosperity? To so much as put this question presupposes that we can, in fact, modify the structure within which our mutual interdependence takes form. The question itself denies by implication the validity of the proposition that we are locked into an inevitable process of historical necessity as well as the one that suggests that we, and our institutions, are products of a biological and cultural evolution that we disturb only at our peril. The social philosopher has a moral obligation to believe that social reform is possible, and that discussion can be helpful both in tempering the romantic yearnings for perfectibility and in suggesting avenues for practical constructive change.

In this paper, I shall attempt to place modern political economy in what I consider to be its appropriate role in such an ongoing discussion. I shall first identify ideas that must be discarded if such a role is ever to be attained. In this respect, I distinguish three related strands: the heritage of classical utilitarianism, the ubiquituous and pervasive engineering urge, and the elitist mentality. Scourged of these demons, the potential contributions of modern political economy to the ongoing normative discussion of the ultimate question can be sketched.

II. The Utilitarian Calculus

It is unfortunate that Benthamite utilitarianism emerged to obfuscate the central ideas of classical political economy before these ideas had permeated into the general public consciousness. The calculus of pleasure and pain came to be attached to the evaluation of the market process, with the predicted result that the fundamental philosophical argument for markets was almost lost from mind for over a century. Markets are basically *political* institutions, and they serve to allow persons to interact voluntarily one with another without the detailed supervision of the state. Markets should never have been evaluated primarily and instrumentally for their ability as institutions to maximize pleasure over pain, or indeed to maximize anything else that is interpersonally comparable.

Modern neo-classical economics did, of course, finally escape from the philosophical straightjacket imposed by the Benthamite utilitarian calculus. Unfortunately, however, it retained the maximization paradigm as a central element in models of individual behavior, a retention that seemed to create a methodological void between individual "economizing" and social or political "economizing." There seemed nothing that the economists could legitimately say about the organization of social interdependence. Without a utilitarian value scale, the notion of efficiency in resource use seemed empty of normative content.

Pareto was rediscovered to have offered what seemed to be a way out of the dilemma, and theoretical welfare economics emerged, an economics that seemed to incorporate normative content within an absolutely minimal set of ethical presuppositions. Application of the Pareto criterion for the classification of both social states and shifts in these states did not require interpersonal comparisons of utilities or the conversion of individual utilities into some unique social dimension. Individuals might be modelled as maximizing their own utilities (or anything else), but so long as the Pareto criterion remains satisfied, a state could be judged Pareto optimal or efficient. And so long as the criterion applied to a move or shift was met, such a move could be classified as Pareto superior.

Economists remained unsatisfied with the Pareto construction, however, for at least two distinct reasons, both of which, in some sense, relate to the utilitarian heritage of the whole discipline of economics. With no social value standard, there is no social maximand. Alternative structural arrangements cannot be arrayed on some better-to-worse scalar. And, furthermore, an arrangement meeting the Pareto criterion does so because of the particular configuration of the individually claimed endowments that describe such an arrangement. It follows that there exists a sub-infinity of positions or sets of arrangements that meet the simple Pareto test. Relative to the robust utilitarian norm, the Pareto criterion allowed the economist to say very little. And, importantly, the Pareto construction closed off any potentiality of evaluating distributions of individual endowments or claims. Given any distribution, or, more generally, any definition of individuals, the Pareto norm introduces some normative content into the economists' examination of institutions, even if this content remains severely limited. But, as among differing distributions, the norm remains silent. As I shall summarize in Section III below, economists moved quickly, and sometimes confusedly, to remedy this presumed deficiency in the Paretian normative apparatus.

A second, and distinctly different, problem with the Pareto norm also finds its origins in the utilitarian heritage. Utilitarianism fosters a delusion of quantitative measurability that did not disappear with the demise of interpersonal comparability. Even if it is acknowledged that Mr. A's "utility" is not comparable with Mr. B's "utility," analysis proceeded as if Mr. A's "utility" is itself an objectively measurable and quantifiable magnitude. After all, "utility" is defined as "that which a maximizer maximizes," and the maximization paradigm implies a quantifiable maximand. The difficulties of any crude or simplistic measurement of individual utilities were, of course, recognized, but the basic dimensionality issue remained obscured. Economists who were reluctant to measure individual utilities directly were, nonetheless, willing to introduce cardinally measurable arguments into individual utility functions. Once this step is taken, the application of the Pareto norm can be made without relation to observed individual evaluation, which, methodologically, becomes equivalent to a reintroduction of the apparently discarded utilitarian calculus.

The point here is perhaps sufficiently subtle to warrant simple illustration. Consider a community with two persons, A and B, along with an external observer economist. There are two producible commodities, X and Y, and two inputs, those from A and those from B, designated as a and b. The quantities of commodities may be changed by variations in inputs supplied. The utility functions of A and B contain, at most, four arguments, X, Y, a, and b. If the economist signs the arguments, with X and Y signed positive, and a signed negatively for A, and b signed negatively for B, arrangements may be arrayed in accordance with the Pareto norm. There may be an arrangement that enables *both* A and B to secure more X *and* more Y while supplying less a and less b than that arrangement observed to be in existence. The economist seems to be able to say that a shift from the existing arrangement to the alternative one is a Pareto improvement.

The quasi-utilitarian step is that which allows the economist first to identify and then to sign the arguments in individual utility functions. If this step can be taken, the economist must presume to know something about individual utilities, and it seems but a small step from this to the presumption that he knows all. The indirect quantification of individual value scales through the specification of arguments in utility functions was encouraged, and its methodological status obscured, by the mathematization of economics, which was, itself, fostered by the maximization paradigm.

It seemed possible, at the apogee of theoretical welfare economics at mid-century, to lay down objectively meaningful conditions that must be met if an allocation is to satisfy the Pareto norm of optimality or efficiency. From this perspective, it seemed to be possible for the economist observer to make diagnoses of market failures and to suggest specific changes that might be Pareto superior. As the illustration above suggests, however, all is not so simple. What if the identification and the signing of the arguments in individual utility functions are all wrong? What if Mr. A does not positively value X, and, indeed, X is a "bad" rather than a "good" in his utility function? And, suppose that Mr. B enjoys working; hence *b* is a "good" rather than a "bad," as postulated in the exercise. Once such questions as these are raised, even the limited scope of Paretian welfare analysis seems to be largely emptied of normative substance.

It is at this point that Wicksell comes to the rescue but not in a manner that satisfied the modern welfare theorist. If the Paretian construction is translated into the Wicksellian framework, the economist escapes from the apparent necessity to know anything about individual functions. I shall return to this interpretation of normative political economy below in Section VI.

III. The Engineering Urge

I listed the engineering urge as one of three related strands of intellectual motivation that must be eliminated if political economy, and the work of its disciplinary practitioners, can assume an appropriate role in social philosophy. I use "engineering" here rather than the more inclusive words "science" or "scientific" because it conveys more accurately the behavioral implications. In an ultimate sense, all science is aimed at control, at assistance in the solving of problems, but at least at the level of academic endeavor, scientists may seek knowledge for its own sake. By contrast, the engineers find their *raison d'être* in solving problems or, at one stage removed, in suggesting solutions to decision-makers faced with problems. It is in this sense that modern economists have sought pervasively to assume roles as putative problem solvers, as policy advocates, as advisers to governments, directly or indirectly.

I noted above that modern economists were unhappy with the Paretian construction because they considered the construction to be insufficiently robust. They did not accept the implied inability to say anything about distributional arrangements, and they did not like the sub-infinity of optimal positions forced upon them by the feedback dependence of classifications on distributions. Relatively early in theoretical welfare economics, attempts were made to get beyond the Paretian limits by introducing the "social welfare function," a construction that was aimed precisely at allowing the economist to make normative evaluations of distributional arrangements. The Paretian construction was incorporated into the new edifice, but the social welfare function was designed to enable its user to rank or array among themselves all states or positions that meet the lower-level Pareto norm.

It should have been clear from the outset, from the very meaning of the Pareto criterion and especially if interpreted in Wicksellian terms, that no unique social welfare function could be derived that allowed for an expression of individuals' values and which remained internally consistent in its orderings. Nonetheless, Arrow's formal proof was required to establish this proposition, and, despite the widespread acceptance of such proof, economists continued, and continue, to utilize the social welfare function as a device that seemed to offer a basis for normative statements. Why did this practice persist so long, and why does it still persist? Why did economists reintroduce essentially the same evaluation procedures that were used by the utilitarians and which seemed thoroughly discredited? Presumably they did so, at least in part, by their urge to be able to offer what seemed to be "scientific" solutions to what seemed to be social problems. They wanted to be able to proceed in a manner analogous to that of their academic colleagues in engineering. Even when, at one level of discourse, these economists would acknowledge that there are as many social welfare functions as there are members of the community, they continued to use the ordering constructions. Empty as these might be, the exercise appeared to give satisfaction to those economists who were, and are, intellectually at sea without some engineering paradigm within which to ply their trade.

A second, and totally different, reflection of the basic engineering urge among modern economists also warrants brief attention here. And, at a practical level, this expression may swamp in significance the one previously discussed. Fully acknowledging that no evaluative norms can be applied to distributional arrangements and, also, that the arrangements that exist determine the meaning of the efficiency scale, some economists have proceeded to use the scale as a policy norm. That is to say, the slogan has been "a dollar's worth is a dollar's worth, full speed ahead, and ignore the distributional consequences!"

All of the serious cost-benefit analysis that has been central to much applied economics in the decades since World War II can be interpreted to fall within this classification. Many man-hours of economists have been turned to the evaluation of public investment projects on the basis of this methodology. Note that this applied welfare economics, like its counterpart labelled theoretical welfare economics, presumes the legitimacy of the quasi-utilitarian step made when arguments in individual utility functions are defined and signed. In the work under the rubric here discussed, this step is straightforward. Individuals are postulated to be net wealth maximizers, and, for the collectivity, that which is presumed to be maximand is the aggregate net wealth, as measured in monetary values. With such a measuring rod in hand, the economist indeed becomes the "social engineer."

IV. The Elitist Mentality

The economists who have worked or who work within either of the two research programs sketched above have been and remain highly sophisticated analysts. Why have they remained so reluctant to acknowledge the fragility of the epistemological foundations for their exercises? In part, they remain utilitarians; in part, they seek roles as engineers. But equally important is what I have called an elitist mentality, that describes not only the economists but almost the inclusive membership of the modern academy, along with that of the intelligentsia broadly defined. There has been a general unwillingness to accept the implications of the rejection of classical utilitarianism. Economists, along with their peers, have been unable to evacuate the putative claim to normative knowledge that seemed to be offered by the utilitarian delusion. They continue to think themselves superior in normative wisdom to ordinary persons who possess none of the requisite analytical skills.

I am not directly concerned here with the cruder forms of elitism, represented by paternalistic and patronizing attitudes of members of the academic-intellectual establishment toward the great unwashed. Economists, as such, have not been nearly so flagrant in espousing these attitudes as their peers in other disciplines. The elitist mentality that I want to identify and to discuss is much more subtle, and those scholars whose attitude is described need have no conscious sense of being themselves elitist in any of the standard uses of the term. And, indeed, my terminology may be deemed misleading, since I am discussing a general characterization of politics, broadly defined, as a truth-discovery process.

To the extent that the purpose of collective action, of "politics," is interpreted, even if unconsciously, to be a seeking after "truth," it follows that those who engage themselves more actively in the process, and especially in the intellectual inquiries accompanying the process, are somehow "closer" to "that which is to be discovered" than those who remain passive in their behavior and their reflections. It is as if all who engage in "politics" are "scientists," while those who do not directly participate are "non-scientists." And just as the layman defers to the scientist in all matters appropriate to science, so the non-participant in politics "should" defer to those who participate in the discourses on matters of the political realm.

The economist who models his behavior in an analogue to the scientist must be confident that his investment in human capital yields a positive return. If, indeed, there is a "most efficient" set of structural arrangements "out there" waiting to be discovered by economic research analysis, the economist is surely more capable of suggesting possible changes that will move the community toward that desideratum than is the person who claims no prior knowledge.

To rid modern political economy of this "scientistic" mind-set, which is subtly different from the more simple engineering urge already discussed, requires much more than the rejection of utilitarianism. What is required is a fundamental reshaping of the research program of the whole discipline of "politics," of which economics and political economy are but component parts.

V. The Principle of Spontaneous Order

I suggested that political economy assumes its proper place in social philosophy only if the three related strands or elements identified in the neoclassical orthodoxy can be removed from the mind-set of those who remain within the disciplinary boundaries. I also suggested that developments in the research program of political economy late in this century have been such as to allow this place to be assumed. In defending this statement, I am obliged to outline what political economy is and how it can make its contribution to the more inclusive and ongoing dialogue.

As indicated earlier, the central principle of classical political economy remains untouchable. The principle demonstrates that the separate actions of individuals may be coordinated through a structure of interrelated markets contained within a legal-governmental system that enforces property rights and contracts. The implications of this principle for social philosophy are straightforward. To the extent that individual actions can be coordinated by decentralized organization of emergent markets, the necessity for political coordination and/or reconciliation is reduced. To the extent that markets work, there is no need for the state. Markets allow persons to interact, one with another, in a regime that combines freedom and order, provided only that the state supply the protective legal umbrella.

Note that the exposition of this central principle of political economy does not require any identification of arguments in individual utility or preference functions or any summation of individual values in some unique social dimension. Individuals coordinate their efforts so as to achieve mutual gains, as they individually define the content of such gains. And, importantly, there is no need for individuals to agree explicitly or implicitly on an allocation or a distribution. These emerge as results of a process of trading, and individual preferences are exerted, not on the characteristics of such end-states, but instead on the subjectively defined objects of each person's own value scale, a scale that may, itself, emerge only as trade takes place. The market allows each participant to seek to further "that which he wants," given the constraints that he confronts, and "that which A wants" need not be brought into agreement with "that which B wants" at all. Indeed, the efficacy of market process is located in its facilitation of the satisfaction of divergent preferences.

The principle of the spontaneous order of the market process depends critically, however, on some explicit presuppositions that cannot be neglected in any systematic philosophical treatment. The organization of markets coordinates separate individual activities within the protective umbrella of a legal order without a specification of arguments in utility functions, but it does require that individuals themselves are defined in terms of some set of initial endowments, claims, rights, or characteristics.

Who is an individual? Who is a person? Who is a potential market participant? Response to these questions may seem, at first glance, to be as difficult as response to that which the classical utilitarian purports to answer: What does an individual want?

There is, nonetheless, a quantum difference between the epistemological requirements in the two cases. The utilitarian who would define the arguments in individual preference functions presumes a degree of psychological knowledge that is internal, whereas the non-utilitarian requires nothing beyond an empirical identification of the acting subject. The *individual* or "that entity which engages in potential exchange" can be conceptually defined by the legal structure that sets out allowable limits on behavior. The individual, in this context, is that choosing-acting unit that may voluntarily exchange or trade his legal endowments, rights, or claims, including those to the produce of his own application of personal talents (work) with others for some reciprocal offering (money, other claims, other inputs in a joint venture).

The argument here does suggest, however, that a legal-governmental order, one that contains within its allowable limits of enforceability some specification of the distribution of rights and claims among individuals, is logically prior to any meaningful discussions of the process of market interaction among persons. Note that this priority of the legally protected assignment of rights does not carry the implication that the state, itself, is empowered arbitrarily to modify this assignment.

The central principle of political economy remains valid under *any* observed or imagined assignment of rights and claims. To the extent that individuals are *separately* assigned any legally protected rights or claims and voluntary contractual exchanges in these separately assigned rights and claims are enforced, emergent exchange arrangements will generate results that will maximize the values of the persons within the constraints described by their initial assignment. The principle applies equally to the production, sale, and final distribution of goods from the small garden plots of persons in the Soviet Union to the production, sale, and final distribution of the far wider range of goods and services that are allowed in Western economies.

The normative thrust of the principle depends critically on two presuppositions, one empirical, the other ethical. The empirical presupposition states that units of the human species are separable in a meaningful and observable sense. That is to say, just as we can talk about separate dogs, cats, or trees, we can talk about separate persons as independently existent biological units. The presupposition simply calls attention to the elemental fact of what we might call "natural partitionability" within the species. The ethical pre-supposition states that these "natural individuals" are the ultimate sources of valuation, clearly much more controversial than its empirical counterpart. If, however, individuals are not acknowledged to be the sources of value, the central principle of political economy has no normative meaning. If some external or supra-individual value standard is postulated, the coordination processes of the exchange network need not produce results that have any meaningful relationship to such standard. Or, if some individuals' values are somehow deemed to be "superior" to those of others, there is no valuation process implicit in market equilibrium.

Even upon acceptance of these presuppositions, however, there may exist a sub-infinity of possible assignments of rights and claims among persons. The particular assignment that describes a *status quo* is, in some fundamen-tal sense, arbitrary. Given any such assignment, the decentralized market or exchange order operates so as to further the values of the individual partici-pants, so defined, whatever these values might be. But the question remains: Can the political economist offer any normative guidance in the assignment of rights and claims among persons?

VI. The Wicksellian Criterion for Institutional Change

Having shed the utilitarian value standard, and having accepted the presup-positions that individuals who can be identified are the sources of value, the political economist cannot array differing institutional structures, including assignments of individuals' rights and claims, in accordance with any non-individualistic value scale. He cannot call on some criterion of "efficiency" unless he takes the quasi-utilitarian step noted earlier.

The contractarian framework advanced by Knut Wicksell can be helpful at precisely this point.[1] The political economist may call on his specialized talents to isolate and to identify changes in the institutional structure that might meet the Pareto test for superiority, interpreted in Wicksellian terms. Given any assignment of rights to persons, the political economist may ad-

---

1. See Knut Wicksell, *Finanztheoretische Untersuchungen,* Jena (Gustav Fischer) 1896.

vance an hypothesis to the effect that *all* persons in the community can be made better off, by their own reckoning, by a proffered shift in institutional arrangements. This hypothesis can then be put to the test; if arrangements can be worked out so that all members of the community agree to make the change, the test is passed; the hypothesis is corroborated. If the test fails, the political economist returns to his drawing board and searches for alternative rearrangements or, finally if none are found, he concludes that that which he observes is optimal in the Pareto-Wicksell sense.[2]

Care must be taken, however, not to claim too much for the contractarian escape route offered in the Wicksellian construction. The political structure of modern societies is such that suggested reforms in institutions can rarely, if ever, be put to the Wicksellian unanimity test. And, indeed, we might argue, at the more fundamental level of rules for constitutional decision-making, that the Wicksellian test, in itself, would not probably be Wicksell-efficient.[3] Where then does this leave the political economist who remains unwilling to take the quasi-utilitarian step? If he cannot actually carry out the Wicksellian test and observe the results, he is left with the notion of conceptual agreement. And critics have suggested that attempts to define changes upon which "persons might have agreed," if tests were possible, are on all fours with attempts to define and sign arguments in individual utility functions.

The Wicksellian contractarian framework seems, nonetheless, superior for normative purposes to the quasi-utilitarian framework of orthodox welfare economics because it allows for a sharper conceptual separation of value-enhancing and distributional changes to be made. In a sense, of course, the Wicksellian approach to normative economics is a straightforward extension of the exchange nexus. In working out the requisite compromises, side-payments, deals, many-issues adjustments that may be necessary to secure general consent to a proposed institutional shift, individual participants are essentially exchanging elements of a vector that describes the total package. And to the extent that such compromises are possible, we are assured that

2. The role for the political economist sketched here was first advanced in an early paper, "Positive Economics, Welfare Economics, and Political Economy," *Journal of Law and Economics*, 2 (1959), 124–38. Reprinted in J. Buchanan: *Fiscal Theory and Political Economy*, Chapel Hill (University of North Carolina Press) 1960, 105–24.

3. See James M. Buchanan and Gordon Tullock: *The Calculus of Consent*, Ann Arbor (University of Michigan Press) 1962.

the change finally made is value-enhancing. But the Wicksellian procedure dictates that pure redistribution, defined in utility dimensions, simply cannot occur with general consent of all parties. No such implication can be drawn from the application of utilitarian procedures, which has been the source of much of the confusion in normative discourse.

VII. Justice and the *Status Quo*

Because political economy, as such, cannot contribute directly to the normative discussion about alternative assignments of rights and claims among persons, that is, about pure distributional issues, we may be tempted to conclude that its role in social philosophy is severely limited. To the extent that social philosophy concentrates on considerations of distributive or social justice, where can political economy be of assistance? The implied relegation to secondary place in relevant discussion would be premature, however, once we recognize that very little of the observed discussion of "social justice" by philosophers other than political economists has more than remote relevance to any ultimate choice. Far too frequently, social philosophers have implicitly presumed that their normative discussions of idealized principles of justice are applicable to social worlds that we inhabit. There are two related flaws in such a presumption. First, no person, agency, or collectivity chooses among differing assignments of rights and claims, as such. Secondly, we live and interact one with another in historical time and place. We cannot jump out of our history and commence again.

I have often argued that any discussion of institutional change must embody the recognition that *we start from here,* and that *here* defines both place and time. There is a distribution of rights, endowments, and claims among persons, along with historically determined rules that dictate limits on exchanges in such rights. The distribution is an existential reality. It is that which exists; there is, and could be, no other.

Considerations of justice in distribution must, therefore, be couched in terms of possible *changes* from the *status quo.* And in this context, the two presuppositions advanced earlier will simply not permit normative judgements in any *redistributional* change to be made. The basis for this somewhat shocking (and disturbing to many) result is that any reduction in the expressed or revealed well-being of one person or group for the purpose of enhancing the well-being of another person or group, unless it is wholly voluntary (in which case it could not be called redistribution), can be "legitimized" only by resort to some standard of valuation external to and independent of the valuations of the individuals involved in the social interaction.

I should emphasize that the acknowledgement of an inability to evaluate genuinely redistributional changes in the *status quo* on other than purely individual scales should not be interpreted as providing some ethical-moral defense of that assignment of rights and claims that exist. By any individual's private value scale, the existing assignment may be worse than a whole set of alternatives. The absence of the potential for voluntary or agreed-on consent to change indicates only that the existing assignment is the unique point in the directionally divergent individual scalars.

VIII. Rules, End-States, and Contractarian Reform

The role for political economy, now interpreted in the Wicksellian-contractarian paradigm, need not be so limited as the above discussion may suggest to those who think of distributional issues exclusively or primarily in end-state terms. As noted earlier, "distributions," as such, are not "chosen" by any person or group. Distributions emerge from the operation of framework rules or institutions within which separate persons interact. The potential objects for collective choice, and hence for reform or change, are these rules or institutions. Differing rules will, of course, generate differing predicted patterns of distribution, often in some stochastically defined sense.

Precisely because rules are the objects for collective choice, the scope for potential agreed-on contractual change is considerably more inclusive than that which might be applicable for end-state comparisons. That is to say, it is easier for persons to agree on rules which will, in their turn, allow differing patterns of end-state distributions to emerge, than it is for persons to agree on end-states themselves. Or, to put the point differently, the focus of attention on rules serves to relegate overt redistributional conflict to secondary stages of consideration.

The basic reason why agreement can emerge more readily upon a choice of rules or processes than upon end-state assignments lies in the relatively greater uncertainty about individuals' identifiable positions under the operations of alternative rules. Almost by definition, an individual's own position in an end-state is well identified. By comparison, the operation of a quasi-permanent rule that generates stochastic patterns of end-states, each with distributional characteristics, necessarily makes it difficult for the individual to identify and predict accurately just what his own position might be. Because of this inherent uncertainty, the individual will be led to evaluate alternative sets of rules in accordance with a somewhat more inclusive sense of his own interest than that which might inform his simple choice among well identified end-states.[4]

In a contractarian and rule-oriented perspective, therefore, it is possible that consensus on a set of institutional arrangements will emerge that will, in operation, embody interpersonal transfers that may be loosely described as redistributional. But it is critically important that this "constitutional redistribution" be categorically distinguished from post-constitutional "political redistribution," which can never be normatively sanctioned. Note, however, that the normative argument in support of arrangements that embody constitutional redistribution stems from the agreement on these arrangements in the constitutional or rule-making dialogue. Such argument does not, and cannot, stem from any external and supra-individualistic value scale.

IX. Political Economy in Social Philosophy

Political economy is a necessary ingredient in any informed discussion of the ultimate question of social philosophy. It need not, of course, be sufficient. As conceptualized in the contractarian-constitutionalist paradigm, political economy offers a coherent structure within which the interactions of persons may be analyzed. It allows the generalization and extension of the exchange

---

4. Elements of the analyses of Buchanan-Tullock, Rawls, and Nozick are combined in the position outlined here. In *The Calculus of Consent* (1962), Tullock and I examined the choice among political decision rules, and we discussed the prospect for agreement on rules that is enhanced by the uncertainty of individuals' positions under the operations of alternative arrangements. John Rawls in *A Theory of Justice*, Cambridge (Harvard University Press) 1971, introduced the veil of ignorance, rather than uncertainty, to analyze prospects for ultimate contractual agreement on basic principles of justice. Robert Nozick in *Anarchy, State, and Utopia*, New York (Basic Books) 1974, developed the basic distinction between choices among processes and choices among end-states.

model of market interaction to the more encompassing institutions of politics and governance. As with the simpler exchange models of markets, specific results can neither be positively predicted nor normatively evaluated. That which emerges emerges, and evaluative criteria can be applied only to processes of the interaction, and not to the characteristics of the end-states that are generated.

The structure is not normatively empty, however, and institutional arrangements that incorporate or allow for the coercive overriding of individual values do not find ready legitimation in the contractarian, or generalized exchange, framework. Legitimacy can be derived only, at one level or another, from the voluntary consent of individuals. But the fundamental question, Who is an individual? remains exogenous to the whole contractarian exercise. In this context, political economy, along with contract theory, depends critically on the two presuppositions noted earlier in the paper. If there are "natural persons" in some biological sense, what are the margins for extension? Are there "natural boundaries" that separate persons, one from another? Are there "natural rights"? These questions remain relevant even for the social philosopher who staunchly holds to a methodologically individualist position. But, are individuals the only sources of value? Do extra-individual sources exist? Are there moral absolutes?

Political economists can contribute only indirectly to the discussion on such grand questions. Such discussion becomes meaningful, however, only if it is informed by an understanding of the principles of political economy.

An Individualistic Theory
of Political Process

The "theory" or "approach" presented in this paper represents an extension of the tools, methods, and procedures utilized by the economist to an analysis of politics. Like the political scientist, the economist studies social organization. But the economist does so, or should do so, differently. He studies the emergence of market and exchange relationships out of the choice processes of individual participants. Orthodox neoclassical economic theory gives a central position to the theory of individual choice behavior; and the textbooks normally begin with an analysis of individual demand for goods and services. Upon this theory of individual choice behavior, a theory of interaction among individuals and groups is constructed. The organization that comes into being as a result of individuals participating variously in exchange processes is called "the economy." This organization, this economy, as such, has no independent existence apart from the interaction of individual participants in it. It has no goals, no purposive intent.[1] It is properly a social organization, but it is not a social organism. The word *individualistic* in the title of this paper is the opposite of the word *organismic*, and it classifies the approach taken in terms of methodology, not in terms of ideology.

In the individualistic approach, the polity is examined as a social organi-

From *Varieties of Political Theory,* ed. David Easton (Englewood Cliffs: Prentice-Hall, 1966), 25–37. Reprinted by permission.

1. As Gunnar Myrdal pointed out in his fundamental methodological critique, many economists have erred in inferring "social" content in the results of the market economy, without making explicit value statements. See *The Political Element in the Development of Economic Theory* (London: Routledge and Kegan Paul, Ltd., 1953).

zation in a manner similar to that in which the economy has traditionally been analyzed. The political structure is conceived as something that *emerges* from the choice processes of individual participants. This approach to politics is not, of course, novel. The whole of the contractarian tradition can, in one sense, be classified as falling within this approach. It nevertheless seems to be true that individual behavior in participating in and in determining the outcome of political process has been relatively neglected by political scientists. Many of these scholars continue to assume that, somehow and somewhere, there exists a "public interest" or "general interest" that is divorced from the interests of the individual participants. In their behavior in the economic process, private people, as consumers, workers, investors, and entrepreneurs, are assumed to have differing tastes, desires, and values. And the economy represents the institutional or organizational response to the need to satisfy simultaneously this manifold set of wants. By contrast, and with important exceptions, when individuals participate in the formation of social or collective decisions, they are assumed to be somehow identical. Political process has not been sufficiently examined as a means through which separate and differing individual and group interests come to be reconciled, although major contributions have been made in this country by the so-called Bentley school.

This school aside, political process has continued to be viewed as a means through which "right" or "correct" decisions are reached. Political decisions are, for the most part, still conceived as "truth judgments"; the primary task of political decision making becomes that of discovering the "true" public interest. When collective choices reduce to mutually exclusive, either-or, decisions, this "truth judgment" model has some validity. The basic issue is whether or not it is the appropriate model for analyzing the ordinary day-to-day operation of a democratic political structure. The approach to be developed here is based on the presumption that it is not, and that the political process in democratic society can best be examined by interpreting it as a means of reconciling divergent interests. The theory is one of "individualist democracy" as opposed to "idealist democracy," in the terms used by T. D. Weldon.[2]

The acceptance of this individualistic model as the appropriate one for

2. T. D. Weldon, *States and Morals* (New York: McGraw-Hill Book Company, 1947).

analysis involves value judgment in two separate respects. As one who accepts the traditions of Western society, I think that we should treat the human individual as the basic philosophical entity, and that we should conceive the state as if it were ultimately derivative from individual consent. The second value judgment, which is more important for the purposes of this paper, is a judgment about facts, a "characterizing value judgment," to use Nagel's term; it may be accepted independent of any judgment concerning the philosophy of the state. It involves the empirical judgment that political process can be "factored down" to the level of individual choices.

This statement need not, of course, involve the claim of exclusive, or even predominant, relevance for the individualistic model in making predictions about political decision processes. In the scientific house there are many mansions, and, in analyzing politics, there is surely room for alternative models. For some purposes, an organic model may be helpful; for others, a ruling-class or force theory of the state. And, in many instances, a model that bypasses the individual and begins with the interplay of group interests may yield fully satisfactory predictions. At base, it is claimed only that the model which derives the whole political process from the decisions made by individual persons, who are assumed to behave rationally, explains elements of politics that seem awkward in other models by providing some "explanations" of reality that are not consistent with alternative theories.

At this point, a familiar methodological difficulty arises, one that caused a certain ambivalence in the more extensive treatment of this approach to politics that Gordon Tullock and I have published.[3] What is required of a "theory" of politics? There are two possible answers to this question. "Theory" may, first of all, be conceived of as a logical structure, an "explanation," which allows meaningful statements to be made and which helps to establish some uniformity in thinking without producing conceptually refutable hypotheses. At this level, which may be called that of "logical theory," all that is required in the individualistic model is that interests differ, and that individuals act in accordance with these separate interests. There is no need to examine the nature of these differences in individual and group wants. All that is required for the formal structure of a theory is the presumption that dif-

---

3. *The Calculus of Consent: Logical Foundations of Constitutional Democracy* (Ann Arbor: University of Michigan Press, 1962).

ferent individuals want to accomplish different things through the political mechanism. This "logical theory" of individualist democracy can be helpful in understanding the processes through which persons and groups compromise and reconcile their differences in a system of political order.

For a genuinely predictive theory of politics, however, more is needed. If by "theory" we mean the development of hypotheses about behavior in the political process that can be conceptually refuted by observation of real-world events, some additional constraints must be placed on the manner in which separate interests differ. The most familiar of these constraints, again taken from economics, is the hypothesis that individuals act in politics as they are assumed to act in the predictive theory of markets, so as to maximize their expected utility, and that their behavior in doing so is measurable in terms of some objectively identifiable magnitude such as personal income or wealth. In politics, this "positive" theory implies that individuals, and groups, act so as to further their economic positions. For example, California farmers vote for Congressmen who vote for Federal funds for irrigation projects; and owners of trucking firms vote for Congressmen who vote for highway expenditure projects. Clearly, this hypothesis has at least *some* explanatory value. Alternative constraints on the pattern of individual differences could, of course, be imposed; hypotheses could be drawn, and the implications tested.

It should be emphasized that the acceptance of the individualistic approach to politics need not imply acceptance of the hypothesis that men and groups, even in a first approximation, act narrowly to further identifiable self-interest. As a logical theory of political behavior, the model is equally applicable to a world of altruists and to a world of egoists, although the testable hypotheses would of course sharply differ in the two cases. The logical construction can be applied even to a world of saints, so long as their separate visions of the "good society" differ. The model is inapplicable only to a world where separate individual interests really do not exist, but, instead, are somehow transcended in some supraindividual set of goals.

What contribution can the individualistic approach make to an understanding of politics? The underlying proposition is that individual interests differ. Starting from this, what happens to the "public interest"? Does it exist, and, if it does, how can individual interests be reconciled with it? The standard approach in political science seems to have been that of beginning with the "public interest," defined perhaps in terms of what the modern welfare economists refer to as a "social welfare function." The whole problem of "politics and morals," of "political obligation" arises out of attempts to get people to accept the "public interest" as their own. In other words, the reconciliation, if there is any, between private and public interests must come about through some moral force that the latter exerts on individual behavior. Political behavior of the individual becomes, in this familiar approach, necessarily moral behavior.

This whole conception of politics is foreign to the approach that is summarized in this paper. There exists no "social welfare function," no "public interest," as such in a society of freely choosing individuals, and there seems no reason to invent such a conception for analytical convenience. This does not imply, however, that political process reduces to a simple struggle for power among individuals and groups, which may be analyzed systematically and scientifically, but about which nothing can be said normatively. It is precisely at this stage that the individualistic model can rescue the "public interest," indirectly, through the essential separation between the constitutional and the operational stages of political decision. The clarification of this separation, and the implications that may be derived from an understanding of it, is the central contribution that the model can make to political theory.

It is necessary to distinguish sharply between day-to-day political decision making, where the struggle often does reduce simply to that among conflicting individual-group interests, and "constitutional" decision making, where individuals may be thought of as participating in choices on the set of rules under which subsequent day-to-day decisions are to be made. This second set of decisions, of choices, which may be called the "constitutional," is the important one, and, at this stage, it becomes possible to reconcile separate individual interests with something that could, with some legitimacy, be called the "public interest" were it not for the confusion that this particular usage might generate.

The center of attention becomes the mental calculus of the individual as he is confronted with a choice among alternative rules for the reaching of subsequent political decisions—that is to say, as he is confronted with a genuinely constitutional issue. The individual does not know, nor is he able to predict, what particular issues will be presented subsequent to the adoption of the rule. And, even if he can predict with some accuracy the sort of issues that may arise, he could hardly predict his own position vis-à-vis the other members of the group. Faced with such uncertainty, how does he proceed to choose among alternative rules? He must, in the nature of the case, try to select a rule that will work reasonably well for an unpredictable series of events and in terms of his own personal situation that he will assume to be more or less randomly distributed. Simple self-interest dictates that the individual try to rank alternative rules and institutions for collective decision making. The essential element here is the recognition that self-interest, at the level of decisions on rules or on institutions that are expected to remain in effect for long time periods, imposes on the individual an attitude and a behavior pattern that are not identical with those which the same self-interest would dictate in particular choices on specific political issues.

The members of the group may, of course, disagree on the rules, as they discuss these at the constitutional level of decision. A consensus on the ranking of alternative institutional schemes will not necessarily emerge. But it is precisely at this constitutional stage that discussion in some meaningful sense can take place. It is at this stage where analysis and argument can be helpful in resolving differences of opinion. No moral issue is introduced in this procedure; there is no dilemma that requires the individual to choose between furtherance of his own self-interest, as he perceives it, and some vague "public interest" as sensed by others than himself, with a view toward preserving social harmony. The reconciliation that is possible here is achieved through the fact that self-interest, as the individual himself perceives this, becomes less and less identifiable in any objectively measurable sense, for the individual is removed from the moment of pure conflict.

The analogy with the choosing of rules for an ordinary game is helpful, as my colleague Rutledge Vining has repeatedly emphasized. Consider the individual who participates in a poker game. At the start of an evening's play, rules under which play is to proceed are discussed and debated. There is no departure from pure self-interest required for the individual to choose rules that will, in fact, be predicted to result in a reasonably "fair" game. Not knowing in advance how the cards will be distributed over a whole series of particular plays, the participant will, in his own interest, be motivated to choose rules that will make the game "fair," that is, "in the general interest of the group." Various players or prospective players may, of course, disagree on the precise content of the rules that are required to produce "fair" games.

But these differences will be based, not so much on differences in identifiable self-interest, but on differences in characterizing value judgments concerning the working properties of alternative rules, that is to say, concerning the frequency distribution of predicted outcomes. Ultimate agreement may not be possible, and the game may not be played. But it seems that genuine compromise, genuine consensus, is much more likely to result in this sort of situation than at that stage where, by necessity and invention, individual positions come to be directly opposed, one to the other.

At the constitutional level of discourse, unanimity or consensus becomes important, not because there is something sacrosanct about unanimity per se, but for the simple reason that it provides the *only* criterion through which improvements in rules and institutions can, in fact, be judged without the introduction of an explicit value scale. Lacking an explicit social welfare function, there is no external or exogenous means of evaluating possible changes in the rules or institutions that describe an existing political structure. And, if agreement on possible changes in these cannot be secured, how are the interests of the separate individuals or groups to be weighed, one against the other? Agreement becomes the only possible test, and if this does not, or cannot, exist, there is simply nothing that can be said. Disagreement precludes any conclusion. But it should be again emphasized that the standard arguments against the application of the unanimity rule do not apply with equal force at the constitutional level and at the operational level of choice. Where individual and group interests are demonstrably in pure conflict, agreement is not possible, and some rule other than unanimity must normally be introduced to resolve the issue. But where individual and group interests are not clearly defined, where disagreement is based largely on conflicting interpretations concerning the working properties of alternative institutions, discussion and compromise leading to general agreement seem possible.

If observed agreement, or unanimity, provides the only criterion that enables an evaluation of changes in the rules for making political decisions, the question of the starting point becomes important. What position is in being, and what changes are to be considered? Obviously time is wasted if discussion is limited to a hypothetical group of individuals considering the original organization of a political society. The interpretation of the contract theory as applying to such a situation has, I think, plagued much of the critical discussion concerning this theory, and it has obscured the basic validity of the contract approach. A polity exists; it seems best to start from an existing political entity which may best be described in terms of the institutional-constitutional rules for reaching decisions. What is to be sought, therefore, is a criterion for evaluating changes in these existing rules. By saying that agreement or unanimity is the only meaningful criterion in the individualistic context, I of course stand accused of building into the model a defense of the *status quo*. The unique position given to this criterion seems to suggest that whatever exists is "right," until and unless everyone agrees to make a change, emphasizing, of course, that changes in rules are the sort discussed.

Several points must be made in response to this entirely reasonable interpretation that may be placed on the approach to political process that has been sketched out briefly here. In the first place, it should be noted that no statement at all is made or implied about what is or is not "right," "just," or "correct." The model is based on an explicit disavowal of any personal imputation of moral-ethical values into the system. Secondly, and more important, analysis must start from somewhere, and the existing set of rules and institutions is the only place from which it is possible to start. There is no implication that this position is personally desirable. But if we seek, dispassionately, to evaluate changes, there is no other place from which we may begin. Each and every one of us who looks at the existing political structure might prefer the world to be different from what it is now; but, until and unless general agreement can be reached on making changes, any modification of what exists must involve coercion of some persons by others.

And this means that some choice be made as to which individuals or groups are to be allowed to coerce others, a choice that simply cannot be made without the introduction of external value scales. This need not, of course, inhibit more general discussion. Value scales can be introduced on a personal and necessarily arbitrary basis, and statements can be made about "socially desired" changes in an existing set of rules. The steps are outside of the model of political process that can be properly called the "individualistic" model. But this is not equivalent to saying that these extraindividualistic models, and whatever theories or hypotheses that they may produce, are somehow "improper." They are simply beyond the pale of this discussion.

Additional clarification may be forthcoming if we return to the poker-game analogy. Assume that play has continued under an agreed-on set of rules for an hour, during which some participants have gained and others lost. A proposal is made to change the rules. The change considered must be from the existing set. Those proposing change may consider the rules wholly unfair and improper, but unless they are prepared to enforce their will on others, they can improve the rules only by securing agreement. Those who accumulated gains under the established rules will not necessarily be averse to reasonable proposals for change. Their positions on a future sequence of plays remain uncertain, and the fact that they have been gaining under one set of rules in no way insures that they will continue to do so. For these reasons, general agreement or consensus becomes possible on changes in rules for future play, as contrasted with the impossibility of agreement on some modified division of gains on a particular play. Clearly, proposals to change the rules of the game through general agreement belong to a different realm of discourse than proposals to change the results that have been generated under an existing set of rules, presumably in accordance with some externally determined value judgment.

Efforts to remain as clear as possible of externally imposed value judgments, to attempt to construct a theory of politics without interjecting interpersonal comparisons, may seem strained and tedious to political scientists. It should again be noted, however, that the approach here taken is derived from theoretical welfare economics. The unanimity criterion is merely the translation into political terms of the familiar Pareto criterion for evaluating changes in policy or in classifying positions.[4] Few economists have extended

---

4. This criterion states that a position is "optimal" or "efficient" when any change from that position will damage at least one person in the group. There are, of course, an infinite number of positions that may be classified as "optimal." The criterion is useful only for identifying nonoptimal positions. The same criterion may be applied to changes or proposals for change. If a move or change is such that at least one member in the relevant group is made "better off" while no one is made "worse off," the change is "optimal" in Pareto's sense. If a move or change damages at least one person, it is "nonoptimal." If an initial position is "nonoptimal," there must be at least one means of shifting to an "optimal" position in an "optimal" way. The relationship of this construction to the unanimity rule is a direct one once it is admitted that the only way in which an individual can be assured to be made "better off" is as a result of his own observed behavior in making choices.

this criterion to the evaluation of rules or institutions, where it seems considerably more applicable than it does in connection with unique events.[5]

There is an important distinction that is of some significance in understanding the constitutional approach to political rules, one that follows directly from the economist's proclivity to consider human interaction in terms of exchanges. This is the distinction between a zero-sum and a positive-sum game, to use modern, and highly suitable, terminology. In other words, it is necessary to emphasize the difference between situations of pure conflict among individuals and groups and situations that include conflict but also embody mutual possibilities for gain. At the operational level of day-to-day politics, where interests of individuals and groups may be sharply identified and delineated, the pure-conflict or zero-sum model can yield useful explanations, as William Riker has demonstrated in his recent work on coalition formation.[6] At the constitutional level of decision, however, where selections must be made among alternative rules, and where individual and group interests are not clearly identified, the situation is not properly described by pure conflict models. Participation in the "great game of politics" must, on balance, be mutually beneficial to all parties, or else revolution would ensue. The game is best conceived as positive-sum. But the game analogy remains relevant. Conflict is not wholly eliminated, and "pure" cooperation (all players on the same side) does not describe the situation.

The ordinary exchange relationship seems to be the appropriate model at this level. Gains can be realized through reaching agreements, and these gains accrue to *all* parties to the relationship, although the distribution of these gains will depend on relative bargaining strengths. Perfect symmetry need not be a property of the result. Unless gains can be secured by *all* parties there is, of course, no possibility that a genuinely voluntary agreement can be attained. Ordinary exchanges, as well as ordinary games, are essentially voluntary because participants are free to withdraw from or to refrain from entering the association. Should the political relationship be viewed, at base, as essentially a voluntary one? That is, of course, the heart of the matter, and the individualistic approach or "theory" of politics comes down squarely on

---

5. For a discussion of this extension, see my "The Relevance of Pareto Optimality," *Journal of Conflict Resolution,* 6 (December, 1962), 341–54.

6. *The Theory of Political Coalitions* (New Haven: Yale University Press, 1962).

the affirmative side of this question. At the ultimate constitutional level, it seems difficult to talk about political organization unless the structure is assumed to be derived, in some way, from individual consent. If this is not accepted, the basis for any judgment becomes purely personal.

The discussion, to this point, has been devoted largely to presenting a frame of reference within which political process may be examined. The emphasis has been deliberate, for it is the shift in the frame of reference, and not the particulars of analysis, that is the important element in the individualistic approach. It remains, however, to discuss some of the implications that may be drawn from the approach.

It is perhaps evident that the approach is quite consistent with a pragmatic and pluralistic conception of existing political institutions. The test of an institution is whether or not it is predicted to work, not in a unique situation or in a unique period of time, but over a whole sequence of events, over a whole span of time. Workability is not, however, to be measured in terms of accomplishing specifically postulated goals for political action. Such goals are nonexistent in the model. Workability of an institution means the efficacy or efficiency of the institution in accomplishing, for the individual, those purposes or goals, unpredictable at any particular moment of time, that he may desire to achieve from collective action over a sequence of future periods.

Some predictions must be made concerning the adaptability of the institution under varying circumstances. The final estimation of the net efficiency of an institution involves both positive and negative accounts. The political rule or institution must be examined for its positive efficacy in promoting the results that the individual desires to see achieved through political process. But the same rule or institution must be examined also for its negative potentiality for promoting results or outcomes that the individual does not desire. Common sense suggests that different institutions or different rules will be recommended for different types of political decisions.

Tullock and I have analyzed one such institution—the simple majority voting rule—in part for its own intrinsic interest, and, in part, as illustrative of the sort of approach to the various political decision rules that the individualistic conception suggests.[7] Our approach implied that majority voting is not to be prejudged at the outset. It is one possible decision rule among

7. See *The Calculus of Consent.*

many, and it must stand the test of efficiency when compared to alternative decision rules and institutions. What are the costs of allowing political decisions to be made by majority voting rules? What are the benefits? The point is that these familiar questions should be approached from the vantage point of the individual participant in political process, the citizen-voter-taxpayer-beneficiary. Clearly, if the decision involves choosing among predictable outcomes of a unique, once-and-for-all variety, the single individual could estimate the desirability or undesirability of majority voting rules quite simply by determining whether or not his own opinion is supported by a majority of his fellows. But again, it is not at this level or stage of decision that the rule itself should be evaluated. The individual should be conceived as participating in a "constitutional" decision that ultimately chooses majority rule, or some alternative, on the basis of its predicted effects in producing a whole sequence of outcomes, the particular configurations of which are largely unpredictable.

This "constitutional" choice among political rules and institutions can be subjected to rigorous general analysis that is helpful in indicating the elements that must enter into the individual's final decision. Let us return to the familiar questions concerning the benefits and costs to be expected under the institution of simple majority voting. The individual will recognize that, on a certain number of occasions, he will find himself in the minority, and that, on such occasions, he will be subjected to exploitation by the majority coalition; net costs will be imposed upon him. On the other hand, he will recognize that majority rule is one reasonably simple way of getting decisions made, of getting results accomplished through political process, without excessively high costs of decision. Weighing these two sides of the account, he may rationally choose majority rule as "optimal" for certain types of political decisions.

He may, however, reject majority rule for other types of political decisions; he may expect either some less-than-majority rule or some greater-than-majority rule to be more "efficient." His final choice among such rules or institutions will depend on a large number of factors. Prominent among these will be such things as the expected distribution of his own "interest" or "preference" as related to those of his fellows over the expected sequence of issues to be presented and the expected intensity of this interest on particular sorts of issues. For many aspects of collective organization, where the important consideration becomes the general establishment and acceptance of some rule rather than no rule, the individual may, at the "constitutional" stage, quite rationally choose to delegate final authority to particular individuals in the group. For example, majority rule is obviously inefficient as a means of determining traffic regulations; this task is normally delegated to the bureaucratic apparatus. By contrast, for decisions that can significantly affect human life and property, the individual may choose to accept some "constitutional" constraint that requires greater-than-majority agreement. On such issues, he expects the intensity of his own interest to be such that majority rule will not be acceptable. The familiar constitutional protection of human rights can be "explained" in this way. At a more mundane level, the most familiar example of this sort of thinking is the requirement for variance in municipal zoning laws. Here, in many cases, some greater-than-majority agreement is required to approve proposed changes.

That majority voting is only one among many possibly efficient or inefficient institutions through which political choices are made in a rationally organized democratic structure is recognized in existing political institutions, as the few examples cited above suggest. But this fact seems to be less well established in the literature of political analysis. The divergence here stems, in part, from the "truth judgment" approach to democratic choice that has been previously mentioned. If political decision-structures are viewed, at base, as institutional means of arriving at "correct" decisions, rather than as means of simply reconciling differing individual and group interests, a wholly different conceptual framework of analysis is required. If this essentially nonindividualistic view of politics is accepted, the choice among decision-making institutions must be made on the basis of comparative efficiency in making decisions in terms of some externally established criteria.

Such an approach seems to provide the basis for arguments that decisions had best be left to "experts," to the bureaucrats, who will be able to choose "correctly" with greater efficiency. This is the current antithesis to the individualistic approach to democratic process, and the choice between these fundamentally opposed analytical models can be made only on the acceptance of explicit value judgment. If individual valuations and preferences are to be allowed to count—and this admittedly requires an explicit value judgment—and so long as individuals and groups differ in what they desire to see collectively accomplished, no conceivable computing technique can replace the constitutionally constrained institutions of representative democracy.

One additional implication of the individualistic approach to politics serves to sharpen its contrast with the "truth judgment" model. One of the fundamental "constitutional" decisions that any group must make concerns the appropriate areas of human activity that are to be subject to collective organization. How much collectivization is to be allowed? The answer to this question clearly depends in the individualistic model on the rules and institutions that are to prevail in the operation of the collectivized sector. The decisions as to the degree of collectivization and the choice among alternative decision-making institutions are interdependent. It becomes impossible to determine whether or not a particular activity should or should not be collectivized, on efficiency grounds, until the choice among decision rules is taken into account. This, too, is an obvious but important point that is often overlooked. Collectivization of an activity, say, education, may be highly desirable in a community that is to reach decisions under institutions of majority rule, but highly undesirable in a community that is subjected to dictatorial controls.

The "theory" of democratic political process that has been sketched in this paper suggests a shift in research emphasis. There is required a painstaking and rigorous analysis of existing decision-making institutions in terms of their operation over periods of time and on numbers of issues sufficient to permit meaningful judgments to be made. Both in economics and in politics, attempts must be made to develop theories of institutional structures and to test the hypotheses derived from these theories against real-world observations. The existing set of institutions surely includes some that are grossly inefficient, as well as others that are highly efficient, even within the limits of an individualistic model. Analysis can highlight these differences and explore the predicted working properties of alternative institutions. This research emphasis follows from an acceptance of the "efficiency" notion that emerges from the individualistic model. Efficiency is not to be defined independent of the choice calculus of the individual citizen as participant in political process.

Appendix

The "individualistic" approach to a theory of political process actually represents only one of several strands of recently converging research, which, when taken together promise significant contributions in the social sciences over the next decade. The theory of the firm, which is of course central to orthodox economic analysis, is only now being re-examined under the assumption that a business firm is not to be studied as a single person, but as an organization within which the several persons involved variously interact one with another. Bureaucratic structures, within or without government, are similarly under theoretical reappraisal, and the conflicts between individual and organizational goals and the impact of these conflicts on behavior and performance have come to be recognized as important elements of scientific investigation. And there are many other similar examples.

Contributions from organization theory, information theory, the theory of teams, statistical decision theory, game theory, learning theory, theoretical welfare economics, pure theory of government finance, and others point toward a fundamental revision of existing orthodoxy, and an emerging consensus on what may be called a general theory of social structures, which will surely include political organization as only one among an array of forms. These developments should help to break down the barriers among the disciplinary specializations in the social sciences, barriers which have been, at best, arbitrarily erected and maintained.

Constitutional Democracy, Individual Liberty, and Political Equality

I. Introduction

In this century, "democracy" is a positively charged emotive term. It is employed in putative description of political regimes that vary widely in structure, purpose, and operation. Few regimes are to be found that openly claim status as "nondemocratic," and even those regimes that avoid total distortion of language often promise movement toward "democratic" procedures. From observed usage alone, therefore, the term seems to be largely empty of discriminatory content. Any meaningful discussion of alternative political structure must commence with an examination and evaluation of fundamental normative precepts of political philosophy. It is necessary to get behind the emotive connotation of "democracy" and to look at the philosophical origins of the whole conception.

I shall suggest that "democracy" emerges as a uniquely desired political ordering of interaction only in a particular set of circumstances. This set requires acceptance of specific philosophical presuppositions along with an understanding of the workings of the institutions of politics, broadly defined. So understood, the term "constitutional" *must* be prefixed to the term "democracy" if the latter is to be sustainable in an internally consistent normative argument. Stated in somewhat more concrete detail, my ar-

From *Jahrbuch für Neue Politische Okonomie* Band 4 (1985): 35–47. Reprinted by permission of the publisher.

gument is that "democracy" assumes evaluative significance only under the presupposition that individual liberty is, itself, of value, and, further, that effective political equality, which is the operative principle of democracy, can be meaningfully secured only if the range and scope of collective-political action are constrained or limited by constitutional boundaries. As indicated, there are two separate elements in my argument; the first may be classified to be broadly philosophical in nature; the second is intensely practical and draws on much of the modern research in public choice and related areas of inquiry.

In Section II, I discuss the philosophical or epistemological presuppositions without which "democracy" or "democratic procedures" would find no normative foundations. In Sections III and IV, and accepting the initial presupposition, I discuss the relationship between the normative principle of political equality and the structure of political organization. In Section V, I discuss problems of constitutional design, especially as this topic is informed by modern public choice theory. In Section VII, I treat the issue of limits to the range of political decisions or actions, and I evaluate the state of modern discussion. Finally, in Section VIII, I offer summary conclusions.[1]

II. Individual Persons as Sources of Value

The first and most critical presupposition that provides a foundation for any genuine democratic theory is that which locates sources of value exclusively in individuals. If there exist, or if there are presumed to exist, nonindividualistic sources of value, democratic political procedures become, at best,

1. I have discussed the central subject matter of this paper in several prior published works, although not, of course, in precisely the manner developed here. For a more general understanding of my position, I suggest the following works be consulted: James M. Buchanan and Gordon Tullock, *The Calculus of Consent* (Ann Arbor: University of Michigan Press, 1962); James M. Buchanan, *The Limits of Liberty* (Chicago: University of Chicago Press, 1975; German translation, *Grenzen der Freiheit* [Tübingen: J. C. B. Mohr, 1984]); James M. Buchanan, *Freedom in Constitutional Contract* (College Station: Texas A&M University Press, 1978); Geoffrey Brennan and James Buchanan, *The Reason of Rules* (Cambridge University Press, forthcoming).

Also see *Constitutional Economics: Containing the Economic Powers of Government*, edited by Richard McKenzie (Lexington: Lexington Books, 1984). This volume of conference papers is directly relevant to the subject matter of this paper.

one set of possible instruments for discovering such independent values, a set that may not be any more efficient than several other alternatives. Much of the so-called "political theory," through the centuries, has been developed in such a nonindividualistic tradition. In this tradition, politics, broadly and inclusively defined, involves a search for "truth," and the activity of politics in its modern conceptualization becomes analogous to that of science, an activity that is acknowledged to be a discovery process.[2]

It should be evident that democratic procedures, which involve at least some counting of heads, some use of individually expressed preferences over alternatives, are not directly related to the search for some independently existing and abstract objective of "politics," an objective that is presumed omnipresent in the whole of the nonindividualistic tradition in political theorizing. In some settings, a counting of heads, along with a discussion among ordinary persons, may be judged to be instrumentally superior to the delegation of authority to a single expert or to a group of experts. In other settings, however, the reverse pattern of decision authority may well be deemed more desirable in the sense of its ability to generate efficient patterns of results. The use of the judge and the jury in criminal law cases illustrates this point well. The guilt or innocence of the accused must be determined by some institutional process. In some legal structures, the use of a multi-person jury, operating within well-defined voting rules, may be more efficacious in yielding "correct" results over a sequence. In other legal structures, the power of decision is lodged in a single agent, a judge, who is considered to be more capable of rendering "correct" verdicts. There is no *a priori* basis for a claim that either one of these two institutional means of determining guilt or innocence is instrumentally superior to the other.

By extension of this argument, it should be clear that if the existence of some independent political objective, whether this be called "truth" or "the common good," is implicitly postulated, and if politics is intellectually modelled as the search for this objective, then ordinary electoral processes that are widely interpreted to describe "democracy" need not be judged to be ei-

---

2. For an elaboration of the potentially dangerous implications from modelling politics as science, see my paper "The Potential for Tyranny in Politics as Science." Prepared for Liberty Fund Conference on "Orwell: 1984," Cambridge, England, August 1984.

ther necessary or desirable. Effective political decision-making authority may be lodged in a committee of experts, a set of philosopher-kings, a single party's ruling clique, a military junta, or a single monarch, any one of which structures may be held better able to attain "that which is good for all members of the community" than ordinary electoral processes with inclusive voting franchise. In this way, the institutional form or structure of governance is divorced from process, and "democracy" can be reintroduced, not as process at all, but as an emotively charged term designed putatively to distinguish between alternative end-objects for politics. Hence, a ruling committee can lay claim to "democracy" if it acts "for the good sought by the people," as opposed to acting "for the interests of the ruling class," with the proviso, of course, that the definition of what is good "for the people" is made by the ruling committee.

The authoritarian-totalitarian regimes that cloak their activities in the rhetoric of "democracy" are a natural outgrowth of the nonindividualistic tradition of a political theory that has been advanced at least since the ancient Greeks. My argument stems from the conviction that there is no generalizable *instrumental defense* of democratic political procedures. A normative case in support of electoral processes, where individual preferences are counted, must be noninstrumental. That which is sought for in politics is not, and cannot be, that which exists independent of the values of the individuals who make up the political community. The object or aim of politics is the furtherance or achievement of the separate and several objects of the individuals who participate variously in the collective enterprise. There is, and can be, no other object if we are to develop a general normative defense of democratic governance, understood in the process sense of the term.

If the suggested presupposition is accepted, that is, if individuals are presumed to be the only ultimate source of evaluation, the argument for electoral processes as means through which values (preferences, interests) may be expressed becomes straightforward. Here the question is not one of how to find or to discover "truth" through politics; it is not one of determining what is the "best" one from among several political options; it is not the quest for "the common good." Here the question is, instead, one of using the institution of politics, or governance, as means through which separate persons, as members of an organized political community, may jointly achieve their individually desired purposes. In this individualistic and contractarian model for politics, that which emerges from the interaction process is, quite simply, that which emerges. It is inappropriate to classify any one outcome or end-state as "better than" another. There is no supra-individual scalar that can be introduced as a criterion for any such ranking.

In this model of politics, any method of decision making that does *not* incorporate the expressed preferences of all persons in the polity, at least in some ultimate sense, must involve overt discrimination. Those who participate in the collective or group decision process have the opportunity to express *their own evaluations* of the alternatives that are confronted. Those who are not allowed to participate have no such opportunity; their preferences and interests must go unrepresented. Note that the operation of nonelectoral processes of decision is categorically different in this model and in the truth-discovery model previously discussed. The activity of a ruling committee or junta, conceived as a search for an independently existing objective, may find instrumental defense. The same activity, conceived as the expression and subsequent imposition of the values of the self-chosen elite, finds no comparable normative support.

The individualist-contractarian model of politics, for the reasons noted, cannot incorporate discriminatory limits on participation, regardless of the relative size of the decision-making group. The normative argument advanced above may seem acceptable in application to a small committee or junta, but it may, initially, seem to be attenuated in application to large number constituencies. Suppose, for example, that democratic electoral procedures are observed to operate, but that only one-half (say, males) of the adult members of the polity are franchised. In the truth or goodness discovery model of politics, this system may be expected to yield results that are approximately identical to those that would be generated under inclusive franchise. Hence, there would be little to choose as between inclusive and discriminatory franchise. By contrast, in the individualistic-contractarian model, the values of those persons who remain disenfranchised cannot be reflected in the results from the very fact of nonparticipation.

The normative argument for democratic electoral processes, as a means of allowing individuals to express their own values, the only values that exist, becomes, at the same time, an argument for an inclusive franchise or, more generally, for individual political equality.

III. Political Equality and the Potential
for Conflict among Individual Values

With the presupposition that individuals are the only sources of value, the normative argument for universal adult franchise and for electoral process in which all persons participate seems to emerge. The extension and application of this argument to the institutions of politics and governance remain to be examined. Serious errors have been made in too hasty extensions of the argument, as I shall demonstrate in the following discussion.

If there are no nonindividualistic sources of value "out there," waiting to be discovered in the truth or goodness discovery enterprise of politics, we should expect that individuals, as separate conscious beings, will have differing values, interests, and preferences, at least within wide limits. Politics, inclusively defined, involves the whole set of activities in which separate persons participate as a collective body or organization. That is to say, politics and governance involve the determination of rules, institutional structure, and particular outcomes that are to be applied to all persons in the collective. There is, by definition, a single political choice among relevant alternatives that are confronted. In the terminology of modern economics, politics, by definition, involves "publicness," whether "public good" or "public bad."

The singularity and commonality of political decision are extremely important, and make it necessary to distinguish effective political equality from nominal political equality. Because of the possible conflict among separate individual interests and values, any political decision must override at least some of those who participate in the process. Nominal political equality insures only that all persons may participate equally in the ultimate choices to be made. This point is perhaps best illustrated in a setting where all persons vote in a referendum on a single issue, with the collective outcome to be settled by simple majority rule. All persons equally express their preferences as between two outcomes presented; but those who are out-voted find that their own desired outcome is not selected. They must acquiesce in a result that runs counter to their own interests or values. Clearly, with respect to the particular choice examined, those whose interests are submerged gain little or nothing from their participation in the electoral procedure.

Here it is necessary to introduce a second and complementary philosophical presupposition, and one that is a direct implication of the first. If individuals are the only sources of value, it follows by implication if not directly that the satisfaction of individual values carries positive normative weight. That is to say, a situation in which individual preferences are met becomes normatively superior to a situation in which preferences are overruled, other things equal. From this straightforward statement, implications for political organization may be drawn.

Consider the simple referendum example, one in which the preferences of a majority for alternative A are satisfied, while the preferences of a minority for alternative B are overruled. Clearly such a result is normatively inferior to one in which alternative A could be chosen for members of the majority and alternative B could be chosen for members of the minority, if, indeed, such a result should be structurally-institutionally possible. The normative principle that individual values should be allowed to find expression in results necessarily has implications for the design of political institutions. Conflicts among separate individual values should be reduced or eliminated to the maximum extent that is possible. And, since conflicts of interests depend, in part, on the structure within which interaction takes place, there are direct implications for structural design.

Return to the referendum example, and suppose that the objects for choice are: A, which is a holiday in June, and B, which is a holiday in August. As the example suggests, if this pairwise comparison is treated as a mutually exclusive choice between two "public goods," conflict necessarily arises. But as the illustration also suggests, conflict need not be present unless there is some nonreducible "publicness" involved. That is to say, A and B, as defined, need not be mutually exclusive alternatives for the whole membership of the polity. Unless there are compelling reasons for the requirement that all persons take the same holiday, conflicts among individual values may be eliminated by the elementary expedient of allowing those who wish to take the holiday in June and those others who so desire to take the holiday in August. This solution guarantees effective equality in the satisfaction of individual preferences. It clearly goes well beyond the minimal equality that participation in the voting process insures. To the extent that the potential for conflict among individual values and preferences can be reduced by structural design, there will be less need to be concerned about the requirement that individuals, whose interests are overruled in collective decisions, must voluntarily acquiesce so long as they possess rights of participation.

IV. Democracy within Limits: The Logic of Constitutional Constraints

The elevation of individual values to a central normative significance in any comprehensive political theory has, therefore, direct implications for the institutional structure of human interaction. If conflict among separate interests is a variable, alternative structures of interaction may be ordered in a meaningful fashion. "Democracy," defined as a process that allows equal expression of separate individual values in choices that are *necessarily* mutually exclusive and that necessarily generate results applicable to all members of the polity, may be severely limited in scope and range. Such limitation is a mark of the political "success" of the social interaction process, inclusively considered, rather than the opposite. Indeed, the perversity of much modern discussion is well illustrated by the claim that the extension of "democracy" to previously nonpoliticized areas of interaction is somehow praiseworthy, when, of course, such extension is a signal that the potential for interpersonal and intergroup conflict is enhanced rather than reduced.

The normative argument for democratic decision procedures of decision making would be substantially weakened, if not totally eliminated, if *all* forms of social interaction should be either actually or potentially considered to fall within the range of political choice. If all activities should be politicized, individuals would, of course, find some normative value in guaranteed rights of equal participation in the choice process, that is, in electoral institutions, but there would also be the certainty that individual interests would be thwarted in many separate areas of activity. An evaluative comparison between a procedural democracy that is literally unlimited in this sense and other governmental forms that explicitly limit the range of politicization, even if the choices made within that range are nondemocratic, may well cut in favor of the second alternative. The normative case for democratic procedures emerges strongly only if it is understood that the range over which political-collective decisions are to be made is appropriately constrained. The attachment of the word "constitutional" as a prefix to "democracy," with the implied meaning that this carries with it if properly interpreted, immeasurably strengthens the normative case. This conclusion follows even if we are willing to make the assumption that genuinely unlimited politicization could, indeed, remain procedurally democratic, rather than shift inexorably toward totalitarian reality cloaked in democratic rhetoric.

It is, of course, no accident that constitutional democracy, as an observed governmental form, emerged in the post-Enlightenment period, and that it found intellectual support in the 18th-century discovery of the spontaneous coordination properties of the market economy. Simply stated, the principle of spontaneous coordination suggests that the economy operates so as to allow separate individual interests to be reconciled peacefully without any need for political determination of the allocation of resources, the choices of products, and the distribution of goods. The range of necessary political decisions on economic matters is dramatically reduced in a polity that gives a predominant place to a market or enterprise economy.

The economy will not, of course, organize itself in total independence of the political-legal order. There is a necessary political role involved in enforcing individuals' rights and contracts, and in producing those goods and services that are inherently public or collective in nature, including the legal system itself. The role of politics in this severely limited sense was well recognized by the classical economists who discovered and promulgated the ordering principle of the market economy.

There exist, however, no "natural" barriers that will emerge to insure that politics, as it actually operates, will stay within the limits defined by any "public goods" requirement. Indeed, quite the opposite seems to characterize political reality. There seems to arise a "natural" proclivity for individuals, groups, and the political entrepreneurs representing them, to extend the range and scope of collective-political action beyond any conceivable publicness boundaries, if publicness is defined in any economically meaningful sense. (Any politicization of an activity converts what might have been private into a public activity. Hence, politics always involves publicness, artificially defined.) The arms, agencies, and authority of the state will be utilized to secure, or in attempts to secure, differential gains for members of particular coalitions, with little or no regard for normatively appropriate boundaries on governmental action.

Such overextension can be prevented only if the range and scope for politics, for collective, governmental, or state activity is subjected to enforceable constitutional constraints. As I have already suggested, there seems to be relatively little normative support for democratic electoral procedures, as such, until and unless some limits are placed on the range of activities over which politics may operate.

V. Defining the Limits: The Problem of Constitutional Design

The general principle that politics should be limited by constitutional rules may be readily accepted, and for the reasons discussed in Section IV above. The translation of this principle into political practice is quite a different matter. There are no technologically sharp dividing lines between those activities that involve public goods and those possible activities that can, with proper institutional design, be left to nonpolitical interaction processes, such as the market. As I have indicated earlier, the fundamental role for politics, inclusively defined, is that of providing the legal framework within which individuals can go about their ordinary business of seeking to further the values they choose to seek, without overt conflict. The enforcement of rights and contracts is a necessary task for government in any liberal regime. The argument extends quite normally to the guarantee of internal and external order.

Beyond such minimal-state or protective-state limits, however, there exists a broad area for potential political activity that may or may not be admissible with appropriately defined constitutional constraints. Should or should not there be an explicit role for collective action in setting the value of the monetary unit? In enforcing and insuring that the economy is effectively competitive? In regulating natural monopolies? In preserving environmental amenities? In protecting health and safety? In promoting equality of opportunity, especially through the support of education? In alleviating poverty?

It is precisely in such areas as these that the problem of constitutional design is squarely met. There may be consensus on the legitimacy of governmental action in the maintenance of order (the protective state), and on the illegitimacy of governmental action in the regulation and control of purely private behavior, such as the individual's choice of his location, occupation, and consumption bundle. At the same time, there may arise intense dispute about the range for the potential governmental role over the whole set of in-between activities, such as those listed.

Persons who may broadly be classified as "social democrats" will want governments to remain free of any constitutional constraints on the activities falling within this set. By comparison, persons who may be broadly classified as "liberal," in the European sense, or as "libertarian," in the modern American usage, will want governments to be constitutionally restricted over at least some subset of the activities noted.

I shall neither criticize nor defend a particular dividing line between those activities that may be appropriately politicized and those that should be left free from politics. I do want to suggest, however, that, quite apart from fundamental ideological persuasion, the degree to which any person will, ideally, seek to limit the activity of government by constitutional constraints depends on the *predictive model of politics* that informs his analysis.

VI. The Implication of Modern Public Choice Theory for Constitutional Design

The theory of public choice becomes directly relevant for my discussion at this point. This theory provides at least the elements of a predictive model, or models, of how democratic electoral politics works in reality. Public choice examines the behavior of persons as they take on varying roles as "public choosers," as actual or potential voters, as organizers or members of pressure groups, as party leaders, as aspiring or elected politicians, as bureaucrats. And the theory allows us to make some predictions about patterns of outcomes that may be generated under varying sets of institutional rules through which final collective-political decisions are reached.

There are direct normative implications of public choice theory for the issues of constitutional design previously discussed. Those who have previously accepted, if often unconsciously, a naively romantic model of political activity, and who may, on that account, have remained largely unconcerned about effective constitutional constraints on governments, can scarcely do so once the full impact of modern public choice theory is acknowledged. In a very real sense, public choice theory offers a "theory of governmental-political failure" that is on all fours with the "theory of market failure" that emerged from the theoretical welfare economics of the 1950's. By comparison with the conventional wisdom of the 1960's, there can no longer be a prima facie case for political-governmental intrusion into the whole range of in-between activities that fail to be handled ideally by the operation of the non-politicized market. The whole question of limits here must be addressed pragmatically, in part on a case-by-case basis, and in part through a long-term and reflective consideration of the costs and benefits that are predicted under alternative regimes of democratic procedures.

VII. Constitutional Guarantees of Democratic Procedures and of the Political Limits

Those persons who object to the explicit introduction of or an extension of constitutional limits over the range and scope of political activity often, at the same time, strongly support constitutional guarantees of democratic decision-making procedures, as such. In the literal sense, therefore, these persons are also "constitutionalists," and they would acknowledge the necessity of affixing the word "constitutional" to "democracy." Without effective guarantees of electoral processes, a majority coalition, once in office, could, of course, simply abolish all elections and establish itself in permanent authority. In this context, those persons who most strongly oppose constitutional constraints on the activities of governments accept the necessity of constitutional constraints on the procedures of politics. There are few who claim to adhere to democratic values, however these values may be described, who are not, at the same time, constitutionalists of one sort or another. There is then no inherent or internal inconsistency in the position that urges the imposition of constraints on the range of activities open to political authority. Just as a majority coalition may, unless it is restricted, abolish electoral feedbacks that insure the potential for rotation in office, so may any effectively operating political coalition seek to extend its authority beyond any plausibly acceptable boundaries described by the publicness notion.

Even when the basic analysis here is accepted, however, and even when the operating flaws in both nonpolitical and political interactions are understood, there will remain the prospect for disagreement over constitutional design. Only those who might yet retain a romantically naive faith in the progress of "social science" could expect convergence of opinion on the proper range of governmental action. The argument that has persisted for centuries is not likely to be resolved in any emergence of "scientific consensus." At its best, scientific analysis can reduce the level of intellectual conflict.

Nonetheless, spokesmen for modern public choice theory can, I think, legitimately claim that the "state of the debate" has been considerably advanced over the course of the post-middle decades of this century. To the extent that the issues are discussed as issues of constitutional design rather than issues of policy choice with little or no regard to the rules and institutions within which choices are made, the dialogue has taken a major leap forward, by almost any criteria. To discuss policy alternatives or options independent of processes in which policy choices take place almost necessarily involves reversion to or maintenance of the notion that nonindividualistic sources of value and valuation exist, whether these be expressed as the efficiency criteria of the economists or as the common-good vector of the philosophers. Quite apart from the introduction of an external value scale, however, any discussion of policy choices independent of rules must embody the romantic conception that individual decision-makers, in their roles as "public choosers," will totally disregard the incentives offered by the rules structure and that they will, somehow, be guided only by whatever scalar ordering exists to inform their behavior.

By comparison and by contrast, consider the level and content of the normative argument among constitutionalists who continue to disagree about the appropriate limits on state or political action. The argument here is based on the presupposition that there exist no nonindividualistic values, and also that individuals will respond to the incentives that they confront. The argument further incorporates the modern analysis of how differing rules and institutions of public choice affect the incentives for persons who participate.

The normative argument then reduces to one that involves an ultimate choice among alternative structures of rules (to constitutional choice), rules that will, in turn, serve to limit collective action. As I noted earlier, we need not expect consensus, even among those who work within the given presuppositions and who are informed by essentially the same analysis. Productive dialogue can proceed, however, unencumbered by the excesses of romantic folly that have wrought such havoc in the intellectualized discussions of "democracy" over the ages.

Such a constructive dialogue must embody some attempts to derive plausibly acceptable criteria for constitutional choices. If alternative sets of rules are the ultimate objects of choice, how are these rules to be ordered? What is the scalar here? Or, even at one stage further back in the discourse, what principles are to guide the construction of an ordering of alternative sets of rules? It is, I think, an indication of intellectual progress when we can point to modern efforts to examine precisely these issues.[3]

VIII. Democracy in Constitutional Perspective

In summation of my argument in this paper, let me suggest that "democracy" assumes normative meaning only in a constitutional perspective. And I suggest further that those who limit meaningful usage of the term to those political regimes that embody electoral processes in which individuals participate as ultimate public choosers, must implicitly if not explicitly adopt such a perspective. Surely it would be difficult to locate a "nonconstitutional democrat," a person who does, indeed, value the rights of persons to participate in collective action but who, at the same time, does not seek to limit the range of political behavior, even to the extent of incorporating guarantees that rights to participate are maintained.

The philosophical presuppositions that are implicit in any normative argument for constitutional democracy are by no means universally shared, even by persons in effectively democratic regimes, and even by those scholars whose task it is to clarify and to explain the intellectual underpinnings of social reality. There is widespread intellectual confusion, even at the level of academic "political theory" (or perhaps especially at this level). However, until and unless we can unpack and sort out the intellectual foundations, there is relatively little to be gained in engaging in debates at the stage of choice among policy alternatives.

As I have noted, progress has been and is being made in the academic-intellectual-philosophical discussion. "Constitutional democracy" is now a meaningful term, with positive normative weight, for more people than was the case in the middle years of this century. With time, and with luck, those of us who profess to be the academic-intellectual defenders of constitutional

3. For the first question, see Buchanan and Tullock, *The Calculus of Consent*, op. cit., and subsequent discussion. Also, for a modern treatment, see Brennan and Buchanan, *The Reason of Rules*, op. cit. For the second question, see John Rawls, *A Theory of Justice* (Cambridge: Harvard University Press, 1971), along with the vast literature that this seminal book has spawned.

democracy, as the uniquely preferred regime of political-social-economic order, may find that our ivory-tower conceptions can measure up, in broad terms, to the inchoate sentiments of ordinary persons everywhere, sentiments that place liberty from political oppression very high on any value scale.

Equality as Fact and Norm

Economists often introduce the simplifying assumption that all persons are equal or identical in order to make their abstract models of human interaction more tractable. In a world-of-equals, analysis of the behavioral responses of a single person yields results that are automatically generalizable to the whole community. Models embodying these assumptions may retain explanatory value even when their descriptively unreal nature is fully recognized. The predictive potential is enhanced when the equality or identity assumptions can be restricted to selected characteristics or attributes. Any generalized prediction in social science implies as its basis a theoretical model that embodies elements of an equality assumption. If individuals differ, one from the other, in *all* attributes, social science becomes impossible. In an ideal sense, the role of the social scientist is limited to explanation and prediction, and it does not extend to the formulation of norms for social organization. Nonetheless, the underlying purpose of scientific explanation must be acknowledged to be improvement. Those who participate in social and institutional reform (including social scientists in other roles than scientific) act on the basis of some vision of social process. This vision is shaped by the scientists' explanatory models.

In this paper I shall argue that the continuing debate between the individualist and the collectivist may be grounded on divergent visions of social

From *Ethics* 81 (April 1971): 228–40. Copyright 1971 by The University of Chicago. All rights reserved. Reprinted by permission of the University of Chicago Press, publisher.

An earlier version of this paper was presented in a seminar discussion at San Diego State College in April 1969. This version was prepared for presentation at the annual meeting of the Southern Economic Association, November 1970. I am indebted to my colleague Gordon Tullock for helpful comments on earlier drafts.

process and not necessarily or fundamentally on differing ultimate values. Further, I shall demonstrate how the basic difference may reduce to one involving the implicit assumptions made about personal equality and inequality. The individualist and the collectivist select different attributes of equality to be dominant characteristics in their model visions of social interaction. To the extent that this hypothesis holds, the issue between the two political philosophies may be primarily empirical. Saying this is not to imply that the issue is amenable to straightforward resolution. If, however, agreement could be reached on the sources of disagreement, prospects for constructive dialogue might be enhanced.

The discussion is intended to be general, but it has direct relevance to the current social scene. The social discontent in evidence in East and West can be interpreted as providing empirical refutation, even if indirectly, of one variant of the equality assumption. Individuals seem to be rejecting the implied equality of collectivism. Whether or not this rejection is or may be coupled with an increased acceptance of the implied equality of individualism remains an open question.

I. The Attributes of Equality

Economists state their assumptions somewhat more carefully than their fellow social scientists, and it will be helpful to commence with the economists' specifications for a world-of-equals. Normally, they discuss two separate attributes of identity or equality among individuals. One of these relates to the demand or consumption side of personal behavior and the other relates to the supply or producing side. For the demand or consumption side these are summarized in the interchangeable terms *preferences, tastes, utility functions;* for the supply or producing side in the terms *factor* or *resource endowments, capacities, production-transformation possibilities.* In a full world-of-equals model, persons are postulated to be identical in both attributes—in preferences and in factor endowments or capacities. For some purposes, economists find it useful to retain the equality assumption on the utility-function or preferences side while dropping the corollary assumption on the capacities side. For example, an equal-preferences model has proven helpful in "explaining" some of the widely observed fiscal institutions in modern societies. For other purposes, the economist finds it helpful to drop the assumption of equal preferences while retaining that about equal capacities. This is essentially the model employed for explaining those interoccupational wage or salary differentials that are "equalizing."

My reference here to economists' frequent use of models that embody assumptions about individual equality should not be interpreted as suggesting that such restrictions are necessary in the central models of economic theory. For the most part, this theory is developed in a context of inequality among persons, with respect to both utility functions and resource endowments. As economic theory assists in informing an overall or comprehensive vision of the socioeconomic interaction process, however, the relative patterns of inequality that are assumed to be present in the two attributes may well exercise significant influence. While acknowledging interpersonal inequalities in both preferences and capacities, the normative implications of specific institutional-organizational structures may depend critically on the relative degree of inequality imputed to each attribute. Roughly similar results may be predicted with theoretical models that implicitly embody widely differing assumptions, and existing empirical techniques remain far from that level of sophistication that would be required for definitive testing.

II. Equality in Preferences and in Capacities

Initially I shall discuss the all-market and the all-collective organizational alternatives under a pure world-of-equals assumption. All persons are assumed to be identical, both in preferences and in capacities. Identity in preferences means that all persons classify "goods" and "bads" in the same way, and, furthermore, that they make the same subjective trade-offs among the separate arguments in these two sets. In formal economic theory, the arguments in the utility functions of individuals are normally limited to "economic" goods and bads. For our purposes, equality in preferences or tastes should be extended to encompass "noneconomic" arguments. Identity in preferences implies not only that all persons place the same relative evaluation on apples, oranges, and smog, but, also, that they place the same relative evaluation on reduced military posture in the Far East and increased military posture in the Middle East.

A rigorous definition of identity in capacities or endowments is less familiar and considerably more complex. In a static context, identity among persons in endowments means that each one confronts the same production-transformation prospects. Each person commences with the same set of "goods" and "bads," and he faces the same prospects of "trading" these one with another. This static definition is overly restrictive, however, because of the intertemporal interdependence of individual choices about the utilization of capacities. By choosing to use his initial endowment in one way rather than another at one point in time, a person can permanently increase or decrease his endowment or capacity. Any reasonable definition of identity in endowments or in capacities must, therefore, specify that persons face the same production-transformation possibilities at some designated point in time, normally before the start of the income-earning period, which would presumably be at some moment of career or occupational choice. Only with some such definition as this can the capacity-equality assumption have much relevance independent from the preferences assumption. Defined in this way, individuals may actually differ in resource capabilities, human and nonhuman, at any one point in time even though the model postulates strict identity. The actual differences at any point in time must be attainable by the exercise of individual choice dating from the initial point at which capacities were in fact identical. We should note that this definitional complexity does not arise in the pure world-of-equals model. When we postulate identity in utility functions, this implies that all persons will choose to use their capacities identically and hence will remain identical through time. However, when we drop this assumption of identity in preferences in later discussion, the definitional extension of the equal-capacity assumption becomes essential.

In the pure world-of-equals, embodying both identity among all persons in preferences and identity among all persons in capacities, similar results are generated under widely differing institutional-organizational arrangements. Hence, the "constitutional" choice among separate social structures is not an important consideration. To demonstrate this, we may compare and contrast collectivist and noncollectivist or individualistic organization of an economy under the extreme equality assumption.

Let us assume that the production of all goods and services is organized through a market process in which all persons remain free to make whatever producing-trading-consuming decisions that they desire. If we assume only that contracts are enforced and that fraud is effectively policed, this economy will be characterized by substantial identity in final consumption patterns among all individuals.[1]

Let us compare this result with that which might be predicted to emerge under a dramatically different organizational structure. We assume now that the economy is fully collectivized. All decisions are made through a collective or political choice process. If we assume only that arbitrary exploitation or personal discrimination is effectively prevented, this structure, regardless of the particular decision rule that is adopted, will generate results that are quite similar to those that characterize the all-market economy. This similarity in results between these wholly different organizational alternatives may appear surprising. It stems basically from the equality assumption under the restrictions imposed on each decision process.

In the all-collective economy, the effective prevention of arbitrary discrimination requires that each person be treated in the same manner as his equals, which in this case means that all persons are treated identically regardless of the collective decisions that are made. This applies for the cost as well as for the benefit side, and means that no person can, through his membership in a dominant political coalition, secure gains at the expense of his equals outside the coalition. Every decision rule produces results that are the same as those that would emerge under a rule that requires unanimous consent. An example may be helpful here. Suppose that one man is appointed as dictator; he is authorized to make all decisions in the community. He will, of course, choose among alternatives on the basis of his own preferences, but since his preferences are identical with those of everyone else, he will make the same choices that everyone else will desire that he make. He could secure

---

1. In an extreme variant of this model which embodies constant returns to scale of production over all ranges of output for all goods, this economy would be without trade. In such a setting, each person becomes a complete microcosm of the whole society. In the less-restricted setting where constant returns are not assumed, individuals will be led to specialize in production, and differentials in wages and in salaries will emerge that will offset the relative advantages of the several occupations. To the extent that such differentials in income emerge, individuals can differ, one from another, in command over final product, and full identity in consumption patterns will be violated. Such differentials are required, however, to keep persons on the same utility levels. If we assume away the differences in the subjective advantages of differing occupations, this complexity will not arise.

differential personal gains from his dictatorship position only if he should somehow discriminate between his own position and those of his fellow equals. Under genuine nondiscriminatory collectivism, this is not possible. All decision rules generate, therefore, the same results.[2]

The no-discrimination requirement for the all-collective economy serves the same purpose as the no-fraud requirement for the all-market economy. If fraud becomes possible in market dealings among persons, even among those who are initially assumed to be equal, some must assume the role of the defrauders and some must become victims of fraud. The differential ability to defraud along with the differential ability to secure personal gains through political or collective discrimination violate the basic equality assumption. This assumption is critical for the comparative purposes that this analysis embodies.

With the nondiscriminatory qualification, the all-collective economy will generate an equality among all persons in final consumption patterns just as will the all-market economy. Collective agreement on this pattern will be reached readily, and, significantly, all persons will acquiesce in the chosen results since they will mirror their own preferences regardless of the decision rule. The important conclusion for our purposes is that the all-collective and the all-market economy produce roughly the same results.[3] These sharply divergent institutional-organizational alternatives generate significant differences in results only to the extent that men differ one from another.

III. Differential Preferences and Equal Capacities

The question becomes: How do men differ, and how will differences over particular attributes modify these comparative results? The dichotomy of at-

2. For a further discussion of this proposition, see my *Demand and Supply of Public Goods* (Chicago: Rand McNally & Co., 1968), 164–66.

3. Both models will generate equality in final consumption patterns among all persons, but the actual mix of goods and services produced may be slightly different due to the technology of consumption. If there are genuine advantages to be secured from jointness in consumption (genuine "public goods" in the modern sense), goods embodying such jointness might not be produced in the all-market economy, at least to the same extent that they would be produced in the all-collective economy. Even this difference would disappear if transactions costs should be absent. In any case, this complexity need not concern us here.

tributes is helpful. We shall first compare the organizational alternatives in a model that embodies the assumption that all persons remain identical in capacities, as earlier defined, but where they are allowed to differ in preferences. Individual utility functions are no longer the same. In one sense, and as the analysis will reveal, this is the economists' standard model. In many economic applications, "the individual" is described by his preference scale or his utility function.

Let us consider, as before, an all-market structure qualified only by the enforcement of contracts and the policing of fraud. Since individuals now have different tastes, their final consumption patterns will not be uniform. Trade will be observed to take place until each person commands that set of consumption goods and services which most nearly satisfies his own unique trade-offs. The assumption that persons remain equal in capacity insures that the differences among final consumption bundles stem almost exclusively from the postulated differences in preferences.[4] For reasons noted earlier, individuals at a given point in time may face different production-transformation possibilities even in this equal-capacities model. To the extent that they do so, real incomes, and hence command over final product, may differ. But such differences as these arise themselves from the individuals' own decisions made earlier about increasing or running down initially held endowments.

The differences in final consumption bundles that would be observed in the all-market economy in this model cannot be interpreted as having been imposed by forces external to the individuals. These differences reflect the inherent individualities of the persons that are involved and nothing more. In such a context, it seems evident that "greater equality" carries little meaning, and that it could hardly be advanced seriously as a norm for social change.

Let us now change the postulated organizational structure while remaining within the differential-preferences–equal-capacities model. Assume that an all-collective constitution is in being. All decisions concerning the allocation and the utilization of resources are made in a collective or political process. As before, we also postulate that there is an effective restriction against arbitrary discrimination among persons or groups. In this setting,

---

4. The "almost" is inserted to allow for the differentials discussed in n. 1.

individuals would tend to be provided with uniform patterns of final consumption, despite their differences in tastes. The central characteristic of nondiscriminatory collectivism is universality or uniformity in treatment.[5] The particular characteristics of the consumption bundle that will be provided uniformly to all persons will depend on the rule through which collective decisions are made. When the collective decision rule is that of simple majority voting, the person or persons whose preferences are median for the whole community will tend to be controlling. Under other decision rules, the preferences of the median member of the effective electorate will dominate the outcomes. Under single-person dictatorship this reduces, of course, to his own preferences. The outcome depends on the rules for making group choice, and, in any case, individualized expressions of preference or taste could not be predicted to emerge under any rule. In the final solution, large numbers of persons must remain dissatisfied by the common standards of consumption that are imposed. The uniformity in consumption bundles is achieved only through the repression of individual differences in tastes.

As this organizational scheme would actually work, individuals would have strong incentives to retrade goods and services among themselves after some initial collective or governmental distribution. To the extent that such retrading takes place, individualized tastes could be expressed. If this sort of trading were allowed, however, we should be outside the range of our all-collective model. For comparative purposes, it seems best to restrict analysis to a pure collective model, in which all such retrading as this would be prohibited.

As the description of this differential-preferences–equal-capacities model should make clear, it provides the strongest case for adopting the market process as the organizational norm. The imposed equalities in final consumption patterns that collectivism produces take on no normative features.

5. Somewhat surprisingly, the implications of this uniformity-universality characteristic of nondiscriminatory collectivism were not fully discussed in the traditional economic analysis of socialist organization. Several recent papers have been aimed at filling this gap (see Gordon Tullock, "Social Cost and Government Action," *American Economic Review* 59 [May 1969]: 189–97; Yoram Barzel, "Two Propositions on the Optimum Level of Producing Collective Goods," *Public Choice* 6 [Spring 1969]: 31–38; C. M. Lindsay, "Medical Care and the Economics of Sharing," *Economica* 36 [November 1969]: 351–69; along with my own "Notes for an Economic Theory of Socialism," *Public Choice* 8 [Spring 1970]: 29–44).

For those who place strong positive value on individual freedom of expression, on individual and personal liberty in their conception of the "good society," the market offers major advantages over its collectivist counterpart. It allows individuals to express their separate preferences while these are necessarily stifled, to greater or lesser degree, under wholesale collectivization of activity. Conversely, for those who may value individual freedom somewhat less intensely and who place relatively more weight on distributional equality, the collectivist alternative offers relatively little advantage here. The distributional inequalities in final consumption that characterize the market results in this framework do not arise from differences in initial endowments. "Distributive justice" simply cannot be invoked in ethical support of a collectively imposed set of uniformities in consumption. Insofar as the equalities in capacities, the assumption of this model, are equalities in fact, equality in consumption cannot be introduced as a norm.

Only one minor qualification need be added. To make these conclusions generally acceptable, we should include in individual capacities the ability to "be lucky." If there are significant uncertainties present, individuals with equal initial endowments may find their final consumption possibilities determined, in part, by sheer luck. An argument may be advanced in support of equalization to correct partially for such fortuitous differentials. Realistically, of course, comparable or even greater uncertainty would be present under the collectivist alternative.

IV. Equal Preferences and Differential Capacities

We may proceed predictably in our analysis by reversing the assumptions about equality. We now assume that all persons in the community are identical in tastes or preferences but that they differ in capacities or endowments, human and nonhuman. We shall examine the results to be predicted under the contrasting institutional structures.

In an effectively working market process, individuals would be observed to consume different final consumption bundles despite the initially postulated identity in utility functions. The position that a particular person attains on his utility surface will depend on his resource or factor endowments (including luck), and this model postulates that these endowments differ as among separate persons. The market continues to allow for a full expression of individualized preferences, but these are restricted by the initial differentials in capacities.

These results may be compared with those predicted to emerge under the all-collective structure. As previously emphasized, there will be a tendency here for individuals to be provided with uniform consumption bundles. Interestingly, if all persons find themselves in this model with identical sets of "goods," there would be no overt dissatisfaction at this stage. Even if all prohibitions on retrading were eliminated here, none would be observed to take place. The reason is, of course, the postulated equality in tastes among all persons in the group. In the final equilibrium produced by the all-collective structure, which would be characterized by consumption uniformity, individuals are not directly coerced into an acceptance of a final-goods package that is contrary to their own preferences.

This suggests that the results of the all-collective structure or process under this model's set of assumptions would be more stable in some political-sociological sense than those emerging in the earlier model. This is correct, but an important consideration that has been so far neglected must now be explicitly discussed. The decision-making process in the all-collective structure under equal preferences and differential capacities must be examined closely. In one sense what is required here is a more careful specification of the differential-capacities assumption in this setting. In the earlier definition, we limited capacity to production-transformation prospects that faced the individual, production-transformation prospects for producing-exchanging "economic" goods and services. We said nothing about the capacities of persons in the political process. In one respect, we have assumed throughout our analysis that all persons possess equal capacities to influence collectively determined outcomes. This "political equality" assumption is the basis for the postulated uniformity in consumption under collective organization. If differences among persons in capacities to produce economic values are accompanied by differences in capacities to produce values through the political process, the market and the collective-decision structure would tend to generate roughly the same results in all cases. In the model under consideration in this section, we want to retain the assumption about equality in "political capacity" but to allow for differential capacities to produce economic values. If we then impose uniformity in consumption as a result of collective decision making, we must require that individuals, with different economic capacities, make differing contributions to costs. Obviously, if capacities to produce goods and services differ among persons, and if these capacities are to be fully utilized, the equalization of final consumption bundles among all persons must involve differential shares in the costs of producing those goods that are produced.

Understanding may be facilitated here if we compare this all-collective result with that result discussed earlier under the differential-preferences–equal-capacities model in Section III. In the latter, individuals would presumably be subjected to nondiscriminatory "tax payments," and because capacities are identical, these are roughly the same for each person. Individuals are unhappy or dissatisfied with the all-collective structure because of the imposed uniformities in consumption bundles in the face of differing tastes. By contrast, under the model treated in this section, individuals acquiesce in the consumption bundles that are uniformly imposed under all-collective decision making because their utility functions are the same. Those whose capacities are superior may remain unhappy in the fact that their own imposed contribution to total production exceeds those made by others. But since capacities or endowments cannot be directly exchanged, there is no available means for redress.[6] The same thing can be put in the language of theoretical welfare economics or of game theory. The all-collective results in the equal-preferences–differential-capacities model treated in this section need not be, but conceptually could be, Pareto optimal. Hence, in such case any proposals for change would become analogous to plays in a zero-sum game. By contrast, the all-collective results in the differential-preferences–equal-capacities model treated in Section III must be nonoptimal. Proposals to modify these results can conceptually secure unanimous consent of all parties; the game is positive sum.

It should be clear from the discussion that the collectivist has an immensely stronger argument in this equal-preferences–differential-capacities model than he does in its converse examined in Section III. The costs of enforcing collectively chosen outcomes are lower, which is the same as saying that these outcomes are more stable. Relative to the situation predictable in

6. This statement would have to be qualified to the extent that persons have locational alternatives available to them. If persons can migrate to other communities, if they can "vote with their feet," indirect trade can take place.

the converse setting, the collectivist also stands on firmer economic ground here. He cannot, of course, carry the day even in this case on pure efficiency criteria, but the possible inefficiencies of collectivism are relatively less significant.

The individualist's arguments are likewise relatively less potent here. Insofar as individual preferences are, in fact, identical, his argument for allowing differential expressions of these is undermined. His support of market process that stems normatively from the supposition that "men are different" rests solely on the initial differences in capacities or endowments. The end objectives, the "goods" that men seek, are identical for all men. Their differences in final attainment under unfettered market interaction stem almost exclusively from differences in the means with which they are provided. It is here that "distributive justice" takes on significant ethical properties. The individualist who defends market organization will rarely argue for inequalities in final consumption bundles that arise solely from capacity differences. His defense of the market must rest largely, if not exclusively, on efficiency grounds; he must advance quite different arguments from those that seem effective in the equal-capacities model.

V. The World of Unequals

It is, of course, recognized that individuals differ, one from the other, in both of the essential attributes discussed. Men are unequal in preferences; they do not possess identical utility functions. Men also differ in capacities; even at some defined point in time, inequality in endowments (human and nonhuman) is characteristic of the real world. It is also evident that no social reformer proposes either an all-market or an all-collective institutional arrangement. The continuing debate between the collectivist and the individualist concerns the appropriate dividing line between market and collective order, always within a structure that includes both a private and a public or governmental sector.

Analytically, however, the extreme models about personal equality and about institutional structure are suggestive. They may indicate some of the implicit empirical biases of those who stand on opposing sides of the arguments about social reform. The individualist who seeks to shift the organizational spectrum toward the market pole, who seeks to decollectivize activities currently in the public sector, may interpret and explain the inequalities that he observes on the basis of differences among persons in preferences, including preferences about capacity utilization (e.g., choices for work versus leisure, spending versus saving, etc.), at least to a relatively greater extent than his collectivist counterpart.[7] To the extent that he acknowledges capacity-generated inequalities in distribution, the individualist is likely to propose reforms that are aimed at equalizing initial endowments or at least mitigating extreme inequalities. He seeks reform and social changes that have as their objective the achievement of some plausibly satisfactory approximation to the model examined in Section III. In contraposition, the collectivist, who seeks to shift the organizational spectrum in the opposing direction, who seeks to remove still more activities from the market process and to collectivize them, may interpret and explain the inequalities that he observes (the same reality confronted by the individualist) on the basis of individual differences in inherent capacities, at least to some relatively greater extent than does the individualist. If he could conceive of equalized capacities, the collectivist would probably predict the emergence of what he might consider to be only trivial differences in final consumption patterns, differences that he might attribute to whim and fashion rather than to genuine tastes or values. In this vision of the world, each individual really does want the same things; the inequalities that are observed must, therefore, reflect capacity differentials. As he comes to propose reforms, the collectivist may pay relatively little attention to capacity equalization, per se. He may consider attempts to make individuals equal in initial endowments, attempts to "equalize opportunities," to be both indirect and inefficient means to secure distributive justice. In his vision, even the most massive of such attempts may produce limited results. He agrees with Plato and disagrees with Adam Smith about the differences between the common street porter and the

---

7. An alternative hypothesis would allow the individualist to attribute observed inequalities among persons to the same sources as does his collectivist counterpart but to be more pessimistic about the possibilities of removing such inequalities through collective action. The whole set of problems raised by the prospects of effectively controlling bureaucratic hierarchies cannot be neglected, but these are not central to the main theme of this paper.

philosopher. Within the limits of plausible social-collective effort, the collectivist prefers direct equalization of consumption in terms of specific goods and services.

The individualist and the collectivist are likely to settle for differing social compromises in the world of pervasive inequality. Institutions that overtly and explicitly perpetuate inequalities in endowments and capacities are subject to the individualist's most severe attacks. He will tend to place confiscatory inheritance taxation high on his scale for social reform. He will lend his support to massive public outlays on general education, and he will support selective programs to eliminate poverty. He will tend to oppose an "establishment," and he will oppose the political ambitions of the Kennedys and the Rockefellers. The collectivist will, by comparison, acquiesce in a continuing and pervasive inequality in capacities if he can secure a sufficient measure of consumption equalization. His reform efforts are concentrated on collectivizing activities as a means of securing uniformity. He will tend to advocate a nationally collectivized health service, extensive programs for public housing, public recreation facilities, public libraries, publicly financed cultural programs, publicly operated as well as public-financed education, public television broadcasting.

This summary is not intended to suggest that individuals can be found who fit perfectly into either the individualist or the collectivist mold. Within himself, an individual may be a mixture of the two positions that I have compared. What I am trying to demonstrate is that the manner in which human or personal inequality is interpreted, which is essentially an empirical estimation, may be an important influence on a person's views on social policy. Social scientists have perhaps been too prone to reduce disagreements on policy to value arguments. Ideally considered, the "good society" of the individualist may not be much different from that of the collectivist. Practicably, however, because of the differences in interpretation of inequality, these may remain poles apart.

VI. Evidence and Its Implications

The unrest and dissent that are characteristic of young persons everywhere can be interpreted as a rejection of the collectivist attempts to impose conformity. It would be hard to explain this behavioral revolution by any appeal to endowment or capacity differentials. The shift in attitudes reflects the expression of personal differences in tastes, notably as among groups. The students simply have different preference functions from those of their elders. They choose to live differently.

All of this may be considered as a refutation of the equal-preferences hypothesis. It cannot be interpreted as corroboration of the equal-capacities hypothesis. If "socialism is dead" as a potentially viable social structure, there is still no sign that individualism can emerge in its stead. The reaction against conformism, against centralization, against bureaucracy—these may possibly result in some limitations on the range of collective control over man's actions. This may provide some opportunity for reforms aimed at reducing inequalities in capacities, and the greater emphasis now being placed on selectivity in governmental programs may reflect some of this. Even with such policy reforms, however, there is no basis for predicting that any equal-capacities hypothesis will be proved. Facts cannot be made into fable, and we must recognize that, in spite of policy, individuals may differ significantly in inherent personal capacities to create values. Empirically, Plato's hypothesis of inequality may not be refuted, no matter how much we might prefer Adam Smith's. The inequalities that we see may stem from both attributes, and satisfactorily corrective measures may be beyond the scope of social policy.

Where does this leave the social philosopher? A subsidiary theme of this paper is that modern social philosophy, in either its individualist or its collectivist variant, depends critically on one or the other of the equality hypotheses. The ideal world of the individualist contains persons who are basically the same in capacity, and modern democratic and economic institutions in the West were established on the hypothesis that empirical reality can be adjusted to provide a satisfactorily close approximation to that ideal. The ideal world of the socialist contains individuals who are equal in basic tastes, and socialist institutions were established on the hypothesis that empirical reality can be adjusted to reflect this equality despite differing capacities.

What happens when people refuse to accept the distributional inequalities that a practicably working capitalist structure requires while at the same time they refuse to accept the restrictions on personal freedom that a practicably working collectivism requires? The assorted compromises represented by the mixed social systems of the mid-twentieth century may collapse and from differing directions.

I write as an individualist who yet has little faith in the ultimate corroboration of the equal-capacity hypothesis. From this vantage point, the route toward social stability may involve an increased willingness to tolerate major divergences between our ideals and reality, a recognition that we must proceed "as if" our implied hypothesis is fact, even when we acknowledge that it has little empirical foundation. With Thomas Jefferson, we must sense that in order to treat men "as equals" it may be necessary to tolerate considerable inequality. My counterpart is the collectivist who yet acknowledges that individuals do want different things for themselves. From his vantage point, the route toward greater social stability may involve the more intensive conditioning of individuals to make them accept the conformity that collectivism must impose. In order to secure the distributive equality that he seeks, he must acknowledge that it may be necessary to introduce the inequality in treatment that coercion embodies.

Both the individualist and the collectivist, as I have used these terms here, place positive values on personal freedom and on equality. These basic values may be given different weights and the empirical reading of the world may differ, but neither the individualist nor the collectivist desires to impose his own standards on the rest of society. In this idealized sense, both are democrats; neither is elitist. Within more broadly defined individualist and collectivist categories, however, elitists abound. Many persons propose a smaller public sector primarily because they do not like what is being provided; they should be quite willing to support an enlarged governmental role in society provided only that they could dictate its pattern. Similarly, and perhaps more commonly, many collectivists are *dirigistes* first and democratic socialists second. They support an extension of state activity because they see in this a means of imposing their own social values on others. The elitist values neither personal freedom nor distributional equality. If either of these values is to be preserved, even at some tolerably acceptable levels of attainment, the nonelitists in both the individualist and the socialist camps may find it necessary to come to some provisional agreement.

Political Equality
and Private Property
The Distributional Paradox

Introduction

In this chapter I shall advance an explanatory hypothesis concerning widely held attitudes toward the distributive outcomes produced in an economy that is organized largely on market or exchange principles. I shall argue that these attitudes stem from an emergent contradiction within modern liberal individualism, a contradiction that can be neither readily resolved nor easily ignored. Public property rights, embodied in the voting franchise, have come into being through modern political institutions, in both their idealized and operative forms. We seek to use these rights to modify the distribution or assignment of private property among persons and families to conform with vague ideals of equality, while at the same time we try to limit the encroachment of the State on spheres of private action.

Political equality among persons, defined in terms of the voting franchise, is basically inconsistent with continuing economic differences. The individual's right to vote, held on an equal basis with other people, implies an ultimate equality in a political claim to all wealth in society. Observed economic inequalities among persons must therefore be subject to predicted political intrusion. But this political thrust toward the elimination of economic differences, toward economic equality, is at the same time inconsistent with in-

From *Markets and Morals*, ed. Gerald Dworkin, Gordon Bermant, and Peter Brown (Washington: Hemisphere Publishing, 1977), 69–84. Reprinted by permission of the publisher.

dividual freedom from the State. "Political equality to use power within appropriately defined limits" may be reconciled with "the legal protection of private property within appropriately defined limits," but the delicate balance that is required to accomplish this reconciliation may be overreached. The attempt to allow the full exercising of public property rights held equally by all participants in democratic order may produce ill-conceived interventions in market adjustment to the disadvantage of everyone.

Many of those who criticize the distributive results of a market economy draw the wrong implications about causal elements and hence seem largely to misdirect their emphases. They should not, basically, be concerned about the distribution of the potentially realizable surplus that market exchanges bring into being—the only distribution that is, strictly speaking, attributable to the market process. The institution generating the distribution of these gains from trade is a misconceived target.[1] What these critics are concerned about is, instead, the pretrade or premarket distribution of endowments, talents, and capacities (of *wealth* defined to include human as well as nonhuman capital), which is a much more important element in determining the observed posttrade distribution than the market itself. To make the market, as a social organization, responsible for the imputation of premarket positions confuses the issue, especially in terms of implications for social and political policy. The market takes persons as they are, differences and all, and allows *mutual* gains to be secured. Distributional attention should be focused on pretrade or premarket positions of persons and families, with the recognition that, under any conceivable distribution, whether this be "natural," historically determined, or arbitrarily imposed, the market process itself insures mutuality of gain.

---

1. Dissatisfaction with the distributive outcomes in a market economy has traditionally been central to the socialist critique of markets. For a sophisticated statement, see M. Dobb, *Welfare Economics and the Economics of Socialism* (Cambridge: Cambridge University Press, 1969), especially pp. 24–25. But the critique has by no means been limited to socialists. Many economists who support market organization acknowledge the validity of the socialist critique concerning distribution and implicitly suggest that the distributional outcomes observed are, in fact, attributable to the market process. James Meade is one of the few exceptions; he explicitly separates the distribution of ownership of property (the *premarket endowments distribution* in my terminology here) from the distribution of incomes that emerges from the market process, as such; see J. E. Meade, *Efficiency, Equity, and the Ownership of Property* (Cambridge: Harvard University Press, 1965).

There may be differentials in bargaining power and in bargaining skills that modify the distribution of the net gains from trade within narrow limits. But broadly speaking, the potentially realizable surplus that trade makes possible is shared among all traders, and certainly no trader finds himself made worse off in absolute terms in his posttrade position than in his pretrade position. However, what we observe is postmarket distribution. With no knowledge of premarket disposition of endowments, we are tempted to impute to the exchange process itself causal influence that it simply does not possess. This may, in turn, lead to mistaken and misapplied prohibitions and limitations on the exchange process which may damage all parties, with little or no effects on the distribution of relative endowments and talents.

Equal Endowments

It is helpful to break down the separate causal influences that may generate realized differences among persons in command over final product values. Consider first a model in which all persons possess identical endowments and capacities but in which individual preferences differ;[2] that is to say, all persons enter the market process on an equal basis. Because of differences among utility functions, however, the postmarket distribution of final product values will be unequal. Even in a no-production economy, those persons whose preferences embody somewhat more flexibility among final product items will, on observation, seem to fare better than those whose tastes dictate relatively high evaluations for specific commodities. For the latter, market exchange may involve large sacrifices in initial endowments, in a physically measured sense, in order to attain relatively limited increments in the amounts of those items that are intensely desired. For example, the person in Greenland who has an abiding passion for fresh coconuts will seem demonstrably worse off than a neighbor for whom fish are equally delectable.

If we introduce production from human effort, the market organization of the identical-endowments model will also tend to generate differences in final product allocation that reflect attitudes toward risk. In any single period

2. See J. M. Buchanan, "Equality as Fact and Norm," *Ethics* 81 (April 1971): 228–40, for a discussion that introduces various models of equality among persons.

of observation, some of those persons who are not averse to risk will have "struck it rich" in comparison with those in the community who shun risk. Some gamblers are always rich.

Most important, perhaps, are those persons who place a relatively low value on leisure who will secure a relatively large share of measured end values of produced commodities. There may appear to be substantial differences among persons and families in "real income" in such a market economy because the value of leisure is not normally incorporated in such measures. Finally, chance itself may enter; a "little bit of luck" may create private fortunes, even in the world where endowments and capacities are identical among all persons.[3]

In any of the settings just discussed, there will emerge apparent asymmetries in the postmarket distribution of final consumables. There is, however, no legitimate basis for prohibiting or restricting market exchange in any commodity or service so long as individual preferences are accepted as controlling and so long as consumption externalities are absent. The call girl sells her services because she values them less than that which she can secure in exchange; she does so not because of some relative deprivation in economic endowment, but because this behavior is dictated by her intrinsic pattern of preferences. The same thing applies to the wino who indirectly trades his blood for alcohol.

This identical-endowments model becomes the idealized setting for laissez-faire precepts. In the premarket assignment of endowments and capacities, all persons are economic equals. Observed differences in command over final product value stem exclusively from choice or chance, and there is no contradiction among the trading process, the market, and democratic political order, where each person is assigned an equal share in ultimate political power. Limitations on the exchange process might emerge here, but these would reflect the presence of recognized externalities. There would be no grounds for proposing distributionally motivated interferences with the market process.

---

3. For a general discussion of how the several elements noted here may modify income distribution, see M. Friedman, "Choice, Chance, and the Personal Distribution of Income," *Journal of Political Economy* 61 (August 1953): 277–90.

Differences in Endowments with Equal Preferences

Let us now shift to an alternative model that allows differences among persons in either initial endowments or in capacities to produce values or both. To clarify the discussion, let us now assume that all persons are identical in preferences; utility functions are the same for all individuals.

In this setting, let us say that one person, A, is observed to purchase personal services from another person, B. Both parties clearly gain from the transaction, and any overt restriction on the freely negotiated exchange would probably place both parties in less preferred positions. Individual A, the purchaser of personal services in the example, may be able to secure the services of the other person, B, however, solely because of A's superior initial economic endowment. The result is exemplified quite clearly in the BBC series "Upstairs Downstairs," which has been shown on Public Broadcasting Corporation television programs in the United States. Those who lived "upstairs" in Edwardian England dominated the lives of those who lived "downstairs" (the domestic staff) despite the demonstrable personal superiority of some members of the downstairs group. Given the distribution of initial endowments, that is, the legally sanctioned structure of property rights (which in Edwardian England included rights of class position as well as rights to measurable assets), attempts to restrict market activity would probably have caused damage to all parties. Such attempts, however, have often been observed to take place because of the failure to distinguish carefully between the distribution of property rights and the trading of these rights. To continue with the Edwardian England example, attempts to improve the competitiveness of the market for domestic servants, to introduce potential mobility among prospective employers, might have reduced, and perhaps substantially, the subservience of the domestic servants as a group and individually. Strictly speaking, competitiveness in the structure of markets can eliminate the "master-servant" relationship in a personal sense. But market exchange between persons with vastly different economic endowments may still embody the performance of services by one person for another that would not take place in the absence of such differences. The exchange, as such, may be wholly voluntary, and there may be no economic exploitation in the process. Yet the willingness of one person to perform personal services for the other may stem, at base, from the first person's relatively sparse endowment rather than from any personal preference to pursue such an occupation.

Economists have not been especially helpful in sorting out the confusion here, even if they have recognized the issues. Their domain is that of exchange, or contract, and too often they have seemed content to relegate distributional issues to one side, to separate these all too sharply from allocative questions. But, of course, distribution is what matters in this context, the distribution of relative endowments, of rights, in pretrade or premarket positions. Only within the last two decades have economists commenced to look at property rights in any serious analytical fashion.

Hobbesian Anarchy and the Emergence of Property Rights

But what can economists say? I have recently written a book in which I try to examine the conceptual origins of individual rights from an initial situation of Hobbesian anarchy, the war of each against all.[4] My ultimate purpose in this book is to see what, if anything, we can say about *changes* in an existing distribution of premarket endowments (rights) among separate members of a defined political community. Forcing ourselves to think of the setting for genuine Hobbesian anarchy is helpful, since it prompts the realization that individuals need not be natural equals in the sheer struggle for survival that such anarchy embodies. Individuals would differ in physical strength, in intelligence, in inherent morality. Nonetheless, even when these differences are fully recognized, a *contractual* basis for the emergence of mutually respected rights can be derived.[5] All persons can gain from the negotiation and enforcement of an effective disarmament agreement, as Hobbes recognized and elaborated in his discussion of the basic contract with the

---

4. J. M. Buchanan, *The Limits of Liberty: Between Anarchy and Leviathan* (Chicago: University of Chicago Press, 1975).

5. The use of the Hobbesian model to analyze the potential emergence of a contract does not imply that, descriptively, the interaction among persons in anarchy need be close to that which Hobbes pictured. Behaviorally, persons might exhibit a wide range of traits. Nonetheless, as long as areas of conflict are present, there will be a basis for contractual agreement. There is no need at this level of discussion to specify just how much conflict Hobbesian anarchy would embody.

sovereign. The point is that all persons can secure continuing mutual gains from a legal structure that implies both a definition of the appropriate spheres of individual action and the enforcement of these spheres as defined. There would be, of course, a wide range of outcomes that would satisfy the requirements for mutual gain implicit in the very notion of contract. There is no uniquely determinate outcome of any contractual or trading process, regardless of the number of participants.[6] But the point of emphasis is that any outcome within this set dominates the anarchistic alternative for all members of the community. The structure of rights legally agreed on does, therefore, have a direct relationship to that distribution of consumables that might emerge under anarchy, the *natural distribution*.[7] Once a determinate assignment of rights has been settled, however, there seems to be no prospect for a contractual or an agreed-on rearrangement without some change in the underlying structural elements. Changes from one distribution to another, a distribution of endowments, of rights, within the dominant set become analogous to shifts among outcomes in *n*-person, zero-sum games. Losers must exist alongside winners, and potential losers will not agree to play in advance.

In a purely static and formal model, this might be the end of discussion. But history is not static, and our whole objective is to say something that will contain relevance, however remote, for an evaluation of the current structure that has emerged through historical process. Passage through time necessarily involves changes in the underlying structural parameters that might have provided the basis for any initial contractual agreement. The natural distribution of talents in Hobbesian anarchy, which influences the relative positions of persons in the agreed-on structure of rights, may shift, in a real or in an apparent sense, and this may potentially destroy or threaten to destroy the dominance of an existing claims structure. Recognition of this may prompt contractual renegotiation, with subsequent changes in the distribu-

---

6. In this respect, much of modern economic theory is grossly misleading through its implication that trading outcomes are unique when there exist large numbers of both buyers and sellers. The uniqueness in the economists' models stems from the assumptions made about potential recontracting in a timeless process that converges to equilibrium, assumptions that are not remotely descriptive of any trading process as observed.

7. This term was introduced by Winston Bush; see "Individual Welfare in Anarchy," in *Explorations in the Theory of Anarchy*, ed. G. Tullock (Blacksburg, Va.: Center for Study of Public Choice, 1972).

tion of endowments. I have discussed the potentiality for such renegotiations in some detail elsewhere, and I shall not elaborate the analysis here.[8]

The State as Enforcer

In what follows, I want to examine another potential and perhaps more important variable, that which measures the limits of State action. Even in an idealized and abstract setting, it is difficult to conceive of a complete and unchanging definition or assignment of property rights among persons in a community. Some grey areas where individual rights to do things seem to come into conflict must almost necessarily be present from the onset of any contractual agreement. And this area can surely be predicted to expand through time, as initial delineations prove inapplicable to unforeseen interactions. In this area of potential conflicts of rights, persons are plunged back into something analogous to Hobbesian anarchy; at the edges, predictable order disappears.[9] Indeed, one conceptual measure of civil order lies in the relationship between that set of behavioral interactions that is regulated within well-defined and mutually respected rights and that set which involves interpersonal and intergroup conflicts. Any assignment of rights must, of course, be enforced, and a contract of government may bring into being the enforcer, which we may call the *Protective State*.[10] It is, therefore, a natural consequence that this agency, which is appropriately assigned a limited enforcer role, should also be granted powers of adjudicating conflicts among persons and private groups where claims come into dispute.

Conceptually, the rights of the created agency, the Protective State, are also defined in the initial contract of government in a constitution. As this agency assumes powers to adjudicate claims, however, it necessarily takes on a dominating role. There exists no agency above it to limit its own claims, to protect the rights of persons and groups against encroachment by the enforcing agency itself. This inherent paradox of government has, of

---

8. Buchanan, *The Limits of Liberty.*

9. As Gordon Tullock's appropriately titled essay "The Edge of the Jungle" suggests, civil order always exists alongside potential Hobbesian conflict; see "The Edge of the Jungle," in Tullock, *Explorations in the Theory of Anarchy.*

10. This name is helpful in distinguishing the *Enforcer State* from its complement, that State which provides goods and services publicly, which may be called the *Productive State.*

course, been fully recognized since classical antiquity, but neither historical experience nor philosophical precept has done much toward resolution. To Hobbes, the paradox points necessarily toward the surrender of all rights to the sovereign, a hypothesis that history neither fully corroborates nor fully refutes. To many political philosophers, "limited government" is possible, and experience suggests that this possibility may sometimes be realized.

It is not my intent or purpose here, even if I were fully competent to do so, to discuss the instrumental means and devices through which the activities of government may be limited, through which private property may be made inviolate against claims made upon it by the sovereign. Historically and factually, there have been societies that succeeded in limiting the arbitrary action of those persons who make decisions in the name of the State. Constitutional limits have sometimes been descriptively meaningful, up to a point, despite the frequently observed gradual enhancement of State powers.

In the American setting, the stricture that private property may not be taken without "due process of law" has carried a degree of protection against overtly discriminatory behavior on the part of governments and their officials. This clause of the Constitution has been helpful in allowing individuals and private groups to carry on their ordinary market dealings in an atmosphere of stability and predictability that would not have been present in a setting where rights were subjected to continuous redefinition by governmental agency. Strictly interpreted, however, the due process clause, or its equivalent, would or could allow little or no scope for the exercise of individual rights to political equality. Private property rights, as historically determined, are perhaps far removed from any initial contract or from that natural distribution that might have emerged from some period of acquisition and struggle. But these rights, as existing, would be protected against encroachment, not only from private persons but also from government itself. In a regime of such strict constitutional interpretation, there could be little or no role for the instrumental use of the political process to secure modifications in distributional outcomes. Individuals might be "political equals" in some effective sense, but the allowable scope for political-governmental action would be so circumscribed as to make franchise impotent with respect to the achievement of distributional objectives.[11]

___

11. Even in this restrictive context, political action can insure some net redistribution, provided that the public sector is sufficiently large relative to the private sector. Where

The Exercise of "Public Property Rights"

The historical experience of the United States has embodied increasing demands that distributional outcomes be modified in the direction of greater equality, and an increasing acceptance of the view that positive governmental action toward this end is fully appropriate, representing individuals' exercise of their claimed rights to political equality. Empirically, these demands have seemed too strong to be resisted by a fragile legalism that offered apparent protection to an arbitrary and historically determined pattern of individuals' claims to assets—a pattern that has seemed to many to possess little consensual foundations. Predictably, governments have responded to these demands, and by necessity this has implied increasing restriction on the exercise of legally santioned rights to the use of private property, broadly interpreted. "Political equality," expressed indirectly through the ballot box, came to dominate "private property" protected by the existing legal assignment of claims.

Nonetheless, both the legislative arm of government, which most directly gives expression to the demands of constituents, and the judicial arm, which embodies the enforcement of the legal order, recognized, at least implicitly, the dangers of allowing an emergent Leviathan to go unchained. If old limits were to be overstepped, new limits would have to be designed, new limits that might accomplish the reconciliation between the two conflicting social norms.

It is at this stage in our conjectural history that major mistakes seem to have been made, mistakes that apparently stemmed from a simple misunderstanding of economic principles. These mistakes, or apparent mistakes, have by this time become imbedded in our legal structure. Increasingly, legislatures and courts came to sanction collective or governmental interference with freedom of private contract, with the trading process, as such, while at the same time, they remained reluctant to sanction direct governmental transfers of endowments among persons. To economists, this result was, and is, essentially upside down. As noted earlier, intervention in the

collective or public goods and services are equally available to all consumers, the efficient structure of prices may well involve income wealth–related differentials. If, however, an attempt is made to move beyond these efficiency limits in public goods pricing (that is, if redistributive norms are introduced directly into the fiscal process), the due process clause would be violated on a strict interpretation.

freedom of private persons to make contracts, to trade, must damage all parties. On the other hand and by contrast, a reassignment of endowments in premarket positions is, in the limit, a zero-sum transfer. At least one party gains what the other loses.

This is the origin of the continuing argument between economists and noneconomists over many particular proposals for governmental policy. Regardless of the distributive norms that they might hold, economists will tend to oppose overt interferences with voluntary contract. They will tend to oppose such measures as minimum wage legislation, price and wage controls, rent controls, gasoline rationing, marketing agreements, price supports, closed-shop restrictions, import and export quotas, direct bureaucratic allocations, and prohibitions. If they share distributive norms with those who advance market intervention on such grounds, or if they accept the political necessity of distributionally oriented policy, economists will tend to favor direct transfers of income and wealth, welfare payments in cash rather than in kind, positive and negative income taxation, and wealth taxation. In taking such positions, the economists will, quite correctly, be able to demonstrate that a larger pie, a larger national dividend, will be produced by minimizing the interventions with market processes. Not only may any given set of distributional norms be met more effectively; these norms may even be exceeded if markets are allowed to function freely.

As I noted earlier, however, the economists have been too ready to leave matters roughly at this point. They have been unwilling to acknowledge that there may well be more in the noneconomists' insistence on direct market intervention than there appears to be in the economists' nonpolitical world. As Knut Wicksell wisely pointed out nearly eighty years ago, most economists talk as if they are advising a benevolent despot. But, of course, such a despot is nonexistent. Governments embody the choices and the actions of quite ordinary people, from voters who exercise their ultimate political rights to franchise, through legislative representatives who act for voters and for themselves, to bureaucrats who actually carry out policy decisions, including some of their own. The complex structure that is government cannot readily be controlled at any level, and any target is likely to be missed. Recognizing this, how is the required reconciliation between political equality and private property (individual freedom) to be secured? To go "whole hog" with the economists on distributional policy, to open up prospects for direct transfers of wealth among persons in exchange for the enhanced efficiency promised by nonintervention with market contract does not seem so attractive in this setting. If government is to be used instrumentally to effect direct transfers from "rich" to "poor," what is to prevent this same instrumentality from being used by those in middle-income and wealth coalitions from making direct transfers from others, including the poor, to themselves? There is indeed evidence to suggest that governmental distributional policy as it exists has foundered on just such grounds.[12] If governmental transfer policy is acknowledged to be responsive to the demands of citizens, who exercise their "public property rights" in the voting booth, there is nothing that will restrict this response to only those demands that are ethically motivated by some abstract norms. We cannot conceive of a constitutional rule or precept that would restrict the expression of individual and group interests to enforce consistency with "social values."

Perhaps working politicians, and judges, have shown some wisdom in their apparent reluctance to allow constitutional precepts to be adjusted in such a manner as to allow government to become a massive transfer process. These politicians may have realized that, in the net, the equivalent to transfers of wealth results from governmental activities. And they may also recognize that more direct transfers would increase overall economic efficiency. But here, as in other areas of human interaction, both hypocrisy and illusion may have virtues. By talking as if private property rights are enforceable by legal order while distributional objectives are being furthered by overt governmental interventions in market process, these politicians may have succeeded, up to a point, in distracting attention from the underlying contradiction that must be present. By making the market process the target for policy, they may have obscured the basic conflict that arises when premarket differences among persons in endowments, talents, and capacities to produce values coexist with political equality, defined in terms of voting franchise. By creating an illusion of action, political leaders may produce an acquiescence by potential voters in distributional differences

12. G. Stigler, "Director's Law of Public Income Redistribution," *Journal of Law and Economics* 13 (April 1970): 1–10; G. Tullock, "The Charity of the Uncharitable," *Western Economic Journal* 9 (December 1971): 379–92.

that might otherwise not be tolerated. Hence, private property may be preserved, within limits, despite the potential power of political majorities.

Objection may be raised to my imputation of such sophistication to modern political leaders, but even if their motivations are wholly unconscious the model may retain behavioral content. If it does so, we may briefly look at some of its implications. We should predict that, despite the continuing plaints of the economists, specific and piecemeal intervention with voluntary contract would increase, with little or no desirable distributional consequences, despite the illusion of such results. We should predict continued journalistic and pseudophilosophical attack on the market principle, as such, and on the institutional embodiments of this principle without the formulation of an effective organizational alternative. We should predict a rapidly expanding governmental sector, covering a widely varied set of activities and manned by an increasingly unwieldy and cumbersome bureaucratic apparatus.

The World We Live In

This description is, of course, one that fits the United States today. As an economist, I find this difficult to accept, even as the nth best alternative. I am tempted to rally in support of my fellow professionals, those optimists who call for the enactment of universal negative income taxation in the hope that, once this legislation is on the books, we might be able to dismantle much of the grossly inefficient governmental structure that we currently observe. Only as a public-choice theorist, as an economist who has also done some thinking about how politics actually works, do I draw back here and realize that such is the stuff of utopian dreams. The introduction of the negative income tax would probably enhance rather than resolve the continuing contradiction.

If we lived in a world peopled by human beings who possessed roughly equal capacities to create values but who had been, by historical circumstances, forced into positions characterized by significant differences in nonhuman, physical property claims, reconciliation might be readily attainable. Conceptually, a once-and-for-all reassignment or redistribution of these nonhuman claims might be accomplished, after which the ideal setting for laissez-faire precepts would come into being. A regime of genuine classical liberalism might be within the realm of the imaginable. This is, of course, the world that was dreamed of by the classical liberal philosophers, who did not acknowledge the existence of great capacity differences between themselves and the street porters. Unfortunately, history may suggest that Plato and not Adam Smith understood human differences. A major share of interpersonal endowment differentials may lie in the capacities to produce values, capacities that cannot be equalized by a reassignment of nonhuman assets or claims.

Where does this leave us? In a world where people are not, and cannot be, proximate "natural equals," how can the political equality that is both honored in precept and imbedded in institutional structure be reconciled with the differential rights of individuals to do things with things, the rights of private property? This is the question posed at the outset, and I have tried to explain some of the political behavior that we see in terms of responses to this question. The danger is, of course, that the continuation of current trends will reduce the attainment of both objectives. The attempted exercise of political equality may well produce an increase rather than a decrease in the inequalities among persons and families while, at the same time, reducing the freedom of individuals to dispose of their privately claimed rights. The differences in commands over final product values that we conceptually observe in the marketplace may seem intolerable in a society that gives more than lip service to political democracy. But it may be impossible to reduce these differences substantially without creating equally, if not more, intolerable differences in the power of individuals over each other. Even if she is motivated primarily by relative poverty, the call girl who sells services to one among many potential rich clients retains more freedom than the ordinary citizen who faces the monopoly bureaucrat. Interferences with markets, in the name of citizens, must be made by individuals who act on behalf of governments. The game is negative-sum over a wide range of weights assigned to individual freedom and to equality.

Fairness, Hope, and Justice

I. Rules for a Fair Game

In my book *The Limits of Liberty*[1] I discussed the problem of distribution at some length, but I did not explicitly raise normative issues of "justice." Several critics have interpreted my efforts as supporting the "justice" of the distributional results that emerged from my analysis, but I did not, at least in any conscious sense, consider myself to be offering any such argument. My primary concern in that book was to show that contractarian agreement, at some initial and prelegal stage, might emerge that would involve the definition, the guarantee, and the enforcement of a distribution of rights and claims (endowments) among persons in a community. I was concerned to show that such a distribution of rights and claims is necessarily prior to the simple as well as the complex exchanges that a market economic process embodies, the process which, finally, determines a distribution of end-items or product values, final goods and services, upon which attention tends to be directed when we talk loosely about "distribution."

Though my analysis was essentially positive rather than normative, there are direct implications for the methodology of discussing matters of distributive justice. My whole argument suggested that the focus of attention should be on the distribution of rights and claims prior to or antecedent to the market process itself rather than on some final distribution of social product.

I shall return to this central point later, but let me now plunge directly

From *New Directions in Economic Justice*, ed. Roger Skurski (South Bend, Ind.: University of Notre Dame Press, 1983), 53–89. Reprinted by permission of the publisher.

1. James M. Buchanan, *The Limits of Liberty* (Chicago: University of Chicago Press, 1975).

into my main topic and ask the personalized question: Are the nominal claims to income and wealth that I now hold "just"? Am I "entitled" to these claims which allow me to translate values into measured quantities of goods, services, and real assets produced by others in the economy?

Let me first point to some considerations that must be reckoned with in my answer. Perhaps the most important of these to keep in mind is the relative or relational characteristic of "justice in holdings" or "entitlements." Are the nominal claims that I now hold "just"? Now, let me pose the question differently. Is there anyone else "more entitled" to these holdings than I am? And, even more specifically, are you more "entitled" to my nominal holdings, to the cash in my wallet or in my bank accounts, than I am? If you choose, you may include everyone in the "you" in thinking about this question. Would a revised distribution, with you holding the cash or claims rather than me, be more "just"? Or is the "state" or the "government" somehow more entitled to them? If so, what is "the state"? Who is "the government"? Who is "entitled to act as 'governor' "?

As you can surmise, it becomes very easy to translate all such questions into the oldest and deepest issues in political, moral, and legal philosophy, issues with which we are all familiar. And of course the reason such issues are the oldest and the deepest is that they are the hardest to resolve satisfactorily.

A second consideration, already suggested by the first, involves the prospect of disagreement. Let us suppose, provisionally, that I believe that my entitlement to my holdings is at least as strong, in a moral sense, as that of anyone else. If you accept this judgment—that is, if you acknowledge my relative claim—then we really do not need to argue further about the larger issues of the "moral-ethical" supports for such claims. It is critically important here to recognize that most of our ordinary economic dealing proceeds on the basis of just such a mutual acknowledgment of the justice of the holdings that exist in the status quo. I can go to the university bookstore and buy a book with relatively minor transactions costs because I fully acknowledge the bookstore's claim to ownership of the book before I buy it, while at the same time the bookstore accepts my claim to the cash in my wallet. Neither of us need be concerned at all about "justice" in the large.[2] Serious issues

2. I would like to note at this point that I am leaving off the adjective "distributive" before "justice," but I am exclusively discussing "distributive justice" here as opposed to "commutative justice." The latter is, of course, important in its own right. We can attri-

arise only when disagreement emerges. Let us suppose that I believe I am more entitled to my holdings than you are, but that you do not agree with me. You think that you are really more "entitled" to the cash in my wallet than I am.

If you act out your beliefs, you will simply take my wallet if you have the power to do so, and I will, at the same time, exert every effort to prevent you from so doing. We fight unless one of us is protected in our claims by the force of law, of the state. In my example, if you attempt to take my wallet, I can call the local policeman and he will arrest you. In the foreknowledge of this probable scenario, you may refrain from attempting to take the wallet by force; that is, you may be observed to acquiesce in my holdings while at the same time you may continue to think that you remain more "entitled" to these holdings than I. In this case, you may then seek to modify the existing set of claims by political action that would involve the government levying a tax on me while at the same time making cash transfers to you. If you succeed, I may acquiesce in the tax-and-transfer program, but I shall do so only because I am unable to violate the tax law without probable penalty. The basic conflict remains. We continue to fight by political rather than by more direct means.

In any such fight or conflict, questions of "justice" necessarily get mixed up and intermingled with pure self-interest. You may want to take my wallet simply because you want the money, quite independent from any consideration of entitlement or justice in holdings. If you cannot take the holdings directly, you may be quite willing to let the agency of government do it for you. I may want to keep my holdings because I want to keep them, and I may be quite happy to allow government to prevent you from taking these by force. "Justice" need not enter at all, on either side of the potential conflict. Your utility function may dictate that you would like my money under any conceivable distribution, but you may be constrained from taking these holdings by law. If, however, the law is not effective, either directly or indirectly, you will take the money unless additional constraints are present. And among these additional constraints are your attitudes toward the "justice" of my holdings.[3]

---

bute "injustice" to any institution or rule that would prevent the bookstore and me from making mutually advantageous trades.

3. Let me add clarification at this point, concerning the indirect constraint that law may exercise on behavior. You may be constrained, not by the law directly, but by the fact of the law itself. You may consider it unethical to violate the law, not because the law is just in its object, but simply because it is the law.

We come back, therefore, to agreement. What are the conditions or characteristics that determine whether or not you agree that my holdings are "just," that my entitlements to these holdings are superior to anyone else's? There are, of course, many ways of getting at this question, but I want to concentrate on what we call the contractarian response.

II. Games with Fair Rules

The response may be summarized in the subsidiary question: Can my claims to holdings be interpreted and understood as one component in the outcome of what we might agree is a *fair game?* This question, in turn, raises several subsidiary ones. What is a fair game? What is fairness? Is the game analogy appropriate for interpreting the economic interaction process?

I shall deal with the last question very briefly here. The contractarian position is distinguished from its alternatives by its dependence on criteria that are internal to the individuals who are participants in the interaction. It becomes illegitimate to invoke external criteria for evaluating either processes or end-states. Once this is recognized, the game analogy emerges almost necessarily, with the qualifications as noted in the discussion to follow. For those who do not accept the basic contractarian logic, and who would want to invoke external norms of evaluation, there is little to be said.

Let me, therefore, return to the other questions concerning what is a fair game, and what is the meaning of fairness. The contractarian response, not surprisingly, comes back again to agreement. A "fair rule" is one that is agreed to by the players in advance of play itself, before the particularized positions of the players come to be identified. Note carefully what this definition says: A rule is fair if players agree to it. It does not say that players agree because a rule is fair. That is to say, fairness is defined by agreement; agreement does not converge to some objectively determined fairness.

One way of proceeding from this point would be to discuss the derivation of what we might call "ideally fair rules" or even "plausibly fair rules." That is essentially the approach taken by John Rawls in *A Theory of Justice.*[4] While I have considerable affinity with Rawls, this method of proceeding would take me too far afield for my purposes. I find it useful to commence with an

---

4. John Rawls, *A Theory of Justice* (Cambridge, Mass.: Harvard University Press, 1971).

existing or even an abstracted status quo and to try to use the fairness criteria to determine the possible correspondence between the results, actually or potentially observed, and personal attitudes toward the "justice" of these results. To return to my personal example, could my claims, my current holdings, have emerged as one outcome of a game that we might agree has been carried out under tolerably fair rules?

It is first necessary to look at the factors that might determine distributional results, under real or imagined institutional structures. Anyone who would argue that a person's holdings are "unjust," or indeed that they are "just," by fairness criteria, must presume genuinely monumental knowledge of both economic analysis and statistical interpretation. Too often our academic colleagues, in economics and other disciplines, as well as commentators outside the academy, are unwilling to undertake the chore of understanding how distributional patterns actually might emerge under differing sets of rules. They tend, instead, to stand ready and willing to "jump" directly into evaluative-normative judgments about existing distributions of holdings, and hence about particular personal holdings within these distributions, before they really know what they are talking about. This point is made emphatically by my former colleague at the University of Virginia Professor Rutledge Vining. He has for a long time argued that students of distributions (of any kind) should be forced to understand stochastic patterns, should be thoroughly grounded in the elementary principles of probability theory, before they are allowed to advance evaluative diagnoses.

It is evident that if we take Vining's admonition strictly, none of us could say much of anything about income and wealth distribution. I think that we can, however, take the Vining admonition as a warning to temper all of our efforts at discussing distribution. Here, as elsewhere in economic policy analysis, we must be careful to remain with relevant comparisons. And we can start to lay out the factors that determine the distribution of claims to economic value in differing institutional settings, in different games, under differing rules.

In the United States economy of today, the institutional setting is one that combines markets and politics in an extremely complex web of intersecting and often conflicting relationships. To attempt to model this structure, this game, in any plausibly acceptable manner, even when allowing for highly abstracted models, is beyond my competence or purpose here. I propose, instead, to abstract from the politics, from the manifold governmental influences on distributional patterns in the economy that we observe, and to look directly at the market process, and at the distributional patterns it might generate in the absence of governmental intervention. That is to say, I want to look at a relatively pure market structure, a relatively pure market game, a game operating within a legal-political framework that is limited to the protection of life and property and to the enforcement of contract. For labels here, we can say I shall be discussing distribution in the market economy in a minimal or protective state.

As noted above, this model is not at all realistic, but by examining the distributional patterns that might be predicted to emerge from it, we may begin to get some feel for what we mean by the terms "justice" or "injustice" applied to distributive results, again both terms as interpreted within the fairness conceptions.

One way of avoiding the pitfalls that Vining warns against is to forgo discussion of "distributions," as such, and to stick with the simple personal example introduced earlier. Take a single person, take me. What are the elements or factors that have determined my relative share in the status quo claims to economic value or, rather, would have determined my share in these claims in the relatively pure market economy, as defined?

At this point, let me call on my own professor Frank Knight of the University of Chicago, who said that in a market economy claims are determined by "birth, luck, and effort" and "the least of these is effort." Knight's three determinants offer us a good starting point for discussion, but let me add only one additional determinant, "choice." As you can already envisage, there are interdependencies among these elements. Let me take these four determinants in the following order: choice, luck, effort, and birth.

Choice. Surely my own choices have in part influenced the value of my current claims on economic product or, more generally, my current holdings. It must, I think, be readily acknowledged that any person's claims have been influenced by his own choices, of course with varying degrees of importance. With the proviso noted above, take my own personal history. I chose, deliberately, to undertake an academic career at a time shortly prior to the academic boom of the late 1950s, 1960s, and early 1970s. That is to say, I chose to enter an industry that was shortly to experience extremely rapid growth, with the predictable consequences for the income levels of its participants.

Even before I made this occupational choice, however, I had chosen to continue with my education, even at the cost of forgone earnings (which admittedly were pretty dismal in the late 1930s). I do not, of course, suggest that my various choices along the way were fully informed. In a very real sense, I was personally lucky in these choices, and as I noted above, we cannot really separate some of the determinants I have separately listed. Persons necessarily choose under conditions of great uncertainty, and I could have chosen a declining industry rather than an expanding one, in which case the consequences for my relative income-wealth position would have been quite different.

My purpose is not, however, to discuss in detail the influence of choice on individual or family shares in the claims to total economic value. I want only to suggest here that, insofar as personal differentials in the relative sizes of such claims can be attributed to choices freely made, there is no legitimate argument for assessing such differentials as being "unfair" or "unjust." The wino in Chicago who "might have been" a success had he chosen differently may, it seems to me, appeal to the compassion of his fellows; but he cannot, and should not, be allowed to appeal to their innate sense of "fairness," which has in no way been violated in his own situation.

Luck. Choice merges with and intersects with luck, fortune, or chance as an element that influences the distribution of claims. Though a person may not have deliberately and explicitly chosen to do this or that, his share in the claims to value may have been shifted unexpectedly and dramatically, upward or downward. The farmer who tills the family farm in the standard manner did not choose to have oil discovered under his land. He was simply lucky. Others may be unlucky and see their holdings vanish into nothing by flood, fire, or pestilence. Again, I do not propose to discuss the relative significance of luck in the total imputation of claims to value, in the United States economy of 1980, or anywhere else. My point, once again, is to suggest that, to the extent that luck is the acknowledged causal influence, and provided all persons "could have been" in the game, so to speak, there would seem to be no violation of basic fairness precepts in observed relative differences in the sizes of claims.

Effort. There need be little discussion of effort. To the extent that a person's share in claims is traceable to his own efforts, there must be near-universal agreement, on fairness or any other set of criteria, that his claims are "just." Indeed, we could argue that, in the absence of such effort, there would have been no value existent to claim. In a very real sense, therefore, this value attributable to effort involves no opportunity cost to anyone in the community, even in the narrow context of potential value available for redistribution.

Birth. We are left with birth as the remaining influence or element in determining the distribution of claims, and it is not at all surprising that most of the charges of "injustice" and/or "unfairness" concerning income and wealth distribution arise or are alleged to arise from this source. Few persons could say that the economic game is intrinsically unfair just because some persons are lucky, or because some persons make better choices, or that some persons exert more effort than others. Unfairness in the economic game described by the operation of market institutions within a legal framework of private property and contract tends to be attributed to the distribution of endowments with which persons *enter* the game in the first place, *before* choices are made, *before* luck rolls the economic dice, *before* effort is exerted.

III. The Easter-Egg Hunt—a Market Analogy

I can introduce some of the issues raised indirectly by resort to an analogy, that of the Easter-egg hunt, an analogy that I borrow from my former colleague Professor Richard Wagner of Auburn University. The distributive patterns in a market process are not too different in kind from those of the Easter-egg hunt. In large part, "finders are keepers," and the final division of product depends on the historical accidents of person, time, and place—on luck, talent, capacity, and effort, which were discussed to some extent earlier. But as I noted in connection with effort, there is no fixed sum to be "found"; there is no fixed quantity of total economic value to be somehow shared among all participants. The fact is that unless the hunt is properly organized, many of the eggs will not be found at all. Product of potential value will remain "undiscovered," "unproduced." The person who by luck, talent, or effort finds a cache of eggs is not necessarily "entitled" to keep them in some basically moral sense, but surely no one else, individually or collectively, is similarly "entitled" since, by supposition, the cache might not have been located at all by anyone else.

All of this is, of course, merely a way of emphasizing the positive-sum nature of the competitive economic process. But the attribution of "justice" or "fairness" to the rules of the finders-keepers game depends critically on the presence of one of two conditions. Either there must be many "games in town" *or* the starting positions must be approximately equivalent. There need be little or no concern about relative starting positions if there are "many games in town" so that any player who joins a particular game does so voluntarily and at the same time retains the option of exit from the game. If, however, there is "only one game in town," and if everyone, willy-nilly, must participate, attention is immediately drawn to relative starting positions. Before we can even begin to evaluate results in terms of justice or fairness criteria, the starting positions must be reckoned with. If there are some players endowed initially with superior capacities, which they possess through no choices on their own part, these players will be relatively advantaged in any playing of the game. Our ordinary sense of "fairness" seems to be violated when such players are put on equal terms with those who are relatively less advantaged but who must, nonetheless, participate in the same game.

Must an acceptable fair game, therefore, embody handicaps? Many of us will recall Easter-egg hunts when older and larger children were deliberately handicapped by being placed behind the younger and smaller children, in distance or in time. Presumably, all children must have been entrants in the same hunt; the smaller children were presumed unable to have their own game, at least advantageously. In a sense, this setting offers a reasonably appropriate analogy to social process, at least for my purposes of discussion here.

If there are demonstrable and acknowledged differences in endowments, talents, and capacities, differences that are discernible at or before the effective starting point, there would seem to be persuasive arguments for discriminatory handicapping, even at a reckoned cost in lost social value. But if we postulate an idealized veil of ignorance, in which no person knows what position in the predicted array of initial endowments, talents, and capacities he or she might occupy, expected value is maximized only in the absence of handicaps. Social product is largest by allowing the market process to operate without redistributional encumbrances, and if each person has the same opportunity to secure each share in product value, rational precepts, defined on expected values, seem to reject any discriminatory handicapping at all.

Expected value will not, however, be the only criterion. If the predicted distribution of starting points—defined by endowments, talents, and capacities to produce value—extends over a wide range, then variance matters. Empirical estimates concerning actual as well as perceived differences among persons become important in determining possible departures from expected value maximization. If we agree with Adam Smith about the absence of natural differences between philosophers and porters, the starting-position problem becomes immensely more tractable than it is if we agree with Plato about inherent natural differences. In addition, the relative importance of differentials in starting positions in influencing final shares in consumption value will, of course, affect the attitudes toward possible adjustments in starting positions. That is to say, if choice, luck, and effort dominate birth in the determination of any person's actual command over economic value, the fairness issue in the possible distribution of starting points may be of relatively little import.

This point is, I think, important enough to warrant some elaboration here. The sources of the observed and the imagined differences in command over final product values, at the potential consumption stage, are relevant for any attribution of "justice" or "injustice" to the economic game. Consider a simple two-person example. Suppose, first, that the incomes of A and B are exclusively determined by the initial endowment of each, which for A is double that for B. Hence, A's income is two times that of B. Contrast this setting with one in which initial endowments remain as before, with A's being double B's. Assume now, however, that income shares also depend on choice, luck, and effort. Before these additional determinants enter, the expected value of A's income share will exceed that of B. In observed results, however, B's income share may well exceed that of A. In this setting, there will tend to be less concern about the disparity in initial endowments than in the first.

Two further points need to be made. In the political-economic "game," the inequalities in starting positions that become relevant for considerations of "justice" are inequalities among the opportunities to produce whatever is deemed to be "valuable" for social order and stability. These values need not, and normally would not and should not, include all observed differences among persons in preferences, talents, and endowments. This recognition of the multiplicity of values is closely related to a second point. In the extremely complex "game" that modern social order must represent, capabilities to produce value take on many different forms. In effect, there are many subgames going on simultaneously within the larger "game," each one of which might require a somewhat different mix of endowments and talents for success. "Equality of starting position," even as an ideal, surely does not imply that each person be qualified to enter each and every subgame on all fours with everyone else. Properly interpreted, "equality of opportunity," even as an ideal, must be defined as some rough, and possibly immeasurable, absence of major differences in the ability to produce values in whatever "game" is most appropriate for the particular situation for the person who participates.

With all the qualifications and provisos, however, rules of fairness would seem to suggest some imposition of what we may call handicaps so as to allow an approach to, if not an attainment of, something that might be called equality in starting positions or, more familiarly, equality of opportunity. Before this implication of "justice as fairness" is accepted too readily, however, we must ask and try to answer the awesome question: Who is to do the handicapping? There is no external agent or overlord, no benevolent despot, who can spot the differences among the players in advance and adjust starting positions. And, indeed, the individual who conceives himself to be in some original position behind the Rawlsian veil of ignorance would be foolhardy to turn the handicapping task over to that subset of persons who might be temporarily or permanently assigned powers of political governance over their fellow citizens. Genuinely fair rules might include some equalization of starting positions, but if some of the players are also allowed to serve as umpires, it may well be best to leave off consideration of such rules altogether.

The implementation of handicapping rules, even those upon which conceptual agreement might be reached most easily, presents any community with a formidable institutional dilemma. If those persons who are to be assigned powers of governance are not to be, and cannot be, trusted to use their own discretion in carrying out the rules that are given to them because of some fear that they will exploit these rules for their own self-interest, how can "equality of opportunity" be promoted, even in a limited and proximate sense?

Some resolution of this dilemma may be secured by resort to *constitutional* order, to the selection of institutional rules that are chosen independent of political strife and conflict, and which are designed to be quasi-permanent constraints on the behavior of governments as well as private parties. Constitutional rules may be laid down that establish institutional structures within which some equalization of starting positions may be encouraged. If this constitutional, as opposed to the political, route toward implementation is taken, however, the inability to accomplish any "fine tuning" among possibly widely disparate opportunities must be acknowledged. At best, constitutional design might allow for institutions that take some of the more apparent rough edges off gross inequalities in starting positions. I shall discuss two such institutions in the next two sections.

IV. Constitutional Design and Inequalities

Could a polity that allows intergenerational transfers of assets to proceed unencumbered pass any test of fairness? Such intergenerational transfers are perhaps the most blatant and most overt devices that are seen to create *inequalities* in starting positions, and hence to run directly counter to any objective of equalization. Even when the above-mentioned difficulties of implementation are recognized, some system of taxation of asset transfers would almost surely emerge from any agreement on a set of fair rules. Some such tax structure would seem to be almost a necessary part of any set of starting-position adjustments.

This conclusion is not affected by the various arguments that may be, and have often been, advanced against transfer taxation. It may be fully acknowledged that such taxes are Pareto-inefficient, that saving, capital formation, and economic growth are adversely affected, and that such taxes necessarily interfere with the liberties of those persons who are potential accumulators of wealth and potential donors to their heirs. These arguments do suggest the relevance of some trade-offs between the requirements for fairness in the rules and the objectives for economic efficiency and growth. But they do not imply that the latter objectives somehow dominate or modify those for fairness. They imply only that the fairness objective be tempered by a recognition of the costs of achieving it. Nor does a second, and possibly much more important, set of arguments modify the basic role of transfer taxation in a "fair" society. These arguments are based, first, on the substitutability between wealth in potentially taxable and nontaxable forms, and, second, on the inherent nontaxability of endowments in human capital, endowments that may be transferred genetically. Such nontaxable endowments may well be more significant in determining ultimate command over product value than potentially taxable endowments. If this should be the case, what is the moral-ethical basis for taxing the transfer of nonhuman assets?

As I have noted above, one such reason lies in the blatancy or overtness of such transfers; there is a fundamental ethical difference between nonhuman and human capital, even if modern economists can treat these two elements of endowments equally for their analytical purposes at hand. A second reason lies in the potential taxability itself. To an extent, such taxation, no matter how limited it might be in ultimate effect, represents a movement toward the objective of equality in starting points. The fact that the nontaxable elements in the transfer of endowments exist so as to make this objective ultimately unattainable should lend support rather than opposition to faltering efforts to go on as far as is possible.

A second institution that seems justified on basic fairness criteria, and still within the objective of equalizing starting positions, is publicly—or governmentally—financed education. It might be predicted that this institution would emerge from conceptualized contractual agreement even in recognition of the difficulties of implementation already noted.

The second set of arguments against transfer taxation noted in the preceding section is also applicable here. Natural differentials, in part genetically determined, in human capacities cannot, of course, be offset in their effects by education, even if instruction should somehow be organized with idealized "efficiency," whatever this might mean. But the availability of education serves to reduce rather than to increase the effects of such differences in starting positions in determining relative commands over economic value. In this sense, education acts similarly to transfer taxation.

Economists, and public-finance economists in particular, may have shifted attention away from the central issues when they classify education as a "public" or "collective consumption" service in the formal Samuelsonian sense. In such a schemata, public or governmental financing tends to be justified only to the extent that the benefits spill over or are external to the child that is educated and its immediate family. The whole public-goods approach, however, presumes that persons are "already in the game." A conceptually different justification for publicly financed education emerges when we look at potential adjustments in starting positions, at handicaps aimed at making the game "fair." Note that, in this context, the argument over governmental fi-

nancing is not at all affected by the extent of spillovers or external economies, at least in the ordinary usage of these terms.[5]

As I have emphasized, the taxation of transfers and publicly financed education are not capable of equalizing starting positions even in some proximate manner. Inequalities will remain; opportunities will remain different
for different persons. Nonetheless, these two basic institutions can reduce
the impact of differences, and they can be seen to accomplish this result. To
such an extent, the "game" will be seen to embody criteria of "fairness" in its
rules.

What else might be done from fairness criteria at the starting position
level? In subsequent discussion, I want to concentrate attention on additional aspects of the problem, specifically institutions aimed at insuring
reasonably "fair chances to play." Even if persons may recognize that starting positions can never be equalized, steps can be taken that allow all persons to have the same opportunities to participate. In terms of an example,
the child of a sharecropper can never possess an equal opportunity to become president with that of the child of a billionaire. But institutions can
be organized so that the child of the sharecropper is not overtly *excluded*
from the game, as such. And if he is so much as allowed to play, and by the
same rules, there remains at least some chance that he can win. Later I shall
discuss these aspects of "economic justice" in considerable detail. "Hope"
is an extremely important component of any social order that makes claims
of "justice."

V. Division of the Product

At this juncture, I want to shift from the starting-position problem and to
examine more carefully possible redistributive adjustments in results, or
end-states, in income shares after the economic game is played. Using the

5. I should add a necessary footnote to the discussion at this point concerning the argument for public or governmental *financing* of education as opposed to the more complex extension of a possible argument for governmental provision and organization of
education. I do not propose to discuss such an extension here; I would say only that there
are very strong efficiency-based arguments for limiting government's role to financing,
although some "fairness" arguments may be adduced for governmental provision.

same basic precepts of fairness, what scope for redistributive income transfers exists?

In order to concentrate on end-states, let us provisionally assume that
starting positions, inequalities in opportunities, have been satisfactorily mit-
igated. Nonetheless, the interdependence between the two stages of potential
application of fairness criteria should be kept in mind. To the extent that
starting positions are satisfactorily adjusted, that the game is appropriately
handicapped, there is surely less persuasive argument for any operation of
redistributive transfer among results, and vice versa.

I have previously noted that if differences in results, in relative income
shares, can be attributed to choice, luck, or effort, elementary precepts for ex
ante fairness are not violated. So long as all players enter the game on proximately equal terms and have the chance to play the same rules, the rules are
"fair" in a very fundamental and basic sense. The predicted, and observed,
results may, however, exhibit wide differentials in the shares assigned to
separate persons. The efficiency of the "finders-keepers" rules in maximizing total product value may be acknowledged. But fairness precepts, more
extensively interpreted, may suggest some postproduction *redistribution*.
That is to say, even if the expected values of all income shares should be equal
ex ante, the actual distribution of shares, ex post, may exhibit such variance
as to command rejection on contractarian grounds.

The issues here are, in part, empirical. As noted earlier, the contractarian
logic labels that rule as fair upon which general agreement is reached. And
prospects for agreement depend critically on the expected or predicted pattern of results. With genuine equality of opportunity, what form would the
actual distribution of income shares in a market economy take? I do not
think any of us here can really answer this hypothetical question, and we are
reminded again of the Vining admonition discussed above.

The prospects for agreement on any set of rules also depend upon the
potential acceptability of alternatives. The generalized finders-keepers rules
that are embodied in the market may not meet first-best criteria for "justice,"
at least in the attitudes of most persons, but unless alternative rules exist
upon which more agreement may be secured, these rules may remain superior in some consensual context. That is to say, the distributive rules of the
market may represent some sort of Schelling-point outcome of the concep-

tualized contractual process; there may be no alternative set of rules upon which agreement can be attained. This "defense" of the distributional results of market order has been advanced by Frank Knight and, more recently, by Dan Usher.[6]

There would seem, however, to be no convincing logical argument to demonstrate that distributive rules of the competitive market would *necessarily* emerge from generalized contractarian agreement among potential participants, even under the presumption that starting positions are equalized. The market rules *might* emerge from this postulated setting, but these are only one set of rules from among a larger number of sets. Plausible arguments could be made to the effect that some posttrading, postproduction adjustments in income shares would be embodied in any contractual agreement, at least if the difficulties of implementation should be neglected. The rough edges of market-share distribution might be tempered, so to speak, with some guarantees from those persons whose luck turns sour, even at the expense of those persons who are more fortunate. There is no logical basis for rejecting the Rawlsian "difference principle" as one possible outcome of the contractual agreement. Rawls's error was in suggesting that this principle for redistribution was somehow the unique rule that would, in fact, emerge under his postulated conditions.

For my own part, in both a positive predictive sense and a normatively preferred sense, I should remain relatively undisturbed about the distributional results of competitive market process if rough fairness in the distribution of initial endowments and capacities could be guaranteed. Much of the socialist-inspired criticism of the market economic order has been misdirected. The institutions of the market have been criticized for their failure to produce distributive results that meet stated normative objectives when, in fact, these results are more closely related to disparities in premarket endowments and capacities.

Consider a very simple oranges-and-apples example. Suppose that, as a posttrading result, we observe that Tizio has 16 oranges and 14 apples, whereas Caio has only 3 oranges and 2 apples. This postmarket imputation, taken alone, however, tells us nothing at all about the premarket imputation of endowments. If, before trade, Tizio should have had 19 oranges and 13 apples,

6. See Dan Usher, "The Problem of Equity," mimeographed, Queens University, 1975.

while Caio had no oranges and 3 apples, the trade of one apple for 3 oranges by Caio has surely improved his position, as well as that of Tizio. The distributional impact of this trade is dwarfed in significance by the premarket disparity in endowments.

The market rules are rarely put to the test in situations where differences among premarket endowments and capacities can be neutralized or isolated. If the distinction between the distribution of value potential in premarket positions and the distributional effects of trade, as such, is recognized, several principles command acceptance, whether on fairness or other criteria. Attempts to mitigate distributional inequities or injustice that may be due largely to premarket inequalities should not take the form of interferences with the market process, as such. Minimum-wage laws are perhaps the best example. Such restrictions harm those whom they are designed to benefit. In this, as in many other cases, the distributive justice of Adam Smith's system of natural liberty should be acknowledged and emphasized. Attempts to modify distributional results should be directed at the source of the undesired consequences, which is the distribution of premarket power to create economic values.

VI. Fairness in Political Rules

It is necessary to return to the question posed earlier. Who is to do the adjusting? Who is to impose the handicaps? Precisely because the redistributional arrangements must be chosen and implemented by persons internal to the community involved, the contractarian-constitutional ethic seems to offer the only available standard for evaluation. The "laws and institutions" of society provide a continuing and predictable framework within which individuals interact. It is important that these laws and institutions be seen to be fair, and to do so they must contain features that to some extent rectify differences in opportunities, as previously noted. In this respect, I have already suggested the importance of the taxation of transfers and the governmental financing of education. But, perhaps even more important, the institutions of political decision-making must also be seen to be fair and just. This critical element in any structure embodying "economic justice" tends to be overlooked almost entirely by socialist critics of the market. If political adjustments are to be made, the political game itself must embody precepts of fairness even more stringent than those sometimes attributable to market dealings.

Political adjustments in claims to values can be made to appear fair only on contractarian grounds. That is to say, the arms and agencies of the state, the government, cannot be used directly to transfer incomes and assets from the politically weak to the politically strong under the disguise of achieving "distributive justice" or anything else. The citizenry cannot be fooled by such empty rhetoric. Distributional adjustments that are implemented politically must, first of all, be strictly "constitutional" in the sense that they must be embodied in permanent or quasi-permanent institutions of social order. No short-term legislative or parliamentary manipulation of distributive shares could possibly qualify by genuine fairness criteria. In terms of practical programs, the argument here suggests that a progressive income tax might possibly emerge as one feature of an acceptable fiscal constitution, but the overtly political jiggling with the rate structure to reward political friends and to punish political enemies would, of course, violate all contractarian precepts. Similar conclusions apply to the pandering to politically dominant coalitions by jiggling expenditure programs.

Libertarian critics of efforts to transfer incomes and wealth should concentrate their attacks on the unwarranted use of democratic decision structures. An open society cannot survive if its government is viewed as an instrument for arbitrary transfers among its citizens. On the other hand, libertarians go too far, and reduce the force of their own argument, when they reject genuinely constitutional or framework arrangements that act to promote some rough equality in premarket positions and act so as to knock off the edges of postmarket extremes. The libertarian may defend the distributive rule of the competitive process on standard efficiency grounds, and he may, if he chooses, also develop an ethical argument in support of this rule. But this is not the same thing as defending the distributive results that might be observed in a market economy in which there is no attempt to adjust starting positions. The libertarian who fails to make the distinction between the two separate determinants of observed distributive results makes the same mistake as his socialist counterpart who attacks the market under essentially false pretenses.

Having indicated that (i) institutions of transfer taxation along with

(ii) institutions that involve governmental financing of education are likely to emerge in any agreed-on fair rules, I want now to look at additional institutions that may be required to mitigate particular forms of starting-position inequalities, always as evaluated with basic criteria of fairness.

VII. Justice and Fair Chances

More specifically, I want to elaborate the notion of "fair chances" that I have already touched on only briefly. In a fundamental, but limited, respect, "fair chances" amount to "equal opportunity." Each person is insured that the claims to economic value assigned to him are determined by elements *within himself* and by chance factors that affect all persons *equally*. These criteria do not require equalization of expected values among all persons, evaluated at the starting positions. As suggested, the more restrictive definition of equal opportunity implied in the latter criterion could never be achieved, or even closely approached. But the "fair chances" criterion does require the absence of effects on expected values that are exerted by elements external to the persons themselves and discriminatorily distributed among persons.

It is not easy to articulate the precise meaning of this criterion apart from examples to be introduced below, in which I think the notion becomes evident as well as familiar. Let me say at the outset, however, that I think the criterion of "fair chances," or, in perhaps a more descriptive appellation, "equal treatment," is vitally important in the generation of personal attitudes toward the "justice" of any social order. So long as each person considers himself to have a "fair chance" to play the game, he can hope for a favorable outcome despite his own recognition that the expected value of the outcome for him may remain below that for other players.

Consider my earlier argument to the effect that elementary precepts for ex ante fairness are not violated if income shares can be somehow attributed to choice, luck, or effort. To the extent that the rules allow everyone to play on equal terms, the pattern of outcomes, including the distribution of shares in command over final goods and services, cannot be adjudged to be "unfair." But, as I have also noted, to "play on equal terms" could be strictly interpreted to require that all players possess equal capacities-endowments at the starting point. In this narrow interpretation, and even with the imposition of institutionally appropriate handicapping, the game can never really be labeled to be "fair." But life in civil community means that all persons must, willy-nilly, participate, so what is to be done?

To the extent that a person accepts his own lot in the genetic-cultural distribution of basic or natural capacities and talents, he can also think of this lot as his own "luck," considered in the more inclusive pregame sense of the term. None of us can change his or her genetic-cultural heritage (we cannot choose our own parents). And we may, therefore, look on that heritage that we do have as our own particular "luck in the draw of history," while at the same time we may acknowledge that this heritage may itself be of major importance in determining just where we will stand in the allocation of shares to value in the community. For better or for worse, we may accept the necessity to live with our lot, and especially as the political-economic rules of the game do not seem to operate so as to add to, or to exacerbate, the differences in value shares emergent from the distribution of natural talents.

In order to discuss this distribution of "natural talents" more systematically, let me postulate, for purposes of argument, that all persons in the community make roughly the same quality of choices, have roughly the same luck within the game itself, and exert roughly the same basic effort. In this abstract setting, if the distribution of natural talents or capacities-endowments is known, and if each person can be readily identified in terms of where he or she stands in the distributional array, a distribution of expected values of claims to final values can be mapped as a direct correspondence with the initial distribution of talents-capacities-endowments. As noted earlier, to the extent that choices, luck, and effort vary among persons, this precise mapping between the distribution of starting positions and the distribution of final claims to product value breaks down. Considerable ranges for intersections and overlapping may emerge in the latter distribution as the game is actually played out. And as I suggested previously, there will be a direct relationship between the importance of these "nonnatural" or "nonstarting-point" influences and the perceived "fairness" of the game itself.

We know, however, that persons cannot be readily identified in terms of their "natural talents," their basic capacities to generate economic values, independent of demonstrated or proven performance in the economic game itself. In part at least, and perhaps in large part, the differences in the capacities of persons to create economic value, to produce what we may call "social income," can be seen only in retrospect, after individuals act. To an extent, persons necessarily *enter* the game unidentified and unclassified. Unobserved differences in capacities may exist, and they may be important in determining the distribution of final claims to value, but there may be no way of judging these initial differences until the course has been commenced. The simplistic Easter-egg hunt analogy used above breaks down; the "faster runners" cannot be identified in advance.

If the distribution of assigned claims to final product value could somehow be put off or delayed until full information about comparative productivities is available, there is no particular problem created by the absence of such information during those initial periods when economic activity takes place. But in the economic-political game described by a market economy operating within a legal setting of property and contract, we must think in terms of extended calendar time. Persons could hardly be expected to wait for the length of a working life, or even a relatively small part thereof, before some shares of product value are passed out. Some payments scheme must be worked out and implemented that will assign per-period claims in the absence of full information about relative productivities. During some initial sequence of time periods, which we call a "demonstration period," while individualized productivities are being determined, the market will tend to generate pay assignments, "wages," that are valued at some average for the whole group of entrants from the relevant subgroup. The calendar length of such a demonstration period will, of course, vary significantly among different occupational groupings. For common labor the period may be so short as to be almost insignificant; for professors it may be quite long.

VIII. A Formal Model

At this point, I find it necessary to introduce somewhat more formal analysis through a set of simplified and highly abstract models. Let me first assume that there are N entrants into the working-producing force for a defined set of occupational categories. (I do not want to get into detailed discussion here about wholly "noncompeting" groups, with the distinctions among these being determined by the range of genuinely natural talents and abilities, e.g., artists and athletes.) For purposes of my argument, we may either assume that all potential entrants may enter all occupations, in which case we need not refer to groupings, or, alternatively, we may restrict our analysis to the single set of occupational categories which all of the N entrants considered can enter and in which they can produce meaningful economic results.

The N entrants are cohorts in terms of time profiles; they enter the working-producing force at the same time, say, 1980. Let me postulate that the entrants differ in starting positions, in their basic capacities to produce economic values. If each person in the group of N entrants should make the average quality of personal career choices, if each should have roughly the same luck, and if each should exert roughly the same effort, the array of market-value productivities would follow the array of natural talents, as noted above. Let me plot such a distribution in Figure 1, where, on the abscissa, we measure expected values of economic productivity for the N persons and where numbers of persons are measured on the ordinate.

Let me postulate that the economy is fully competitive. Once information about individual productivities is known, individuals will be able to receive income shares commensurate with their marginal productivities. If this information is available at the outset, and *before* income shares are assigned in any period, no problem arises. Individuals will receive income shares that correspond with those capacities that are inherent in their own endowments. An individual's income share will depend in no way on the inherent capacities-endowments of others than himself.

Assume, however, that neither the entrants themselves nor potential employers have any information about relative individual productivities when

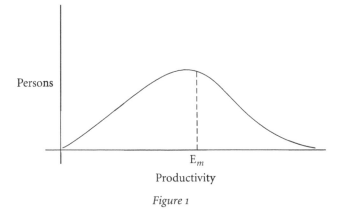

E_m

Productivity

Figure 1

persons are hired. Assume, further, however, that each employer knows that the productivities over the whole group of N entrants are distributed as indicated in Figure 1. Assume that information about individual productivities becomes available at the end of the demonstration period of a single-period duration, say, one year. For simplicity in exposition, assume that this information is available to individuals themselves and to *all* potential employers. There is no need to get into problems of firm-specific information, or problems raised by differences in information as between employee and employer.

For the first period, each of the N entrants, no matter where he might stand in the distributional array, can expect to receive the mean expected value of the whole distribution, say, E_m, in Figure 1. At the end of this period, when full information becomes available, wages will be appropriately adjusted, and, from this point in time, all workers will be paid for marginal value productivities.

In this model, note that each person is *treated equally with his equals*, in terms of identification by basic natural talents and capacities. In the first period, all persons, regardless of their capacities, receive equal shares in value. After the first period, persons in each and every position on the capacity-talent scale secure the value of their own inherent contribution to value in the economy.

I want to argue that this precept or principle: *equal treatment for equals* is a necessary element in any set of rules for social order in a community that makes any claim of "fairness" and that such a principle will tend to emerge from the conceptualized contractual agreements among all persons. John Rawls did not specifically discuss this principle, as such, in his formulation of a theory of justice, although we may read the discussion of his criterion "careers open to talents" as indirectly stating such a principle.[7] In one form or another, such a principle is central in normative tax theory, and it is also analogous to the more general principle of equality before the law. But the

---

7. See Rawls, *Theory of Justice*, 73: ". . . those who are at the same level of talent and ability, and have the same willingness to use them, should have the same prospects of success regardless of their initial place in the social system, that is, irrespective of the income class into which they are born." In his discussion, however, Rawls seems to think that the institutions of transfer taxation and publicly financed education will suffice to satisfy the equal-chances criterion, in the absence, of course, of discriminatory "tastes."

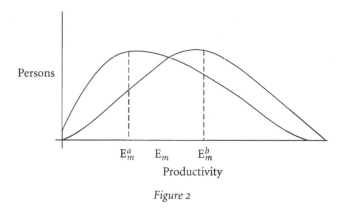

Figure 2

particular application of the equal-treatment principle to the problems of distributive justice has not, to my knowledge, been fully worked out and analyzed.

In the model described above, the principle of "equal treatment" is met, and no further institutional adjustments are suggested. If, however, the model, as described, should obscure elements of the game as actually played, we may predict violation of the principle through the ordinary workings of the competitive market. As an alternative model, suppose, now, that the inclusive array of expected values of productivities for the N entrants is as depicted in Figure 1. The conditions of the model remain as before with one important exception.

Potential employers are now assumed to have *some* information about individual productivities in a probabilistic sense before persons are hired. As before, there is no information available about individuals, as individuals, but there now are assumed to exist certain identifiable characteristics that enable employers to classify persons within two roughly equal-sized sets or groupings.[8] The mean value of productivity differs as between these two sets. Further, employers are assumed to know the array of values, the distribution, for each of the two sets of potential employees. Figure 2 depicts the situation

8. What I call identifiable characteristics are *indices* in the terminology of Michael Spence, which he defines as "unalterably observable characteristics." See Michael Spence, *Market Signaling* (Cambridge, Mass.: Harvard University Press, 1974), chap. 4.

in this model. Note that the range of the two distributions is the same for the two sets of persons; only the mean values differ. As before, assume that the length of the demonstration period is one year, and that, subsequent to this period, all employees, regardless of their initial classification, secure the full value of their marginal contributions to value.

For the initial period, employers in this setting will be forced by competitive pressures to offer different wages or incomes to workers from the two sets, A and B. All entrants from the A group will be paid a wage E_m for the first period, regardless of their ultimate productivity. Similarly, all workers from the B group will be paid E_m for the first period. It is clear that the "equal-treatment" norm is violated here by the workings of the competitive market. Workers from the A group, and identified as such, will receive a lower present value of lifetime earnings than their "equals" in the B group, not because of something inherent in their own individualized "luck in the draw" of natural talents and capacities, but, instead, because they happen to be classified as a member of a group with lower mean productivity. To put the same result differently, an entrant from the A group who makes precisely the same choices, who has precisely the same luck in the game itself, who, for a given wage, exerts precisely the same effort, will secure over his lifetime a net claim to final product value lower than his equal from the B group. He is effectively "penalized" by his membership in the group that happens to exhibit the lower average productivity.

I should emphasize that the competitive market process that generates the violation of the "equal-treatment" norm is efficient, by construction. The differentials in present values between any pair of genuine equals, one from each of the two subgroups, do not reflect *market failure* in any meaningful sense of this term.[9] In the competitive market model that I have postulated here, employers act on the basis of the information that is available to them. Their first-period information is, by assumption, limited to identification by class or group. If a single employer chose deliberately to ignore such information, and chose instead to pay all entrants the mean expected

9. Frank Knight often remarked that it is difficult to know whether critics of competitive markets base their criticisms on failures of markets to be competitive or on the very successes of markets in attaining efficiency.

value for the whole set of N entrants, he could not hire any of the workers from the B group.[10]

Note also that there is no "discrimination," as such, in the model. Employers are presumably interested solely and exclusively in maximizing profits, and they have no tastes or preferences as to the type of input units employed, either individually or as a mix among the two types. Similarly, employees are exclusively interested in wages and are totally indifferent as to who their coworkers might be.

---

10. Akerlof discusses the market phenomena that I have described under the heading "statistical discrimination," which in itself is somewhat misleading since no "discrimination," as such, is involved. In addition, although his discussion is somewhat unclear in this respect, Akerlof seems to suggest that the existence of such phenomena implies inefficiency through the generation of what he refers to as a "low-level equilibrium trap," one that results from the incentives exerted on the behavior of the members of the class or group with relatively lower average qualifications. See George Akerlof, "The Economics of Caste and the Rat Race and Other Woeful Tales," *Quarterly Journal of Economics*, November 1976.

Such incentive effects may, of course, be present which would imply inefficiency. In my model, however, I have explicitly eliminated these effects to insure that there is no inefficiency in the competitive solution.

In his earlier treatment, Kenneth Arrow refers to the differences in perceived qualifications, based on perceived differences in averages, as one explanation for observed differences in wages among differing racial groups. Arrow's whole analysis is marred, however, by his apparent commitment to the presumption that basic productivities among groups cannot differ, even in average terms. See Kenneth Arrow, "Models of Job Discrimination" (chap. 1), and "Some Mathematical Models of Race in the Labor Market" (chap. 6), in *Racial Discrimination in Economic Life*, ed. Anthony H. Pascal (Lexington, Mass.: D. C. Heath, 1972).

In his book *Market Signaling* Michael Spence discusses models in which results analogous to those emerging from the models here seem to be derived. His whole analysis, however, is based on the signaling role of education and on individuals' choices of educational investment. In his discussion Spence, like Arrow, postulates that the actual productivity distributions between the two classes (races in his model) are identical. Differences in treatment of "equals" in separate classes stem from the possible differing levels of educational signals required to establish conditional probabilities for employers. Given an initial, historically determined "prejudice," the expectations of employers and employees alike, over both classes, may prove to be self-reinforcing. See Spence, chaps. 2 and 3.

By contrast, in my model, which postulates actual differences in the mean or average productivities of the two classes, the differential treatment of "equals" arises with no "prejudice" or "discrimination" present, at *any* point in time. For an earlier and more formal presentation of the model introduced here, see E. S. Phelps, "The Statistical Theory of Racism and Sexism," *American Economic Review*, September 1972.

Once the violation of the equal-treatment principle is recognized, a question arises concerning the possible efficiency losses that any interference with the working of competitive markets designed to correct the violation might produce.

Consider the following scenario. Suppose that all potential employers should be required to hire entrants *as if* the initial classification into the A and B groups were not possible. That is to say, suppose that all employers should be constrained to "hire blind," to throw away or ignore information deliberately that had been of potential value to them in the setting described above. Note that, in this new situation, employers could do no more than pay the mean value for the whole set of N entrants for the initial or demonstration period. Despite the fact that all persons in the community, employers and workers alike, recognize that the B workers as a set are, on average, more productive than the A workers as a set, the competitive market will force all wages during the initial period to the level E_m. All workers will be employed, as before, by assumption. Efficiency losses will emerge only to the extent that we allow workers to respond to wage-rate differences by modifying effort (e.g., through changing number of hours worked). If incentives of this sort are allowed, the initial market solution, with mean wages E_a and E_b for the two classes respectively, the A-class workers will work less than they would under the uniform wage, E_m. The B-class workers, on the other hand, will work more at wage E_b ($>E_m$) than at E_m. Since, by construction, the mean productivity of the B-class workers exceeds that of the A-class workers, there will be *some* efficiency loss involved in the shift to the arrangement where all employers pay all workers in N the uniform initial-period wage, E_m. This efficiency loss may, however, be very small.

IX. Implications for Policy

The analysis in the preceding section demonstrates that it becomes conceptually possible to secure satisfaction of the "equal treatment for equals" or "fair chances" criterion with little minor efficiency losses of the sort ordinarily discussed by welfare economists. There may, however, be significant gaps between conceptual possibility and practical implementation. In the model that was specifically analyzed, I simply assumed that information about individual productivities is not available until after a demonstration period is complete, a period during which some wage-payments scheme must be worked out. Clearly, if potential employers could, in some way, secure accurate information about individual productivity before entrants are taken on as employees, there need be no violation of the equal-treatment criterion, even if the two-group identification with differing average productivities continues to hold. In such a full information setting, employers will be led by their profit-seeking behavior to ignore averages over groups and to look exclusively at prospective individual values. Recognition of this result suggests that policy aimed directly at increasing the flow of relevant information concerning prospective employee productivity before employment commences may be of independent value in terms of promoting a basic sense of "fair chances" in the community.

It should, however, be anticipated that some of the elements isolated by the model analyzed above will remain. The equal-treatment principle will not be fully met with improved information. How and to what extent could constraints be imposed on hiring and wage-setting behavior in a fully competitive economy for the purpose of enhancing "fairness"?

If constraints are to be imposed, note that efficiency in results would require that such constraints be *universally applied*. They must bear on each and every employer who faces the set of entrants into the work force. And note that each of these employers will have a continuing private-profit motivation to use the classificatory information that we presume is available to him. To impose the hiring constraints on some employers but not on others or to impose the constraints so loosely that only some employers will be affected will guarantee net-efficiency losses without accomplishing the results intended. Some minimal steps may be taken to deny the information as to class identification to employers. In this sense, legal and administrative rules that dictate that blanks for identifiable characteristics not be filled out may seem justifiable.

Care must also be taken to note precisely the nature of the constraints that would be required to prove effective in promoting genuine equal treatment of equals. A constraint that merely directs potential employers to pay all entrants *equal wages* would be disastrous for *all* entrants from the class described by the relatively low average productivity. This result emerges because, in such a setting, every employer, having the general classificatory information, will on probabilistic grounds find it to his interest to hire entrants *only* from the group with the higher average productivity. Regardless of their ultimate contribution to value, individuals from the group with relatively low average productivity will find it difficult if not impossible to find employment in this setting.

If the "equal treatment for equals" criterion is to be satisfied, equal wages for equally productive persons will have to be paid during the initial demonstration periods as well as for all subsequent periods during which individualized contributions are fully known. But this end-result must be produced by the profit-maximizing response of potential employers within the constraint that entrants be chosen as if they are drawn from the inclusive group and not from identifiable classes within the larger set. In more specific terms, the suggested constraints must take the form of *hiring quotas*, with new entrants taken on in proportion to the relative numbers of the identifiable classes in the inclusive set. In my example, if A and B are equal in size, each being of size $N/2$, each employer should be required to hire equal numbers of entrants from A and from B. In this case, competition would prevent employers from paying differential wages to members of the two groups; he will necessarily pay first-period wages equal to the average productivity expected for all entrants from N, and not from A and/or B.

The hiring quota or constraint in this model should be made to apply *only* to initial or demonstration-period hiring. By our assumption, after this period, full information is available concerning individual productivities, not only to the specific firm that employs particular persons but to other potential employees as well. Average productivities of classes or groups, even if these differ substantially by easily identifiable classes, become totally irrelevant to decisions about continuing employment and relative wage scales. Market competition will insure universalized payment in accordance with relative marginal productivities.

In the distribution of actual productivities as indicated in Figure 2, the firms or industries that employ relatively more high-productivity workers would be anticipated to retain relatively more B-class employees in their work force than firms or industries that require less productive workers. This sort of permanent "imbalance" in the ratios between A-class and B-class employees does not imply any violation of the "equal-treatment" norm. Indeed, quite the contrary. To require that all firms and industries "balance" the work force between the two classes of workers would require that the equal-treatment norm be violated, with the employees from the relatively more productive group, from B in our example, being subjected to "unfair" treatment.

I have tried to be careful in saying that the implications for policy outlined in the previous section depend strictly on the existence of the parameters of the model that was specified. The assumptions of this model are extremely restrictive, and it need not follow that the policy implications suggested are relevant when and if these assumptions are modified. Recall that I assumed (1) that all N entrants in the inclusive group can produce economic value in the employment categories considered; (2) that potential employers initially possess no information at all about the individual productivities to be expected from any entrant; (3) that employers do possess information that allows the N entrants to be subdivided into two readily identifiable classes, that are known to differ in average productivity; (4) that the demonstration period during which information about individual productivity comes to be available is the same for all entrants; (5) that this productivity information is known to all potential employers at the end of the demonstration period; and finally, (6) that the economy is fully competitive.

It is useful at this point to see just how rigid these assumptions are; how might they be relaxed without destroying the validity of the policy implications that were suggested above? The requirement for competition need not be made overly restrictive; the general competitiveness of the economy in some broadly workable sense seems all that would be necessary here. Nor need there be concern about the subdivision into only two readily identifiable classes or groups or about the uniformity of the demonstration period. These assumptions may be modified to allow for several classes with several lengths of demonstration period without changing the structure of the analysis. The assumptions that remain critical to the analytical implications are those which relate to the *absence* of information on relative individual productivities and the *presence* of information about average productivities for classes or groups smaller than the whole set of entrants prior to the work force. These assumptions are critical because it is only on these assumptions that we get profit-seeking employers in a competitive environment differentiating among entrants on the basis of class in the complete absence of information about individual productivity. It is such differentiation that introduces the "unfairness" in the game, that violates the equal-treatment norm, that insures that persons who ultimately demonstrate equality with others in the "natural draw" secure lower present values of claims to product solely because they are members of a class with relatively low average productivity.

The reader will, of course, have noticed that I have deliberately refrained from attaching labels to the classes, but whatever designations seem fitting can be added, whether these be for male-female, black-white, Protestant-Catholic, short-tall, Yankee-redneck, or what have you. I should argue that in the real world, where the assumptions of the formal model are, of course, not present, the policy implications follow generally with respect to hiring practices, provided that potential employers should be observed to make such differentiation by class, provided that those who do so are observed to survive.

Note what the analysis *does not say*. The *average* present values for claims for members of the "less productive" class will, in any case, be lower than the average for the "more productive" class. Satisfaction of the equal-treatment criterion will not modify this basic result. There is no way that a hiring-quota system could, or should, equalize the differing average productivities of members of the various identifiable classes. A hiring-quota system, ideally administered, should do nothing more than insure that the individual, regardless of his ultimate productivity, is not affected in the value of the claims that he secures by factors *external to his own capacities,* which are not equally applicable to all members of the group, inclusively defined.

X. Objections Considered

Objections can be raised to the policy implications and, by inference, to the analysis itself. In particular, since my whole model allows for separate individual shares in product value to be determined, in part, by "natural capacities," and since these are acknowledged to differ among persons, why have I advanced the argument that the "fair-chances" or "equal-treatment" criterion requires blindness only with respect to one feature of a person, namely, his identification as a member of a particular class or group? If "luck in the genetic-cultural draw" is to be accepted, and lived with, in terms of basic individual capacities to produce economic value, why should not this same "luck in the genetic draw" be extended to cover membership in the identifiable class or group? If person A_1 is "unlucky" in that his inherent productive capacity, when demonstrated, falls below that of the mean capacity for the community, can he not also be considered, and so consider himself, to be "unlucky" in having been born to membership in the A group, where persons are, on average, less productive than in the B group? Perhaps to some readers this objection is compelling, but to me there is an element of what I should call *perverse handicapping* in the uncorrected operation of competitive markets in the setting postulated in the model. An individual member of the A group, in my example, is forced to start the race behind his equals, behind those whom he later matches in terms of demonstrated capacity. He has to catch up to be equal, which, in my set of values, becomes inherently "unfair."

A more specific objection may be raised concerning my argument to the effect that the imposition of initial-period hiring quotas may be accompanied with relatively insignificant welfare or efficiency losses, limited essentially to the slight differences in the product value of the offsetting responses of the members of two groups in the model. In the model itself, I assumed that all of the N entrants can be employed, and can produce value, in the "industry" or "set of employment categories" considered. If, for any reason, some persons who might seek entry into the relevant "industry" cannot be employed, there must be some means of rationing places. In such a setting, a legal requirement for all employers to select entrants proportionately from the A and B groups may introduce an additional efficiency loss. The average productivity of persons employed will be lower than the average productivity under the unencumbered operation of the competitive market.

Too much should not be made of this additional efficiency-loss emendation, provided that the market is assumed to be competitive. To the extent that entrants seek to enter occupational-employment categories, they should be able to do so and to secure employment therein if there are no barriers to entry and if wage levels are competitively determined. Problems arise only with genuinely "noncompeting" groups, where threshold differences in natural talents create sharp dividing lines between those who qualify and those who do not, and where there are no genuinely marginal employees who can readily shift into and out of such groups.

On the other hand, implementation of the equal-treatment criterion may involve efficiency loss in situations where, for any reason, artificial and non-market barriers to entry into occupations and employments have been established. If competitive organization is not allowed to determine the number of medical doctors, for example, there may be many more applicants for medical school than there are places. In such a setting, the introduction of quotas among groups or classes of entrants based on some proportion of identifiable characteristics with distinguishable average productivity differentials will produce a higher fail rate (and hence higher cost) than would be the case without such quotas. This amounts to saying that "fairness" costs less in market than in nonmarket settings.

A much more serious objection than any of these discussed to this point lies in the prospect that the policy implications of the whole analysis may be extended and applied in settings where the assumptions of the model are clearly violated, notably to employment and pay structures in which information about individual productivities *is* known to employers. As noted, there is no implication in my analysis that uniform wages should be paid all entrants, even in the initial period, save as a result of the hiring arrangements that make such uniformity a *result* rather than a specific objective. And there is surely no implication that wage rates should be standardized over groups on the basis of elements other than individual productivities, when the latter are ascertained. And, as I suggested earlier, it is a perversion of my argument to suggest that average wages among groups with differing average productivities should somehow be forcibly equalized. Also, as noted earlier, "equal treatment" in the initial hiring stage does not, and cannot, be perverted to mean the maintenance of "balance" in employment, *after* productivities are known.

We must recognize that any projected interference with the working of the competitive market in hiring must be organized and put into being politically—that is, by persons acting on behalf of governments, persons who have their own self-interest to consider, whether this be tenure in office, electoral success, or their own idealized goal for society. Thus the dangers that the implications derived from basically sound analysis will be perverted for use in situations where they simply do not apply, and where, if applied, they will produce damage, both in terms of efficiency and of fairness, must be acknowledged.

Once again, distrust in the ordinary political arrangements suggests resort to genuinely constitutional rules that will, to an extent at least, be immune from ordinary political pressures. But courts, even if nominally bound by rules, can also get confused, especially since the parameters of the cases at hand rarely, if ever, correspond to the conditions of the models that might have been systematically analyzed. The meanderings of the Supreme Court in the recent Bakke and Weber cases attest to this confusion. I find myself sympathetic to the Court's dilemma in both cases. I would not have had this appreciation of the dilemma facing the Court before I worked out the "equal-treatment" principle of this essay. So, at the least, I have learned something.

XI. Appendix

In this Appendix I want to extend the basic analysis developed in previous discussion to a setting in which, for some reason, there is an arbitrary limit on the number of applicants who can secure "employment" in an "industry," a limit that is lower than the total number of applicants, and where the competitive forces of the market are not allowed to operate. I shall develop the argument through the use of stylized models, but my aim is to isolate certain features that bear considerable relevance to familiar policy issues.

1. Consider first a model in which there are only 100 "places" to be filled, but where there are 1,000 applicants. Suppose that there is absolutely no information about individual capacities or productivities, but that the distribution of such capacities is known to take the form depicted in Figure 1. How can the 100 "best" applicants be selected? In this model, it is clear that only by sampling the whole population of applicants can this objective be attained. If this sampling takes the form of a required period of demonstration, the selection process will be costly but necessary.

2. Consider, as a second model, a situation where "entrance tests" can be administered cheaply, and where there is a perfect correspondence between scores on these tests and the observed productivities in periods subsequent to the tests. In this case, the indicated policy is simply to select the 100 persons who score highest on the entrance tests. No one is excluded; the game is fair.

3. As a third model, consider a situation where nothing is known about individual capacities, and where a costly demonstration period is required to determine these. Assume, however, that the set of 1,000 applicants may be divided into two classes, A and B, in terms of some readily identifiable characteristic, and that the average productivities of these two classes are known

to differ, as depicted in Figure 2. If the range of capacities is the same for both groups, all of the 1,000 applicants must be tested before the 100 best qualified can be chosen. Assume that, if such a testing procedure is done, there will be 90 successful applicants from B and only 10 from A. Note that this apparently biased result does not violate the equal-treatment criterion in any way because, at the level of initial testing, all persons are given fair chances to compete. No arbitrary exclusion based on class is involved.

In the setting of this model, however, the temptation to use the class-identification information may be very strong. By testing only from the B group, known to have the relatively higher mean capacity, 90 of the 100 required applicants may be selected. The costs of locating the remaining 10 applicants from the A class will be equal to the costs of getting the 90 from the B class. Further, the capacities of the 10 "best" from the A class, who might be excluded by a sampling limited to the B class, may be only slightly lower than the additional 10 persons who might qualify under the more restricted testing. The benefit-cost calculus may put great pressures on decision-making authorities to sample only from the B group.

To do so, however, would clearly violate the equal-treatment criterion, as discussed above. Potential applicants from the A class, even if they have full knowledge of the probability coefficients, can properly label the game to be unfair, because they would be prohibited entry, even at the demonstration-testing stage.

4. A more complex model involves a combination of the first and second models above. Suppose that no class identification (Model 2) is possible, and that *some* information about individual capacities can be secured from inexpensive entrance examinations, but that this information will prove accurate only within rather broad probability limits. All potential applicants may be given the entrance tests, but, differently from Model 2, the selection of the 100 persons with the highest entrance-test scores will not insure that the 100 "best" persons, in terms of proven capacities, will be chosen. To determine the latter, an additional costly demonstration period must be administered. In this setting, a decision to admit more than 100 persons for the demonstration period may well be warranted. Regardless of the number admitted to the demonstration period, however, so long as scores on the entrance test are used to determine the lower cutoff point, there is no overt violation of the equal-treatment criterion. A person who is excluded because of his low

entrance-test score cannot claim unfairness; he is treated equally with his equal at this level.

5. The most complex model of all is attained by adding the possibility of class identification to the partial information model above. In this setting, there is no violation of the equal-treatment criterion *if the class-identification information is not used.* If applicants to be allowed to enter a demonstration or tryout period are selected purely by entrance-test scores, even if it is known that these scores are grossly imperfect predictors of ultimate capacities, those excluded cannot be justified in possible claims of unfairness.

6. This result depends, however, on the presumption that scores on the entrance test are not biased by class. Suppose, for example, that the differences in the mean test scores for A and B applicants are significantly larger than the differences in the mean values of capacities, when finally determined, although both means vary in the same way. In this situation, even though the entrance-test scores may be the single best predictor of ultimate capacity, the result of the use of this score as the sole criterion to select applicants for the extended demonstration periods will tend to bias the whole selection process to the disadvantage of members of the A class, which is known to be characterized by lower mean test scores and lower mean productivities.

There is no overt violation of the equal-treatment norm here. A person from the A group is not excluded because he or she is a member of that group. And such a person can observe members of the B group with the same test scores as his or her own also being excluded. However, in an indirect sense, basic unfairness can be claimed here, due to the bias in the test. With observed identical test scores, a rejected member of the A applicants will embody a somewhat higher probability of ultimate success than a member of the rejected B applicants with an identical test score. If equals are defined by equal probabilities of success in the extended demonstration period, then identical test scores do not meet the definition. In this particular case, there is a logical argument, based on fairness precepts, for putting the cutoff test score somewhat lower for the A applicants.

7. Whether or not the bias suggested exists is, of course, an empirical question to be determined. Unless it can be shown to exist, there can be no alleged unfairness in a system that relies exclusively on entrance-test scores,

even when everyone recognizes that these scores are imperfect predictors of ultimate capacities. In the models of this Appendix, as in the body of this chapter, unfairness, in the absence of such a test bias, stems *only* from the use of class-identification information.

8. The extensions of the basic equal-treatment analysis summarized in this Appendix are relevant to some of the problems faced by the Supreme Court in the Bakke and Weber cases, perhaps the most important decisions of the decade of the 1970s.[11]

Allen Bakke was successful in his particular claim that he had suffered "reverse discrimination" in the University of California–Davis practice of selecting medical-school entrants. His evidence was that his score on an entrance test was higher than that of blacks who were admitted under a designated quota system. As the analysis above has suggested, Bakke was justified on the "equal-treatment-for-equals" criterion if there was no evidence of the test-score bias discussed in Section 6 above. Even if entrance-test scores could be shown to be quite imperfect predictors of success in medical school, the sole use of such scores to determine success or failure in admission does not violate the fairness precept. In such a setting, there is no argument for the establishment and enforcement of racial quotas, and any attempt to introduce such quotas would violate the fairness norm for members of the relatively high mean-productivity race.

Since no evidence of test-score bias was explicitly introduced, the Court's opinion of the Bakke position seems likely to have been in accordance with applications of the equal-treatment precept. On the other hand, the apparent "hedging" by Justice Powell on the use of race may well have been prompted by considerations of the sort discussed in Section 3 above. The "low-cost" way for a medical school to secure, say, 100 entrants of reasonably high quality, given information about the mean success of persons from identifiable classes, would be to restrict persons by race or class, and to use test scores only within classes. This method of operation would tend to emerge without the slightest preference on the part of anyone for racial or class considerations, per se.

11. *Regents of University of California* v. *Bakke*, 98 S. Ct. 2733 (1978); *United Steelworkers, etc.* v. *Weber*, 99 S. Ct. 2721 (1979).

In the Weber case, the majority of a reduced-sized Court found against Weber's claim of unfair or unequal treatment. In this case, Weber's argument was based on the fact that his seniority ranking was above that of a black applicant who was chosen for a training program based on a proportionate white-black quota arrangement.

The issues raised in *Weber* are considerably more complex than those raised in *Bakke*. It will be useful to see if the basic analysis worked out in previous discussion can be applied so as to offer insights into the Court's genuine dilemma. For purposes of discussion, we presume that the mean productivities of the two races, black and white, were estimated by employers to be as depicted above in Figure 2. In this setting, and prior to any program of affirmative action, Kaiser would have been willing, presumably, to hire blacks initially only if they were available at lower wages (for comparable skill categories); or, if wages were equalized, at higher qualification levels for the same categories. This policy would have emerged on the assumption that uncertainty about individual productivities was necessarily present when hiring decisions were made. (No overt racial discrimination at all would have been involved in such a policy.) Union wage standardization would have, presumably, required equalization of wage rates across all workers in a given category. Hence, a black worker, on being hired, would have represented a *higher* level of qualification (on average) than his white-worker counterpart. Seniority records commence, however, only from the date of initial employment, and these records could not, of course, reflect differential qualification levels at point of entry. It might have been argued, therefore, that a black worker was not the "equal" of the white worker who exhibited the same seniority, and that, because of the difference, the seniority records, standing alone, did not reflect the appropriate criterion of legal equality for selection and advancement to a training program. "Equal treatment" at the level of training-program selection, if designed to offset the initial differential in qualification on employment, might require some quota arrangement, and one that might necessarily have been inconsistent with simple seniority.

The majority of the reduced-sized Court would have been on much more secure grounds in its *Weber* opinion had it chosen to use an argument like that sketched out briefly here. Unfortunately, Justice Brennan, for the majority, did not use such an argument, and instead, relied on an internally con-

tradictory argument that seemed to reflect personally biased judicial legislation. As a result, the opinion was highly vulnerable to the scathing dissent of
Justice Rehnquist. Neither the majority opinion nor the dissent recognized
the potential conflict between the satisfaction of the "equal-treatment" criterion and the commitment against quotas in the discussion of the basic legislation.

PART FIVE

Contractarian Encounters

Rawls on Justice as Fairness

When I first encountered John Rawls' conception of "justice as fairness," I was wholly sympathetic. I interpreted his approach to be closely analogous, even if not identical, to that aimed at explaining the voluntary emergence of "fair games," with widely divergent applications. Stimulated by Frank Knight and, more directly, by Rutledge Vining (both economists who worked independent of and prior to Rawls), I sensed the possible extensions in the explanatory-descriptive power of models for "rules of games," derived in accordance with some criteria of "fairness." As readers of *The Calculus of Consent* recognize, Gordon Tullock and I employed such models in our derivation of the "logical foundations of constitutional democracy" (our subtitle) of a political structure not grossly divergent from that envisioned by the Founding Fathers and embodied in the United States Constitution, at least in its initial conception. For these and other reasons, I looked forward to publication of Rawls' long-promised treatise.

Now that the book has appeared, I find myself less sympathetic with Rawls than I might have anticipated from my early reading of his basic papers. There are two distinct reasons for this temporal difference in assessment, and this review incorporates a two-part argument. Rawls has extended his allegedly contractarian conception and thereby increased its vulnerability. On closer examination, Rawls does not seem to say what I thought he was saying. His approach now appears quite different from that which I shared in 1960.

The second reason for a change in my own reaction to Rawls' work lies

From *Public Choice* 13 (Fall 1972): 123–28. Reprinted by permission of the publisher, Kluwer Academic Publishers.

A review article on John Rawls, *A Theory of Justice* (Cambridge: Harvard University Press, 1971).

in a shift in my own thinking since 1960. I am less of a contractarian, although just where my own position would now be classified remains an open question.

I

Consider several persons voluntarily discussing the rules for an ordinary card game which they are to play. No one can predict the particular run of cards on any series of plays or rounds. These persons attempt to agree on a classification scheme that allows them to separate "fair" and "good" games (defined by sets of rules) from "unfair" and "bad" games. Agreement requires predictions about the working properties of alternative sets of rules, but since these predictions are at least quasi-scientific in nature, there is no self-interest barrier to consensus. For example, a set of rules that insures victory in all subsequent rounds of play to the chance victor of the initial round might be labeled "unfair" and "bad" and the game embodying such rules rejected out of hand. By contrast, a set of rules that guarantees independence among opportunities over separate rounds of play might be classified as "good" and "fair." Or, alternatively, rules that penalize the victor in one round of play over a finite series of subsequent rounds might equally qualify by criteria for "fairness" and "goodness." These simple examples suggest that there may be many sets of rules, many games, that would meet reasonable criteria of both "fairness" and "goodness." As among these, there seems no apparent means of selecting a single "best" set.

It is surely reasonable to extend this essentially contractarian framework to an evaluation and analysis of the whole set of rules, formal and informal, that describe or might describe social interaction. The framework appeals quite naturally to anyone who accepts the individualistic or Kantian precept that human beings are to be treated as ends never as means. This precept implies, in some basic sense, that men are to be treated "as equals." The appropriate question becomes: How would a group of individuals, no one of whom can predict his own position in any of the time segments over which the rules to be chosen are to be operative, go about setting up the socio-political rules of the game? The "veil of ignorance" or uncertainty is the device or requirement that forces participants to consider alternatives on grounds other than identifiable self-interest, narrowly interpreted. In a broader sense, of course, the objective of individual self-interest is served precisely by the criteria for "fairness" and "goodness" in the rules, in the fundamental constitution of society. The important usage of this framework is to evaluate and to analyze existing and proposed social institutions.

It is possible to exclude some existing institutions and some proposed institutional-constitutional changes on such minimal contractarian grounds. Overtly discriminatory restrictions on the franchise, for example, clearly violate the precept of equality among participants. Similarly, the criteria might rule out restrictions on entry into professions. This essentially negative application of the "fairness" criterion can be helpful. But can positive application be other than classificatory? As the simple game examples above suggest, there may exist a whole set of socio-political institutions, embodying among themselves quite different internal characteristics, that qualify on the minimal criteria of "fairness" and "goodness."

Rawls' first principle for a "just" social order is that of equal liberty for all persons. It seems plausible to suggest that any departure from this principle would be rejected in any system that qualifies on the minimal criteria. But Rawls' second major principle seems on much weaker ground. To his first principle of equal liberty, Rawls appends lexicographically his second "difference principle." This states, specifically, that allowable distributional inequalities among persons are acceptable only to the extent that their existence benefits the least-advantaged members of the community. I should accept the hypothesis that a socio-political-economic structure embodying the difference principle meets widely accepted criteria of "fairness." But I should not be prepared to elevate this principle into the ideal position accorded it by Rawls. There may be many other distributional rules that qualify within the acceptable set, classified only by the minimal criteria for "fairness" and "goodness."

Let me illustrate this with an extremely simple numerical example. Two potential players consider alternative positive-sum games, A and B, each of which involves only one round of play. The playoff structure in A is 60:40, while that of B is 80:20. So long as each player has an equal opportunity to win or lose, is there any reason why A should be accepted as "fair" and B as "unfair"? Both games would seem to qualify as "fair" under a broader conception than Rawls would accept.

This is more than a disagreement on detail. By his attempt to make the contractarian approach or model do more than is appropriate, Rawls seems to fall into precisely the same trap as the utilitarians, whom he quite properly criticizes. As he finally admits, Rawls is an idealist, and he seeks to lay down the principles of a "just" social order. He is extremely cautious, and he does allow for much more latitude than most of his idealist colleagues through the ages. But to me he is a bizarre contractarian, despite his self-identification. Perhaps my professional economist's biases show here, but the very essence of contract is the *nonspecification* of outcome by external observers. Traders trade; agreement is reached, agreement that is presumed to be mutually beneficial to the parties. Conceptually at least, there is a subinfinity of possible equilibria along some generalized contract locus. The task of the contractarian social philosopher is to evaluate and to analyze the institutions of the trading process, to lay down criteria for "fairness" in these rules (e.g., that contracts are enforced once made, that fraud is prohibited, that all markets are open, etc.). The task does not involve specifying distributional attributes of outcomes. This unwillingness to allow for a multiplicity of "games," accompanied by a zeal for normative uniqueness, has plagued and continues to plague modern welfare economics. It is singularly unfortunate that Rawls has come so near to what I should classify as a genuine contractarian position while yet remaining so far removed in this most fundamental respect.

Rawls might respond to this criticism by charging that my conception is purely procedural whereas he states explicitly his desire to go beyond procedural limits. In my view, however, there is a direct relationship between a contractarian philosophy of social order and a willingness to be bound by such limits. As contractarian, I cannot, without stepping outside my own limits, lay down precise descriptions of the "just society" or the "good society." I must abide by my own standards and accept as equally "just" whatever outcome emerges from the negotiations among freely contracting persons in an idealized "original position," constrained by the "veil of ignorance."

II

My second reaction is as applicable to my own earlier conception of the contractarian position, implied in the discussion in Part I, as it is to the more vulnerable position espoused by John Rawls. What point is there in talking as if persons will "think themselves" into some idealized version of an "original position" behind a deliberately contrived "veil of ignorance," when we know that, descriptively, the men who must make social choices are not likely to make such an effort? Social choices will continue to be made, as they have always been made, by ordinary mortals, with ordinary passions. Recognizing this, what can be said about ordering rules in terms of criteria for "justice" and "fairness"—whether these criteria be broadly or narrowly drawn? David Hume's stricture that reason must be, and should be, slave to the passions can be helpful here. Precisely because we recognize ourselves to be ordinary men, no different at base from others of our species, we can cultivate an attitude of mutual tolerance and respect for one another, along with a highly skeptical attitude toward anyone who presumes to lay down ideal standards whether or not this is accompanied by proposals collectively to force such standards upon us. But more than this is required. Rules for social order must be evaluated and analyzed, and criteria for orderly change in these rules must be developed. While I can fully appreciate the desire to search for more, the limits seem apparent to me. We can, first of all, emphasize the categorical distinction between "constitutional" choice, the choice from among alternative sets of rules or institutions, and "operational" choice, the choice of policy outcomes within a given constitutional-institutional order. In Rawls' framework, this distinction is not important, and it is not surprising that he largely neglects it. In the more realistic setting that I am suggesting here, the distinction is of critical, indeed crucial, importance. And for reasons closely analogous to those through which Rawls justifies his notion of the original position. In a short-run, operational context, when choices are made within an existing constitutional structure (e.g., a legislative decision on welfare or tax reform), it is folly to expect representatives of the separate constituency interests to act on some idealized principles of "justice." And, indeed, I am not at all sure that we should desire a system where representatives tried to follow such principles, if such were possible. Self-interest can be turned to good account, and even in political process it offers some ultimate protection against ideologues of all stripes.

In the distinct, and conceptually separate, constitutional context, when choices are made among alternative sets of rules, there are at least *some* elements characteristic of the "veil of ignorance." To the extent that rules are considered as permanent or quasi-permanent, designed for operation over a time sequence that remains perhaps open-ended, individual participants in the selection process must be uncertain as to just where their own self-interest lies. They will, to this extent, be motivated to opt for rules and rules changes that embody "fairness" or which at least contain "unfairness" within broad limits. Certain institutional devices may assist in generating the desired uncertainty here, for example, explicitly chosen delays in the implementation of choices, legal precedent, prohibitions of personal aggrandizement from political offices, etc. But despite all this, interests are identifiable even over long terms, and men will act to further them. Rules for social order, as observed, will reflect the struggle among interests, and will rarely, if ever, qualify as "just" in accordance with any idealized criteria.

This raises issues of compliance with or adherence to allegedly "unjust" rules. If consensus is attained, such rules may, of course, be changed. But lacking consensus, who is to decide when criteria of "justice" override the stability of law? We start always from here, not from an "original position," and if men have not previously been guided by agreed-on precepts of justice, what expectation can we have that those to whom we might offer power will behave differently? Conservative or reactionary it may be, but attainable consensus offers the only meaningful principle for genuine constitutional change.

How far is this from Rawls' conception? I do not know, and I cannot tell from a careful reading of this treatise. Would John Rawls allow Earl Warren or his successors to make judgments on their own versions of "justice as fairness" and, in the process, to disregard the embodied predictability of existing constitutional order? I wish that I could be sure that Rawls would answer negatively to this question. If he is advancing "justice as fairness" as a basis for discussion, as an input in some process of reasoning together, with consensus as an ultimate objective as well as constraint, I should grant his work high marks indeed. If, however, he is holding up "justice as fairness" as the embodiment of "truth," which judges and legislators in their "superior wisdom" are to force upon us, Rawls' book deserves to gather dust on the idealist bookshelf.

Is not misguided idealism, operating in disregard of constitutional precepts, a major source of our time's tragedy? When the judiciary is allowed to make "constitutional" choices that cannot secure minimally required legislative assent, and when the judiciary is respected and applauded in the process, the misunderstanding of constitutional democracy has indeed gone far.

And when the people, acting through the legislative arm of government, even find it so much as necessary to begin to discuss reversing court-ordered constitutional change by the amendment process, the confusion has come full circle.

It is perhaps inappropriate and unfair to expect *A Theory of Justice*, a major philosophical treatise, to enlighten us on matters relevant to modern politics. I wonder. The social order that James Madison tried to secure in the United States Constitution, and which was respected for almost two centuries, did not fully embody "justice as fairness." Through time, however, this constitution was adjusted by both a responsive legislature and a responsible judiciary to move closer toward the satisfaction of Rawlsian or alternative precepts of justice. The emergence of unpredictable legal chaos came as the judiciary began to assume the role as guarantors of "justice" in some idealistic sense. Surely we now need a wider recognition of man's inability at playing God. It is a matter for regret that the extension and elaboration of his basically humble and, to this degree, admirable conception of "justice as fairness" led John Rawls away from rather than toward the contribution to social philosophy that this treatise might have represented.

A Hobbesian Interpretation of the Rawlsian Difference Principle

I. Introduction

In this paper I shall offer an interpretation of Professor John Rawls' principle of distributive justice that has not, to my knowledge, been previously developed, despite the lengthening bibliography of Rawlsian-inspired criticism and analysis.[1] Critics of this principle have concentrated attention almost exclusively on the extreme risk-averseness that is implied, and, indeed, the term "maximin principle" has been widely substituted for Rawls' own preferred term "difference principle." In an earlier review article,[2] I expressed misgivings about this principle similar to those of other critics. My own

From *Kyklos* 29, fasc. 1 (1976): 5–25. Copyright 1976 by Blackwell Publishers Ltd. Reprinted by permission of the publisher.

This paper was initially presented at the Second Annual Interlaken Seminar on Analysis and Ideology, Interlaken, Switzerland, in May 1975. It was also presented at the meeting of the Western Economic Association in San Diego, California, in June 1975. The argument of this paper was stimulated directly by Robert Cooter's discussion in his paper "What Is the Public Interest?" (Harvard University, December 1974, mimeographed). Cooter interprets Rawls to say that all persons have rights to equal lots in a just society. From this premise, Cooter is able to derive the difference principle contractually, and without relating it to risk preference. Cooter does not, however, fully integrate this interpretation with the importance that Rawls himself attaches to the original position. At one point in his paper, Cooter argues that the assumption of equal strengths in the original position implies rights to equal lots, but he does not fully explain why this follows. I am indebted to my colleagues Gordon Tullock, Victor Goldberg, Arthur Denzau, and especially to John Rawls, Harvard University, for helpful suggestions.

1. Inspired, of course, by *A Theory of Justice*, Cambridge, Harvard University Press, 1971.

2. "Rawls on Justice as Fairness," *Public Choice*, Vol. 13 (1972), Fall, 123–28.

emphasis was, however, on what I considered to be Rawls' unsatisfactory reconciliation of the two parts of his analysis, "(1) the interpretation of the initial situation and of the problem of choice posed there, and (2) the set of principles which . . . would be agreed to."[3] I argued that Rawls' fundamental contribution lay in his elaboration of the contractarian approach or method, essentially (1) above, and I suggested that both Rawls and his critics should abandon their utilitarian-like search for uniqueness in the outcomes of idealized agreement. As later discussion in this paper will indicate, this remains my own position, but under the interpretation to be advanced here, Rawls' insistence that both parts of his analysis remain essential and complementary can be readily understood. Rawls does not, however, properly describe the assumptions that are required to make his model internally consistent. These assumptions can appropriately be classified as Hobbesian in tone.[4] Some of these assumptions have been drawn more fully by Robert Cooter,[5] but neither he nor Rawls seems to have fully recognized the implications. When these assumptions are carefully presented, the whole Rawlsian construction takes on quite different characteristics from those normally attributed to it.

The interpretation in this paper allows the analysis of Rawls to be related closely with the analysis of Hobbesian anarchy that has been recently developed.[6] In particular, it allows me to relate Rawls' usage of the original position to my own use of the equilibrium position in Hobbesian anarchy as the basis for a hypothetical social contract. The interpretation also places Rawls' construction in a somewhat more positivistic setting than has appeared to be the case.

II. A Crusoe-Friday Model

It will be helpful to present the analysis initially in a highly simplified two-person model in which the dimensionality of agreement is limited to the

---

3. Rawls: op. cit., 15.

4. Rawls does say explicitly that his original position corresponds to the state of nature in traditional contract theory (*A Theory of Justice*, 12). But he does not go beyond this.

5. Cooter: "What Is the Public Interest?" op. cit.

6. See *Explorations in the Theory of Anarchy*, edited by Gordon Tullock, Blacksburg, Center for Study of Public Choice, 1972, and my own book *The Limits of Liberty: Between Anarchy and Leviathan*, Chicago, University of Chicago Press, 1975.

minimum. This model is familiar to economists, and it allows most of the relevant points to be developed. The more complex dimensions of agreement required in full-fledged, even if hypothetical, social contract can be readily appended to this basic "economic" model. I should emphasize, however, that the analysis is intended, as is that of Rawls, to be applicable to the conceptual agreement on the basic structural arrangements of society.

Consider Crusoe and Friday alone on the island. They live in Hobbesian anarchy; no law exists and each person acts on his own to produce and to defend stocks of a single all-purpose consumable commodity, which we may call "fish." Let us assume that, in this setting, the net income of each person amounts to only one or two units per day. Under our interpretation, this is the "original position" from which any idealized contractual agreement emerges.[7] This is not made fully explicit by Rawls, and his discussion does not fully describe the characteristics of the position which would be maintained in the absence of agreement.[8]

Note that I have not assumed that Crusoe and Friday are "natural equals" in the sense that their net incomes in the state of nature are equivalent. This may or may not be the case, and the model should allow for either equal or unequal incomes. I postulate only that a "natural distribution" will come to be established, implying that each person has the strength-ability to maintain whatever position comes to be defined in this equilibrium.[9] In this rude setting, both Crusoe and Friday should recognize the advantages of cooperation, of joint action, of contractual agreement. The critical questions involve the degree of information about the results of cooperative action that

7. Strictly speaking, the "original position" need not be the equilibrium of Hobbesian anarchy. As the discussion below will indicate, the initial position conceptually may be different. However, the knowledge that this Hobbesian equilibrium will be the social state in the absence of agreement must inform the choices of parties, whatever the characteristics of the initial position. Hence, for clarity in discussion it is best to treat the Hobbesian equilibrium as the initial position.

8. However, see Rawls: A Theory of Justice, 103, where he states that in the absence of agreement "no one could have a satisfactory life." In a 1974 response to critics, Rawls says, "[. . .] being in the original position is always to be contrasted with being in society." John Rawls: "Reply to Alexander and Musgrave," Quarterly Journal of Economics, Vol. 88 (1974), November, 638. See also Robert Cooter, op. cit., 27–28.

9. For a formal analysis of the equilibrium natural distribution in Hobbesian anarchy, see the paper by Winston Bush in Explorations in the Theory of Anarchy, op. cit.

the parties may possess in the initial position and the basic technology which cooperative action embodies. As the analysis in this paper will demonstrate, in the Rawlsian framework as here interpreted there must be rather full information about alternative production-distributional alternatives available under cooperation, while remaining within the restriction that individualized positions cannot be fully identified. Also, the interpretation is more readily understood if we assume that cooperative action necessarily introduces a dramatic shift in the technology of producing income or product. The jointness aspects of the basic structure of social arrangements become predominant. By way of a simplified economic illustration, we might say that the Rawlsian model allows Crusoe and Friday to commence fishing with a boat once agreement is reached, whereas in anarchy this degree of cooperation is not possible, and each man has to fish without a boat. The cooperative arrangement involves participation in the provision and use of a genuinely public good. In this framework, it becomes impossible to impute separate income shares to the two parties, Crusoe and Friday, since the whole production is clearly a joint product.

Crusoe and Friday agree to act jointly, to become partners in social arrangements; gross production increases dramatically, but there is no means of imputing separate shares. Furthermore, in the original position and before agreement is reached, although both persons can predict with accuracy the vector of production and distributive shares, neither person can predict what his role in joint production will be. Once joint action is taken, there is one quantity of the good that could be produced under a simultaneous agreement to share equally in income or product. This represents one point on a "production-distribution" possibility frontier. And this equal-sharing regime involves a higher net income for each party than the income attainable in anarchy.[10] There may exist, however, different and larger quantities which could be produced under regimes of unequal sharing. The increase in total output is presumably possible because of the response to income incentives. Agreement could be reached on one of these unequal-share imputa-

---

10. This is not a logical consequence of joint action. It is possible that the increase in total product consequent on joint production can be realized only in regimes of unequal shares. In terms of Figure 1 (page 367), there may be no point *C* on the 45° line that is Pareto-superior to *A*. This result would, however, seem sufficiently bizarre to rule out its serious consideration.

tions only if the income total of the least advantaged is thereby increased over the income total attainable under equal sharing. This is the much discussed "difference principle," and we must try to see precisely why the results indicated by this principle will emerge in the setting postulated.

Each of the two persons can, by withdrawing his cooperation, plunge the system back into Hobbesian anarchy. And this is predicted to be possible by both parties at the time of the initial agreement. The "marginal product" of each man is extremely large, and payment in terms of "marginal productivity" would far more than exhaust the total product. For illustration, think of the situation where Crusoe secures an income of one unit and Friday secures an income of two units in genuine Hobbesian equilibrium. Cooperation promises to yield a total income of twelve units, provided that these are shared equally between the two parties, with each person getting a net income of six units. The "marginal product" of each man is nine units, since this represents the difference in total product between the cooperative outcome and the Hobbesian outcome. Each person can, therefore, enforce the equal-sharing version of the cooperative outcome.

At this point, the veil of ignorance, stressed by Rawls, becomes relevant. In the original position, in Hobbesian anarchy, the persons do not know their respective abilities within the cooperative technology, nor do they know how each will respond to income incentives in participating in joint production. They know only that each of them can, by unilateral action, shift the whole system back into anarchy by the simple expedient of withdrawing cooperation. Conceptually, therefore, it is plausible that an initial stage of agreement will be some common acceptance of the symmetrical sharing outcome. Having reached provisional agreement on this stage, however, the actors may, on further consideration, find that the income positions of *both* persons can be improved by the specific introduction of distributional inequality. Work incentives may be such that unequal sharing will increase total product. This step in the agreement may, but need not, involve the identification of the recipient of the high income. Even if the two persons are identical in their work-effort responses to rewards, an unequal-sharing outcome may still be Pareto-superior to an equal-sharing outcome.[11] Or, per-

11. Consider a situation where the two persons are basically similar but where efficiency requires that one of the two take the role of residual claimant who monitors the

haps more plausibly, there may arise some mutual recognition as to the potential responses to work incentives which allows the person who will secure the high-income share to be identified. In either case, to the extent that envy is absent, there should be contractual unanimity on a shift from Hobbesian anarchy to a set of social arrangements that will maximize the income of the least advantaged.

This scenario places a somewhat different light on the concept of justice inherent in the predicted final outcome. In the original position, acting behind the veil of ignorance, individuals agree on the difference principle of income distribution because they mutually recognize the threat potential possessed by the relatively disadvantaged in any sharing outcome that fails to meet the requirement of Pareto-superiority over the equal-sharing solution.[12] The latter position or solution becomes, in effect, a necessary way station, at least in terms of the agreement, between Hobbesian anarchy and the final position. The existence of many possible unequal-sharing outcomes that are Pareto-superior to the original position but which may not be Pareto-superior to the equal-sharing position under social cooperation becomes irrelevant. Behind the veil of ignorance, neither person would accept unequal-sharing arrangements that do not dominate, in the Pareto sense, the equal-sharing regime.

Note that this argument does not, at any point, rely on risk-averseness and, indeed, in this argument, it seems wrong to substitute the term "maximin principle" for "difference principle." The parties in the original position are not considering alternative production-distribution arrangements in the sense conceived by most of Rawls' critics. They are considering alternative social structures, all of which require the cooperation of *all* parties for continued viability. The arrangement chosen must satisfy minimal requirements of justice if it is expected to be maintained. For this reason, the arrangement

---

performance of the other. On problems of organization raised by the recognition that monitoring must take place, see A. A. Alchian and Harold Demsetz: "Production, Information Costs, and Economic Organization," *American Economic Review,* Vol. 62 (1972), December, 777–95.

12. At one point in his argument, Rawls comes very close to making this the basis for his whole construction. See Rawls: *A Theory of Justice,* 15. See also Rawls: "Reply to Alexander and Musgrave," 647 ff.

that qualifies may, but need not, maximize *expected* utility for a person who remains behind the "veil of ignorance" in the "original position." There may be general agreement that the arrangement dictated by the expected utility criterion would not be maintainable as a system of social cooperation, as a joint contractual venture, for the simple reason that the least advantaged, whoever this might be, would not stand for it. And this potential behavior might well be predicted at the time of the initial agreement.[13]

We may illustrate the analysis arithmetically in our simplified Crusoe-Friday model. Four situations may be specified: (1) Hobbesian anarchy, (2) equal sharing under joint production, (3) unequal sharing advantageous to the least advantaged under joint production, a Rawlsian solution, and (4) the utilitarian solution where total product or income is maximized. These situations may be shown in Table 1 below. In this illustration, expected income (10.5) is higher under IV than under III (9), on the equiprobability assumption which seems plausible enough in this setting. But rational choice makers in the initial position, in I, will eschew the selection of those institutions required for IV because of their shared prediction that these institutions will not be viable. The person who finds himself on the short end in IV, with an income of only five units, will be predicted to act to force the system back to that of equal shares, where his income moves up to six units. He can enforce this threat here, since his continued cooperation is required in what is essentially a joint venture.

Table 1

Setting	Technology	Total Product	Shares of Crusoe-Friday
I. Hobbesian anarchy (the original position)	Independent production	3	1:2
II. Equal sharing	Joint production	12	6:6
III. Unequal sharing, Rawlsian	Joint production	18	11:7
IV. Unequal sharing, utilitarian	Joint production	21	16:5

13. See Rawls: *A Theory of Justice*, 175 ff., and also Rawls: "Reply to Alexander and Musgrave," 652–53.

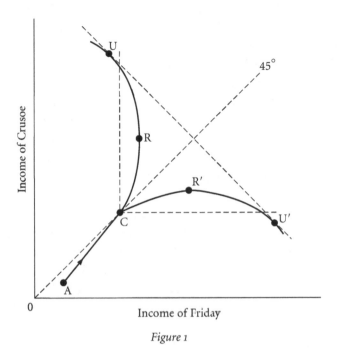

Figure 1

III. Geometrical Analysis

We can remain within the two-person model and present these results geo-
metrically, using a construction that is an emendation of that introduced by
Rawls.[14] This allows us to clarify the distinction between the Rawlsian solution, as here interpreted, and the utilitarian solution. In Figure 1 the incomes
of the two persons are measured on the two axes. The initial situation is the
equilibrium natural distinction in Hobbesian anarchy, shown at point *A* in
Figure 1, where Friday secures the higher income of two units. The equal-
sharing outcome when joint action is undertaken, upon contractual agreement to engage in a cooperative venture, is shown at *C*.[15] Note that, as illustrated, this represents a dramatic increase in total product, and, hence,
in the income of each party. This position becomes, in the process of agreement, a way station toward agreement on a more complex arrangement

14. See Rawls: *A Theory of Justice*, 76–77.
15. See Footnote 10 above.

which might involve unequal shares. Both parties can improve their income positions by northeastward moves from C. The Rawlsian solution is shown at R or R', both of which might be considered equally likely if there is genuine ignorance as to roles in the original position. The shift from C to R (or R') is a Pareto-superior move, and hence one upon which agreement should be forthcoming at the time of the initial agreement. Considered as a discrete and lumpy set of alternatives, any point along the curve northeast of C (on either curve) can qualify on Rawlsian precepts. But if the whole set of possibilities is examined, the single point for step-wise agreement would seem to be that shown at R (or R').

The total income of the two-person community is maximized at U (or U'), the utilitarian outcome. And, under an equiprobability assumption (with the outcome at U equally likely with that at U'), expected utility for each person is maximized by the selection of the institutional regime that will generate this result. Note, however, that in U (or U') the low-income partner in the cooperative enterprise secures less than in the much *less* productive equal-sharing regime. In the original position, each party must surely ask himself something about the viability-enforceability of any contractual agreement that might be reached. In particular, he must ask whether or not the "least-advantaged" person, himself or the other, will readily acquiesce in a regime that generates an outcome such as that shown at U (or U'). Will a person not predict that, finding himself in the low-income role at U (or U'), he might threaten, directly or indirectly, to plunge the whole system of social cooperation back into anarchy unless he secures at least that which he can guarantee in the equal-shares regime? Hence, rejection of the utilitarian regime in the initial position emerges from the rational choices of participants who recognize the extreme vulnerability of such a regime to the threat potential held by the low-income party, whoever this might be.[16]

---

16. Objection may be raised here to suggest that the threat potential is symmetrical over all parties. A return to Hobbesian anarchy will harm both persons; hence, why should the threat potential of the least-advantaged person be especially considered? My argument, as well as that of Rawls, presupposes that persons do act from other than purely utilitarian motives, that "justice," as perceived, does matter.

IV. From Two to Many Persons

As we shift from a two-person to a many-person setting, the limitations of the difference principle of distribution become somewhat more evident. In the two-person example discussed, the dependence of the cooperative gains on the continuing acquiescence of each of the two parties is reasonable, especially when the technological shift from noncooperative to cooperative behavior is assumed to produce relatively large increases in total product. Consider, however, a society of *n* persons. As before, the original or initial position is one of Hobbesian anarchy, where the life of each person is "poor, nasty, brutish, and short." There is no requirement that the net incomes of each person be substantially equal in this setting; all that is required is that each person secures a sustainable income that is dramatically lower than that which he might expect to secure under a regime of social cooperation. Why should the rational choice of a distributional rule be represented by agreement on a position analogous to R or R' in the two-person case, depicted in Figure 1?

To generate this result it is necessary to assume that *any* person who might find himself in the role of least advantaged can, by withdrawing his cooperation, plunge *all* of the other persons back into Hobbesian anarchy, back to the setting in which all incomes are dramatically reduced. That is to say, the whole structure of the society, as a society generating real income for its members, must be vulnerable to almost total disruption by the defection of any one member. In a sense, this is the extreme converse of the idealized competitive equilibrium. In the latter, the withdrawal of effort by any one person has, in the limit, no effect on the welfare, the income levels, of other persons. The total product of the group falls by precisely the amount of the marginal contribution which the person who withdraws previously added to total product. The income receipts of persons remaining in the game are not modified by marginal changes in the number of players. In the limiting case at the other extreme considered here, the withdrawal of any one member of the team essentially reduces the whole product of cooperative endeavor to zero.[17] In in-between cases, where there are increasing returns to numbers,

---

17. Consider the utilitarian solution, a non-Rawlsian production-distribution that may be in the core of the game, in that *no* coalition can secure gains by defecting from

the withdrawal of a person will reduce the amount available to others (there will be externalities), and these may be small or large depending on the shape of the total returns function. The marginal product of each man may exceed the average product, in which case the threat potential of any one person will vary depending on the size of the divergence.

A model of increasing returns may be plausible if there are extreme advantages of joint action, if the structural arrangements of society require the cooperation of all members for their productivity in generating net incomes or product. An assumption to this effect may be an inference of Rawls' analysis, as here interpreted. But additional argument may be adduced in favor of its relevance for the objectives that John Rawls set for himself. Ask the question: Under what conditions can a social group, a community, insure against its vulnerability to disruption by a tiny minority, or even by a single person? The immediate answer is that it can do so by adopting, establishing, and enforcing laws, legal rights, which limit, and sometimes severely, the ability of noncooperative persons to disrupt the functioning of the basic structural order of the society. In a system without laws, without punishment for violation, without a police force, it is not at all implausible to suggest that a single dissident can indeed wreak havoc on all of his fellows.

In this context, Rawls may be implying that he is not principally interested in a society with policemen.[18] In a meaningful, if overly restricted sense, such a society cannot meet reasonable criteria for justice. In this sense, Rawls may be trying to lay down distributional rules or principles that will insure against defection in the absence of law and law enforcement. The Rawlsian world that satisfies the norms of justice can remain an anarchy, an ideal one that is ordered by the willing acquiescence of all persons, including those who are least advantaged. Interpreted in this light, we can place the

---

the cooperative arrangements. However, *any* coalition, including one-person coalitions, may impose major damages on *all* others in the group by defection. In this case, the stability properties often attributed to the core may be absent. A distribution satisfying Rawlsian norms may not meet the requirements for the core, but it possesses the additional feature that the threat of defection, even if wholly successful, probably cannot secure an improvement in the position of *any* coalition.

18. See, for example, Rawls: *A Theory of Justice,* 261 and 576–77. However, when he discusses the free rider problem in connection with the provision of public goods, Rawls seems to accept the necessity of an enforcing agent. See 266 ff.

whole Rawlsian construction in more obvious relevance to the events of the modern world.

This relevance is, of course, enhanced when we extend the difference principle from the level of the single person to that of groups. This possible extension is related to the implicit assumptions made about the potential enforceability of law in the community. For example, in the original position, a person may rationally choose on the basis of an assumption that potentially dissident isolated persons, or even very small organized groups, will not be able to disrupt the orderly functioning of society, will not be able to reduce its productivity dramatically, in which case there would be no Hobbesian-like argument for applying the difference principle within these limits. On the other hand, rational choice in an original position might well incorporate the assumption that a potentially dissident large minority, or a majority, of persons, finding themselves in disadvantaged positions relative to those of a small minority of high-income persons, would abandon the support without which legal order could not survive. Indeed, in such a setting, the majority may simply enforce a distribution akin to that suggested by the difference principle, quite independent of what should be chosen in the original position.[19]

There is, of course, no need to adopt this large-group model for applying the difference principle. The point to be stressed is that there is a specific re-

---

19. The argument concerning predictions about majority behavior here turns the argument advanced by Buchanan and Bush on its head, so to speak. In this earlier paper, we suggested that the Rawlsian distributional principle, even if chosen in the original position, would not be enforced in the postconstitutional stage unless a majority of the community's members secure benefits of transfers. Underneath our analysis, however, was the presumption that, independent of Rawlsian transfers, persons can secure incomes in the private sector which may, if anything, generate a higher total product than with transfers. We did not consider the prospects that, without transfers, the whole social structure might either collapse or be seriously eroded, prospects that emerge explicitly when we interpret Rawls in the Hobbesian framework. See James M. Buchanan and Winston C. Bush: "Political Constraints on Contractual Redistribution," *American Economic Review,* Vol. 44 (1974), May, 153–61. Note, also, that Sidney Alexander adopted essentially the same view when he suggested that the advantaged would be able to maintain their positions. See his "Social Evaluations Through Notional Choice," *Quarterly Journal of Economics,* Vol. 88 (1974), November, 615.

lationship between the presumption made about the enforceability of law and the range over which the distributional principle adopted is to be extended. Realistically, dissidence of a relatively large minority may promise social chaos, in which case care must be taken lest a group of this size should emerge in postconstitutional sequence with income less than it might expect to secure under an equal-sharing regime.

V. Informational Requirements and Outcomes under Alternative Contractual Settings

The informational requirements for rational choice in the original position are severe in the interpretation placed on the Rawlsian analysis here. Individuals must be fully informed as to the alternative positions available to the society under cooperative action, positions described by a vector of total production and distributive shares. They cannot, however, know anything at all about their own roles or situations relative to those of others in the community. As Robert Cooter suggests, an individual must know everything in general and nothing in particular.[20] If these requirements are accepted, and if the norms of justice are interpreted as elements of a social order in the absence of enforcement institutions, rational agreement on the difference principle of income distribution becomes logically predictable.

We may, however, accept the original position as the meaningful basis for contractual agreement and seek to derive norms for social order without resort to such restrictive requirements for information. It is reasonable to suggest that, in the equilibrium of Hobbesian anarchy, persons are largely ignorant about the gross productivity of cooperative endeavor. Their initial step toward improvement in their status may lie in their recognition that mutual gains will be forthcoming from a simple definition of rights, a drawing of boundaries on allowable behavior concerning both persons and things. Having acknowledged this potentiality for mutual gains, however, the persons may also recognize the necessity for some enforcement of whatever rights are agreed. Each man will know that, without some means of enforcement, each person will have a free rider incentive to violate the agreed-on

20. Cooter: 25.

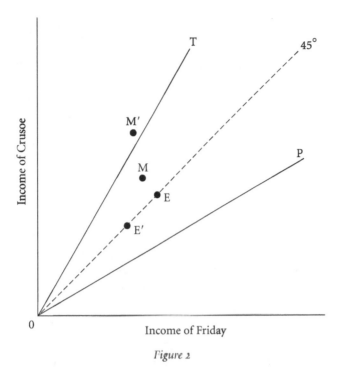

Figure 2

terms, to defect from the social contract. This will prompt, as a part of the rationally chosen initial agreement, some contractual structure of enforcement that will insure that costs are imposed on those who violate its terms.[21]

Once these steps are taken, the structural arrangements of society are complete, and persons can produce income and product independently or jointly, as efficiency considerations dictate. They may, however, also recognize distributional considerations at the time of the original agreement. They may seek to insure that broad bounds or limits be placed on the degree of distributional disparities which might emerge under the operation of the social institutions chosen. These limits may be drawn without knowledge of the production-distribution feasibility set.

This may be illustrated, again for the two-person model, in Figure 2. Cru-

---

21. This summarizes the analysis of the hypothetical contractual process that is developed in detail in my book *The Limits of Liberty*, op. cit.

soe and Friday commence in Hobbesian anarchy, the same original position as that described for Figure 1. In this different framework for analysis, however, the two parties cannot predict the locus of possibilities as in the Rawlsian setting for Figure 1. Instead, the parties know only that substantial gains can be secured from an agreed-on structure of rights. But they also seek to insure that final outcomes fall within certain distributional limits. For purposes of discussion, let us say that the two persons agree that one shall not receive a net income more than two times that of the other. The allowable range of income distribution is then bounded by the rays T and P in Figure 2.

Suppose, now, that a position such as M is attained under the set of institutions chosen in the original position. There is no way of knowing how this position stands with respect to the Rawlsian criterion for distributive justice. If, in fact, point E should be an alternative possibility, M would not qualify as just under Rawlsian precepts. If, however, E' should be the equal-shares outcome that lies on the feasibility locus, then point M would in fact meet the requirements of the difference principle. Note also that the distributional boundaries emergent from an agreement of this sort may involve either more or less ultimate income inequality than that implicit in a Rawlsian contract. For example, if the distribution M' should emerge, it might qualify as acceptable under Rawlsian precepts if E' is the equal-shares prospect, but M' would not qualify under the insurance criterion offered here as an alternative set of terms in the original contract.

VI. The Fragility of Social Order

The consideration of an alternative contractual framework in the preceding section was, in one sense, a digression from the main argument of this paper, the Hobbesian interpretation of the difference principle. Economists in particular have been unwilling to look behind their benign assumptions, so to speak, and to examine the vulnerability of the socio-economic-political structure to disruption. Economists, intellectuals, and politicians alike have tended to concentrate their attention on flaws in the social process that seem amenable to easy correction, on the implicit and almost unrecognized assumption that remaining elements in society are indubitably fixed. It is, for example, relatively straightforward for economists to call attention to the external diseconomies generated by industrial discharges in our streams or internal combustion engine discharges in the air and for politicians to enact legislation imposing regulation or, on occasion, penalty taxes.[22] It must surely be recognized, however, that the reduction in real income, meaningfully measured, produced by the increase in crime probably exceeds manyfold the damage caused by, say, water pollution. The quality of life in major American cities since World War II has been affected more by crime in the streets than by smog. And where are the economists who bring into their simplistic welfare analytics the potential for social damage wrought by industry-wide strikes, notably those in public utility and public service enterprises?

Honest assessment of life about us should suggest that there has been an erosion in the structure of legal order, in the acknowledged rights of persons, and that, indeed, modern society has come to be more and more vulnerable to disruption and the threat of disruption. Increasing interdependence is acknowledged, but the increasing vulnerability that this interdependence brings with it has not yet been properly incorporated into our thinking.

It is at this point that the contribution of Rawls, as here interpreted, can be extremely valuable. In this view, Rawls is not, as many of his critics have charged, providing a philosophical-ideological basis for egalitarian income-wealth transfers superimposed on a market order.[23] Rawls warns repeatedly that this is not what he is about, and that he is trying to derive principles for the establishment of the basic structure of society itself. The assumption natural to the thinking of economists to the effect that a market-determined distribution would emerge *de novo* and that this distribution would always be available for use as a benchmark from which transfer policy might be discussed, is inappropriate in the Rawlsian analysis. This point is clarified under the interpretation advanced in this paper where the benchmark, the position

22. For a public-choice explanation for the political dominance of direct regulation rather than taxes, see James M. Buchanan and Gordon Tullock: "Polluters' Profits and Political Response: Direct Controls versus Taxes," *American Economic Review*, Vol. 65 (1975), March, 139–47.

23. This view of Rawls' work is shared both by those who welcome the implied argument for egalitarian transfers and by those who oppose it. For one of the most severely negative reactions, see Robert Nisbet: "The Pursuit of Equality," *The Public Interest*, Vol. 35 (1974), Spring, 103–20.

that is the effective alternative in the absence of agreement, is defined as the equilibrium in Hobbesian anarchy. Instead of presenting a sophisticated rationalization for egalitarian transfers in a sociopolitical order which, in its basic structure, is implicitly assumed to be invariant, Rawls may be viewed as attempting to call attention to the increasing vulnerability of this structure to disruption.

I should emphasize that this interpretation represents an attempt to bring Rawls' efforts more closely in line with my own. We share a set of quasi-Kantian, contractarian presuppositions as opposed to a Benthamite utilitarian conception. In the latter respect, the various attempts that have been made to treat Rawls' whole effort as little more than the derivation of a "social welfare function" reflect misunderstanding of his basic construction.[24] To a contractarian, there exists no means of evaluating alternative positions of society external to the conceptual agreement among actual or potential participants. In the utilitarian calculus, no matter how sophisticated its mathematics, the original position is a redundancy. To the contractarian, the original position provides the basis from which the social structure must be derived, the starting point for analysis. The veil of ignorance becomes the device which allows agreement to become possible since, behind this veil, individuals cannot predict their own narrowly defined self-interest. As Rawls clearly suggests, his construction does *not* depend on persons acting on the basis of motives other than self-interest. The original position forces them, in effect, to choose on the basis of precepts of fairness because these precepts, in that setting, are consistent with self-interest.

My earlier criticism of Rawls' book was based on the notion that the presentation and elaboration of the idealized contractarian process was his important contribution, and that his complementary argument concerning just what precepts for justice might emerge from this process was both narrow and distracting. In the alternative interpretation that I have tried to develop in this paper, the tie-in between the two parts of Rawls' construction becomes logically consistent. The specification of the particular norms of jus-

---

24. For a recent example of this nature, see Sidney Alexander: "Social Evaluation Through Notional Choice," *Quarterly Journal of Economics*, Vol. 88 (1974), November, 597–624.

tice emerges from a recognition of the difficulties in and even the necessity for enforcement.

Empirical questions become important in assessing the significance of Rawls' construction for possible institutional reforms. How interdependent have persons become in complex social order? How vulnerable is the system to disruption? These questions are tied together by the efficacy of legal institutions. One cannot begin to answer these questions without making predictions about the willingness and ability of decision-makers to enforce nominally defined rights and to punish violators of these rights. If attitudes in the society of the 1970s are such as to make individuals in positions of authority unwilling to punish defection, continued drift toward the chaos of anarchy must be predicted.[25]

How might this drift be arrested? My own efforts have been directed toward the prospects that general attitudes might be shifted so that all persons and groups come to recognize the mutual advantages to be secured from a renewed consensual agreement on rights and from effective enforcement of these rights. Rawls may be, in one sense, more pessimistic about the prospects for social stability. Enforcement may not be possible unless the prevailing distribution meets norms of justice, and notably those summarized in the difference principle. Whereas I might look upon the breakdown of legal enforcement institutions in terms of a loss of political will, Rawls might look on the same set of facts as a demonstration that the precepts of a just society are not present.

As noted earlier, the interpretation that this paper places on Rawls' analysis and construction is more positive than may seem warranted. Parts of his argument may be read to suggest that individuals *should not* abide by the distribution of rights assigned in the existing legal order unless this distribution conforms to the norms for justice. And persons in the original position *should not* agree on a set of social arrangements that are predicted to place strains on individual norms of adherence and support. This more normative setting is consistent with Rawls' ambiguity and ambivalence on

25. For a general discussion of the problem here, see my paper "The Samaritan's Dilemma," in *Morality, Altruism and Economic Theory*, ed. by E. S. Phelps, New York, Russell Sage Foundation, 1975, 71–86.

enforcement and punishment. But this leaves open the definition of the norms themselves. The difference principle can be identified as emerging from contractual agreement in the initial position only if the participants make the positive prediction that least-advantaged persons and/or groups will, in fact, withdraw their cooperation in certain situations and that the threat of this withdrawal will be effective.

The Matrix of Contractarian Justice

James M. Buchanan and Loren E. Lomasky

I

There are no first principles etched in stone from which all moral philosophers must take their bearings. We must deliberately *choose* our point of departure in any attempt to respond to the question: "Must any defensible theory of justice incorporate a commitment both to personal liberty and to economic equality?" Basic to our own approach is a suspicion of seers and visionaries who espy an external source of values independent from human choices. We presuppose, instead, that political philosophy commences with *individual* evaluation.[1] A near-corollary of this presupposition is that *each* individual's preferences ought to be taken into account equally with those of others. That is, we suppose that there is no *privileged evaluator,* whose preferences are accorded decisive weight. *Conceptual unanimity* as a criterion for institutional evaluation follows naturally from the other two presuppositions. If there is neither an external standard of value nor a corps of resident value experts, only unanimity can ultimately be satisfactory as a test of social desirability. Our perspective then is *subjectivist, individualist,* and *unanimitarian.*

From *Social Philosophy and Policy* 2 (Autumn 1984): 12–32. Reprinted by permission of the publisher.

We are indebted to Geoffrey Brennan for helpful comments on an earlier draft.

1. External values may be rejected as an appropriate foundation for political philosophy either because such values are held not to exist or because, even if existent, they cannot be invoked for epistemological or moral reasons. We need not make a commitment to either of these positions, although, of course, the difference between them may be significant in other contexts.

These presuppositions inform our *contractarian* analysis. There are, however, two separate contractarian traditions that we shall find useful to distinguish, the "Hobbesian" and the "Rawlsian." In the first, persons find themselves in the anarchistic war of each against all. They contract away their natural liberties in exchange for the order that civil society—through its sovereign—affords. In this contracting process, individuals are assumed to possess full self-knowledge; they know who they are, what conceptions of the good they hold, and what their endowments are. The contractual solutions that emerge will necessarily reflect this knowledge.

The Rawlsian contractual process is distinguishable from the Hobbesian primarily through the introduction of the veil of ignorance. Individuals in the original position lack knowledge of their own features in post-contractual stages, including their conceptions of the good. They are unable to identify their roles in patterns of interaction that emerge under the set of institutions selected.

In Section II, we examine a highly simplified model of Hobbesian contract. Our purpose is not to derive substantive normative results.[2] Here we limit analysis to the demonstration that the equilibrium outcome may be one in which both parties are better off than in the pre-contractual state but in which they enjoy unequal quantities of economic goods and liberties. If either of these inequalities seems to violate our pre-analytical sense of justice, this clash will, in itself, offer reasons to examine an alternative contractarian setting.

In Section III, we start from the Rawlsian original position. We shall assume a general familiarity with the analysis in *A Theory of Justice*,[3] and we shall ignore issues involved with the conceptual status of "choice" behind the veil. Our interest, here, lies in the results that may be derived from the idealized Rawlsian setting, not with the epistemological coherence of that setting itself. More specifically, we want to answer the question: What must be built into Rawlsian choice to generate principles of justice that are similar to those derived by Rawls himself? We shall focus primary attention on the

2. Both of us have discussed such derivations elsewhere. See James M. Buchanan, *The Limits of Liberty* (Chicago: University of Chicago Press, 1975), and Loren Lomasky, "Personal Projects as the Foundations for Basic Rights," *Social Philosophy and Policy*, Spring 1984, 1(2).

3. John Rawls, *A Theory of Justice* (Cambridge: Harvard University Press, 1971).

principle of maximal equal liberty, rather than on the difference principle of distribution. Moreover, we will show that individuals in the choice process must concern themselves with *relative liberties* as well as with *absolute liberties*. Section IV specifically examines the demonstration of the equal liberty condition, and Section V offers our observations on the assignment of value to relative liberty as opposed to relative economic position. It will be concluded that the case for equality of basic liberties is much stronger than any case for equality in economic goods.

We emphasize that our purpose is *not* that of offering yet another commentary on Rawls or, for that matter, on Hobbes. Our intention is, instead, to explore the place that liberty and economic equality occupy in contractarian theories of justice. Substantive questions concerning contractual agreement motivate our analysis rather than any intention to reinterpret distinguished philosophers. And, as the analysis will demonstrate, our results will differ substantially from those presented by these two seminal contractarians. Those who demur from our interpretation of texts may change our labels to "quasi-Hobbes" and "quasi-Rawls" at their own choosing.

II. Hobbesian Contract

In Hobbesian anarchy, individuals are entirely free from socially contrived constraints on their ability to pursue that which they want to pursue. In this sense, the state of nature affords maximal natural liberty. But, of course, anarchic equal liberty offers hardly an idyllic existence. The solitary predator is an object of predation by others, and the fear of sudden, violent death is never far away. A large share of an individual's resources will be invested in attempts to avoid this worst of fates, but without assurance of success. Hobbesian anarchy almost cries out for amelioration. A leap into order can be accomplished if persons trade off natural liberty for security. The result is the achievement of a contractual equilibrium, one in which all parties to the contract are immeasurably better off than they were in anarchy.

The process is illustrated in the highly simplified two-person model in Figure 1. The position at I depicts the setting in Hobbesian anarchy, where both persons "enjoy" *maximum* and *equal* natural liberty. There are no formal constraints on behavior. Each person is at liberty to do as he chooses; but the *power* of each person to accomplish his own desires is restricted by

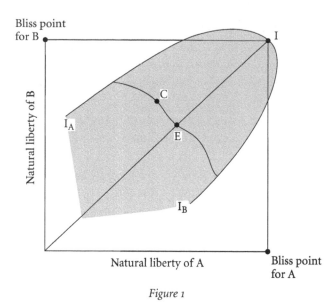

Figure 1

the liberty of the other. From the initial position at I, there are mutual advantages to be secured by a trade of liberties. Individual A may agree to give up some (or indeed possibly all) of his natural liberties in exchange for B's giving up some of his own. The area of the shaded lozenge in the construction of Figure 1 represents the potentialities for mutual gain.

Assume that agreement is reached on position C. Since C is, by construction, on the contract locus, it is in the set of non-dominated positions. No further agreement is possible.[4] Note, however, that C is not on the diagonal, positions along which would reflect equal liberty for both persons. The contractually attained position could, of course, have been shown at E. But there would seem to be no basis for a presumption that the agreed upon equilibrium will lie on the diagonal. The two persons, A and B, know their natural endowments and also their own preferences. As they interact one with another, each will acquire information concerning the other's assets and vul-

---

4. The problem of enforcement of any contractual agreement is, of course, one of intense importance in both the Hobbesian and the Rawlsian models of contract. We do not examine enforcement in this paper, although we recognize that this problem must occupy a crucial place in any comprehensive theory of justice.

nerabilities. If persons find themselves to be natural unequals in predatory ability and/or demand for deference, the equilibrium emergent from contract will tend to reflect such inequalities. Only if A and B are natural equals in these relevant respects will it be likely that the final equilibrium will lie along the diagonal.

There is no presumption of such natural equality and, hence, no inference that contractual agreement will feature equal liberty. Persons tend to differ in strength, guile, fortitude, ruthlessness, and bargaining skills. It would be exceptional if they should agree on arrangements embodying equal liberty. But this fact poses a problem for the normative status of Hobbesian contract: rational agreement may produce results that sharply diverge from pre-analytical intuitions to the effect that political justice must, at the very least, incorporate equality of basic liberties.

We suspect that Hobbes himself had some such intuitions, and that is why he attempted to impose conditions on the contractors that would insure attainment of a position on the diagonal.[5] Hobbes depicts persons in the state of nature as being equally vulnerable to the terrors of anarchy, downplaying the prospect that some are more vulnerable than others. But perhaps Hobbes also recognized that such a presumption was unconvincing, and for that reason he posited a further condition intended to guarantee equal liberties in contractual agreement:

> If nature therefore have made men equal, that equality is to be acknowledged; or if nature have made men unequal; yet because men that think themselves equal, will not enter into conditions of peace, but upon equal terms, such equality must be admitted. And therefore for the ninth law of nature I put this, that every man acknowledge another for his equal by nature. The breach of this precept is pride.[6]

By assertion, this statement constrains the feasible set of outcomes to the diagonal in Figure 1, or its n-person counterpart. Persons are vain, and they

---

5. With the notable exception of the Sovereign, who enjoys immeasurably greater liberty and power than anyone else. It is as if Hobbes believed that, by placing only one unequal in a position of power over a whole set of equals, he could dispel criticism that his outcome lacks formal justice. Critics historically have not been mollified.

6. Thomas Hobbes, *Leviathan*, ed. Michael Oakeshott (New York: Collier Macmillan, 1962), 120.

will not assent to any arrangement that limits one person's liberties more than those of others. With reference to the construction in Figure 1, C would be unacceptable to A because in C, A is required to give up more of his natural liberty than B.[7]

The argument is not compelling. We are required not only to believe that each person displays vanity, but that this behavioral characteristic is lexically prior to all other motivations such that persons are unwilling to trade off even the slightest departure from equal liberty for other gains. This characterization is psychologically implausible, and especially so in the stark setting of the state of nature, where the indulgence of vanity would seem a dangerous luxury. Bargains need not be equal along any stipulated dimension for it to be the case that all parties are thereby made better off. Hobbes recognizes this in his argument for the emergence of a compact that allows one person, the Sovereign, to tower over all others. Were personal vanity so critically important, this most glaring of inequalities could scarcely be tolerated.

Our purpose in this section is not primarily to criticize a Hobbesian politics. It is, instead, to indicate just how difficult it is to ground a requirement of equal liberty within Hobbesian contract theory. Because persons may prove to be natural unequals along the relevant dimensions, it is reasonable to conjecture that civil society will not eradicate, and may indeed reinforce, such inequality. If this result is unsatisfactory for any conception of justice, the conditions of contract must be established so that individuals are either unable or unwilling to transform their natural advantages into a civil regime that embodies unequal basic liberties.

III. Rawlsian Contract

How did John Rawls reformulate contractarian procedures so as to generate his two principles of justice: that of *maximum equal liberty,* and lexicographically appended to it, the *difference principle* of distribution? What is necessary to produce these results?

---

7. The whole construction of preferences, indicated by the set of indifference curves in Figure 1, could not be as depicted under the Hobbesian constraint. Under the latter, no positions would dominate I, for A and B, except those on the 45-degree line.

The meaning of liberty

The first point to be made here is that the meaning of liberty is quite different as between the Hobbesian and the Rawlsian constructions. From the discussion above, it is clear that, if Rawls should have defined liberty analogously to Hobbes, the principle of "most extensive equal liberty" could be satisfied only in anarchy. It seems evident that Rawls' whole discussion applies to a comparison of institutional alternatives (or to a comparison of principles of justice that institutional alternatives represent) all of which fall within the limits of *civil order*. In contrast to Hobbes, Rawls does not compare order with anarchy; his task is a comparison of alternative social orders.

To be meaningful and useful in this comparison, the Hobbesian notion of "natural liberty" must be supplemented by what we can call "civil liberty." Rawls' own discussion as to the precise meaning he gives to "liberty" is not entirely clear, and we do not propose an exegetical effort, here. For our own analysis of the Rawlsian contract, however, it is necessary that we introduce a working definition of "liberty," even if we do not seek to defend this definition more generally. We shall define "liberty" as the absence of constraints on the individual's choice among options. We want to restrict our definition to what has sometimes been called "negative" liberty; we do not want to confuse discussion by introducing the power of the individual to accomplish his desires with liberty itself.[8]

Even within this restricted definition of liberty, however, the dimension described as "liberty in civil order" is different from that dimension de-

---

8. Proponents of a conception of positive liberty maintain that person P has the liberty to do x if and only if no one or no social institution constrains P from doing x, *and* if it is the case that P has the ability to do x (i.e., does not lack the means necessary for doing x). On this conception, if someone lacks the means to take a round-the-world cruise, then that person is not at liberty to take the cruise even though no individual or institution is constraining such travel. We believe this to represent a serious conceptual confusion. Not all morally valuable commodities are liberties and, in particular, *power* or *ability* should not be conflated with liberty. Perhaps more to the point, it seems impossible to read Rawls as putting forth a positive conception of liberty. He distinguishes basic liberties (afforded by the first principle of justice) from the other primary goods to be allocated via the difference principle. Since the latter are instrumental to persons' abilities to pursue successfully their chosen conceptions of the good, Rawls is clearly not identifying liberty with the ability to secure desired outcomes.

scribed as "liberty in anarchy." In civil order, the person who has liberty in person or property enjoys that liberty correlatively with a set of duties on the part of other persons to respect such liberty, duties which are enforceable by the agency of the collectivity. To use Amartya Sen's example, a person has the liberty to sleep on his back or his belly, and accompanying this liberty is the duty of other persons not to constrain the sleeping habits of the person in question.[9]

We can measure, at least ordinally, the predicted levels of liberty that will be available to persons under differing institutional regimes. (That is not to deny that there will be some genuinely hard cases.) Without attempting too much precision here, we can surely say that a regime that constrains a person in his sleeping habits, other things equal, offers such person a lower level of liberty than a regime that includes no such constraints.

THE RAWLSIAN VECTOR

Persons who find themselves, place themselves, or are placed behind the veil of ignorance have no knowledge of their future preferences. They know, however, that once they emerge from behind the veil under the set of arrangements chosen, they will have conceptions of the good that they will want to realize. Moreover, they know that what they choose to incorporate within their agreement will affect their subsequent abilities to act upon their various conceptions. We suggest that persons behind the veil be understood as assigning positive values to each of three components of what we shall label the "Rawlsian vector," namely, *absolute liberty, relative liberty,* and *economic goods.* From this central postulate, it is possible to derive the choice of institutions that embody Rawls' two principles of justice (although, as our analysis will show, the difference principle is less robust than Rawls seems to believe). This derivation may be accomplished without resort to utility-function logic, and, hence, without making the whole construction vulnerable to essentially irrelevant criticism concerning relative degrees of

---

9. The two dimensions are not, of course, independent one from another. An increase in civil liberty of one person necessarily involves a reduction in the natural liberty of others since the duty to refrain from interfering constitutes a limit in natural liberty. That is why natural liberty and civil liberty are both to be regarded as components of liberty *sans phrase.*

risk averseness. The construction remains, however, open to criticisms that challenge directly the three components of the vector, and particularly those that question the independent status of relative liberty in the absence of like status for relative economic position.

There is no numeraire or common denominator such as "utility" that allows the three components to be collapsed into a single measure. Over all ranges of possible levels of quantity, each of the "goods" is assumed to be valued in the predicted sense, but a contractor does not know how much absolute liberty he is willing to trade off for more relative liberty, or how much of either he would be willing to give up for more economic goods. That does not preclude the possible recognition by the individual behind the veil of ignorance that, once the institutional structure is in place, and once roles are identified, persons who then know what they want may evaluate the three components relative to each other. But, behind the veil, the individual remains as uncertain about these future trade-offs within the post-constitutional decision calculus as he does about what his own role will be.

In this model of choice, therefore, the alternatives (which are represented as predicted patterns of achievement levels of the three separate components for each party) can be arrayed only by three scalars identified for each person, one scalar for the absolute level of liberty, one for the level of liberty relative to that of others, and one for the level of economic goods. An alternative can be judged to be preferred to or better than another only if it carries a higher predicted measure for *all* three components and for *all* persons. Note that the scalars are not utility indicators; they are measures of objectively determinate predicted levels or quantities of the components specified.

The three components of the Rawlsian vector may be defined more carefully. *Absolute liberty* ordinally measures the size of the set of activities that the individual is permitted to exercise in the knowledge that other persons, privately or collectively, will not introduce constraints or interferences. Note, in this connection, that the absolute liberty of the individual is restricted even if he participates fully in the reaching of the collective decisions that impose the constraints.[10] For our purposes, we may assume that, for collectively imposed constraints, the individual "votes" on how his own and oth-

---

10. See Robert Nozick's "Tale of the Slave," notably stage nine. *Anarchy, State, and Utopia* (New York: Basic Books, 1974), 290–92.

ers' behavior may be limited. Because he is one among many, however, the single person exerts negligible influence on any collective outcome.[11]

Relative liberty is a ratio between absolute liberties. This scalar measures the absolute liberty possessed by an individual relative to that enjoyed by other persons in the community. If all persons have equal absolute liberty, relative liberty is standardized over all persons with a value of unity. If absolute liberty differs among separate persons, the scalar measure for relative liberty exceeds unity for those with the higher absolute liberty and falls below unity for those with lower absolute liberty.

Economic goods are measured in bundles of "commodities" predicted to be available to the individual, bundles of "commodities" that are deemed generally desirable and positively valued for the maintenance of acceptable life standards (food, clothing, shelter, etc.).

THE MATRIX OF LIBERTY

We shall now introduce a drastically simplified illustration of a two-person interaction, represented in the four-by-four matrix of Figure 2. The row and column dimensions are scalars for the absolute liberties of the two persons, A and B. And, since relative liberty is defined as a ratio between absolute liberties, only positions along the diagonal of the matrix reflect *equal liberty*.

Each cell of the matrix summarizes a separate institutional arrangement that may be chosen behind the veil of ignorance. Each cell contains the predicted "payoffs" for each of the two persons, the terms in the left bracket indicating payoffs for A, those in the right bracket the payoffs for B. Each bracket contains the predicted payoff, under the particular institutional alternatives depicted, for each of the three separate components of the Rawlsian vector. The top number in each bracket (Roman) depicts the predicted level of absolute liberty attainable under each of the institutional alternatives considered. The middle number in each bracket measures predicted levels of

11. In this respect, the two-person models used to illustrate the analysis later may be misleading if not properly interpreted. In the strict two-person model, a single individual's vote is not without direct consequences for the collective outcome. Hence, it is necessary to keep in mind that the two-person example is designed to be illustrative of the more inclusive many-person setting.

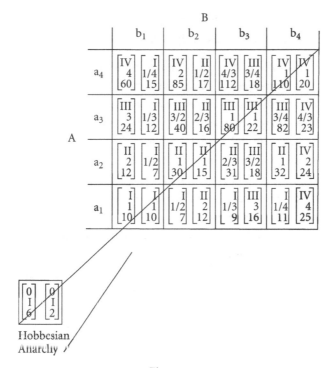

Figure 2

relative liberty. The bottom number measures predicted levels of economic goods, reduced to a single ordinal dimension.

As we suggested earlier, the dimension for absolute liberty that is relevant for Rawlsian choice is not the same as that relevant for the Hobbesian choice examined in Section II. In the latter, recall that natural liberty is maximal only in anarchy, where there is a total absence of formal constraints. In the Rawlsian context, however, absolute liberty, now defined as "liberty in civil society," is essentially nonexistent in genuine Hobbesian anarchy. Any institutional arrangements worthy of consideration behind the veil will dominate Hobbesian anarchy in terms of predicted levels of liberty, as now redefined. In Figure 2, therefore, the position of Hobbesian anarchy is placed outside of the central matrix to be analyzed.

The central matrix contains sixteen possible institutional arrangements; the four-by-four limit being, of course, arbitrary. Before examining the choice calculus of an individual, it is necessary to describe the illustrative construction more fully, at least in its stylized sense.

a_1 or b_1—The behavior of the individual, A or B, is almost exclusively controlled by decisions reached by the collectivity, acting as a unit. The individual's sphere of activities over which he may exercise private choice is minimal. He is allowed no private property holdings.

a_2 or b_2—The behavior of the individual, A or B, is extensively if not exclusively controlled by decisions of the collectivity, acting as a unit. The individual's sphere of activities over which he exercises private choice is severely restricted. The individual possesses private property but over a tightly limited domain.

a_3 or b_3—The behavior of the individual, A or B, is subjected to a relatively large number of collectively imposed decisions, but his private property holdings are not directly restricted, and the individual is able to exercise private choice over a widely defined range of activities.

a_4 or b_4—The behavior of the individual, A or B, is not directly subjected to collectively imposed decisions except to the extent that is determined by recognition of and respect for the personal and property rights of other persons. The range and scope for the exercise of individual or private choice is maximal.

As we define absolute liberty in the Rawlsian setting, the scalar for A for this component increased from a_1 through a_4 (and from b_1 through b_4 for B). Relative liberty is defined as the ratio of absolute liberties and is readily computed once absolute liberties are specified. Predicted values for the third component of the Rawlsian vector (economic goods) will depend on the predicted working properties of the institutions that are considered to be the effective alternatives, and particularly those properties relating to the production and the generation of economic goods along with predicted distributional patterns.

THE RAWLSIAN CHOICE

Consider, now, the choice calculus of the individual behind the veil of ignorance as he examines the alternatives depicted in Figure 2. Recall our earlier statement to the effect that, without some knowledge of the post-veil trade-offs among the three valued components one alternative can be deemed preferable to another only if the dominance relationship is established for both persons and for all three valued components of the vector. An examination of the matrix reveals that there is no one cell that dominates all other cells in these respects, that simultaneously maximizes each of the three components for both A and B.

One step toward resolution of the choice may be taken, however, once it is recognized that, in the total absence of any agreement on some set of institutional arrangements, Hobbesian anarchy will necessarily emerge. In a real sense, this Hobbesian position becomes a benchmark from which all considerations of alternatives commence. If this benchmark is acknowledged, the dominance relationships can now come back into play. The alternatives to be considered must dominate the Hobbesian benchmark; the predicted values for the three components, for both persons, must exceed those predicted to be descriptive of Hobbesian anarchy.

Examination of Figure 2, as constructed, reveals that there are many positions described in the central matrix that dominate the Hobbesian benchmark for both parties in predicted levels of both absolute liberty and economic goods. Note, however, that only positions *along the diagonal* warrant serious consideration in terms of the third vector component, *relative liberty*. All such positions are characterized by *equal liberty*, and, hence, in this valued vector component, are equivalent to Hobbesian anarchy. In all off-diagonal positions, one of the two parties must predictably enjoy less relative liberty than the other, and, hence, less than he expects to enjoy in the Hobbesian setting.

If this initial step is taken, the relevant Rawlsian comparison reduces to that between the four cells: a_1b_1,[12] a_2b_2, a_3b_3, and a_4b_4. Note, however, that

---

12. Libertarian critics, in particular, may suggest that individuals will predictably enjoy lower levels of absolute liberty, even as defined in the Rawlsian sense, in the collectivist, highly regimented order described in a_1b_1 than they might expect to enjoy in genuine Hobbesian anarchy. There are two ways that we might counter such critics. We could point out that the illustrative descriptions in Figure 2 are designed to serve our expository purposes and are not meant to be actual settings, even as summarized. We might then redefine a_1b_1 to be that social order that dominates Hobbesian anarchy, in the sense dis-

once the set is reduced to these four alternatives, the dominance relationship can again be brought into play. Both a_1b_1 and a_2b_2 are dominated by a_3b_3 and a_4b_4. Both persons are expected to secure higher levels of all of the three valued components in either of the latter two positions than in either of the former two positions.

The effective Rawlsian choice then reduces to a simple pairwise comparison: a_3b_3 and a_4b_4. These are the elements in the non-dominated set. Let us examine these two alternatives more fully. As stylized in the illustrative construction of Figure 2, note that both parties expect to enjoy higher levels of absolute liberty in a_4b_4 than in a_3b_3, while, of course, they expect to secure equal liberty in both positions. Also, as constructed, the predicted aggregate of economic goods in a_4b_4 exceeds that of a_3b_3. Given the Rawlsian vector, as defined, however, the aggregate level of economic goods nowhere enters the relevant calculus. The dominance relationship fails to distinguish between a_3b_3 and a_4b_4 because, for one of the persons, B in the illustration, the predicted level of economic goods is higher in the former than in the latter.

Without some further restriction, there is no purely contractarian basis for selecting an alternative from the reduced set of two. That is to say, if we interpret the veil of ignorance to imply the impossibility of predicting trade-offs among the three valued components of the vector and, further, to include these three components and only these, as criteria for evaluation, there is no means of discriminating between the two alternatives that are left in the set.

This result carries through for Rawls himself *if we limit consideration to a barebones statement of his two principles of justice.* Indeed, our construction in this Section may be interpreted as little more than a presentation of the two principles in a somewhat more precise form than that which Rawls gives us. The initial statement of his two principles is familiar:

> First, each person is to have an equal right to the most extensive basic liberty compatible with a similar liberty for others.

---

cussed, but which embodies lower levels of absolute liberty than any other alternative that is considered to be within the Rawlsian choice set.

More straightforwardly, but less rigorously, we might simply postulate that the threshold values of the economic goods component in Hobbesian anarchy are so low that there is a presumptive, non-dominance argument for ruling this position out of account.

Second, social and economic inequalities are to be arranged so that they are both (a) reasonably expected to be to everyone's advantage, and (b) attached to positions and offices open to all. (*A Theory of Justice*, p. 60.)

If this were all there were to it, there would be no trade-off among the components inherent in the principles, and hence no choice between a_3b_3 and a_4b_4 (Figure 2) would be possible. But Rawls goes beyond these initial statements, and he does indeed introduce a suggested trade-off when he adds that the first of the two principles is lexically prior to the second.

These principles are to be arranged in a serial order with the first principle prior to the second. This ordering means that a departure from the institutions of equal liberty required by the first principle cannot be justified by, or compensated for, by greater social and economic advantages. (*A Theory of Justice*, p. 61.)

With this lexical ordering of his two principles, Rawlsian choice must involve the selection of a_4b_4 over a_3b_3. Note that, in a_4b_4, both persons are predicted to enjoy higher levels of absolute liberty than in a_3b_3. Only in the former, therefore, do both parties enjoy the "most extensive basic liberty," or "greatest equal liberty" (p. 124). The fact that, on cursory examination, a_3b_3 seems to meet the requirement of the difference principle becomes totally irrelevant for the choice. Only if absolute liberty is wholly eliminated from the calculus or if the lexical priority of the two principles is reversed would a selection of a_3b_3 be indicated. If, however, absolute liberty is to count and if we are to take the words "most extensive" and "greatest" seriously, the alternative described in cell a_4b_4 in our illustration becomes the "Rawlsian solution" that necessarily emerges from choice behind the veil of ignorance, despite the apparent failure of Rawls himself to emphasize this result.[13] But

13. It may be charged that we have connived to tinker with the Rawlsian choice situation so as to conjure up a set of institutional arrangements for a political-legal order that seems to describe something like a Nozickean minimal state. We should argue that a careful carrying out of the Rawlsian contractual exercise does produce a political order that, in a formal sense, is far closer to the minimal state than most commentators on Rawls have seemed to recognize. The discussion in Section V advances this finding. However, this result is a consequence of taking seriously the conditions Rawls stipulates as characterizing his contractors. Why, then, does Rawls himself not recognize the quasi-libertarian structure of the institutions he recommends as just? Perhaps, the absence

if absolute liberty is to be valued, and the first principle is to be lexically prior to the second, how can the difference principle for distribution of economic goods, which has commanded so much attention from the Rawlsian critics, be applicable at all?

Simplified constructions simplify, and ours in Figure 2 is no exception in this respect. In order to clarify our exposition of the analysis, we have packed many variables in the three component vector payoffs depicted. Each set of institutional arrangements, very broadly defined, may contain within itself countless variations in institutional detail, variations that will make a difference for the payoff in predicted levels of distribution of economic goods in particular. Consider the a_4b_4 cell as an example. We may assume that this set of arrangements, broadly defined, may embody differing details (e.g., differing assignments of property rights) that will alter the economic goods payoff to A and to B. That which is specified by the explicit payoffs in Figure 2 can be reinterpreted as that one of this subset which maximizes the economics goods predicted to be available to the least advantaged of the two persons. That is to say, the difference principle is applied at a level of institutional detail *prior* to the construction of the payoff vectors reflected in the presentation of Figure 2. This relegation of the difference principle to within-institutional categories seems fully consonant with Rawls' own assignment of lexical priority to the principle of maximal equal liberty.

We shall not summarize Rawls' own arguments in support of assigning lexical priority to liberty.[14] We note only that in these arguments Rawls relies much more than in other parts of his analysis on empirical conjectures about the shape of utility functions and upon the context of application. He suggests that the marginal value of extensions of liberty relative to economic goods increases rapidly as a society's stock of wealth increases. Not surprisingly, Rawls' more radical critics tend to find this aspect of his argument un-

---

of clarity here arises because Rawls does not clearly define the precise nature and scope of liberty. Consequently, the implications for social arrangements of the first principle of justice remain murky.

The extent to which the formally defined "Rawlsian solution," in a_4b_4, resembles, in practical application, the Nozickean minimal state, *as this state is normally perceived*, will depend on the range and scope of "interpersonal" externalities, broadly defined, as these are predicted behind the veil of ignorance.

14. See *A Theory of Justice*, especially pp. 243–51 and 541–48.

satisfactory. We, on the other hand, find it largely satisfactory as a rationale for the priority of liberty in societies where wealth levels approach those of Western democracies. But, in our view, Rawls does not need to limit his argument so much as he does. The weight of history and economic theory is sufficient to establish the dictum that a regime of personal liberty is necessary for the amassing of large quantities of economic goods, and for the tolerable distribution of such goods among the people. Maximum liberty is *desirable* on grounds of justice for rich countries; it is *necessary* for poor countries on grounds both of justice and of economic efficiency.

To summarize: we have supposed that persons in the original position are rationally committed to having a care for absolute liberty, relative liberty, and the quantity of economic goods. By means of a further stipulation, that liberty in civil society is more inclusive than Hobbesian natural liberty, we suggested that the Hobbesian benchmark is properly excludable from the relevant choice set while remaining as a basis from which consideration of alternatives commences. Finally, by relying on Rawls' own considerations concerning the grounds for ascribing priority to liberty, we hit on a_4b_4 as the uniquely appropriate solution to Rawlsian contract. It should be reemphasized that this is our interpretation of the Rawlsian game, and it may not coincide with Rawls' interpretation.

IV. Why Equal Liberty?

We have demonstrated how something akin to the Rawlsian solution might be reached through the contractual process that Rawls defined. The discussion suggests the critical importance of the three separate components of the Rawlsian vector, but at the same time it suggests that the whole construction is vulnerable to criticism of the postulate that these components—and only these—are relevant.

We see little reason to question the postulate that individuals predict that positive value will be placed on both absolute liberty and economic goods. But why should relative liberty take on such importance? Is this merely another case where selection of premises is made with an eye on desired results? If we bring to the contractual process the presupposition that relative liberty is valued, then equal liberty will ultimately be derived as a condition for agreement to be reached. Is the Rawlsian contract superior to the Hobbesian in this respect? Does the shift behind the veil allow a derivation of equal liberty that does not emerge without the veil?

To get at these questions, it is useful to consider the possible clash between absolute liberty and relative liberty. Suppose that, behind the veil, it is predicted that a feasible set of arrangements exists that will offer all parties higher levels of absolute liberty, but, by definition, these higher levels come at a cost of imposing differentials among the parties. The problem may be illustrated in Figure 3, where point E depicts the setting of maximum equal liberty and where point F depicts a predictably attainable solution. By definition, no point on the diagonal northeast of E is feasible. Which set of institutions would be selected behind the veil of ignorance?

This question challenges the preliminary stipulation made above that only positions along the diagonal would be included in the relevant choice set. This stipulation might seem indicated if all departures from the position on the diagonal that feature maximum equal liberty would necessarily involve lower levels of absolute liberty for at least some parties. As the construction in Figure 3 suggests, however, this need not be so. Critics may, of course, claim on *empirical* grounds that no social arrangements exist that yield all

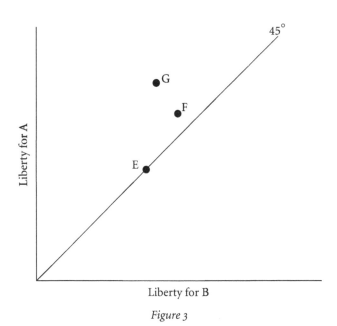

Figure 3

parties higher levels of absolute liberty than those attained under the equal liberty constraint. But on the formal level of analysis, there seems no basis for ruling out such prospects.[15]

How is the possibility of trade-offs of relative liberty for absolute liberty best conceived within a Rawlsian perspective? An analogy to the difference principle for economic goods suggests itself.

Such a principle maintains that equality should be the rule unless inequality improves the position of the least advantaged. Each party is to secure equal basic liberty except where all persons can benefit from some inequality in liberty, and that, among the feasible alternatives meeting the first requirement, one is to be chosen that makes the least advantaged (in terms of basic liberties) best off. Again referring to Figure 3, if both F and G are feasible alternatives to E, then the difference principle for liberty would state that F is to be preferred since B, the person who differentially enjoys lower basic liberty, is better off in F than in G.

If such a difference principle for liberty is adopted, there would be no need to build relative liberty as a separate component into the Rawlsian vector. In that case, however, we would have no initial assurance that the contractual process would generate a regime characterized by equal basic liberties. This result would seem to be almost as embarrassing in the Rawlsian contract as in the Hobbesian. Can we buttress the former in ways unavailable to the Hobbesian?

Several prospects are open. First, it can be argued that an off-diagonal re-

15. One basis for arguing that such prospects may not emerge would be a presupposition that there are no "natural" differences among individuals. But this presupposition would be unsupportable on any formal grounds. If such natural differences are allowed as possibilities, even behind the veil of ignorance, there may be predictions that institutional regimes that "treat individuals differently" with respect to allowable spheres of liberty may generate greater liberties for all parties.

Suppose, as an example, that there are "naturally" two types of persons, one of whom behaves morally toward others, the other of whom remains amoral. Behind the veil, of course, the chooser does not know which of these types he or she may be. Maximum equal liberty may be attained only in a regime that imposes relatively severe constraints on individuals' freedom of action. It may prove possible, however, that *everyone's* freedom of action may be extended by a regime that allows differential treatment for the moral and the amoral persons, once these two types are fully identified in the institutional operational sequence.

sult is less objectionable if it emerges from Rawlsian than from Hobbesian contract. In both arrangements, the more favored parties enjoy an *ex post* advantage in relative liberty. However, in the Rawlsian setting, contractors do not know their own identities, and each regards himself, *ex ante*, as equally likely to be favored to enjoy greater relative liberty. The Rawlsian contract is like a fair lottery in that it can be judged to be equitable *ex ante* despite the existence *ex post* of differential treatment.

Second, it can be argued that the Rawlsian vector need not assign independent status to relative liberty; the contractual process will, nonetheless, produce results as if such status has been assigned. In a two-person setting, suppose that A and B know that, once they emerge from behind the veil, each will value absolute liberty. Suppose, however, that they do not know whether or not they will place a value on relative liberty. A prudent course for the contractor to take would be to select arrangements that are predicted to distribute liberties equally rather than unequally, to select, say, position E rather than position F in Figure 3. If, post-constitutionally, individuals discover that they are indifferent to relative liberty, or regard it as much less crucial than absolute liberty, they can then agree *in period* so as to bring about the differential liberty allocation (assuming that the payoffs for both persons in economic goods are also satisfactory to both). In this case, the contractors lose nothing by the initial constitutional choice of the arrangement that promises equal liberties.

The reverse is not the case. Suppose that the contractors agree, constitutionally, to the arrangement that promises the highest level of absolute liberty to the person least advantaged in liberty (position F in Figure 3). Subsequently, beyond the veil, however, suppose that they find that each cares much for relative liberty. No agreement could then be made to bring about an institutional shift from F to the regime characterized by equal liberties, E. B would be eager to make such a shift, but A would veto it because it would lower both his level of absolute liberty and his level of relative liberty. There is an asymmetry in the prospects for post-constitutional change that suggests that persons behind the veil who have no reason to know whether they will or will not assign positive value to relative liberty should act *as if* relative liberty will be valued.

A third argument is indirectly related to the second, although it does not depend in any way on uncertainty about post-constitutional evaluation of relative liberty. Even if the contractors predict with certainty that, post-constitutionally, A and B would agree to make a shift to the set of arrangements that promise higher levels of absolute liberty to both, at the expense of some differentials in relative liberty, they may prefer, on grounds of *autonomy,* to select the equal liberty arrangements at the basic constitutional stage. Individuals will assign value to the retention of in-period autonomous choice to the extent that such retention does not involve major opportunity cost. They may predict that post-constitutionally they will enjoy enhanced self-esteem by having retained the option to remain under the equal liberty set of arrangements, even if they are sure, in advance and behind the veil, that agreement will be reached on abandoning the equal liberty precept.[16]

The lines of reasoning above at least partially meet the charge that Rawlsian contract is vulnerable in assigning overriding importance to relative liberty. We acknowledge, however, that this component of the Rawlsian vector is more problematic than the other two components. What this means is that the intuition that justice requires the assignment of equal basic liberties is also problematic.

We have been surprised to find how little has been said by Rawls, by Hobbes, and by others in justification of the equal liberty proviso. The issue here demands a closer examination. For example, libertarian philosophers profess unlimited support for a regime of liberty, a regime in which absolute liberties are maximal and in which these liberties are equal among persons. But what if these two requirements diverge? What if maximal liberty requires

---

16. A critic might demur, claiming that autonomy is simply a function of *who decides,* not whether decision is made in-period rather than at a constitutional level. However, the manner in which a decision is made may have a bearing on the autonomy of the one who decides. The conditions of constitutional choice are significantly different from those of in-period choice. The former is made anonymously and with no knowledge of particularities. One brings about an outcome that will be an outcome for oneself in one way or another, but what that way is remains unknown. The latter choice is made in full knowledge of who one is and what one wants. It is determinate; one is not merely accepting some outcome or other, in which one's own role is unknown, but *this outcome.* We maintain that this amounts to a significant difference in degree of autonomy exercised. One who knows what he is bringing about for himself and who acts intentionally to produce that result acts autonomously in a way no Rawlsian contractor can.

that liberties be differentially distributed? Is this "libertarian dilemma" to be resolved by giving priority to the rule of law (equal liberty) or to absolute liberty? So far as we know, the issue has not been addressed, let alone satisfactorily resolved.

V. Equal Liberty, Economic Equality, and the Difference Principle

Persons are presumed to value both absolute liberty and their absolute level of economic goods. The concern for liberty was extended so as to include relative liberty within the Rawlsian vector. Does not parity require a similar introduction of relative economic status? With this question, the egalitarian voices his chief complaint against our version of the Rawlsian construction.

We are under no illusion that we can settle, once and for all, the dispute between the libertarian and the egalitarian. We acknowledge that our interpretation of the Rawlsian contract does assign greater importance to relative liberty than to relative economic status. The critic might charge, however, that much of the argument set forth in defense of the equal assignment of basic liberties could be transformed into like arguments for equal assignments of economic goods. We are, therefore, under some obligation to show how the analogy between relative liberty and relative economic position breaks down. There is at least one crucial point at which the egalitarian's plea for parity is at risk.

As the examples make clear, and as ordinary common sense indicates, a choice of institutions that assign maximum equal liberties to all persons will insure results that involve at least some, and perhaps significant, inequalities in the distribution of economic goods. It is clear, however, that implementation of the equal maximum liberty principle does not, in itself, consign any particular person to any particular rung on the economic ladder. Some persons will be more talented than others, some will be lucky, and these persons will prosper relative to their fellows. But, behind the veil, no one trades off a known quantity of economic goods for a stock of liberty.

Suppose now that an overriding concern for relative economic position should dominate institutional-constitutional choice. With reference to Figure 2, observe that such a concern would be fully realized only in cell a_1b_1. Strict equality with respect to both liberty and economic goods prevails, but absolute liberty is thereby minimized. To select a_1b_1 because of an overriding concern for relative economic status is *to abdicate for oneself and for everyone else any appreciable claim to absolute liberty*. On the other hand, to choose institutions that incorporate maximum equal liberty implies that *some* persons will have lower quantities of economic goods than others. But to opt for equality in economic goods means that *everyone's* liberty is minimized. Because persons are predicted to value absolute liberty, they have reason to deny to relative economic status a dimension within the basic Rawlsian vector.

The critic may, of course, suggest that this result is an artifact of the construction. He may suggest that the assignment of the lowest level of absolute liberty to the cell in which economic goods are equalized is arbitrary, that liberty and equality really thrive together.

We totally reject this criticism. Although almost every other particular feature of Figure 2 is arbitrary, this one is not. To guarantee a continuing order of strict economic equality requires continuous interference by collective institutions.[17] Persons will not be allowed to engage in activities that lead to differences in access to economic goods. "Liberty upsets patterns," says Nozick,[18] and, somewhat more directly to our point, patterns upset liberty. A choice of institutions that is dominated by a concern for relative economic status *will* land persons in cell a_1b_1. Liberties *will* be forgone by everyone, and the stock of economic goods will predictably be low.

For this reason and others that could be adduced, we reject the contention that there is an essential equivalence between a presumption in favor of relative liberty and one in favor of relative economic position. It is simply far costlier behind the veil to impose a regime of economic equality than to impose a regime of maximum equal liberty.

As has already been suggested, the difference principle does not occupy a central place in our analysis, despite the attention that it has received in the whole Rawlsian discussion. As was indicated, this principle is applicable only at a level of institutional choice that is far less general than the choice we have analyzed here. Such relegation of the difference principle to the level of insti-

---

17. This conclusion requires that these collective institutions operate ideally. In any realizable context, of course, collective ventures aimed at promoting economic equality introduce inequalities of their own, both in liberties and in access to economic goods.

18. Nozick, *Anarchy, State, and Utopia*, 160.

tutional detail stems, expectedly, from the lexical priority of the maximum equal liberty principle, a priority which we take directly from Rawls. If institutional choice is constrained in the first instance by a proviso that equal liberty is to be maximized, scope remains for redistributional arrangements only *within the institutional choice emergent from the satisfaction of the proviso.*

Our analysis of the contractual process that generates the maximal equal liberty principle yields by-product implications for the basic economic organization of society. Maximal equal liberty would seem to require that all persons be free to enter and to exit from private contracts, to make voluntary exchanges without collective constraint, and to enter any occupational category. A society that even comes close to meeting the requirement for maximal equal liberty would, necessarily, have to be organized along the lines of a competitive economy in a constitutionally restricted democracy. Any socialist implementation of the principle of collective, centralized ownership-direction of production would violate the principle of justice. For that reason, we reject the following construal of the Rawlsian theory:

> It is necessary, then, to recognize that market institutions are common to both private-property and socialist regimes, and to distinguish between the allocative and the distributive function of prices. Since under socialism the means of production and natural resources are publicly owned, the distributive function is greatly restricted, whereas a private-property system uses prices in varying degrees for both purposes. *Which of these systems and the many intermediate forms most fully answers to the requirements of justice cannot, I think, be determined in advance. There is presumably no general answer to this question. . . .*[19]

The author of the above lines is John Rawls. The seminal proponent of the Rawlsian contract himself seems to have misapplied his own principles, a result that might have been avoided by the introduction of the Rawlsian vector in the matrix of contractarian justice.

---

19. Rawls, *A Theory of Justice*, 273–74 (italics supplied).

Notes on Justice in Contract

After more than half a century of eclipse, social philosophy has reemerged into a position of respectability, within both the sometimes scarred halls of ivy and the pages of highbrow journals. The catalyst in this resurgence was John Rawls's book *A Theory of Justice*, published in 1971. In half a decade we have seen literally scores of critical papers, pro and con, devoted to the Rawlsian argument, several of which have been collected in special issues of journals in philosophy, political science, economics, sociology, law, and perhaps others. At least two books have appeared to counter Rawls, and we cannot yet begin to count the doctoral research projects that in one form or another incorporate Rawlsian criteria as basic reference points.

In this chapter, I shall discuss the Rawlsian conception of justice from my own perspective, which is that of a professional (and academic) economist whose interests have shifted increasingly toward basic issues in social philosophy. I consider myself sympathetic to Rawls's attempt, as I interpret it, while at the same time I remain sharply critical of the image of Rawls that has been so widely promulgated by both his friendly and his unfriendly critics.

Rawls's book has sparked an interest in conceptions of justice undreamed of a decade past. But Rawls's decisive contribution tends to be obscured by an unwarranted concentration of attention on the second of the specific Rawlsian principles, the difference or maximin principle of distribution. I have argued previously that this distributional principle is only one from among a set of possible outcomes that might emerge from a genuine Rawlsian process of evaluation, any one of which would be equally deserving of

From *Freedom in Constitutional Contract: Perspectives of a Political Economist* (College Station: Texas A&M University Press, 1977): 123–34. Reprinted by permission of the publisher.

the attribute of justice. That is, in my interpretation of the Rawlsian framework, the attribution of justice is directly derived from process or procedural criteria instead of any nonprocedural or independent assessment of end states, utilitarian or otherwise.[1] This is, of course, the contractarian element in the Rawlsian construction, an element that is wholly unnecessary, and has been held to be so,[2] in those interpretations which themselves incorporate end-state principles. Rawls himself is not without some ambiguity on the point at issue here, and it might be argued that a fully consistent contractarian position should have dictated that its advocate stop short of enunciating specific "principles" that are not, in themselves, embodiments of process.[3] In chapter 14, I shall suggest an explanation of why Rawls was led to suggest the difference principle. At this point I want to discuss in some detail the moral and ethical foundations of contract.

The Contractarian Imperative

Why is it necessary to introduce the notion of "social contract" in discussions of the moral foundations of the state? Only the incredibly naïve among social philosophers could ever have offered a literal contractarian explanation for the historical emergence of governments. If positive explanation is ruled out, however, what is the purpose of introducing an admittedly hypothetical construction?

Ultimately, the social contract offers the only bridge between the consent of those who are governed and the possible or potential legitimacy of the entity that purports to exercise powers of governance. If, however, people have not, in fact, consented to the set of rules—the laws and institutions—in be-

1. For this reason I find it difficult to accept the applicability of Robert Nozick's persuasive general attack on end-state or patterned criteria of distribution to Rawls's basic arguments, an applicability that seems clearly to be implied in Nozick's treatment. See Robert Nozick, *Anarchy, State, and Utopia*. In this connection I should note that H. Scott Gordon, in his paper reviewing Rawls's and Nozick's books as well as my own, places all three of us in the procedural criteria group. See H. Scott Gordon, "The New Contractarians," *Journal of Political Economy* 84 (June, 1976): 573–90.

2. See, for example, Sidney Alexander, "Social Evaluations through Notional Choice," *Quarterly Journal of Economics* 88 (November, 1974): 597–624.

3. This was a central theme of my initial review article, "Rawls on Justice as Fairness," *Public Choice* 13 (Fall, 1972): 123–29.

ing, what value is there in an imaginary construction which sets up hypothetical consent as a criterion for making evaluative judgments? The answer to this question can best be stated in opportunity-cost terms. What are the alternatives to the hypothetical social contract or quasi-contract? I shall discuss briefly four possibilities, although other variants might be introduced, and of course there are ambiguities in drawing sharp dividing lines among categories of this sort.

ANARCHISM

In the first approach, which I shall call an anarchist perspective, there is no legitimacy in governance, and it is folly and deception that prompt us to search for an attribute that cannot exist. The state, anywhere and everywhere and regardless of its internal structure, exists for and lives upon the coercion of some persons by other persons. Contractual agreements may emerge voluntarily from interpersonal agreements, but these cannot be used as bases for a normative theory of a nonvoluntary state. This vision of reality has considerable appeal, especially as an ideal, but even here it offers little other than a naïve utopianism under plausible assumptions about the behavior of observable human beings, and it offers no prospect of meaningful improvement by stages. If all state action is equally illegitimate, how can we expect to dismantle the existing structure save by total revolution?

EVOLUTIONISM

In the second perspective, the whole complex of "laws and institutions" that define the social order, including those of government, is viewed as the outcome of a process of historical evolution. There is no constructive conception of "the state" or "the law" in any overall sense, and indeed, the very possibility of such conceptions is explicitly denied. The institutional results observed at any point in time are generated by the particular adjustments made by people to the various situations they confront. The English common law provides the archetype for this "invisible-hand explanation" of the state. The spontaneous coordination of the competitive market, which is perhaps the basic principle of economic theory and which has been central to this discipline since Adam Smith, is extended to include the emergence of legal-political-governmental structures.

By inference, if not directly, the results of this social evolutionary process are held to be efficient, if not in a static or equilibrium sense at least in the sense of moving gradually toward more efficient forms. In consequence, the existing structure is not readily amenable to improvement by "constructive rationalists." People should, therefore, acquiesce in and accept the existing institutions of society because of their acknowledged inability to generate improvements from any grand design for reform. In this perspective, an entitlement conception of justice may emerge, as with Nozick. A less extended variant, exemplified in Hayek, may stop short of attributing "justice" to the status quo.

Marxism

A third, and familiar, perspective is the Marxian one, in which the state, in all of its institutional features, is simplistically interpreted as the embodied power of the dominant economic class. The instruments of government and the law are everywhere viewed as having been designed and as being used for the purpose of oppressing the working classes. Although this "explanation" carries with it strong moral overtones, these need not be present in its purest versions. The state cannot be "reformed"; it is an inherent part of the ongoing class struggle. There is surprisingly little treatment of the state "after the revolution," and some presumed stability in the power structure that is to emerge after the "withering away" of the bourgeois state seems inconsistent with the basic Hegelian framework. (Somewhat interestingly, the Marxian perspective incorporates elements of each of the three other noncontractarian views. Its denial of legitimacy to any activities of the state in being resembles that of the anarchist; its reliance on historical process has much in common with that of the evolutionist; its claim to "scientific truth" is, in itself, transcendental.)

Transcendentalism

In this perspective most often encountered in social philosophy, criteria for the legitimacy of the state, or for "justice" more generally considered, must be derived from values that exist or that may be discovered independent of the individual participants for whom the criteria are exercised. These values may be found in nature, in science, in reason, or from God. In any case, they are deemed to exist by the discernment of the witch doctors and/or the wise of every age and every land. Political-moral philosophy involves a never-ending search for these immutable "truths" that somehow transcend man and his independent and autonomous capacity for judgment. In such a perspective, consent is largely irrelevant.

Despite the dominance of this perspective in both traditional and modern social philosophy and social science (including political economy and welfare economics), I find it less appealing than the other noncontractarian alternatives, and especially that of the anarchist. I find the rejection of the legitimacy of any rule more congenial than the claim of any man to have discovered "truth" in values on his own or the claim that the state itself is God. The discourse among such claimants to wisdom cannot be expected to be other than a continuing, possibly entertaining, but also possibly deadly dispute.

THE CONTRACTARIAN PERSPECTIVE

The four perspectives sketched out briefly above, and other variants of them, are not the only options that are available. The contractarian perspective or approach finds its value precisely in the deficiencies of its putative substitutes. It is necessarily somewhat more ambiguous in application, less clearly defined than some of its alternatives. Its potential use is inherently difficult, but not impossible. It is subject to abuse. Almost any conceivable activity of the state, either as observed or as imagined, may be explained as a conceptually possible outcome of some sort of "social contract." The problems here should not, however, be allowed to obscure the relative superiority of this perspective over its alternatives. Only some set of contractarian precepts or principles can resolve the problem of obligation of the individual in political society. A person can abide by the "laws and institutions" in existence if he can evaluate them as structural features that might have emerged from a social contract in which he might have participated.

Only the contractarian can effectively discriminate among the activities of the state, among the laws, without recourse to external evaluation. The following summation of the alternative perspectives may be helpful here:

1. To the anarchist all law is illegitimate.
2. To the evolutionist all existing law is legitimate and, by inference, just.
3. To the Marxist all existing law is instrumental to further the interests of the dominant economic class.
4. To the transcendentalist that law is legitimate, and just, which meets the external ethical criteria chosen for him by the witch doctors.
5. To the contractarian that law is legitimate, and just, which might have emerged from a genuine social contract in which he might have participated. That law is illegitimate, and unjust, which finds no such contractual basis.

Justice as Fairness

The notion of "justice as fairness" emerges almost directly from the contractarian perspective, while it carries little or no meaning in alternative perspectives. As a person observes the arms and instruments of the state, the institutions and practices of the law, how can he apply the suggested contractarian criteria? He cannot directly infer from his own relative position anything about the "justice" of the social order. Almost by necessity he is forced to examine the working properties of the whole structure, of the game itself, in the recognition that he is only one among many participants and that the observed results are those that reflect outcomes from a limited number of rounds of play. Relatively little sophistication is required to see, further, that probabilistic elements will enter importantly into the pattern of any set of observable outcomes. The question becomes: Could these results have emerged from a set of rules, a game, that might be deemed "fair"? But this moves the question backward to the one involving the meaning of "fairness" itself.

At this point I want to introduce some elementary economics, since I think that this disciplinary base does provide a better lead-in to an understanding of the contractarian approach and especially to the "fairness" criterion than almost anything else. Consider a very simple example in which there are two traders, A and B, each of whom is initially endowed with stocks of two consumption goods, X and Y (apples and oranges, if you will). We observe these persons to trade, to exchange goods, and we observe the attainment of some end-state result, an equilibrium. Trading stops, and the relative endowments of the two goods will have been modified by the process. How might we evaluate the outcome? There is no way to compare one outcome with another directly. Almost by necessity we are led to suggest that *any* outcome is acceptable as long as the trading process itself involves genuinely voluntary agreement among the persons, neither one of whom defrauds or coerces the other. As economists we say that which emerges from such voluntary trading is "efficient," and we are quite willing to define efficiency in terms of the expressed evaluations of participants in such processes.

It is a relatively small step which would allow us to replace the word "efficient" with "just" in application to the trading example.[4] We could easily say that that result or outcome is "just" which reflects the voluntary agreement of participants. And we move only a bit further to say that an outcome is "just" when the process that produced it is "fair," with voluntary agreement being the central property of "fairness."

Suppose, however, that we cannot directly observe a trading process; we cannot see traders agree one with another. We can observe only what appears to be an arbitrary distribution of endowments, of claims, along with a governmental-legal-institutional structure that sets out rules within which these claims may be enforced and within which further trades may modify the distribution among persons. How can we evaluate this observed complex structure against criteria of either "efficiency" or "justice," since the process through which it has been generated remains inherently unobservable and necessarily hidden in history? It is at this point that something akin to Rawls's "original position" must be introduced. We must ask ourselves whether or not the outcomes that we can observe, or could observe, could have been generated by a set of rules which might have been agreed upon in some conceptualized rule-making or constitutional stage of decision.

4. Adam Smith did use the word "just" in application to voluntary trading. And his system of "natural liberty" was evaluated in terms of justice as well as efficiency. Economists since Smith have perhaps concentrated too much on the efficiency properties of markets and have neglected the application of norms for justice. On this, see my "The Justice of Natural Liberty," *Journal of Legal Studies* 5 (January, 1976): 1–16.

Note specifically that we do not ask the historical question of whether or not such a stage of decision can be identified and whether or not such agreement did or did not take place. When the purpose of the contractarian analysis is limited to that of evaluation, this question becomes largely irrelevant. As they may be observed in existence, the various institutions of social order may have evolved independent of design or intent; they may have been imposed by some despotic regime; they may reflect prior adherence to a prevailing set of ethical standards. The precise origins of institutions may be indirectly helpful, but an evaluation of these institutions for potential reform need not be related directly to their history. The contractarian perspective, when carefully applied, allows us to evaluate institutions in a discriminating fashion regardless of origins.

I should emphasize once again that it is the conceptual agreement among all participants at the constitutional stage or in some original position that is the essential element of fairness. And here the elementary economics or exchange analogy is helpful; any rule is "fair" that is agreed to by all players. This statement is subtly, but significantly, different from the statement that fair rules will be agreed to by all rational players. "Fairness," as an attribute of rules, is defined by agreement; it is not, and cannot be, defined independent of agreement, or at least of conceptual agreement. From this definition it follows, or should follow, that uniqueness is not an expected property of outcomes qualifying under fairness criteria. Once again the simple exchange analogy is useful. Any one of a very large number of final, posttrading distributions of goods may be deemed to be "just." Even behind a genuine veil of ignorance, persons in original positions might unanimously agree to any one of a large set of possible rules for social order, any one of several sets of "principles of justice." There should be no presumption that the Rawlsian test must produce unanimous agreement on a unique set of principles.[5]

An example may be helpful in clarifying this point. In the United States we observe the traffic rule that requires us to drive on the right. In Great Britain we see a rule dictating that we drive on the left. Either one of these rules may have emerged from the unanimous agreement of the relevant partici-

---

5. H. Scott Gordon, in "The New Contractarians," 576, incorrectly interprets the veil-of-ignorance, original-position setting to be one which must necessarily produce agreement on a unique set of principles.

pants in some hypothesized constitutional stage of deliberation. That rule upon which agreement emerges, partly by chance, can be classified as "fair" for that set of participants and for others who, in later periods, find themselves confronted with such a rule as a part of their ongoing social order. I shall return to this absence of uniqueness, because it is here that Rawls himself produced ambiguity by extending his basic construction in a manner that has caused the construction itself to be widely misinterpreted.

Comparative Institutional Evaluation *versus* Idealization of Principles

At this point it is necessary to distinguish two separate ways of using the basic contractarian construction, including the "justice as fairness" norm. In a loose sense this distinction represents the difference between my own efforts and those of Rawls, both of which seem to share essentially equivalent contractarian foundations. In the first we may utilize the contractarian framework to evaluate the existing institutions of social order, in the small or in the large. In *The Calculus of Consent* Gordon Tullock and I looked at the rules for making collective decisions. In his book *The Logic of the Law* Tullock applied essentially the same method to some of the more specific legal institutions. The method here is one of comparative institutional analysis and evaluation. It starts from abstracted models of institutions that are observed to be in existence, and it attempts to evaluate these models against contractarian standards. There is no direct requirement that the practitioner set up idealized principles.[6]

The second way of using the basic contractarian construction is to try first to derive ideal principles, independent of any evaluation of those rules that might be observed to exist. This is the Rawls approach, and the basic question posed concerns what can be predicted to emerge from agreement among reflective men placed behind the veil of ignorance in the original po-

---

6. The contrasting methods may be illustrated by Adam Smith on the one hand and modern economists on the other. Adam Smith looked at the economic institutions about him and tried to determine whether or not they were consistent with his principle of natural liberty. Modern economists first set up elaborate models of theoretically perfect market systems before even beginning to consider the operation of the institutions that they observe.

sition. This approach is presumably an effective way of organizing one's thoughts about first principles, and it does allow the philosopher to place himself in an imagined setting that requires no appeal to transcendental norms. The question posed is deeper than those presented in the alternative method suggested, but this depth is secured only at the expense of distance from reality. If the philosopher remains unwilling to place existing institutions on some agenda for critical scrutiny, he must make the heroic effort of deriving first principles, from scratch as it were. This now explains to me why John Rawls felt it necessary to go beyond an emphasis on process or procedure, to go beyond his earlier definitions of "justice as fairness." Failure to have done so would have left his construction open-ended and without content precisely because of the nonobservability of any constitutional agreement, precisely because men could never, in fact, be placed behind the veil of ignorance.

Such an extension beyond process was not, however, achieved without major cost. In his attempts to define the specific principles of justice that could be predicted to emerge from conceptual agreement among reflective persons in an original position, Rawls found it necessary to discuss end states, notably in his elaboration of the difference principle of distribution of primary social goods. Since it is logically easy to separate end-state and procedural criteria, it is not at all surprising that Rawls's critics, pro and con, interpreted his effort as one that involved the erection of an unnecessary contractarian superstructure for the end state that he desired to advance for independent reasons. To both his presumed egalitarian "friends" and his presumed antiegalitarian "enemies," Rawls's central emphasis on process is largely obscured.

How might such misinterpretations have been avoided, while still retaining content in some sketch of contractarian principles of justice? In my view, Rawls might have been more successful in getting his message across had he used the fairness criterion to *reject* specific principles of justice (the entitlement principle advanced by Nozick?),[7] even if such principles might have to

---

7. It would seem difficult to bring an entitlement theory of justice in distribution of holdings within the contractarian fairness framework. Would reflective persons, behind a veil of ignorance, adopt and agree on rules for a game in which the cards are never re-

have been invented or imagined for the purpose of demonstrating the operational content of the contractarian construction. This use would have allowed for the emergence of alternative principles within an acceptable set, any one of which might have been alleged to emerge from conceptual agreement. The difference, or maximin, principle of distribution of primary social goods might, in this way, have been presented not as *the* unique principle of justice, the unique rule emergent from agreement, but as *one* possible rule in a set of plausibly acceptable alternatives. The maximization of expected utility, the rule that economists have most often posed in opposition to the difference rule, might have, in this way, been allowed to occupy its claimed place in the Rawlsian spotlight, along with other rules—for example, those embodying an "insurance" motive—that might seem less egalitarian when adjudged in end-state terms.

The Relevance of Rawls

In my view Rawls is not merely a transcendentalist in contractarian cloth. As my discussion in chapter 14 below will suggest, under one interpretation, the difference principle emerges as a part of a normative "theory of order," and, indeed, it could have been advanced independent of a normative "theory of justice." To the extent that persons and groups are motivated by self-interest, even demonstrably "unfair" games may remain viable if something akin to the difference principle of distribution is implemented. The "bread and circuses" component of acquiescence in governance should never be overlooked. And some of those critics who have interpreted Rawls as having provided the intellectual bases for straightforward socialist schemes of income and wealth redistribution seem to have overlooked the lexically superior principle of equal liberty.

But Rawls's concern is with justice in addition to order, and perhaps his objective might be stated more accurately as that of defining the principles

---

shuffled? In such a game everything would depend on the first-round allocation, and even if the participants remain wholly uncertain about their own position relative to others, it seems unlikely that so much would be left to depend on a single round. At least such a game would tend to become much less interesting than others that involve an occasional reshuffling, even if it is partial.

for a "just social order." His central achievement is the derivation of both of his principles from the contractarian process without introducing logically contradictory end-state normative criteria. This is not to suggest that alternative principles might not have been derived under somewhat differing assumptions. Properly interpreted, the Rawlsian principles for a just social order remain "good" because they reflect conceptual agreement among persons in an original position; they are not "good" because they satisfy transcendental norms of "goodness" as defined by Rawls or by anyone else.

Although his central vision of "justice as fairness" was developed in the 1950's, we must recall that *A Theory of Justice* was largely written during the 1960's. Along with the rest of us, John Rawls observed an American society that seemed to be becoming increasingly vulnerable to disruption. As the reception of his book has amply shown, the time was ripe for a thorough examination of our philosophical foundations. To his credit Rawls was unwilling to play at being God, the preoccupation of so many of his colleagues, in philosophy and other intellectual disciplines. And therein lies the relevance of his work. Unless we are to be rescued by a "savior" or "saviors" who will enslave us all, modern men and women must reform their own institutions. Rules can be changed while the game continues to be played, but few players are willing to delegate decisions on such changes to the self-anointed witch doctors. In such case the changes can be implemented only through agreement, and agreement can be reached only when all players test proposals against their own conceptions of fairness.

An American society that was initially grounded in contract may live off its capital for a while longer. Men and women may retain some of the freedoms that history has bequeathed to them. But this capital must depreciate with time, and we stand in real danger that a loss of understanding of our contractarian foundations will place us in a situation comparable to that which faced the Romans when they sought to build the Arch of Constantine. Without some contractarian basis there is no free social order possible. Rawls has contributed greatly to what I have called a "contractarian revival." It would indeed be tragic if his central contribution in this respect should be neglected in some gadarene rush toward end-state norms of measured equality, norms which can be advanced only by an unlimited Leviathan.

The Libertarian Legitimacy
of the State

I was somewhat disturbed by the widespread reception of Robert Nozick's much-acclaimed book by the intellectual-academic community in the United States.[1] I was concerned lest Nozick should succeed or appear to succeed in tying together a libertarian position with an entitlement theory of distributive justice. This tie-in, should it be accomplished, would discredit, and substantially destroy, the moral appeal of the basic libertarian position. It would leave those of us who remain steadfastly libertarian, but who refuse to base precepts of justice on some chance distribution of endowments, without an intellectual constituency and with a continuing challenge to defend our position against charges of internal inconsistency or outright contradiction. These early fears were, I think, unfounded, because the weakness in Nozick's construction becomes increasingly apparent on critical reflection. The nonentitlement libertarian need not be forced into intellectual retreat by Nozick, whose effort may be viewed, on later evaluation, as an interesting digression on the continuing discourse stimulated in large part by the acclaimed, if widely misinterpreted, work of Nozick's colleague John Rawls.[2]

Nozick's central concern is the moral legitimacy of state or governmental control over the lives of individuals. He looks about him, as indeed anyone must, and sees a maze of quite arbitrary interventions, both regulative and

From *Freedom in Constitutional Contract: Perspectives of a Political Economist* (College Station: Texas A&M University Press, 1977): 50–63. Reprinted by permission of the publisher.

1. Robert Nozick, *Anarchy, State, and Utopia.* For my early reaction, see the review article "Utopia, the Minimal State, and Entitlement," *Public Choice* 23 (Fall, 1975): 121–26.

2. See John Rawls, *A Theory of Justice.*

redistributive, which are seldom called into question at the most fundamental philosophical level. Rather than directing his considerable intellectual energies toward the margins of Leviathan's existing reach, Nozick chooses to go back to essentials. He properly defines the first question in political philosophy to be that concerning the very existence of anything that might be called a state.

The Minimal State

This approach leads him to examine, first, the arguments of those who reject the moral legitimacy of any state. His first explicit objective is, therefore, to demonstrate that a minimal state will qualify as morally legitimate, a demonstration that is specifically aimed at undermining the opposing claims of the libertarian anarchists (notably Murray Rothbard).[3] Nozick derives this minimal state by means of what he calls an "invisible-hand explanation." Through a series of ordinary marketlike exchanges a dominant protective firm or association will emerge, selling its services (protection for persons and property) to individuals who will look upon its activities as no different than the activities of butchers, bakers, and candlestick makers.

In order to understand why Nozick devotes a major share of his book to this complex conceptual derivation, which may seem bizarre, it is useful to review briefly the position of his implicit adversary, the libertarian anarchist. This anarchist is a peculiarly American breed, an anarchist who allows for private property rights and for market exchange and who extends his defense of laissez-faire even to the supply and competitive organization of the policing function. There is no state in his idealized conception of the world, and there are competing firms which offer policing services available to all.[4] Nozick accepts this paradigm, but he recognizes the inherent instability of the system. What will happen when clients of one agency or association are damaged by clients of another agency or claim to be damaged? Conflicts may occur, and one agency will win. Persons who have previously been clients of losing agencies will desert and commence purchasing their protection from

3. Murray Rothbard, *For a New Liberty.*
4. For a summary discussion of the history of these ideas, see Laurence Moss, "Private Property Anarchism: An American Variant," in *Further Explorations in the Theory of Anarchy,* ed. Gordon Tullock, 1–33.

winning agencies. In this manner a single protective agency or association will eventually come to dominate the market for policing services over a territory. Independent persons who refuse to purchase protection from anyone may remain outside the scope of the dominant agency, but such independents cannot be allowed to punish clients of the agency on their own. They must be coerced into not punishing. In order to legitimize this coercion, these persons must be compensated, but only to the extent that their deprivation warrants.

The dominant protective agency, as derived from this construction, will maintain domestic tranquility. Persons and possessions will be secure against aggression. The agency will, however, have all of the characteristics of a protective or "night watchman" state, and it might as well be labeled as such. But what is the value of this derivation? How is Nozick's derivation superior to the more familiar and more straightforward contractarian one, which requires only that persons agree to establish a protective state? I shall return to this question, but it will be useful first to summarize Nozick's subsequent application of his minimal-state derivation.

He is concerned to show that the minimal state, so derived, is legitimate, while at the same time showing that no extensions beyond these limits are legitimate. Without the latter purpose, the complex analysis of the minimal state would hardly seem worth the bother. Nozick's direct target in the second of these aims would seem to be the massive governmental apparatus that we observe, although his intellectual target is the construction of John Rawls, who derives "principles of justice" on basic contractarian grounds. Although the argument is not explicitly developed, Nozick apparently feels that any resort to contractarian norms opens up the prospect of justification for almost unlimited coercive action on the part of government. Presumably he would reject the attempted use of the contractarian model to classify legitimate and illegitimate spheres of collective or governmental action. I shall return to this central issue, but only after some treatment of Nozick's own derivation of principles of justice, the derivation that is central to his critique of Rawlsian norms.

Distributive Justice

Nozick is highly critical of all end-state or patterned conceptions of distributive justice. In this his argument seems wholly convincing. We cannot infer "injustice" from any examination of end-state results. Any attribution surely depends on the process through which an observed result or sequence of results is generated. An observed pattern of absolute equality could scarcely be classified to be "just" if we know that this result has been achieved by mutual theft. Nozick, who is exceptionally good with examples, offers his Wilt Chamberlain story to demonstrate this principle. He first allows his reader-critic to postulate his own idealized end-state distribution, be it absolute equality or anything else, with basketball player Wilt Chamberlain being among the members of the group. Nozick then asks us to evaluate the results that will emerge when many persons express their desire to see Wilt Chamberlain play basketball and voluntarily purchase his services. In the process, Chamberlain secures an income of $250,000 annually, much more than anyone else in the community, and in the process the initially postulated ideal distribution is, of course, violated. But can Chamberlain's earnings be adjudged unjust when the process which has generated the result seems clearly to be unobjectionable?

The example seems convincing, but an apparently slight modification will change its implications dramatically. Suppose now that Chamberlain is not a member of the community initially and, instead, assume that he lives alone on an island off the coast, unable to market his potentially valued services unless he secures an immigration visa. His alternative prospects are worth only $1,000 in real value. Chamberlain will pay up to $249,000 for the privilege of selling his superior and highly valued athletic skills to members of the community. The initial members of the community may collect and distribute these rents among themselves, equally or in any one of many other ways. Or, if swept by generosity, they may even return to Wilt Chamberlain a pro rata share of his rental value, a value generated by his opportunity to sell his services to members of the community.

A second and different example that does not involve the question of initial membership in the community may be helpful. Consider a group of twenty fishermen, each with his own boat and equipment. These people differ in talents and also in their willingness to work hard, and on any particular day they will also differ in luck. It could be predicted that the distribution of the total fish catch among the twenty men would exhibit inequalities among differing individuals. Contrast this case with a setting in which the twenty fishermen combine to charter a large boat with accompanying gear, with each man assuming some assigned station on the boat throughout the day.

As in the other case, there will be differences in catch among the separate fishermen. But the argument for some explicit social or group redistribution in the second case seems overwhelmingly stronger than in the first case. In the second case the individual fisherman, *on his own,* may be able to secure only a very small fraction of the income that he might be able to secure as a member of the larger group effort. The social product of the jointly used capital, the large boat, may loom large relative to the social product of the individual fishermen, taken separately and independently.

The difference between the first and second cases in either of our two examples here isolates a profound gap between Nozick's position and that of someone who acknowledges the productivity of the whole set of laws and institutions that describes an observed social order. Nozick explicitly accepts as his starting point a Lockean state of nature, a situation in which there are well-defined and generally accepted natural limits to persons and possessions. By inference, although he does not directly discuss this point, Nozick suggests that the economic value of a person's total endowment is modified by the shift from anarchy to the minimal state only by the reduction in predation. There are no gains from social interdependence as such.

The conceptual validity of this whole framework depends critically on the acceptability of the initial situation. If we can jump over, or assume away the basic set of issues that arise in attempting to define and to describe an initial distribution of individuals' "rights," "boundaries," or "limits," most of the problems disappear. There should be relatively little quarrel with Nozick's Wilt Chamberlain example, as he has posed it. The end-state results, whatever they might be, that emerge from the ordinary market process should be acceptable both because the process itself seems unobjectionable and because the initial-state situation is explicitly defined to be acceptable. Nozick imposes the process onto an initial situation that is defined to eliminate problems of regress. But this imposition tends to distract attention from the direct interrelationship that is all-important. Nozick does not fully resolve the question: What happens when a fully acceptable process is superimposed onto an initial distribution that embodies none of the attributes of desirability such as justice or fairness?[5] In this case it becomes much more difficult to sort out the two elements of the interaction.

---

5. Nozick recognizes this question in his discussion of possible rectification of entitlements that were acquired unjustly, but his treatment of it remains ambiguous.

This question has been a source of continuing confusion in the socialist critique of market organization. Much of that critique has concentrated on the undesirable qualities of the distributive results that emerge from market process, with the implications that those results thereby imply a condemnation of the workings of market exchanges. But the argument is confused because it fails to make the necessary distinction between the initial or premarket distribution of endowments or capacities among persons and the postmarket results, a distinction that reflects the workings of the voluntary exchange process. The socialist critique should be directed not at the market process at all, but at the initial distribution of premarket endowments and capacities. The market process, per se, generates *mutual* gains to *all* participants, surely a desirable attribute under widely divergent ethical standards.[6]

Nozick's argument seems to me to confuse the issue here through his exclusive insistence on process as opposed to end-state results. Much of the apparent criticism of end states is indirectly aimed at the preprocess situation instead of the process as such, at the preprocess distribution of endowments or capacities instead of the market organization. Nozick, of course, fully recognizes the dependence of his whole structure on some satisfactory resolution of the "starting point" problem. And it is here that he explicitly invokes his "entitlement" criterion for justice. By this criterion, a person's holdings are just provided only that they have been acquired justly, that is, by an acceptable process. Hence, in the example, Wilt Chamberlain's holdings of $250,000 are just because, as postulated, he has acquired them through a process of voluntary sale of services which others value highly.

But something seems amiss here. Recall that Chamberlain was assumed to start from an initial situation in which the distribution was adjudged to be just, a preexchange distribution of endowments deemed acceptable. *All* persons secure gains from the exchange process in which Wilt Chamberlain supplies his services to willing purchasers. *All* members of the community are made "better off," by their own expressions of preference, than they would have been had the exchange not taken place. But there may well exist many alternative trading arrangements under which Chamberlain's services

6. I have discussed this basic distinction in some detail in my paper "Political Equality and Private Property: The Distributional Paradox," in *Markets and Morals*, ed. G. Dworkin, G. Berwent, and P. Brown.

might be made available to the members of the community and in which *all* persons, including Chamberlain, would benefit, that would involve differing distributions of the rental value of his scarce talents. In our earlier variation on Nozick's example, Chamberlain secured only slightly more than $1,000, while the community's remaining members shared the $249,000 in any one of a large number of ways.

Let us change our earlier variation on Nozick's example to allow Chamberlain to be a member of the community from the outset. Now suppose that through a wholly voluntary set of agreements all prospective purchasers of Chamberlain's services appoint a single agent to deal with Chamberlain. As a result, he agrees to provide services for, say, $10,000, with the rental value of $240,000 being available for general distribution to all consumers.[7] What would be Nozick's reaction to this end result? There has been no coercion; hence, he would have to imply that the holdings that are observed are just. But this set of entitlements would be quite different from those which suggest that Chamberlain get $250,000. Must we conclude from this modified example that the entitlement theory or criterion of justice allows almost any one of many possible end states to be classified as just? This much Nozick will accept, but will he accept the further implication that the processes of acquisition which pass muster are themselves almost open-ended? Surely if end states as widely variant as the two we have postulated can be reached by fully acceptable processes, the content of the entitlement theory of justice seems minimal.

How would Nozick respond to this charge? He could hardly call upon the forces of his minimal state to coerce prospective purchasers so that the appointment of a single bargaining agent would not be allowed. Freedom of association is surely to be allowed in Nozick's utopia. Yet if this much is admitted, the end-state results may describe almost any conceivable pattern of distribution, depending on the institutions of voluntary exchange that emerge from personal interactions. No one set of institutions would seem to warrant priority over any other on Nozick's criterion.

Would there be any set of conditions under which an entitlement theory,

---

7. A real-world example is offered in the United States by the National Collegiate Athletic Association, which effectively prevents university and college athletes from securing more than a small fraction of their full rental values.

properly applied, would indicate that Chamberlain must retain the full amount of his rental value, the $250,000 in Nozick's original example? This question gets me back to my alternative example of the twenty fishermen, each of whom operates his own boat and equipment. If social interdependence is not, in itself, of economic value, there is no way in which the owner of a valued resource or talent can be made to surrender some portion of rental value unless he is coerced. If, in fact, Chamberlain's opportunities to earn real income, on his own and outside the market nexus provided to him by the community, approach or equal those opportunities which operation inside that nexus offers him, there is no rental value which is unique to the community as such. Chamberlain would, in this case, be able to secure the full value of his services merely by threatening to withdraw them and operating on his own, as his own economy.[8]

This reasoning suggests the general principle that a person's minimally guaranteed holdings under the effective operation of a minimally protective state will be definitionally equivalent to those holdings that he can enforce in an n-person noncooperative game. Should Chamberlain's services be withdrawn from the market nexus, the value of total product in the economy falls by $250,000, and production on his own can replace only $1,000 of this amount. But is the $249,000 rental value properly attributable to Chamberlain personally or to the cooperative setting within which his valued services are made available to others in the community? The so-called entitlement criterion for justice in holdings tells us nothing here, and Nozick acknowledges that in many cases the criterion must allow for widely divergent end-state results, any one of which may be equally deserving to be called just.

Social Rent

If we carry this line of argument just one step further, however, we must recognize that a person's ability to subsist literally on his own outside the mod-

---

8. This is, of course, the idea behind the solution concept of the core in n-person game theory. In our example if Chamberlain can earn as much on his own, completely outside the economic nexus, as he can within the community, the distribution according him the full rental value, and only this distribution, qualifies as a core solution. On the other hand, if he has no opportunities outside the economic nexus, *any* distribution of the rental value satisfies core requirements.

ern economic nexus may be absent. In such case *any* return, *any* income share above zero, requires the cooperation of others as provided by the possibility of participation in an interdependent economy. In this context, therefore, any income share, and, by implication, every income share, whether it be from the sale of labor services, from the sale or lease of capital assets, or from anything else, is "social rent," which may be divided or distributed any number of ways, any one of which may be justified on entitlement grounds. Care must be taken at this point to distinguish the notion of social rent defined here from the more familiar categories of rent normally discussed in economic theory. All income becomes "social rent" if individuals have no option except to remain within the interdependent economy. This rule does not, however, imply that all income or even a large portion of it is purely "Ricardian rent." Differing patterns of distributing income among persons may modify the allocation of resources among uses within the economy, and considerations of efficiency would normally be expected to emerge to place bounds or limits on the set of potentially admissible distributions. But the explicit introduction of efficiency norms would require something other than a minimally protective state. Within the structural confines of Nozick's analysis, therefore, the designation of all, or substantially all, income as "social rent" seems necessary.[9]

This problem of indeterminacy does not concern Nozick, because his underlying presumption seems to be that something akin to a competitive market order will emerge naturally or spontaneously under the operation of the minimally protective state almost independent of either the starting point or the underlying technological characteristics of the society. Hence, the end-state distribution to which the entitlement criterion is applied becomes something that approximates a marginal productivity imputation, as it is traditionally defined in economic theory. Somewhat indirectly, therefore, Nozick's entitlement conception becomes a vehicle for reviving the argument that attributes ethically desirable properties to the distributive outcomes of a competitive market order.

---

9. This is not the place to discuss the concept of "social rent" in greater detail. The concept is obviously related to the whole theory of competitive and monopoly governmental structures and to the notion of "voting with the feet" by migration among governments.

Laws and Institutions

There are two basic problems with this underlying presumption, the first of which arises out of Nozick's minimal-state limits while the second of which is more traditional. In the first place, Nozick's construction does not allow for laws and institutions that are deliberately designed to promote competitive and deter noncompetitive contractual agreements among parties. Freely associating individuals, within the confines of the minimally protective state, may exchange restrictive as well as productive agreements. Despite the dreams of some of the more enthusiastic laissez-faire theorists, and despite the acknowledged role of the state historically in restricting competition, there seems to be no grounds for the faith that the "natural" forces at work in an economy will insure a workably competitive order, independent of specific institutional arrangements designed to promote this end. There will, of course, be pressures to undermine any restrictive agreements that emerge. But in a world of rapidly changing technology, the distributional gains from the attainment and operation of monopolistic and cartellike agreements may attract significant resources into the invention and implementation of such agreements, even when it is fully recognized that state protection is wholly absent.[10]

A second and more familiar difficulty lies in Nozick's implicit bridge between a workably competitive economic order, with its implied marginal productivity distribution of income shares, and the ethical legitimacy of this distribution, even if it is accomplished indirectly through the process-oriented entitlement criterion. Even if the first problem noted above is wholly neglected, and even if we assume that a workably competitive economy will tend to emerge and be maintained under the legal framework of Nozick's minimally protective state, the range of end-state distributive results that might fall within this domain is wide indeed. The fortunes of the Rockefeller family would be as "just" as the chance rewards of the peculiar talents of professional athletes and entertainment celebrities. On careful examination, Nozick's argument seems to prop up a highly questionable criterion of distributive justice. If "entitlement" is defined to allow almost any

---

10. On the points made in this paragraph, see Frank H. Knight, *Risk, Uncertainty, and Profit*, 193.

conceivable end-state result to emerge and to be legitimatized, Nozick probably would have been on stronger grounds to make his argument explicitly in terms of the justice of the status quo.[11]

The alternative route that might have been taken is to acknowledge that the minimal state alone will not insure the workability of a competitive economic order and that even should it do so, there might be limits beyond which the distributive results would prove unacceptable. This route would, however, introduce explicit discussion of the design of the laws and institutions along with their possible contractual derivation from the constitutional stage of agreement among persons. This route is, of course, the way that both John Rawls and I have proceeded. Rawls attempts to derive "principles of justice" from the contractual process that takes place when persons choose among and agree upon alternative institutions from behind the "veil of ignorance."[12] In his conception, any institution that emerges from such a contractual process is "just." In this construction, process serves much the same function as it does in Nozick's more limited analysis, and it is difficult to understand why Nozick places such importance on the process through which holdings are acquired by persons and rejects categorically the possibility that through a wholly voluntary process these same persons may agree to operate within defined rules and institutions, which may well include some that restrict the range of possible distributive outcomes. Admittedly, Rawls himself creates considerable confusion and ambiguity in his own discussion by moving beyond the process through which rules are chosen and attempting to specify the content of the rules themselves. It is not my purpose here, however, to elaborate on the Rawlsian construction.

My point is mainly that of emphasizing the use of process, as opposed to end-state results, in both Nozick's and Rawls's constructions. For Rawls, as

11. Although I have not evoked criteria of "justice," I have argued that because the status quo distribution of rights offers the only conceivable starting point for improvement or reform, attempts should be made to work out mutually agreeable contracts which insure to *all* participants a position at least equal to that enjoyed at the starting point. See my *The Limits of Liberty: Between Anarchy and Leviathan*. Hayek makes the different, but related, point that attempts to achieve what he calls the "mirage of social justice" may be condemned as likely to do more harm than good, without, however, attributing "justice" to that distribution of rights which is observed to exist at any point in time. See F. A. Hayek, *Law, Legislation, and Liberty*, vol. 2, *The Mirage of Social Justice*.

12. Rawls, *Theory of Justice*.

for contractarians generally, that which emerges from contractual agreement is just, and such rules and institutions might, in fact, range from something akin to the Rawlsian difference principle on the one hand to some Nozickian defense of emerging entitlements on the other. Nozick, by comparison, makes no attempt to discuss the process of choosing institutions. Instead he suggests that *any* end-state result that emerges from a just process is itself just, but this conception is restricted to a postconstitutional or postrule level of consideration. Nozick simply does not allow for a process through which laws, rules, and institutions are explicitly chosen by members of the group. And by implication he does not allow for a method through which existing laws, rules, and institutions may be evaluated with a view toward possible reform or improvement. In this sense, therefore, Nozick leaves aside or ignores most of the problems that concern Rawls and that have concerned other social philosophers through the ages.

Nozick's whole attempt must, I think, be judged a failure.[13] Nonetheless, I can appreciate both the problem that he tried to resolve and the immensity of the task. It may be helpful for me to put the problem in my own personal terms. I find myself being required, by force of law, to give up a large share of my annual income, almost all of which is labor income or salary, to the support of the state, which I feel powerless to control. My vote will not affect the governmental decisions that are relevant for my position. At first glance I seem to be in the last stage of Nozick's "Tale of the Slave."[14] Much of the government's activity is clearly illegitimate by my own standards of evaluation. But I cannot, with Nozick, go all the way and classify all government beyond protection of life and property as illegitimate for the reasons indicated. In attempting to do this, I run squarely into the Hobbesian problem. What is mine and thine? I recognize that I cannot subsist without the cooperation of my fellows; I do not possess an effective option of withdrawing completely from the economic nexus. Hence, independent of the continuing social contract, as represented in the whole legal-constitutional-political-

13. For a comparable conclusion by one of his peers within philosophy, see the outstanding review article by Josiah Lee Auspitz, "Libertarianism without Law," *Commentary* 60 (September, 1975): 76–84.

14. Nozick, *Anarchy, State, and Utopia*, 290–92.

economic structure, I cannot enforce a claim to that particular share of income or property which I currently command.

But that which I can enforce is vitally important, and recognition of this fact allows me to resolve Nozick's "Tale of the Slave" to my own satisfaction. I can enforce those elements of income or utility that I can secure by my total or partial withdrawal from the economic nexus. Even if potential emigration is neglected, I can reduce my income tax liability by not earning income, to the extent that I choose. In so doing I am effectively opting out of the system. And as long as I retain this option, I cannot classify myself as a slave subject to the will of the bureaucratic-demagogic master that modern democratic process seems to represent. The critical step toward becoming a slave would be that which denies me this option, which either imposes a tax on my potential earning power or requires that I do forced labor for the collectivity. Nozick's "Tale of the Slave" is cleverly presented, but it tends to be misleading because Nozick does not make the categorical distinction that I have noted here. In his last stages of the tale he does not indicate whether or not the collectivity retains the power to require labor on the part of the individual, a power that is categorically distinct from the power to impose taxes on earnings from labor.[15] In his more general discussion Nozick does not appear to think that such a distinction is significant.[16]

The failure to make this distinction, if it should come to characterize the attitudes of many people, can have tragic consequences. If modern Americans and Western Europeans come to view the exactions of the modern welfare state as not different in kind from those depicted in Solzhenitsyn's *Gulag*

15. Conscription is, therefore, categorically different from a personal income tax, although the difference tends to be overlooked by economists who analyze conscription as a form of tax. The fact that in the United States conscription has been imposed suggests that in some potential sense American citizens may not be beyond the confines of Nozick's stages of slavery. On the other hand, the fact that the draft did, during the Vietnam war, arouse opposition that was demonstrably different from that aroused by punitive income taxation suggests that American citizens do make the distinction.

16. Indirectly, Nozick's descriptions of Utopia as a world of competing clubs embodies limits on "social rents" and, hence, on the degree of governmental power over the individual. I have not examined the relationship between this description of Utopia and the more general norms of justice advanced by Nozick, nor does he develop this relationship in detail. Such an effort would, nonetheless, seem to represent a useful extension.

Archipelago, the subsequent alienation can itself become a force for reducing the distinction in fact. We cannot, and we should not, try to escape from our own responsibility for controlling the Leviathans that we have allowed to grow, only in part as a result of our own creation. Nozick's noble but misguided effort to brand all extensions of state power beyond minimal state limits as illegitimate may backfire if the effects should be those of reducing our willingness to take on such a responsibility. *Some* extensions of state power are more illegitimate than others. The contractarian-libertarian can at least try to establish plausibly acceptable criteria for discrimination.

Utopia, the Minimal State,
and Entitlement

Robert Nozick's important book *Anarchy, State, and Utopia* treats three major topics that are superficially distinct but closely related at a more fundamental level of analysis.[1] In their order of presentation, these are (1) the moral legitimacy of the minimal state and the moral illegitimacy of any other state, (2) the entitlement theory of distributive justice, and (3) a framework for Utopia. I shall discuss these topics in the order of the appeal of Nozick's argument to me, that is, in the order (3), (1), and (2). His discussion of a utopian framework is familiar, attractive, and hopefully convincing. Despite the possibility of identifying important gaps in the analysis, I can accept much of the argument for the minimal state. But I find Nozick's entitlement theory of justice to be unconvincing.

A Libertarian Framework for Utopia

Economists will recognize Nozick's framework for Utopia as the world of competitive clubs (associations), with voluntary entry and exit. The Tiebout theory of local government and the related theory of clubs were initially analyzed in terms of their efficiency-generating attributes, and most of the sub-

From *Public Choice* 23 (Fall 1975): 121–26. Reprinted by permission of the publisher, Kluwer Academic Publishers.

This is a review article of Robert Nozick, *Anarchy, State, and Utopia* (New York: Basic Books, 1974). I am indebted to my colleagues Nicolaus Tideman, Gordon Tullock, and Richard Wagner for helpful comments.

1. Robert Nozick, *Anarchy, State, and Utopia* (New York: Basic Books, 1974).

sequent discussion has been within this setting.[2] Dennis Mueller has also called attention to the equity aspects of these models, aspects that economists have largely neglected.[3] Nozick's contribution here lies in shifting the analysis of competitive clubs to the most fundamental realm of discourse, the comparative evaluation of idealized social orders.

Nozick asks the reader to dream for himself an ideal world, constrained only by the recognition that other men, real and imagined, can dream their own worlds. This rules out the self-interested temptation to invent a Utopia where others bend to the dreamer's will. In this conceptual setting, Nozick describes a world in which each person holds membership in that club which most satisfies his desires, securing a net value from his membership that is at least equal to the value of his contribution to other members. Nozick does not, and should not, lay down constraints on the limits of club action, and his model allows for widely divergent ranges of activities. So long as persons may voluntarily emigrate and form new clubs or, if permitted, join other existing clubs, there are no moral arguments against the particular activities of any group. In this analysis, and particularly as he moves from the idealized to the real world, Nozick does not fully consider problems raised by the definition of rights of members, by the possible absence of effective entrepreneurship, by the presence of scale economies or diseconomies including threshold limits and transactions costs, by the potential for interpersonal discrimination. He acknowledges the incompleteness of his model, however, and his discussion lends itself admirably to elaboration and extension by more specialized scholars.

The Minimal State

These clubs are not "states," in Nozick's usage, and they are, along with their individual members, presumably subject to the constraints of the minimal state which is exhaustively discussed earlier in the book. Nozick's initial objective is the refutation of the anarchists' claim that any state is immoral. He

2. C. M. Tiebout, "A Pure Theory of Local Government Expenditure," *Journal of Political Economy* 64 (October 1956): 416–24, and James M. Buchanan, "An Economic Theory of Clubs," *Economica* 32 (February 1965): 1–14.

3. Dennis Mueller, "Achieving the Just Polity," *American Economic Review* 64 (May 1974): 147–52.

tries to show that an entity with the required properties of a state will emerge spontaneously from a sequence of morally acceptable actions by persons. Nozick places emphasis on this invisible-hand explanation of the state, and he specifically introduces the analogue to the spontaneous coordination of the market.

The starting point is Locke's state of nature, in which each person has certain natural rights (more on this below). Anarchy cannot prevail because each person will recognize that some will try to violate the rights of others. Enforcement and punishment will be necessary, and specialists in these tasks will emerge. Individuals will purchase the services of protective associations, and, in the ordinary course of things, one association will come to a dominant, but not exclusive, position in the community. To this point, there is no problem. Nozick's conjectural history is essentially a positive model of rational individual behavior. The next critical step, however, is the derivation of exclusivity for one protective association, even in the absence of voluntary purchase of its services by all persons in the community. To take this step, Nozick switches to an explicitly normative model and invokes criteria of morality to evaluate behavior. Through a very complex argument which involves the risks associated with allowing independents to punish clients of the protective agency, risks to all clients and not only to those who are guilty, Nozick justifies the prohibition of independents' rights to punish on allegedly moral grounds. But this prohibition, in itself, would violate the natural rights of the independents; hence they must be compensated which may, in turn, require that the agency tax its own clients. The compensation will normally take the form of offers to provide the protective services of the agency to nonclients at below-cost prices.

The last part of the argument is not congenial to the public-choice economist, who is not likely to be primarily interested in morality, which must be recognized as Nozick's principal domain. The discussion does expose the contractarian presuppositions of the whole public-choice framework. In the latter, the legitimacy of collective action is derived from voluntary agreement, from contract among individuals with defined rights. The institution of free and voluntary exchange is generalized to suggest contractual origins of collective action. And even if this aspect is not emphasized, "moral legitimacy" is thereby accorded to those activities of collectivities that embody observed agreement on the part of all persons in the membership.

Although he does not discuss the point explicitly, Nozick presumably rejects contractarian explanations of the state on the grounds that these become apologies for coercion. And, to Nozick, coercion is the primary attribute of the state. The contractarian is on admittedly weak ground when he uses his criteria to evaluate existing institutions, which demonstrably embody coercion, on the "as if" presumption of contractual origins. This is notably the case when the argument is not informed by a categorical distinction between the constitutional and the postconstitutional stages of agreement, a distinction that I have repeatedly urged on fellow social philosophers. Nozick does not seem cognizant of this distinction, especially when he discusses Rawls' possible response to criticisms of the directly redistributive measures dictated by Rawlsian precepts of justice. Rawls' possible argument to the effect that these precepts are designed to be applicable at the *macro* level of structure and, therefore, that *micro* level objections are unfounded, is held to be invalid by Nozick. While the Rawlsian macro-micro terminology is highly misleading, there is no inconsistency when the distinction is understood in the constitutional-postconstitutional context. Contractual agreement may be reached on rules that operate in subsequent periods so as to embody apparent coercion.

The Entitlement Theory of Justice

In Part II of the book, Nozick is concerned with defense of the minimal state against all arguments for extension, holding that all extensions violate the natural rights of persons. His analysis is, however, devoted almost exclusively to the state's possible role in redistribution, which is, of course, the most difficult of all extensions to defend. Nozick simply leaves out of account the provision of public goods (Musgrave's allocation branch), the "economic theory of the state," which may be contractually derived. He does so, presumably, on the anticontractarian grounds noted above, although the possible benefits to be realized from joint or cooperative ventures tend to be neglected throughout the analysis.

Nozick presents an entitlement theory of distributive justice, which states that any distribution of holdings is just if it has been acquired justly. The *process* of acquisition and transfer of holdings becomes the central focus of attention and not the particular characteristics of any distribution. I share

Nozick's criticism of what he calls "time-slice" principles of justice, principles whose criteria are drawn from end results independent of process. On the other hand, Nozick's own principle of entitlement seems to me to be open to comparable criticism because it, too, looks at an existent distribution and then applies historical criteria to determine its moral acceptability. But why is a young Kennedy or Rockefeller "entitled" to an inheritance merely because it was voluntarily bequeathed to him?[4] What "natural right" is taken from him when such transfers are limited? And why does it matter at all whether the property so bequeathed was acquired justly or unjustly? As Bernard Williams noted in his earlier review,[5] Nozick's moral evaluation of process would suggest that most of America properly belongs to the Indians (perhaps Marlon Brando has something after all).

This sort of question exposes the weak link in Nozick's whole logical structure, his defense of the starting point in Locke's state of nature, where persons are defined with claims to certain "natural rights," with respect both to physical objects and to other persons. Nozick's efforts in this respect are no more successful than those of Murray Rothbard and David Friedman.[6]

Why must a starting point be defined at all? One ultimate purpose may be of locating some basis for evaluating the social order that we observe. In a very real sense, the starting point is always the *status quo*, and proposals for improvement must be informed by this existential reality. Conceptual origins are helpful, however, to the extent that they aid in the evaluation. It will be useful to outline three recent usages of conceptual origins of social order. These are (1) Nozick's state of nature defined in Lockean terms where each person has certain natural rights, (2) the "original position" posited by John Rawls, in which persons put on the "veil of ignorance,"[7] and (3) the natural equilibrium in Hobbesian anarchy, which I have used as a basis for analysis.[8]

---

4. This is admittedly an extreme example with perhaps unfair emotional overtones. Nozick's argument becomes much more persuasive if it could, somehow, be limited to apply to the distribution of earnings based on relative effort. But it is precisely the extreme examples that make the moral acceptance of the entitlement theory so difficult.

5. *Times Literary Supplement,* 17 January 1975.

6. Murray Rothbard, *For a New Liberty* (New York: Macmillan, 1974), and David Friedman, *The Machinery of Freedom* (New York: Harper, 1973).

7. John A. Rawls, *A Theory of Justice* (Cambridge: Harvard University Press, 1971).

8. J. M. Buchanan, *The Limits of Liberty: Between Anarchy and Leviathan* (Chicago: University of Chicago Press, 1975).

If distributive justice is to be applied to possible imputations of holdings only in terms of the process through which these imputations have been created or have evolved, and if the moral acceptability of this process is the ultimate test, it becomes essential that some morally justifiable starting point be described. This is Nozick's schemata, with Locke's state of nature in which persons possess natural rights assuming the central role.

If, by contrast, criteria for the justice or injustice of social arrangements are derived from the contractual process through which these arrangements have been chosen, or might have been chosen, the origin must be defined in such a way as to make general agreement possible. If agreement is to emerge from self-interest, individuals' roles cannot be identifiable. (We agree on "fair" rules for a game only in the setting in which our own positions are uncertain.) This is the purpose of Rawls' original position. Although ambiguities in Rawls' presentation must be acknowledged, Nozick's criticism of the Rawlsian principles on the grounds that these are derived from end-result norms seems to me to be misplaced. (Unfortunately, many of the interpretations of Rawls' principles do treat these strictly as end-result norms.)

Finally, if the purpose is not that of making moral judgments about the existing social order, but instead is that of seeking the basis for mutually advantageous changes in the socio-legal-political structure of society, it is helpful to think of conceptual origins in which men are observed to be unequal in the distribution of endowments. In this context I have found the natural equilibrium in a Hobbesian rather than a Lockean state of nature to offer productive insights. In the former, rights are not defined, and individuals may differ in strengths and abilities. The protective state that emerges from the basic constitutional contract in this setting need not itself be Hobbesian. In my derivation, this state is similar to the minimal state described by Nozick. In my analysis, however, all persons are brought into the protective umbrella, are brought under law and are subjected to punishment on violation of law, because they retain no rights by remaining outside the contract. My contractarian model does not, however, allow the state to be closed off at these limits. If contractual agreements emerge for the provision of jointly consumed public goods, there may be a role for a productive as well as for a protective state. These need not, however, have common boundaries, and the desired provision of public goods may be organized through clubs or associations (local governmental units) among which migration is possible.

Aside from utility interdependence, however, direct redistributive action is not conceptually possible within the strict contractarian framework if attention is confined to the postconstitutional level. However, at the constitutional stage, where individual income and wealth positions are not known, structural arrangements may be agreed upon that will allow for apparent redistribution at the postconstitutional stage.[9] In this respect, my own derivation can be made consistent with the Rawlsian process, although not with particular principles.

Nozick's wholly different approach forces me to acknowledge the basic weakness in the contractarian approach, noted above. There is a fundamental difference between those institutions embodying apparent coercion that may be conceptually legitimatized as having emerged from contractual agreement and those institutions, again embodying apparent coercion, that have been observed to emerge from actual agreement. And, of course, the latter are rare indeed. Nonetheless, I should still argue that the contractarian approach does generate criteria that disqualify certain intrusions on individual liberty. "Could we have reached agreement?" seems to me to be a more appealing intellectual question and a more discriminating instrument for evaluation than "did this violate someone's natural rights?" And surely "can we reach agreement?" offers a more satisfactory prospect for achieving meaningful change than "what do we have the right to do?" Agreement is operationally testable; men fight over disputes about rights.

To establish morally legitimate claims to rights, Nozick would have us look at the process of acquisition. In a world where the minimal state exists, and where its own limits are widely accepted, this might be a meaningful approach. But why should agreement emerge when the claims that seem justified by Nozick's process conflict with individual rights that seem to be embodied in the democratic franchise of the supraminimal state? How can Nozick expect his argument for the minimal state to be convincing until and unless he first unravels, also through agreement, the maze of conflicting "public entitlements" that membership in the modern state seems to carry with it?

The multiplicity of conflicting claims should not be overemphasized.

9. James M. Buchanan and Gordon Tullock, *The Calculus of Consent* (Ann Arbor: University of Michigan Press, 1962).

Within limits, the social process remains orderly, and thereby reasonably productive. Had Nozick grounded his entitlement theory of rights, not on norms of justice but on those of productive social order, his whole analysis would have been more readily acceptable. If men can agree on rights, the problem of social order is largely resolved. I am not convinced that Nozick's argument does much toward securing such agreement. And if I, who share so many of Nozick's libertarian presuppositions, am not persuaded, how can he expect to fare with his peers in the Cambridge (Massachusetts) intellectual establishment?

The Gauthier Enterprise

I. Introduction

I take it as my assignment to criticize the Gauthier enterprise. At the outset, however, I should express my general agreement with David Gauthier's normative vision of a liberal social order, including the place that individual principles of morality hold in such an order. Whether the enterprise is, ultimately, judged to have succeeded or to have failed depends on the standards applied. Considered as a coherent grounding of such a social order in the rational-choice behavior of persons, the enterprise fails. Considered as an extended argument implying that persons should (and possibly must) adopt the moral stance embodied in the Gauthier structure, the enterprise is, I think, largely successful. Considered as a set of empirically falsifiable propositions suggesting that persons do, indeed, choose as the Gauthier precepts dictate, the enterprise offers Humean hope rather than Hobbesian despair.

Morals by Agreement[1] is developed in conceptually separate parts, which are made to seem more integrated than they need to be. The first, and most extensive, part of the book involves Gauthier's attempt to ground cooperative behavior in rational choice. In strategic interactions between persons *who possess defined and mutually respected initial rights,* the argument is that it becomes rational for each person to adopt a cooperative strategy. This part of the analysis falls within the theory of bargaining, and it is presented as

From *Social Philosophy and Policy* 5 (Spring 1988): 75–94. Reprinted by permission of the publisher.

I am indebted to my colleagues David Levy, Hartmut Kliemt, Jennifer Roback, Viktor Vanberg, and Karen Vaughn for helpful comments.

1. David Gauthier, *Morals by Agreement* (Oxford: Oxford University Press, 1985). Subsequent references will be by page numbers in the text.

such. The second part of the book, and much the more difficult part, attempts to extend aspects of the same argument to the *definition and assignment of initial rights* to persons.

I shall discuss the first of these two parts of Gauthier's argument in Sections II, III, and IV, with each section devoted to elaboration of a separate criticism. In Section V, I shall discuss the second part of the Gauthier enterprise involving the definition of rights. In Section VI, I shall present particularized criticism of the whole analysis that emerges from my disciplinary location as an economist. Finally, in Section VII, I shall discuss Gauthier's general perspective on social order.

II. Cooperation and the Definition of Community

As I noted, Gauthier presents his analysis of rational cooperation in the first part of his book as a contribution to the theory of bargaining. He seeks to demonstrate that the individual, who recognizes himself to be in a strategic interaction, will rationally choose that pattern of behavior that generates the cooperative outcome or solution. This demonstration is opposed to that which suggests that cooperative behavior in dilemma-like settings must exhibit a departure from individual rationality, defined as individualized utility maximization. Gauthier does not, of course, question the straightforward analytics of nonzero-sum games and the translation of objectified payoffs into their utility equivalents. His criticism is more general and, as carefully developed in his argumentation, it does carry considerable appeal. The individual, when placed in such an interaction setting, will exclude the off-diagonal or behaviorally asymmetric cells from his realm of feasible solutions. He will do so not out of any altruistic concern for his counterpart in the interaction, and not out of any expectation of repeated plays, but out of his rationally grounded interest in his own payoff. The temptation to "take advantage" that emerges as the motivating force in orthodox treatments of dilemma-setting behavior is suppressed in an extended rational-choice structure that embodies adherence to cooperative strategies as utility enhancing. Morals by agreement do not require other-regardingness or resort to supraindividualistic norms.

Descriptively, the Gauthier analysis applies to many areas of human interaction. I have often referred to the ordered anarchy that seems to define behavior in ordinary informal social relationships. We do not, as individuals, take advantage of each other each and every time that the occasion allows it. We do behave in accordance with precepts of mutual respect, and we brand as deviant the person who violates the mutuality norm.

There exist alternatives to the Gauthier enterprise that offer explanations for this behavior. Hayek suggests that we tend to behave in accord with certain codes of conduct, certain rules, that have emerged in a long process of cultural evolution, and that these codes or rules for behavior cannot be interpreted as products of any rational calculus.[2] These rules evolve spontaneously and direct our actions even though we cannot, consciously, understand them. I shall not discuss the Hayekian argument further here; I shall say only that in any relevant comparison my own sympathies lie with Gauthier. Generally, I applaud rational-choice reductionism, especially in its promise for ultimate institutional reform. Acquiescence before the inevitability of spontaneous evolution is a stance that holds, for me, little appeal.

My first, and most fundamental, criticism of the whole Gauthier enterprise lies, therefore, *within* the postulated structure of the argument.[3] I shall leave to the game theorists any dispute concerning the appropriate definition of technical rationality.[4] In the setting of *Morals by Agreement,* and for purposes of my argument here, I shall accept the essential elements in the Gauthier demonstration. My concern is nontechnically definitional. What does cooperative behavior mean in complex interaction settings that involve several possible interpretations of the set of players in the game, several, and competing, interpretations of the relevant community of persons within the strategic interaction, members of which might be "taken advantage of" by departures from cooperative strategies of behavior?

2. See F. A. Hayek, *Law, Legislation and Liberty,* especially Vol. 3, *The Political Order of a Free People* (Chicago: University of Chicago Press, 1979).

3. There are, of course, other approaches to explanation that do not rely on evolutionary processes and that do not involve incorporating behavior within the rational-choice framework, as this is normally defined. These approaches usually involve redefinitions of the arguments in individual utility functions. For one such recent effort in this direction, see Dennis Mueller, "Rational Egoism versus Adaptive Egoism as a Fundamental Postulate for a Descriptive Theory of Human Behavior," Presidential Address, Public Choice Society, Baltimore, Maryland, March 1986 (Mimeographed, University of Maryland, 1986).

4. See Russell Hardin's paper in this issue, which largely concentrates on such issues.

My point may be illustrated most directly with reference to the *Prisoners' Dilemma* in its classic, exemplary formulation where two prisoners are apprehended and suspected of a crime, but where there exists no hard evidence. The prisoners are led by the structure of the payoff matrix to confess to the crime. They do so, in the familiar argument, because they adopt individualized utility-maximizing strategies. The Gauthier enterprise seeks to supplant the elementary logic here and to suggest that the prisoners will not confess, but that they will, instead, act on a rationally generated disposition to cooperate.

Or so it would seem. But does the Gauthier enterprise really imply a nonconfession strategy on the part of the individual prisoner in a literally interpreted version of the classic dilemma? The relevance of this question is immediately obvious when we observe that the "Confess-Confess" cell of the payoff matrix is presumed to be the *socially optimal* solution. The payoff structure with which the two prisoners are confronted is deliberately designed to offer incentives to the prisoners, who are presumed to have committed the crime for which they are charged, such that their predicted behavior becomes compatible with the socially desired outcome. The inclusive community, which includes those who are potential victims of crime as well as those who are potential criminals (partially intersecting sets) presumably selects an institutional-constitutional structure that imposes the dilemma on those apprehended upon the commission of crimes. If the Gauthier precepts for rationality are generalized over the whole community, should the individual prisoner confess?

The point can be clarified with a numerical illustration developed for instructional purposes by my colleague Charles Rowley, an illustration that will also prove useful in the analysis of Section III. In Figures 1 and 2, payoff matrices are presented for two identical firms that produce and sell a single product. The algebraically defined cost and demand functions that generate these payoffs are specified in Figure 1.

In the two-by-two matrix of Figure 1, each firm has available two courses of action. A firm may behave cooperatively vis-à-vis the other firm, or it may act independently. If both firms adopt the cooperative strategy, the joint profit is maximized, as shown in Cell I of the matrix.

Is such cooperative strategy dictated by the Gauthier norm? If the firms cooperate one with another, joint profits are maximized, but consumers of

FIRM 2

		Produce $\frac{1}{2}$ profit-maximizing output	Adjust output independently (Cournot)
FIRM 1	Produce $\frac{1}{2}$ profit-maximizing output	I $4050, $4050	II $3375, $4500
	Adjust output independently (Cournot)	III $4500, $3375	IV $3600, $3600

Figure 1. Two-firm, two-strategy interaction (profits in dollars; industry demand function: $p = 200 - q_1 - q_2$; firm cost function: $c_i = 20q_i$, where $i = 1, 2$)

the product suffer. Price is higher because output is restricted. Consumers are, in this setting, being "taken advantage of" by the colluding duopolists. The Gauthier argument to the effect that cooperative behavior emerges from a rationally generated disposition based on a recognition of the strategic setting seems highly plausible when the interaction between the two firms taken in isolation is examined. The same argument, however, becomes implausible in the extreme when the community of interaction is extended to include consumers as well as the two firms. The same behavior that is defined to be cooperative in the one community becomes noncooperative in the differently defined community.[5]

This is not a minor difficulty with the Gauthier construction. The problem of definition of the community of strategic interaction is a general one that cannot be readily avoided. There is no "natural community" for the application of the rationally generated morality by agreement. Anthropologists and moral philosophers have long recognized the distinction between the norms for behavior of individuals toward members of the tribe and those for behavior toward strangers. The shift into what Hayek has called the "great

---

5. Only after I completed a draft of this paper did my colleague Viktor Vanberg point out to me that an earlier criticism of a paper by Gauthier contains essentially the same argument that I have presented in this Section, even to the extent of utilizing the same examples. See E. Ullman-Margalit, *The Emergence of Norms* (Oxford: Clarendon Press, 1977), 41–45.

society" and what I have called "moral order" requires behavioral traits that are close cousins of those emerging from the Gauthier analysis.[6] My concern is with his attempted derivation of these norms from game theoretic or bargaining interactions in which the cooperative solutions are perhaps too readily identified. I have the same concern with the attempts to derive the evolution of cooperation from game-like settings.[7,8]

III. Cooperation and the Size of the Community

A closely related but conceptually distinct criticism involves the prospects for cooperative behavior on the part of an individual in a setting where the interaction clearly involves more than a critically small number of actors. Assume that there is no problem of subgroup versus inclusive-group cooperation, as discussed in Section II.

Here, the methodological constraints imposed by the analytical setting of elementary game theory should be emphasized. Simple two-person games can, at best, offer insights into sources of behavior that may be generalized to large-number settings. The interaction of persons in two-person settings, taken literally, remains of relatively little interest. As the number of choosing-behaving units in an interaction increases, there is an exponential increase in the prospects for noncooperative behavior on the part of at least one of the parties. The relationship between the selection of cooperative strategies and the size of the group does not emerge from Gauthier's analysis.

Gauthier's prescriptive rule is that a player should adopt a cooperative strategy if his expected payoff from this pattern of behavior is higher than his expected payoff from the solution that embodies independent utility-

---

6. See my "Moral Community, Moral Order, or Moral Anarchy," included in my book *Liberty, Market and State* (Brighton, England: Wheatsheaf Books, 1986), 108–21.

7. See Robert Axelrod, *The Evolution of Cooperation* (New York: Basic Books, 1984).

8. Critics have suggested that a disposition toward cooperative behavior, whether rationally or evolutionarily grounded, describes the behavior of persons generally, quite independent of the setting of interaction. The prisoners do not confess; the duopolists maximize joint profits. In this view, it becomes inappropriate to evaluate the results of such behavior against any notion of generalized "optimality" of "efficiency" for a more inclusive group. If this line of defense is taken, however, "cooperation," as such, may or may not be judged a character trait deserving of positive evaluation in all settings. Resolution of the dilemma present in subgames may create a dilemma in more inclusive games.

maximizing behavior by all parties (*MA*, p. 166). The rule does require that the probabilities of other players' choices of strategies be considered, but only for purposes of avoiding being "taken advantage of" rather than for those of "taking advantage." The prospects for attaining the off-diagonal cells in the simple two-person matrix are reckoned with, but only with reference to the lower of the paired payoffs in these cells.

The application of the Gauthier rule as well as the dependence of the strategy choice on numbers may be illustrated in the numerical example of Figure 1. (And, for present purposes, consider the firms in isolation from other possible players in the more inclusive economic game.) The Gauthier rule is that a firm should adopt the cooperative strategy if the expected value of the payoff is greater than that indicated in Cell IV, where all parties adjust behavior independently. Suppose that, in the two-firm model depicted, Firm 1 expects cooperative behavior on the part of Firm 2 with a probability coefficient of one-half. In this case, the Gauthier rule would dictate cooperation because ($4050 plus $3375)/2 exceeds $3600. The expected value from cooperation is $3718; that from independent adjustment is $3600.

Suppose, however, that there are three identical firms rather than two, with product demand and firm cost functions unchanged. In this setting, even if the expectation remains that each firm will behave cooperatively with the *same* probability coefficient of one-half, the Gauthier rule will dictate adoption of a noncooperative strategy. The computations yield an expected value of *$1950* from cooperation against an expected value of *$2025* from independent adjustment of behavior. (Details of the computations are provided in the Appendix.) In order for the Gauthier rule to dictate continued adherence to a cooperative strategy as numbers in the interaction increase, the probability of any one player adopting the cooperative strategy must *increase,* which seems to counter common-sense notions about the way persons behave.

The numerical example extends the numbers only from a two-party to a three-party interaction. As numbers increase beyond small-number limits, the prospects for cooperative behavior, even on the part of those persons who try to behave in accordance with Gauthier's rational morality, will disappear in many situations. This apparent flaw is critical to the Gauthier enterprise, because it is the potential breakdown of the ordinary two-person relationships of the competitive market that gives rise to the necessity of some morality that exhibits comparable properties of reciprocation without concern. Coase-like bargaining can be depended on in small-number spill-over relationships; it is precisely the difficulties of market-like bargaining that create the problem in large-number settings.

IV. The Rationality of Retribution

A third criticism is closely related to those discussed in Sections II and III above. In the Gauthier idealization of society, individuals rationally take on a disposition that prompts them to refrain from taking strategic advantage of others when such advantage seems profitable in the orthodox utility-maximization sense. The functioning of this social order requires general adherence to such rational morality by a sufficiently large number of the community's members to make both free-riding and parasitic behavior the exception rather than the norm.

In this construction there is no room for whom we may call the moral entrepreneur; there is no means through which the individual, acting singly, can enforce the precepts of rational morality on others. The whole enterprise would seem to be more promising if it incorporated some role for individual entrepreneurship.

If we are willing, with Gauthier, to jettison orthodox utility maximization as a necessary and central feature of the very definition of rational behavior, we may ask why the extension of rationality need stop at the point where the individual takes on the disposition not to take advantage of others in strategic interactions. Could not arguments be advanced on Gauthier-like bases for the possible development of a rationally generated disposition to behave *retributively* toward those persons who violate the contractarian precepts? Why not punish those who depart from the cooperative norms?

The virtue of this extension of something akin to the Gauthier enterprise lies in its ability to incorporate a role for the individual as moral entrepreneur, as enforcer of cooperative norms for behavior on the part of others. The attainment and maintenance of the cooperative solutions to strategic interactions can be guaranteed by adherence to rationality by a much smaller set of the community's overall membership than that required under Gauthier's more limited model.

The point may be illustrated in the matrix of Figure 2, which adds a row

FIRM 2

		Produce ½ profit-maximizing output	Adjust output independently (Cournot)	Produce ½ competitive output
	Produce ½ profit-max output	I $4050, $4050	II $3375, $4500	III $2025, $4050
FIRM 1	Adjust output independently	IV $4500, $3375	V $3600, $3600	VI $1800, $2700
	Produce ½ competitive output	VII $4050, $2025	VIII $2700, $1800	IX $0, $0

Figure 2

and column to the matrix employed in Figure 1. The example is identical with that of Figure 1; there are two identical firms producing a homogeneous good. For present purposes, I shall ignore any concern about consumers, as expressed in Section II. The row and column additions indicate the payoffs to the two firms when one or the other firm, or both, adopt what we may call a retributive strategy. In this case, we define such a strategy to be production of one-half of the industry output that will satisfy the requirement that marginal cost equal price. When both firms adopt this strategy, profits fall to zero, which is the competitive solution where the benefits to consumers are maximal.

Is it not as plausible to impute as rational, a strategy that dictates such retributive behavior to the firm upon observance of noncooperative behavior on the part of the other party as it is to impute comparison with the independent adjustment position as the benchmark or fallback option? Look carefully at the numbers in the matrix cells of Figure 2. Suppose that the two firms are initially in the cooperative solution of Cell I, but that Firm 2 tries to take advantage and shifts the outcome to Cell II. If Firm 1 recognizes this potential for deviance on the part of Firm 2, it may have built into its response pattern a disposition to impose punishment; it shifts the solution to Cell VIII, where the payoff to Firm 2 is reduced considerably below that attainable in independent adjustment (Cell V).

By comparison with the simple tit-for-tat sequence confined to the four upper left cells of the matrix, the potentially deviant party, in this case Firm 2, is guaranteed a net loss in the sequence of plays. By contrast, and ignoring discounting, Firm 2 breaks even in the tit-for-tat sequence, as does Firm 1, the enforcer. By communicating that it has rationally disposed itself to behave retributively, and making this strategy credible to Firm 2, the enforcing firm has established an incentive structure such that the cooperative solution will tend to be maintained without explicit adherence to any cooperative strategy on the part of Firm 2. The latter knows that it must lose in the sequence to be followed out if it departs from cooperation; it also knows that it loses relatively to Firm 1 in the process, although Firm 1 will also suffer losses.

I shall not extend the argument further since I have discussed this sort of strategic behavior elsewhere under the labels "samaritan's dilemma" and "punishment dilemma."[9] My reason for bringing this discussion to bear on the Gauthier enterprise is to suggest that, once the model extends rationality beyond the limits of orthodox utility maximization, there seems no reason why rationality may not be attributed to a retributive strategy as well as to the more restricted reciprocal strategy advanced by Gauthier.

I am not clear concerning Gauthier's possible response to this third criticism of his argument. He may well accept, in certain cases, the extension of the rationality norm to retribution. He does suggest that deterrence is rational, and that it remains rational to carry out even a failed threat. I agree. But he does not sufficiently emphasize that a retributive strategy is not an initiating threat strategy. The enforcer does not threaten others so long as they behave cooperatively. To communicate a strategy that will punish those who might take advantage is quite different from a strategy that employs threats as a means of taking advantage. Nor does Gauthier recognize that the retributive strategy, by comparison with his strategy of reciprocation, can produce social stability without the necessity of general adherence on the part of most parties to interaction.[10]

---

9. See "The Samaritan's Dilemma," in *Freedom in Constitutional Contract* (College Station: Texas A&M University Press, 1977), 169–80; "The Punishment Dilemma," Ch. 8 in *The Limits of Liberty* (Chicago: University of Chicago Press, 1975), 130–46.

10. I have limited the discussion to behavior that involves the threat of punishment for individual departure from a pattern of cooperative behavior. A more inclusive treatment

V. The Definition of a Person

The criticisms advanced in Sections II, III, and IV are independent of any derivation of a theory of rights. So long as there exists some mutually acknowledged set of initial positions from which social interaction commences, precepts for individual behavior within this interaction may be analyzed. The Gauthier enterprise would, indeed, have been ambitious even if it had been limited to this extent. The enterprise goes much further, however, and includes the effort to outline a normative theory of rights, a theory that derives the definition of the initial positions from which rational bargainers start.

I find this part of Gauthier's work to be basically incoherent. My criticism can best be discussed with reference to Gauthier's treatment of my own argument as developed in my book *The Limits of Liberty*. I employed the concept of the "natural equilibrium" distribution in Hobbesian anarchy. This distribution is that which tends to emerge in the total absence of agreed-upon or accepted rules defining individuals' rights, endowments, or boundaries. I argued that this distributional equilibrium offered the only base point from which conceptual agreement among persons on some delineation of rights, some assignment of things and acts to "mine and thine" categories, could be grounded. Such agreement emerges because parties recognize that there are gains to be secured from a cessation of investment of resources in predation and defense. A set of rights comes to be established prior to the emergence of exchanges of these rights among holders, a second stage of contract that will further increase expected utilities.

David Gauthier fully understands and appreciates my analysis, including its purpose in my enterprise. For his own enterprise, however, he is critical of my construction because of its alleged failure to incorporate some recognition of the illegitimacy of coercion in the preagreement or Hobbesian setting. Gauthier's criticism is superficially appealing, and I should acknowledge here that it is probably shared by most of the philosophers who examined my argument. Why should the slave, who is coerced by the master in the preagreement equilibrium, agree on terms of a contract that will permanently pre-

---

would, of course, include moral indoctrination of the ordinary sort, designed to instill feelings of guilt and shame in those persons who might otherwise be inclined to defect.

serve the preagreement advantage of the master? Despite the fact that both master and slave improve their positions by a removal of restrictions in exchange for continued work for the master on the part of the slave, Gauthier argues that no such agreement could be justified from a rationally based morality.

The Gauthier criticism fails because, in my view, it does not account for the basis of the alleged coercion in the anarchistic setting. Why should the slave be in the master's chains? Clearly, he is enslaved only because of some inability to enforce more favorable terms of existence. The slave does not, presumably, possess a viable exit option, one that would allow him to carry on with an independent and isolated existence. There is no benchmark of independent existence that will define the presence or absence of coercion. If the slave cannot survive independently, can he be said to be coerced? Suppose, however, that the slave could have lived independently, but that he has been captured against his will. Despite our civilized sense that the master's act of enslavement is unjust, hardheaded analysis here must conclude that independent existence for the slave was not feasible, and that any such existence was fantasy, given the presence of the potential master.

Gauthier's reluctance to accept the preagreement base for the measure of cooperative surplus stems, in part, from his desire to make his precept of rational morality extend to include compliance with agreements or contracts once they are made. The slave who had been captured against his will in the preagreement setting would never, rationally, comply with the terms of an agreement that would preserve the advantages of the master. Note, however, that the extension of rationality discussed above in Section IV can extend to compliance. Recognizing the prospect that the slave might not rationally comply with an agreement, the master, before agreeing to terms, can communicate to the slave that any departure from the terms will bring punishment. And, indeed, the agreement itself may include the establishment of an effective enforcement agency.

I acknowledge that my own construction is conceptually *explanatory* in a sense that Gauthier may not intend for his justificatory alternative. For his purposes, the independent existence of the individual provides the normative benchmark from which cooperative gains are counted. In my enterprise, by contrast, parties to potential contract commence from some status quo definition of initial positions because, quite simply, there is no other place from which to start. This existential acceptance of the status quo, of that which is, has no explicit normative content and implies neither approbation nor condemnation by any criteria of distributive justice. My contractarian explanation allows me to justify the emergence of institutions of cooperation, and with respect to the constraints on individual behavior within these institutions, I should find some Gauthier-like rule to be necessary, whether this rule be adhered to voluntarily or enforced by the sovereign. My analysis embodies the justice of natural liberty, to employ Adam Smith's fine terminology, and at some levels there are parallels with the apparently more inclusive and more ambitious Gauthier enterprise. I commence from the status quo distribution of rights, and I do not apply criteria of justice to this distribution. My emphasis is almost exclusively placed on the *process* through which potential changes may be made, rather than on either the starting point or the end point of change. Gauthier extends his justificatory analysis to the initial distribution from which cooperation commences, and he seeks to establish that the distribution qualifying as "just" is only indirectly related to that which may exist. Although his enterprise here does not require rectification as extensive as that of Robert Nozick (see below), the definitional problems raised by the Lockean proviso in Gauthier's usage are more serious than those required by Nozick. Past injustice must remain potentially relevant in both enterprises.

How is past injustice defined? For present purposes, let me address this question within Gauthier's justificatory framework. A person has been unjustly treated if he has been taken advantage of, if his well-being has been reduced below that level which he might have attained in an independent and isolated existence totally apart from those persons with whom he has been forced to interact. Some version of a secession criterion for exploitation is useful, and, indeed, it is one that I have also invoked in recent papers.[11] But it is surely heroic to imply that the individually attainable level of well-being in isolation from social interaction is more than a tiny fraction of that which is secured by almost anyone in complex modern society. The secession criterion, even if it extended to apply to groups rather than to individuals singly, may offer little or no support to those critics of the existing distribution

---

11. "The Ethical Limits of Taxation," *Scandinavian Journal of Economics*, vol. 86 (1984), 102–14; "Secession and the Sharing of Surplus," with Roger Faith (mimeographed 1985).

of rights among persons, and hence little or no warrant for differential bias in the sharing of cooperative gains to rectify past injustice.

In concrete application, the Gauthier version of the Lockean proviso may be empty in the sense that it generates results equivalent to those that emerge, much more simply, from my own existential usage of the status quo. Consider an example. *Neither* the relatively rich man *nor* the relatively poor man could earn more than a pittance in isolation from the social exchange nexus. Any person's "natural talents" are specific to the social exchange nexus in which he finds himself. Almost all of the income enjoyed by any person stems from the cooperative surplus produced by social interaction. Despite observed wide disparity in levels of well-being in the status quo, the observed distribution falls well within the inclusive bargaining set outlined from the initial positions defined by Gauthier's proviso.

If we seek to go behind "the justice of natural liberty," it is necessary squarely to face up to the distribution of rights and endowments, as such. It is, of course, legitimate to inquire into the separate stages in the historical process through which the status quo distribution has been generated. And contractarian criteria of fairness may be applied to any or all of such stages. To label a single stage of development in the historical process as "unfair" (e.g., the capture and bondage of slaves) may imply some noncontractarian attribution of "unfairness" to the end state defined by *that which exists.* But such an attribution does not, in any way, remove the normative legitimacy of evaluating potential changes from *that which exists* in terms of procedural criteria for fairness (actual or hypothetical agreements) that are equivalent to those procedures that may have applied historically to earlier stages in the process. Rectificatory redistribution, if effectuated, must, as a process, involve violation of the contractarian or agreement criteria for fairness, and it is on this process that my own emphasis lies.

As observed, the status quo distribution has been generated through a complex process of political-legal evolution, deliberative political action, preference shifts, economic development, and social change. Is it appropriate to ask to what extent does the observed pattern embody precepts of fairness? And if fairness criteria have been violated at earlier stages of the process that generated that which exists, do these historical violations in themselves offer justification for violations in some process of rectification? Or is it best to concentrate on the process as it operates from the here and now?

I submit that the contractarian exercise does not require rectification of prior injustices before application to relevant forward-looking questions. The relevant questions must, ultimately, be answered empirically, with reference to the general attitudes expressed by the community's members. "Equal chances," "fair shakes," "equal treatment for equals," "play by the same rules," "equality before the law," "careers open to talents"—these seem to me to be principles of procedural fairness that find widespread acceptance. They are fully consistent with, and indeed are required by, the Gauthier enterprise, including the appended Lockean proviso.

As I noted earlier, rectificatory redistribution may be nonexistent even on full acceptance of the Gauthier argument. By contrast, Gauthier's characterization of the market as a morally free zone may be misinterpreted as an indirect defense of the distributive patterns emergent from market interactions. Close examination of his argument reveals that persons are to be justified (by the proviso) in receiving only the values of their external marginal product, values that exclude rents.[12] As his discussion (*MA*, p. 276) makes clear, the baseball free agent who may earn $500,000 from each of several major league clubs is not "entitled" to this total. If his nonbaseball alternative is the $20,000 salary of a truck driver, the $480,000 is rent that emerges only from the exchange nexus and is, therefore, subject to sharing in accordance with the Gauthier bargaining norm, minimax relative concession. If, in turn, the genuinely isolated prospect for the person is not $20,000 but $5000, the inclusive measure of rent increases to $495,000. As this numerical example suggests, application of the Gauthier norm may require very substantial distributive departures from those patterns that are emergent from the market process as it operates.

If rents assume major quantitative significance in the reward structure of the market, the Gauthier precept for the sharing of the overall cooperative surplus may seem to be both equally arbitrary with and not too different from the familiar difference principle advanced by Rawls. Implicitly, Rawls assumes that the isolated individual can produce no value and that all ob-

---

served income is "social rent." In the absence of incentive-induced feedbacks on the production of value, the Rawlsian principle generates equality. The Gauthier principle generates inequality only as related to differentials in the capacities of persons to produce values in isolation one from another. In practical application, the two positions seem much closer than Gauthier's discussion might suggest.

Although they disagree on the specific sharing principle, both David Gauthier and John Rawls seek to go beyond the criterial usage of contractual agreement as the test for distributive fairness. Both philosophers seek to define "that principle upon which contractors will agree," a step that I have tried consistently to avoid. My own contractarianism is, therefore, more limited, and it enables me to acknowledge that any one of several sharing principles may emerge from an ideally conceptualized agreement, including those of Rawls, Gauthier, and others that embody much less redistributive thrust.

VI. The Market as a Moral Free Zone

The idealized relationship between the individual buyer and the individual seller in competitive market exchange is a cornerstone of the Gauthier enterprise. In this relationship, mutual gains from trade (cooperation) are realized, and these gains are shared between the parties in a determinate manner, without other-regardingness on the part of either party, without resort to transcendental moral norms, and without costly investment in bargaining. As so idealized, it is not surprising that this basic market relationship appeals to David Gauthier, the modern moral philosopher, in much the same way that it appealed to Adam Smith, the moral philosopher of the eighteenth century. (A damning indictment of twentieth-century moral philosophy emerges when we recognize that David Gauthier's appreciation of the moral content of the exchange relationship is the exception rather than rule within the set of his disciplinary peers.)

The crowning discovery of the eighteenth century lay in the recognition that the spontaneous coordination properties of the market remove dilemma-like opposition of interests among persons from wide areas of social interaction, thereby eliminating the necessity of pervasive and overriding political direction of individual activity. Adam Smith stressed, however, that these properties of the market, properties that allow for the self-interested behavior of persons yet generate socially beneficial results, require an environmental setting of the appropriate "laws and institutions." Individual rights must be guaranteed; contracts must be enforced; fraud in exchange must be prevented. There need be no inconsistency between the enterprise of Adam Smith and that of David Gauthier. Smith might well agree with Gauthier's implied inference that the formal structure of the law must be complemented by a rational morality that incorporates reciprocal respect among persons in the relevant nexus. Adam Smith, along with most of the economists who have followed him, might be more skeptical than Gauthier concerning the relative importance of the two influences. We recall Smith's differentiation between the behavior of the Dutch merchant constrained by the discipline of continuous dealing and that of the once-encountered rude Scots highlander.[13]

Although he does not make the point directly, Gauthier's analysis implies that the set of social relationships classified as "the market" will more or less emerge naturally from the self-interested behavior of participants and, further, that within this set of relationships there arises no possible conflict between the precepts for rational morality and straightforward utility maximization. A participant in exchange will refrain from taking advantage, from cheating on the agreed terms of trade. If, however, we should remove the protective legal umbrella, Adam Smith's "laws and institutions," the basic elements of the Prisoners' Dilemma appear in even the simplest of exchange relationships. The whole of the Gauthier enterprise would have been strengthened by an explicit recognition that the market relationship offers the exemplar of rational morality, rather than a "morally free zone." As Adam Smith emphasized, men *trade;* animals do not, despite recent empirical evidence demonstrating that animals have well-ordered utility functions and that they exhibit some sense of property rights. Is not the very existence of exchange the best proof that something like Gauthier's rational morality applies to normal behavior within market relationships?[14]

There is, of course, a major difference between the idealized market relationship in which each participant is a price taker and those relationships

13. See Adam Smith, *Lectures on Jurisprudence* (Oxford: Clarendon Press, 1978), 538.
14. I am indebted to my colleague David Levy for discussion on these points.

characterized by the absence of exogeneously determined terms of trade. In the competitive setting, the dilemma-like elements of potential conflict arise only with respect to the prospects for gains from cheating in carrying out the terms of contract, the type of cheating that cannot be wholly prevented except in the imagined abstractions of the general equilibrium economists, abstractions that Gauthier seems to have imbibed somewhat too uncritically. In general equilibrium, producers' rents are absent, and all owners of inputs secure returns equal to opportunity costs. But, as the discussion of rents indicated in Section V above, opportunity cost *within* the market nexus is far removed from opportunity cost outside the nexus. As presented, Gauthier's argument suggests that distributional conflicts arise only in noncompetitive settings where prices are indeterminate. In any less abstracted conceptualization of market process, both producers' and consumers' rents are ubiquitous, and the apparent distributive neutrality of markets emergent from Gauthier's sharing norm disappears.

For basically the same reasons, Gauthier is too enthusiastic about the properties of the market in its institutional role as the eliminator of externalities *in the sense required by his enterprise*. So long as the inclusive economic nexus can be factored down into simple two-person or two-unit buyer-seller deals, there is no requirement that the rational morality of the two parties do more than secure some sharing of the cooperative surplus. The morality must extend to take on a heavier burden only in those settings where "markets fail" in the sense that such a factoring down cannot take place, or where there are external effects on persons who are not primary participants in the simple exchange processes.

The examples are familiar. The discharge of toxic waste into the stream kills the fish. The person who takes such action is "taking advantage" of others with whom he is not primarily dealing, and he must refrain from taking such action by some explicit resort to the rational morality of Gauthier. To the extent that rights are exhaustively assigned, however, the need to call on such an explicit sharing norm is not required. The implication is clear that such externalities are relatively rare.

The market does allow persons to act without direct regard for the interests of others, and, over very extensive areas of interaction, this process does generate results that are welfare-maximizing for the whole community of persons. The market process fails in this respect only in the presence of relevant externalities. But these are only a small subset of the set of all externalities, if this term is defined simply as the imposition of noncompensated harm or benefits on parties who are not primary participants in exchanges. The conventional distinction in theoretical welfare economics is that between *technological* and *pecuniary* externalities, that is, between those actions that directly affect the utility or production functions of parties outside the exchange, and those actions that affect such parties only through changes in terms of trade, or prices. This distinction is broadly recognized also in the traditions of the common law. The market fails in the standard sense when the first sort of externalities are present; the market works only because the second sort of externalities can be disregarded.

The question for moral theory is whether or not there exists a means of making this distinction. The point is closely related to that which has already been discussed in Section II above. How can a person know the difference between the two sorts of noncompensated harms or benefits that his behavior imposes on third parties? An example may be helpful here. Suppose that I enter into simple exchange dealings with construction firms, wholesale grocers, employees, and others and open up a hamburger stand on the corner of Main and Broad streets. In so doing, I impose noncompensated capital losses on the existing owner-operator of the Burger King franchise on the opposite corner. This person is a third party to my transactions, and this third party is harmed by my behavior. This is clearly a *pecuniary* externality. But am I taking advantage of the Burger King franchise in any sense that would require me either to refrain from acting, or to share the cooperative surplus in accordance with some norm? Economic theory tells us that I need not do so, and that any attempt to force me to do so, either in formal law or in a derived morality, would be harmful to the welfare of the community as a whole. To be able to make the required distinction between noncompensated harms and benefits that would and those that would not invoke the application of some rational morality seems beyond the limits of the plausible, even within the acknowledged confines of the Gauthier enterprise.

VII. The Enterprise Assessed

I have advanced several fundamental criticisms of the Gauthier enterprise, based on my understanding of it. These criticisms are intended to be relevant primarily, if not exclusively, to the interpretation of the enterprise as an effort to ground the morality necessary for orderly social interaction in precepts of rational-choice behavior. Recall, however, that this was only one among three sets of standards for evaluating the Gauthier effort that I enunciated in the first paragraph of this paper. By the second set of standards, my judgment of the inclusive enterprise is favorable. I shall defend this judgment in this section, and I shall make a few comments on the third set of standards suggested.

Broadly construed, the Gauthier enterprise represents an attempt to fill a major gap in our understanding and explanation of how we act and how we should act in social relationships one with another. I am convinced that social order, as we know it, would collapse overnight if all persons, or even a large share of persons, should suddenly commence to behave strictly in accordance with the utility-maximizing models of orthodox choice theory, and within the constraints only of formal legal enforcement structures. We need only refer to the statistics of crime and punishment. It is much easier for our formal models to explain why persons commit crimes than it is to explain why persons do not do so.

By comparison with David Gauthier, I am much less concerned with whether or not the behavioral norms required for what I have called the "moral order" can or cannot be grounded in some extension of rational choice. As I have indicated, I am skeptical of his success in this respect. I am concerned, however, with the presence of such norms in the behavior of persons with whom I must interact in the complex socio-political-economic nexus of modern life. Gauthier shares my conviction that the norms emergent from his enterprise, or some that are roughly similar, are necessary for the liberal social order. If his effort is reinterpreted as offering an argument, even if oblique, in support of this proposition it should carry much more weight even to those who remain highly skeptical of his more ambitious enterprise. Clearly, we must understand (to the extent that it is possible) the sources of the moral norms that provide the cement of liberal society if we are to think about constructive improvement or even constructive prevention of further erosion.

So interpreted, Gauthier is a *moral* constructivist, whose enterprise is distinguishable from many other moral philosophers by its individualist-contractarian foundations. By way of comparison, my own position is that of a *constitutional* constructivist, whose enterprise builds on the same individualist-contractarian foundations. But my emphasis is placed on the rules that constrain behavior, rather than on the norms for behavior itself. In this rough classificatory schemata, Rawls combines elements of both moral and constitutional constructivism, still within the contractarian framework. The three of us, Rawls, Gauthier, Buchanan, seem clearly to be closer to each other than either of us is to the nonconstructivism of Nozick or Hayek.

By my third set of standards, I suggest that the Gauthier enterprise offers Humean hope rather than Hobbesian despair. Recall that Hobbes wrote amid the turbulence of revolutionary mid-seventeenth-century England; Hume worked out his ideas in the relatively well-ordered Scotland of the eighteenth century. It is far easier to imagine the empirical reality of a rational morality in the Scotland of David Hume and Adam Smith than it is to model Puritans and Cavaliers as agreeing on precepts for sharing the cooperative surplus. Both Hobbes and Hume were individualist in their rejection of supraindividualist sources of value; one offers reasons for constraints, the other offers reasons for abiding with those that exist.

The enterprise of David Gauthier has both Hobbesian and Humean elements. Does the enterprise presuppose that we live in a social environment nearer to the Scotland of Hume than to the England of Hobbes? Is the community of social interactors sufficiently well defined to make any system of morals by agreement viable? Is a rational morality independent of history, of culture, of institutional-constitutional structure? Perhaps we do have a *moral* obligation to answer these three questions affirmatively.

Arithmetical Appendix

In a shift from the two-firm to the three-firm interaction with product demand and firm cost functions unchanged from the example in Figure 1, joint profit maximizing industry output will, of course, remain unchanged at 90 units. In the three-firm setting, this output will be shared equally among the three identical firms, with each firm producing 30 units. The price remains at \$110 per unit, and each firm's profit becomes \$2700 [(30 $\times$ \$110) $-$ (30 $\times$ \$20)]. This is compared with the \$4050 profit in the two-firm setting. In considering whether to adopt the cooperative strategy by the Gauthier rule, the firm must compare the expected payoff under this strategy with that which is predicted under fully independent adjustment by each of the three firms.

Payoff for Firm 1 if it adopts cooperative strategy

Behavior of Firm 2	Behavior of Firm 3	Prob.	Profit to Firm 1
C	C	1/4	$2700
C	N	1/4	$1800
N	C	1/4	$1800
N	N	1/4	$1500
Expected value of payoff			$1950

Consider, first, the prospects if Firm 1 cooperates, which, in this case, means setting output rate at 30, which is one-third of the joint profit maximizing output. The firm expects that each one of the other two firms will behave cooperatively with a probability of one-half. There are four possibilities, with probabilities indicated below, with C and N referring to cooperative and noncooperative strategy choices.

Values for the profit for Firm 1 are computed by postulating that all firms with N strategies maximize profits subject to the C firm's retention of joint profit-maximizing output.

Payoff to Firm 1 if it adopts independent adjustment
strategy, and same strategy is adopted by other two firms

Expected value of payoff $2025

Value is computed by postulating that each of three firms adjusts output independent of output of other firms.

Constructivism, Cognition, and Value

I appreciate the opportunity to return to Alpbach and to participate in this 1987 forum, both in presenting this lecture and in organizing the workshop on "Ordnungspolitik" with my colleague Professor Viktor Vanberg. I shall look forward to these next days here. The Alpbach European Forum is unique in the world, and it deserves to be widely recognized for its encouragement and stimulation of dialogue and discussion across many academic and scientific disciplines and among scholars and students from many nations and in many languages, for its presupposed understanding of the added impetus provided by the beautiful environmental setting of this place, and, finally, for the sheer "Gemütlichkeit" that seems always to emerge here. Those of you who are here for the first time are, indeed, on the threshold of a fine experience. We owe a continuing debt to our gracious hosts, and especially to Professors Molden and Albert, who make all of this possible for the rest of us.

I was asked to lecture on the general theme of the forum, which is "Cognition and Decision." It is, of course, appropriate that this theme be sufficiently comprehensive to incorporate many variations of emphases reflected in the study groups that are scheduled. I could not, even if I tried to do so, incorporate all elements of such a general theme in a single lecture. I shall make no such attempt here. Instead, I shall try to develop some elements of subject matter that fall within the general theme.

From *Erkenntnis und Entscheidung: Die Wertproblematik in Wissenschaft und Praxis, Europäisches Forum Alpbach 1987,* ed. Otto Molden (Vienna: Österreichisches College, 1988), 36–48. Reprinted by permission of the publisher.

I am indebted to Hartmut Kliemt and Viktor Vanberg for helpful comments.

As some of you who may know my work will have anticipated, I shall concentrate on the choices that we make among rules or institutions that enable us to live in "social order" without conflict while at the same time achieving tolerably acceptable levels of well-being. More specifically, I shall examine the linkage between the knowledge that we possess or may possess about the predicted working properties of alternative sets of rules and the choices that we may make among these sets.

The first step involves the supposition that we do, in fact, choose the constraints within which we carry out our everyday activities, both private and public. That is to say, the rules for social order are not exclusively the product of some process of cultural evolution, rules that we have inherited and that we abide by without understanding their purpose or function. At least within limits, the supposition here is that rules are deliberately "constructed" from the choices of those persons who are to be subject to the constraints that these rules embody.

In channelling the discourse toward constructive choice among sets of rules, I am, as you will recognize, both modifying and going beyond emphasis on cultural evolution associated with the work of Professor F. A. Hayek, a many-times participant of the Alpbach forum, and who, indeed, visited my own study group several times in 1984, my last visit here. I accept, of course, the importance of cultural evolution in the establishment of the rules of social order, and I need not assign weights to the relative significance of evolved and constructed rules. I want only to suggest that, at least along some relevant margins, we can deliberately modify the institutions that constrain our interaction, one with another.

I. Moral Constructivism

The next step in my argument involves a distinction between moral and constitutional constructivism. We have long recognized that constraints on behavior may be moral or extra-moral, or, to put the point differently, may be internal to the psyche of the potential actor or externally imposed. A person may not steal because of internal moral imperative—"it is wrong to steal"; or because of an external sanction—"if I steal I shall suffer punishment."

A moral constructivist seeks to modify behavior by changing the morality of the potential actor. Traditionally, the moralist has sought to urge upon us ethical precepts that are presumably derived from some external source of knowledge—from God, from reason, from natural law. And such precepts have often been introduced explicitly as constraints upon the rationally derived self-interests of actors. I am not a moral philosopher in the sense that I can claim any competence in the derivation of moral or ethical precepts from transcendent sources of knowledge about values. Indeed, I remain highly skeptical about the very existence of such sources of moral values, and, even if I were not, I should remain non-enthusiastic about the efficacy of "moral preaching" in modifying individual behavior patterns.

I am much more sympathetic to a quite different sort of moral constructivism, one that seeks to ground moral precepts for behavior within the rational self-interest of individuals, in the cognition and preferences that exist, rather than in some extra-individualistic sources. We find elements of this second sort of moral constructivism in David Hume and in other leaders of the 18th-century school of Scots moral philosophers. Some elements are also present in Kant's whole enterprise. But I want to concentrate my remarks here on an important new book "Morals by Agreement" (Oxford University Press, 1986), by an American philosopher, David Gauthier. In "Morals by Agreement," Gauthier seeks to demonstrate that a cooperative morality is an essential part of rational choice. In his construction, moral rules do not constrain choices that would otherwise be dictated from considerations of rational utility maximization. Instead, it becomes rational to be moral in dealing with others in settings where reciprocal behavior of others can be anticipated.

Gauthier generalizes the setting described in the classical prisoners' dilemma of modern game theory, and he argues that the choice of a disposition to behave cooperatively is rationally grounded. Despite the existence of several problematic aspects of his technical construction, it does seem to me that Gauthier has moved the argument one stage beyond that at which Hayek's argument finishes. If we acknowledge, as I think we must, that we do, indeed, behave in accordance with rules of conduct that make order in a "great society" possible, we are left with the unanswered question: WHY? Gauthier's construction offers an explanatory answer that does not require the altruism of the moral community, an altruism that is appropriate only to the small-number setting descriptive of our tribal heritage.

In a very real sense, Gauthier is arguing that individuals choose for themselves dispositions or personal behavioral rules that will direct their patterns of choice behavior in a sequence of interactions with others. In my own terms, individuals choose among alternative "moral constitutions"; they choose among alternative constraints rather than among alternative end-states available to them in particularized situations. A reconciliation, of sorts, may be effected between Gauthier and traditional moralists by noting that the rational morality of an individual does require constraints on the open-ended choice options that seem to describe particularized situations. But these constraints are, themselves, a product of, and are chosen by, a rationally based choice calculus at the "higher" level of dispositional alternatives.

The classical dilemma setting may then be misleading. If the payoff matrix is interpreted to reflect the utility payoffs that the individuals actually confront in a single interaction, it cannot be descriptive of that faced by Gauthier's rationally moral person. Having rationally chosen a disposition to cooperate as a binding element of a moral constitution, the individual does not, and cannot, confront the ordinally arrayed payoff structure of the classical dilemma. The off-diagonal cells do not contain the ordinal utility numbers that generate the familiar dominance.

Gauthier's construction is explicitly contractarian, and he suggests that individuals will agree generally on the adoption of dispositions to cooperate reciprocally in interactions that contain the potential for a cooperative surplus. These dispositions will not, however, include the extension of comparable treatment to others who are not similarly disposed. Gauthier's enterprise requires an ability to recognize, within probabilistic limits, those who are free riders and/or parasites, along with a willingness to initiate appropriate non-cooperative behavior toward such persons, from ostracism to retribution.

The cognitive requirements placed on the individual in Gauthier's construction are immense. The individual must, first of all, recognize the potential for cooperative surplus, and he must projectively measure this surplus in a quasi-objectifiable way necessary to allow for share agreement with other parties to interaction. Further, he must identify the limits of the relevant community of potential cooperators. Even if, as Gauthier acknowledges, the exercise is carried out in "ideal theory," as opposed to explanatory analysis, the observed limits on the cognitive capacities of persons as they exist may raise issues of relevance. The ambitious nature of Gauthier's enterprise must be stressed.

Nonetheless, his effort is unique among modern social philosophers in that he does advance a conceptually explanatory framework that allows us to understand how persons might survive and prosper in an "orderly anarchy." I have long argued that much of the observed interaction in Western liberal settings does proceed without formal legalized-politicized constraints. Gauthier's analysis contains elements of explanation, and, because it does so, I welcome it as a contribution that deserves careful attention.

II. Constitutional Constructivism

If we interpret David Gauthier's enterprise as an analysis of the rational bases for the individual's choice of a "moral constitution," a choice that will constrain his non-cooperative proclivities in dilemma-like particular interactions, there is a direct linkage with the "constitutional constructivism" that has, directly or indirectly, occupied much of my own attention for many years, and which is ultimately derivative from the construction of Thomas Hobbes.

Recognizing that we must, as members of a society, interact variously and continuously with others, we may rationally choose to impose constraints upon our own behavior along with that of others, constraints that will operate externally to our own volition, constraints that will be imposed coercively. We may voluntarily and deliberately choose to restrict our own freedom of action, to close off choice options, so long as we are insured that the choices of others are similarly constrained. In choosing such constraints, we are seeking to secure the expected benefits to be derived from the assurance that other persons will, reciprocally, be restricted in their freedom of action. Civic order becomes possible as individual behavior is confined within appropriately defined limits, whether these be internally imposed, à la Gauthier, or externally operative. Law and morals are both complements and substitutes, one for the other. And a rationally based logic of law becomes fully analogous to a rationally based logic of morality in some Gauthier-like framework of analysis.

We have, therefore, three sources of constraints, one of which is non-rational, and two of which have rational choice foundations.

1. "It is wrong to steal."
2. "It is rational to choose a disposition not to steal from persons who reciprocate in their moral attitudes."
3. "It is rational to choose an enforceable law against stealing, applicable for the whole community of persons."

These alternatives need not, of course, be mutually exclusive.

I have discussed the second of these sets of constraints at some length in Section I, in the context of the work of David Gauthier. I want to discuss the third set of constraints in more detail here, and to compare and contrast this alternative with the second. That is to say, I want to compare Gauthier's rational morality with the more familiar rationally derived constitutional contract for political order that embodies coercion of persons in postconstitutional actions.

The critical difference between the two sets of rationally based constraints on individual choice lies in the necessary "externality" that is embodied in any Hobbes-like structure of civil order. Their initial compact or covenant, real or imagined, with the "sovereign" involves the agreed-on submission of the individual, as subject, to the dictates of that person or agency charged with the task of enforcing the agreed-on rules. This subjection of the individual to potential coercive force beyond his own internal precommitments must be present, regardless of the possible predictability and controllability of the agent or agency that might exercise such force. Even if technology should permit the ultimate rule enforcer to take the form of some impersonal robot, the individual, as subject, remains bound by the external constraints programmed in the structure. And, more familiarly, if the ultimate rule enforcer necessarily embodies human agency, the potential for exploitative behavior that extends beyond the limits of consensual-based law must be recognized.

How may the controllers be controlled? Hobbes responded with despair. But historical experience suggests that, in some times and some places and under some circumstances, constitutions can, themselves, bind sovereign governments. Nonetheless, the attention of the constitutional constructivists must be primarily focused on the effective implementation of constraints on the operations of constitutionally authorized and established governments. The protection of the individual from the state, the very agency that he employs to protect him from other persons and to provide him with collective goods and services: such protection becomes the critical challenge for the political philosopher. Even at a level of "ideal theory," there is no satisfactory resolution of this issue.

Unfortunately, this issue is less widely understood today than it was in the 17th or the 18th century. Discussion over two centuries has been plagued by acceptance of what I have elsewhere called "the electoral fallacy," the idea that, so long as governments act "democratically" in accordance with decisions made by duly-elected representatives in parliamentary or legislative assemblies, the individual is sufficiently protected against the overreaching of the state. So long as the individual remains at liberty to participate freely in the electoral process, there need be no cause for the traditional concern over the state's limits. So long as legislative bodies reflect genuine majoritarian preferences, any constitutional constraints on their exercise of authority are unnecessary and may, indeed, be undesirable. I suggest that this whole set of related ideas and attitudes reflects monumental confusion that produces possibly tragic consequences.

As modern public choice theory has demonstrated, the linkage between the individual's participation in the electoral process and insurance against exploitation by the agency of governance is tenuous at best. The individual in a large-number electorate has little or no rationally based interest in the act of participation, in voting, and he has no rational motive for seeking to become informed as to the consequences of alternatives presented for collective choice. Moreover, the potential for majoritarian exploitation of minority interests may well exceed that which is possible in non-majoritarian settings. A practical consequence of the electoral fallacy has been to lend an artificial legitimacy to the overreaching of modern states into spheres of activity that would never have been contractually or consensually ceded to any sovereign.

As I have elsewhere suggested, there is a pressing need for a requisite understanding of the central issues involved in man's relationship to and with the state. This understanding does not emerge "naturally" in the thought processes of modern Western culture, as it seemed to emerge in the political philosophy of the 18th century.

III. Knowledge, Understanding, and Value

In a very real sense, there has been a loss of wisdom between the late 18th and late 20th centuries. We seem to know and to understand less now than we did when David Hume, Adam Smith, Wilhelm von Humboldt, and James Madison lived and worked. But what is it that we know less about? Scientifically, we have, of course, made dramatic progress over the two centuries. The frontiers of knowledge about the physical-natural universe have been enormously expanded. We know much more about almost all aspects of our universe. How is it, then, possible to suggest that we know less, about anything, than we did then?

Lest we presume an unwarranted arrogance, even about matters of pure "science," it is useful to remind ourselves that knowledge about the natural universe has been lost in earlier epochs. The late Roman empire was characterized by less knowledge about many things than the level of cognition attained during Rome's grandeur. Applied to modern times, however, there is no evidence to suggest a loss of technical and scientific knowledge. My reference is to the loss of knowledge about man's relationship to man in organized social community, and particularly about man's relationships to the institutions of the state.

There is an ontological difference between the object of knowledge in the two cases. The natural universe exists, independent of that which man creates. By contrast, the institutions of order may, themselves, be constructed or created by man himself. The difference in "that which we know about" categorically separates the physical from the social scientist. For the former, for the natural scientist, there is, at base, only one reality, a reality that may, of course, be viewed from differing perceptions, but which, nonetheless, is characterized by an exogeneity that is acknowledged to be present by all who claim license as scientists. This reality need not be static, and its formal laws need not be reversible, even in some ideal sense. But the exogeneity of the physical universe remains. In social science, by contrast, the institutional-organizational reality that can be observed empirically is only one among a large set of possible alternatives. Because the institutional-organizational reality is not, and cannot be, exogeneous to the choices of those who are constrained by this reality, we have a source of cognitive differences that cannot arise in natural science. Not only can different scientists view reality from differing perspectives, but, also, different scientists impose differing attributes of exogeneity on the reality itself. The social scientist is almost necessarily a cognitive constructivist in a sense over and beyond the enterprise of the natural scientist. The social scientist would violate his canon of responsibility if he remains quiescent and refuses to consider alternatives to that structure which exists.

The social scientist faces a continuing choice among institutional-organizational arrangements, alternatives to those that exist, to be subjected to scientific and analytical scrutiny. The inclusive research program, which incorporates the extension of one central analytical model to existing and alternative structures cannot, almost by definition, be "scientific" in a strict sense analogous to the natural sciences. Man's actions are not limited to those observed in the existing institutional-organizational setting.

The loss of wisdom between the 18th century and modern times can be located in a general failure to recognize the limits of the feasible sets of institutional-organizational arrangements, limits that are imposed by those elements of stability in "human nature" that so excited the minds of the philosophers of the 18th century. Precisely because they were not bound to that which exists in observed patterns of social relationships, social reformers sought to move structures beyond the realm of the feasible, as dictated by characteristics of natural man. Neither the "new Soviet man" nor the ideally benevolent despot is a resident of any feasible structure of social interaction. The "fatal conceit" (Hayek's term) that was socialism has been revealed for all to see.

Developments in academic discourse since the 1960's offer grounds for hope. Public choice theory's extension of utility-maximizing models of behavior to politics has exposed the romantic illusion of governmental benevolence as well as the electoral fallacy noted above. Critical works by F. A. Hayek, John Passmore, Thomas Sowell, and others have exposed the terrible vulnerability of structures that are based on presumptions of human perfectability. The time is ripe, in 1987, to examine institutional-organizational alternatives that embody an updated 18th-century wisdom or knowledge about the limits of human nature, while remaining cognizant of the dramatic advances in ordinary science. It is time to dream realistic dreams rather than fantasy.

David Gauthier's major effort to ground cooperative morality in a rational choice calculus may be a significant step. A resurgence of interest in and on the Hobbesian issue of controlling the sovereign may offer a productive complementary program. Both "moral constructivism" and "institutional constructivism" may be informed by an understanding and knowledge of the limits of human potential.

Name Index

Subject Index

This book is set in Minion, a typeface designed by Robert Slimbach specifically for digital typesetting. Released by Adobe in 1989, it is a versatile neohumanist face that shows the influence of Slimbach's own calligraphy.

Book design by Louise OFarrell, Gainesville, Fla.
Typography by Impressions Book and Journal Services, Inc., Madison, Wisc.

Printed in the USA
CPSIA information can be obtained
at www.ICGtesting.com
JSHW082148140824
68134JS00014B/128